E-Learning by Design

2nd Edition

By

William Horton

Pfeiffer

A Wiley Imprint
www.pfeiffer.com

Published by Pfeiffer

An Imprint of Wiley

989 Market Street, San Francisco, CA 94103-1741

www.pfeiffer.com

For additional copies/bulk purchases of this book in the U.S. please contact 800-274-4434.

Pfeiffer books and products are available through most bookstores. To contact Pfeiffer directly call our Customer Care Department within the U.S. at 800-274-4434, outside the U.S. at 317-572-3985, fax 317-572-4002, or visit www.pfeiffer.com.

Pfeiffer also publishes its books in a variety of electronic formats. Some content that appears in print may not be available in electronic books.

Library of Congress Cataloging-in-Publication Data

Horton, William K. (William Kendall)
   E-learning by design / William Horton.— 2nd ed.
     p. cm.
   Includes index.
   ISBN 978-0-470-90002-4 (pbk.)
   1. Employees—Training of—Computer-assisted instruction. 2. Computer-assisted instruction—Design. I. Title.
HF5549.5.T7H6357 2011
658.3'124040285—dc22

Book design and composition: William Horton Consulting, Inc.

Printed in the United States of America

Printing 10 9 8 7 6 5 4 3 2 1

Preface

What's new in the 2nd edition?

I must confess that I am the kind of reader who skips over prefaces, acknowledgements, and other throat warming found at the fronts of books. If you are that kind of reader also, go ahead and jump to Chapter 1. It won't hurt my feelings as an author. There are no great revelations here or secret confessions, only a brief description of what's new in this edition and why.

What's different about e-learning?

Since the first edition of *E-learning by Design*, e-learning has evolved rapidly and fringe techniques have moved into the mainstream. Revolutionaries have become bankers.

Underlying and underwriting these changes in e-learning are advances in technology and changes in society.

For one thing, learning games and simulations have gone from being treated as noisy children at a formal dinner to being the life of the party. Proven successes have earned games and simulations serious consideration by even the most conservative designers.

Our ability to search vast information repositories has become universal and commonplace. Many e-book outsell their paper counterparts. Public and private libraries and encyclopedias have grown in number and size. More reliable search engines have made online search a part of technological culture. Google is a verb.

Mechanisms for online collaboration have advanced as well. Name a subject and there is a discussion forum, blog, podcast, or news feed dedicated to it. Global conversations, enabled by social media, arise spontaneously and carom wildly. Politicians tap into these ad hoc discussions to sample the *vox populi*.

Out of this burst of online collaboration burst social networking. Its popularity has given us new technologies, new terminology, and new modes of learning. Well, not really. The technologies and terminology are new, but learning from others is among the most ancient and thoroughly proven modes of learning.

Mobile phones have taken on the functions previously offered by separate personal digital assistants and media players. They are as powerful as many of the laptop computers used for e-learning when the first edition premiered. Today's smart phones are easy to use, rugged, and reliable. And potential learners have one with them all the time.

Some early forms of e-learning, such as virtual-classroom courses, Webinars, and software demonstrations (screencasts) have stabilized. Though they have not advanced in basic capabilities, they have become easier to produce and more predictable to take. They have entered the mainstream and are now helping to define it.

What's new in this book?

To track the changes in technology and society, several sections have been promoted to full chapters. Please congratulate "Games and simulations," "Social learning," and "Mobile learning" on their expanded coverage and much-deserved emphasis. I have tried to avoid the common tendency to trivialize these subjects. I promise you that I do not define mobile learning as dumping desktop courses onto mobile devices or suggest that social learning is nothing more than telling students to ask their social network instead of asking the teacher.

As requested by readers of the first edition, I have fleshed out the instructional design scheme in the first chapter. I was glad to do so because my experience as a consultant, since the first edition, has taught me that most failures of e-learning projects can be traced back to flawed instructional design. I have added an appendix detailing a simple technique to determine what to teach and what to leave out.

Some chapters have moved online at horton.com/eld/. Chapters on designing lessons, strategic decisions that affect the whole course, visual design, and navigation are now online. That allows the paper portion to focus on issues of vital interest to all designers, especially first-line designers with direct responsibility for accomplishing specific learning objectives. The online chapters offer advanced skills and techniques for issues usually dealt with by senior designers and project leaders.

What else? Oh, I have put in new typos to replace the old ones, or at least to keep them company.

So, go on and start reading, skimming, scanning, or however you like to consume books. If you are reading this in a bookstore, go ahead and buy this book. Better still, buy two copies and give one to your boss.

Contents

Designing e-learning

Planning the development of online learning

For tens of thousands of years, human beings have come together to learn and share knowledge. Until recently, we have had to come together at the same time and place. But today, computer and networking technologies have eliminated that requirement. Now anybody can learn anything anywhere at any time. And developers of education can deliver learning when needed, where needed, on any subject, in just the right amount, in the most effective format, and for not much money.

WHAT IS E-LEARNING?

E-learning marshals computer and network technologies to the task of education. Several definitions of e-learning are common. Some people hold that e-learning is limited to what takes place entirely within a Web browser without the need for other software or learning resources. Such a pure definition, though, leaves out many of the truly effective uses of related technologies for learning.

Definition of e-learning

There are a lot of complex definitions of e-learning, so I'll offer you a simple one:

E-learning is the use of electronic technologies to create learning experiences.

This definition is deliberately open-ended, allowing complete freedom as to how these experiences are formulated, organized, and created. Notice that this definition does not mention "courses," for courses are just one way to package e-learning experiences. It also does not mention any particular authoring tool or management system.

Varieties of e-learning

E-learning comes in many forms. You may have taken one or two forms of e-learning, but have you considered them all? Here are some varieties of e-learning to consider:

▶ **Standalone courses**: Courses taken by a solo learner. They are self-paced without interaction with a teacher or classmates. There are numerous examples of standalone courses cited in this book. Search the index for *Using Gantt Charts*, *GALENA Slope Stability Analysis*, and *Vision and the Church.* You can also go to the Web site for this book (horton.com/eld/) to find links to live examples.

▶ **Learning games and simulations**: Learning by performing simulated activities that require exploration and lead to discoveries. We have devoted the whole of Chapter 7 to the discussion of games and simulations. Also go to horton.com/eld/ for links to live examples.

▶ **Mobile learning**: Learning from the world while moving about in the world. Aided by mobile devices, such as smart phones and tablet devices, mobile learners participate in conventional classroom courses and standalone e-learning while out and about. They may also participate in activities where they learn by interacting with objects and people they encounter along the way. Mobile learning is discussed in Chapter 9.

▶ **Social learning**: Learning through interaction with a community of experts and fellow learners. Communication among participants relies on social-networking media such as online discussions, blogging, and text-messaging. See Chapter 8 for advice on designing social learning.

▶ **Virtual-classroom courses**: Online classes structured much like a classroom course, with reading assignments, presentations, discussions via forums and other social media, and homework. They may include synchronous online meetings. Read Chapter 10 for more on designing Webinars and virtual-classroom courses.

And that is just the start. As you read this, clever designers are creating even more forms of e-learning and blending mixtures of the types listed here.

WHAT IS E-LEARNING DESIGN?

E-learning can be the best learning possible—or the worst. It all depends on design.

Creating effective e-learning requires both design and development. They are not the same thing. Design is decision; development is construction. Design governs *what* we do; development governs *how* we carry out those decisions. Design involves judgment, compromise, tradeoff, and creativity. Design is the 1001 decisions, big and small, that affect the outcome of your e-learning project. This book is about design.

Start with good instructional design

Effective e-learning starts with sound instructional design. Instructional design requires selecting, organizing, and specifying the learning experiences necessary to teach somebody something. Good instructional design is independent of the technology or personnel used to create those learning experiences.

Apply just enough instructional design

Instructional design is a vast subject. This humble chapter cannot cover it all. What you will find in this chapter is a streamlined, rapid instructional-design method. It is simple, quick, informal, and pragmatic. Use it as your survival kit when you do not have time or money for more. Or, use it as a check on your longer, more formal process.

Before you fast-forward to another chapter with more screen snapshots and fewer diagrams, take a moment to reflect on this: Unless you get instructional design right, technology can only increase the speed and certainty of failure.

Instructional design determines everything else

Instructional design translates the high-level project goals to choices for technology, content, and everything else. The instructional design of e-learning informs decisions on what authoring tools, management systems, and other technologies to buy or license. Instructional design directs the development of content and the selection of media. It orchestrates decisions on budget, schedule, and other aspects of project development. So, design your instruction *before* buying technology or recruiting new staff members.

Good design can prevent common failures

I've done pedagogical autopsies on a lot of failed e-learning projects over the years and have seen clearly that most failures can be traced back to bad or non-existent instructional design. Such failures are often blamed on defective technology, inadequate budget, lack of time, or insufficient management support. But these causes are really secondary. The project ran out of time, money, and management patience because of common failures of instructional design, such as:

▶ **Trying to teach too much**. Instead of being precisely targeted, objectives were a laundry list of everything every subject-matter expert and manager on the project thought any learner might someday need to know.

▶ **Failing to teach what people really need**. Too often projects try to teach disconnected knowledge when people need applicable skills. Learners do not value such objectives and put little effort into learning them.

▶ **Omitting supporting objectives**. Projects often concentrate on the explicit goals and forget the underlying motivation and fundamental skills necessary to propel and validate learning. Courses are jam-packed with what people should know or understand but deficient in what they must believe or feel.

▶ **Teaching what is easy to teach**. Builders of e-learning often take the easy road and teach what is easy or fun to teach rather than what learners really need. After all, learners are more likely to "like" the course if we make it easy.

▶ **Boring and frustrating learners.** Many projects waste learners' time by teaching what they already know or can easily figure out on their own.

▶ **Forcing people to learn in ways they find awkward and embarrassing**. Sometimes creators of e-learning impose their own preferred learning styles on learners for whom these styles are totally unsuited.

Avoid bad instructional design models

Instructional design is not rocket science—it's harder. And some of its failures are even more spectacular than a cartwheeling Titan IIIC missile. Here are some common methodologies of non-design:

▶ **RAPRAPRAPAWAP**, which stands for read a paper, read a paper, read a paper, and write a paper. It is a sad staple of graduate university courses and constitutes the only instructional design some tenured faculty seem capable of.

▶ **Pack 'em, yak 'em, rack 'em, and track 'em,** which is designed to economically handle large numbers of learners. In it, the institution enrolls large numbers of people ("pack 'em"), lectures to them ("yak 'em"), tests their regurgitative abilities to ensure conformity and compliance ("rack 'em"), and records extensive statistics to create the illusion of learning ("track 'em").

▶ **Warn and scorn** (AKA Cover the Corporate Assets) force marches learners through screens listing relevant laws and regulations and requires them to acknowledge each screen with at least a button click, which the course scrupulously records as proof that it warned employees against forbidden behavior. The cynical goal of such training is so the organization can say, "See, it's not our fault the employee behaved badly." The purpose of such "compliance" courses is not learning or improved behavior but mounting a legal defense.

▶ **Fill in the blanks**. Many designers start out with a template course whose slots they fill with chunks of subject-related content. This strategy is very common among low-cost content developers who use minimum-wage copy-and-paste drones to build courses.

▶ **Wouldn't it be cool if …** (AKA Fad-chasing) consists of trying to impress learners or management by using the latest gizmo or the trendiest technique. Symptoms of this methodology include so-called designers spending more time talking about "wow factor" than about learning—and never completing a project before launching sideways into a quest of the next techno-fad.

Don't expect a guarantee of learning

Some instructional design experts claim that their methodology guarantees successful learning. They lie. We cannot guarantee any outcome involving more than a few human beings. People are simply too unpredictable, and outside factors intrude.

Like it or not, some people are going to fail regardless of what the designer and teacher do. Some cannot be motivated to learn. Some lack basic learning skills. Others struggle with learning disabilities. Intransigent bad attitudes are common. Substance abuse and mental illness are extreme cases. We cannot undo damage done over a lifetime and not already corrected by parents, friends, spouses, bosses, co-workers, psychologists, and decades of schooling.

Only by lowering standards sufficiently ("dummying down the learning") can we ensure that everyone appears to succeed. Doing so usually fails those most likely to master what you teach, apply it effectively, and teach those around them.

Don't blame yourself. Don't play the old butts-in-seats game where learning is evaluated by how many people sit through it. And, don't give up on any learners. Consider whether everyone really needs to learn what you are teaching. Can they learn by other means (p. 36)? Instead of learning the subject, can they succeed by asking or being directed by those you do educate?

Apply design to all units of e-learning

Design must be applied at all levels of e-learning from whole curricula down to individual media components. It is important to understand these units because they influence what design techniques we use. Before proceeding, let's get our terminology straight.

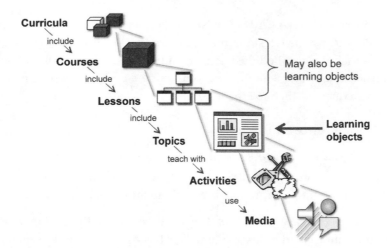

At the top of the pyramid are *curricula*, programs that include related courses that lead to a degree or certificate in a subject area.

A curriculum is typically composed of *courses*, each of which teaches a broad but specific area of a subject. We might also call such units *books* or *knowledge products.* Course-level design issues are discussed in online Chapter 13, *Strategic decisions,* at horton.com/eld/.

Courses are composed of clusters of smaller components called *lessons*. Each lesson is organized to accomplish one of the broad objectives of the course or a cluster of related objectives. Online Chapter 12, *Lessons,* at horton.com/eld/ will help you design lessons.

At a lower level are the individual *topics*; each designed to accomplish a single low-level learning objective. Topics are often designed as self-contained learning objects. For help designing topics, turn to Chapter 6.

Near the bottom level are *learning activities*; each designed to provoke a specific learning experience. Each activity may answer a specific question or make a point, but no single learning activity is sufficient to accomplish a learning objective. Activities are the subject of Chapters 2 through 4. Activities used to measure learning are called tests and are the subject of Chapter 5.

Finally there are the media elements: the words, pictures, voice, music, sound effects, animation, and video that present activities to learners. These are not covered directly in this book.

Courses and lessons may sometimes be designed as learning objects; however, this term is most commonly applied to topics.

Recognize various names for levels

The hierarchy of curriculum, course, lesson, topic, activities, and media is common but not universal. You may encounter a variety of other names for these levels. Let's see some alternatives:

	Quick ID	SCORM	Other names
	Curriculum		Library Program Portfolio
	Course	Content aggregation	Document Book Path
	Lesson	Content aggregation	Chapter Module
	Topic	Sharable content object	Page Learning object Event
	Activities	Asset	Block Teaching point
	Media	Asset	Information object Asset

The SCORM standard (www.adlnet.gov) refers to courses and lessons as *content aggregations*. Topics are called *sharable content objects*, or *SCOs*, for short. Any content below the level of a topic is called an *asset*.

Other names for units are common in specific universities, corporations, tools, and methodologies. For instance, a curriculum might be called a *library*, *program*, or *portfolio*. Instead of course, we might use the term *document*, *book*, or *path*. Lessons are sometimes called *chapters* or *modules*. A topic may be called a page or a *reusable learning object* (*RLO* for short). In virtual-classroom learning, topics equate to events. Activities are roughly equivalent to what some call *blocks* or *teaching points*. Media elements may be called *information objects* or *assets*. If these terms do not match the ones at your organization, do not fret. Just write in your own names for these units.

Time for a real example

Let's see how to apply these levels in the real world. Here is a slice down through a single subject area:

Curriculum:	Master's of Business Administration program.
Course:	"Accounting 101."
Lesson:	"Assets and Liabilities."
Topic:	"Evaluating assets."
Activity:	Using a spreadsheet to calculate the values of assets.
Media	Voice-over animation explaining the concept. Live spreadsheet used in an activity.

DESIGN QUICKLY AND RELIABLY

Earlier in the chapter I promised you a tried and true approach to e-learning design. Well, here it is.

E-learning benefits most from a rapid, cyclical design process. In this section you will find a minimalist, waste-no-time, results-focused approach to specifying e-learning that actually works. This process omits unnecessary steps and concentrates on the design tasks that *really* matter.

In the interest of speedy learning, we'll start with a preview, overview, summary, and job aid all rolled into one. An Adobe PDF version is available at horton.com/eld/. Download it, print it out, and pin it to your wall, where you can refer to it throughout your projects.

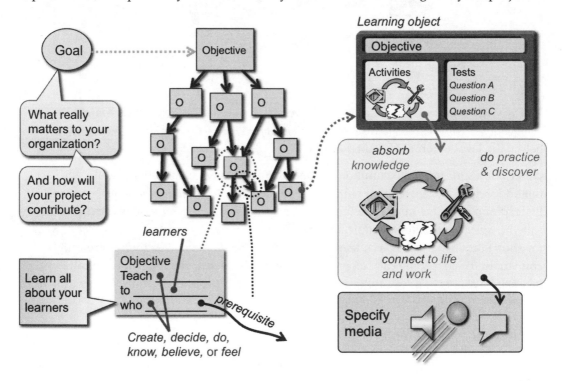

The first step in quick instructional design is to clarify the goal of your project. This is a simple two-step procedure. First you nail down what matters to your organization—the one sponsoring development of learning. Is it profit or public service? Return on investment or reputation?

Next you describe how your project will contribute directly to that organizational goal. If you draw a blank at this point, cancel the project now before wasting resources. Once you do define how your project contributes, you have a solid basis to ask for funding and other support.

The next step is to write the overall learning objective. This objective states how your e-learning changes the learner. It describes the end result of learning. That objective, however, may have prerequisite objectives. And those second-level objectives may have prerequisites as well. You keep identifying prerequisite objectives until you reach the starting abilities of intended learners.

I use a simple formula to state objectives: Teach *blank* to *blank* who *blank*. Typically it takes the form: teach a *subject* to a *group of people* who *know certain things* already. The first slot records what we intend to teach. It is what we want them to create, decide, do, know, believe, or feel. The second slot names the group of learners who must accomplish this objective. It describes a group of learners. The third slot records prerequisites for the objective; for example, what aspects of the subject the learners must already know or what they must be able to do. It may point to other objectives that satisfy these prerequisites.

Each learning objective requires us to design a learning object to accomplish that objective. That object requires two types of content: learning activities and tests.

Tests are questions or other actions to verify that learning occurred and the objective was accomplished.

Learners complete learning activities in order to learn. There are usually three types of learning activities required: the learner *absorbs* knowledge by reading or watching; the learner *does* practice or discovery activities to deepen learning; and learners complete activities designed to *connect* what they are learning to their lives and work.

Only after specifying the activities can we make choices of what media to employ: words, pictures, sounds, and so forth. At this point, we must also keep an open mind. Perhaps the best way to implement the activity is not with electronic media, but with paper and pen. The best way to provoke the needed learning experience may require activities performed away from the computer. Our decisions here may lead us to blend conventional and electronic learning or to use non-learning solutions as well.

Don't worry if this process is not crystal clear or does not seem to cover every possible situation. I will explain each of these steps in more detail and suggest how you can vary it to meet any need.

Identify your underlying goal

Design starts with a goal. You may be designing an office building or a monumental sculpture. You may be designing a rocket or an automobile. You may be designing e-learning. Before you can design any of these things, you must know what it is your design must accomplish.

Rather than start listing the things you will accomplish for learners, think about what you will do for your employer, your sponsor, or your financial backers. What does your organization hope to accomplish? Your goal might look like one of these:

▶ Recertify 150 nuclear power plant operators.
▶ Cut costs of education by 50% over the next year.
▶ Reduce bullying among students in our middle schools.
▶ Quickly prepare a global marketing plan to sell a new line of products.
▶ Cut misdiagnoses of battery failures by 90%.
▶ Earn $200,000 by selling courses.

Keep the organizational goal in mind as you make other decisions. Write this goal on a note card and tack it to your wall. Every day, ask yourself: "How am I helping achieve that goal?"

Ask what matters

Your overall goal tells you what really matters. To clarify this goal, you need to answer two questions.

The first question is "What matters to your organization?" We might phrase the question this way: "For your company, university, department, government, or institution, what is the single most important measure of success?" Try to answer in three words or fewer. That restriction focuses your goal. The goal might be bottom-line profit or return on investment. Or it might be public service or first-rate reputation. On one of our projects, the Gantt Group, a consulting firm specializing in teaching project management, identified their goal as:

> For your organization, what is the single most important measure of success? [3 words maximum]
>
> ### More clients

They figured if they attracted enough clients, revenues and profits would follow.

The second question asks how your project will help accomplish that goal. I am not saying your e-learning will accomplish the goal by itself, but you certainly should be able to state how it will contribute. If you cannot convincingly and honestly argue that your project contributes to the goal, consider canceling the project now. Without such alignment with organizational goals, your project may run out of money, time, and management support. Better to stop now before antagonizing the management of your organization by wasting resources on an endeavor that does not matter to the organization.

Let's look at how this question was answered for the Gantt Group:

> How will your project help accomplish that goal?
>
> *Convince potential clients that understanding Gantt charts can make them more successful project managers (and that the Gantt Group is the source for that understanding).*

The proposed project was aimed at garnering more clients by convincing potential clients that understanding Gantt charts, which are a common tool of project management, could make them more successful and that the Gantt Group was the source for that understanding.

Consider a wide range of goals

Organizational goals are not limited to profit or return-on-investment. Observe what your leaders emphasize as the values and goal of the organization. Here are some possibilities.

Type goal	Description	Measures
Financial	Monetary success of a for-profit or not-for-profit enterprise.	▶ Profit amount and margin. ▶ Cash flow. ▶ Stock price. ▶ Venture capital. ▶ Fundraising.
Intellectual capital	Knowledge the organization controls.	▶ Education level of staff. ▶ Professional experience of staff. ▶ Rates of attracting and retaining talent. ▶ Patents, inventions, and trade secrets.
Customers	Consumers of the organization's services or products.	▶ Accounts, clients, sponsors. ▶ Students. ▶ Market share.
Employees	Staff of the organization.	▶ Retention of essential employees. ▶ Employee morale. ▶ Creativity and positive attitudes.

Type goal	Description	Measures
Operations	Efficiency and speed with which the organization performs its mission.	▶ Time to market. ▶ Cost per unit. ▶ Agility in changing business processes.
Reputation	Public image of an organization.	▶ Industry awards. ▶ Rankings and ratings. ▶ Community-service awards.

Identify the real goals

Don't just read lofty mission statements and listen to flowery speeches by your president. These are often too abstract and usually designed for external consumption only. Instead, do your own research. Here are some techniques to try:

▶ Ask your leaders how they expect you to contribute to the success of your organization. Often we fail to ask for fear of seeming out of touch or feeling we should already know. Most real leaders are delighted with such questions.

▶ Identify what is crucial to survival of your organization or accomplishment of its mission. Do a Web search using keywords of "survival" and "crisis" along with the name of your organization or its market segment.

▶ Observe what areas are being cut back and what areas are expanding within your organization and your industry.

▶ Research what is important to organizations like yours. Consider competing organizations and those in analogous fields.

▶ Consult legally binding statements, such as financial reports and Securities and Exchange Commission reports. Read carefully sections on planned growth and related risks.

Link learning objectives to organizational goals

Create a bridge connecting a high-priority goal of your organization and the learning objectives of your e-learning so both business managers and instructional designers see the value of e-learning to the organization. Notice how this statement provides just such a bridge:

> Misdiagnosing battery failures costs AnCaBattery Company millions of dollars per year in replacement costs and customer good will. Most misdiagnoses occur because customer service technicians (CSTs) cannot identify the underlying problem from the symptoms described by customers. By teaching CSTs to identify the cause of failure, we can reduce misdiagnoses by 90%.

Sad to say, many instructional designers stubbornly refuse to consider the underlying organizational goal when designing instruction. They do not feel that organizational goals are their responsibility. As a result they design courses that accomplish little or else die for lack of organizational support. This is tragic because it only takes two questions to align learning objectives to organizational goals.

Analyze learners' needs and abilities

Whose skills, knowledge, and attitudes are you trying to alter? Before you can design e-learning for people, you must know enough about them to choose the types of learning experience to best teach them. You must assess learners' capabilities, not merely demographics and related stereotypes. Remember, abilities and attitudes matter more than just age, gender, nationality, and economic class.

What capabilities and traits are most important?

▶ **Motivation for learning**. Why would learners devote the time and effort necessary? Is it to accomplish their current job? Or to qualify for a new job? Also consider who pays for the learning: the learner or the learner's employer.

▶ **Psychomotor skills**. What is the level of the learner's perceptual acuity, working memory capacity, and speed and precision of eye-hand coordination? These abilities determine how learners can get information and interact with devices.

▶ **Attitude and mindset**. What are learners' attitudes toward learning and toward authority? Are they introverted or extroverted? Social or solitary?

▶ **Mental discipline**. Do learners have a short or long attention span? Are they easily distracted? Are they self-motivated and self-disciplined? Do they prefer to work alone or with others? Can they skip quickly among simultaneous tasks or do they need to complete one task before moving on to another?

▶ **Communication skills**. How well can they read, listen, speak, and write in the planned language for the course?

▶ **Social skills**. How well do learners work with others? Are they open to criticism? Can they motivate others? Can they offer empathy and support?

▶ **Talents and intelligences**. What basic abilities do learners possess: verbal, visual, logical, mathematical, musical, performance, athletic, intrapersonal, or interpersonal?

▶ **Media preferences**. Which media do learners attend to first: video, graphics, voice, music, or text? Which do they consider primary and which secondary? Which do they treat as more authoritative?

▶ **Background knowledge and experience**. What do potential learners already know about the subject? Do they know the basic principles, vocabulary, and taxonomy of the field? Or are they only familiar with detailed facts and rote procedures without understanding the bigger picture?

- ▶ **Learning conditions**. Where and when will they learn? How much time do they have available for learning? Do they have to learn in short spurts between other activities? Is the environment noisy and distracting?

- ▶ **Locus of control**. What do learners have power over? Can they change their learning environment and conditions? Do they have the ability to apply what they learn in their day-to-day work?

- ▶ **Style of prior education**. What kinds of learning have learners participated in? Which will they find familiar? Which trigger negative associations?

- ▶ **Digital fluency**. Is the potential learner digitally naïve or a digital native? To get a handle on how learners use technology in their lives ask some questions:

  - How do they get their news: through newspapers, television, or newsfeed on a mobile device?

  - How do they communicate with friends and family: by letter, phone, e-mail, or social media?

  - What do they do for fun? For example, do they watch television passively or immerse themselves in video games?

  - What digital skills have they mastered? For example, can they quickly enter text, install and configure application programs, or search for information?

Though you may find it productive or necessary to group learners by shared characteristics, never forget that learners are individuals and no two are exactly the same.

Identify what to teach

Success requires teaching the right things. Try to teach too much and you blow your budget. Teach the wrong things and you accomplish nothing—at least nothing positive.

How do you determine the learning necessary to accomplish an organizational goal? Several forms of analyzing needs are ready at hand. Since needs analysis is a field unto itself with its own courses and books, I will just summarize the techniques here.

Test to identify essentials

Essentialism is a technique to focus learning on essentials needed to accomplish goals— and omitting everything else. When practiced scrupulously, essentialism streamlines education, typically eliminating 90% of the content while still accomplishing the goal better than by using conventional means.

The core of essentialism is testing with potential learners to determine exactly what they need and what they do not need. Learners are given a task to perform. It is a task that those who meet the goals of the learning can accomplish but those who do not meet the goal cannot accomplish. Learners are given no prior training but are given access to resources they will have when they are expected to apply learning in the real world.

Learners work in pairs as they attempt the task. At any time they can ask questions of an expert, who can answer their questions but not volunteer information. The entire session is recorded and analyzed to identify what learners asked about, what they figured out on their own, and what they learned from other sources. After a dozen or so tests, designers have a pretty clear idea of what learners must learn and how they best learn.

Essentialism is especially effective in identifying small misconceptions that block success in a wide range of ideas, as well as spotting places where attitudes, rather than knowledge, is the barrier. I use this technique as my personal secret weapon to cut projects down to size.

Analyze the gap between real and ideal performance

The purpose of most education is to close gaps—gaps between the current state of learning and the goal; for example, between current levels of performance and required levels, between novice and expert behavior, or between unsuccessful and successful work.

Gap analysis asks what is needed to close the gap. What do those at the target level create, decide, or do differently? And, is the difference a result of what they know, believe, or feel?

Probe the gap by interviewing people on both sides of the gap. Especially helpful are supervisors of groups whose members span the gap.

Analyze how work is done

Job analysis examines work to identify its basic components and what each component requires from the worker. Typically an area of work, called a goal, is divided into *jobs*, that is, discrete pieces of work with a clear result. Jobs require *tasks*, which are units of work performed in a continuous span. Tasks, in turn, are made up of a mixture of *decisions* and *actions*.

Once you identify the individual decisions and actions, determine what abilities the learner must acquire to perform each action or make each decision.

Ask "those who should know"

Insight into what people need to learn can come from asking those who routinely interact with them and observe their behavior. Start with the learner and work outward to their bosses, co-workers, subordinates, customers, and clients. If you can ethically do so, consult their personal and professional networks.

For job-related training, be sure to ask immediate supervisors. Simply ask, "What do you want your subordinates to do differently?" If supervisors never mention the subject of your proposed e-learning effort, take that as a warning.

Analyze critical incidents

Critical incidents are important happenings that indicate the potential need or value of learning. Critical incidents include costly failures, widespread mistakes, surprising results, and invaluable successes.

Ask what did people create, decide, or do (or fail to create, decide, or do) to cause incidents? Follow up by asking why. What did they know, believe, or feel (or not know, believe, or feel) that caused them to act as they did?

Do not let the "content committee" decide

The worst way to determine what to teach is to assemble a committee of subject-matter experts and have them list all the things they think learners should learn. Such efforts result in a laundry list of everything every "expert" thinks any learner might need to know, enjoy learning, or should learn as a test of initiation into the profession.

Subject-matter experts are not deliberately dishonest, but they often unconsciously believe that the goal of education is to recreate their level and type of expertise in learners. As a result, subject matter experts list everything they know. Or everything they had to learn "back in the day." Or everything they love about the subject.

Remember, it may be a long time since these experts had to learn the subject. Much of the knowledge they do not routinely apply may be out of date. And, even they do not consciously know much of what they know. They may be unfamiliar with more efficient ways to learn the subject.

Don't ignore subject-matter experts, but do not blindly follow their advice either. Instead of letting them define the course, have them verify the accuracy of the finished e-learning.

Set learning objectives

Good objectives are a mission-critical, sin qua non, must-have, make-or-break requirement for effective e-learning. Forgive me for stacking up so many adjectives, but, without exception, clear objectives make everything go better. In my experience, well over half the failures of e-learning projects could have been prevented by clear objectives.

Everything stems from the objectives. From the objectives, we identify prerequisites, select learning activities, and design tests. Good objectives focus efforts, reduce false starts, and cut waste enormously.

Write your learning objectives

Once you have clarified the goal of your project, you can write the primary learning objective for your project. This objective states what the project will accomplish.

There are many opinions on how to write objectives and complete methodologies on just how to phrase objectives. Search amazon.com for books by Robert Mager or Robert Gagné and you will find some examples. For quick instructional design, however, I use a single, simple formula that works well almost all the time. It states learning objectives in three parts. First, the objective states the intent, that is, what will be taught. Second, it identifies the target learner. Third, it identifies starting requirements.

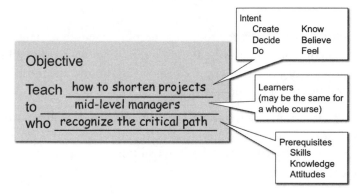

For the example of the course *Using Gantt Charts*, the top-level objective of the course was to teach how to shorten projects. It was to teach this subject to mid-level managers. But those managers had to know how to recognize the critical path in a Gantt chart.

The first slot in our formula records what we want to teach, that is, our intent. For the top objective, it is to create, decide, or do something. For lower-level objectives, it may also be to know, believe, or feel something.

The second slot records the group of people we want to accomplish this intent. If an entire course is aimed at a single group of people, this slot may have the same answer for every objective in the course.

The final slot records the prerequisites necessary to make accomplishing the intent practical. Prerequisites are usually stated as the abilities, knowledge, beliefs, and feelings learners must possess. The prerequisites slot can have multiple answers, but the teach slot has only a single intent.

Each prerequisite may in turn require another objective—with its own prerequisites leading to even more objectives.

What makes a good objective?

Good learning objectives are clear, precise, and worthy. Let's look at each of these requirements.

Clear

A learning objective should be clear to everyone involved with it. The objective must tell the project's management team what you intend to accomplish. It must give the designer of learning activities specific targets to achieve. And it must communicate the "what's in it for me" to the learner.

Precise

The learning objective must specify the required learning in enough detail that we can measure its accomplishment. You may be thinking that what we have just listed as an objective is not complete or precise enough. Correct. Right now, it is more of a goal. But don't worry; we will tighten it up considerably.

My advice is: don't get too precise too soon. Early in a project, it is more important to write down all your objectives briefly than to specify them in excruciating detail. Once you have all your learning "goals" spread out in front of you and have eliminated unnecessary ones, you can flesh them out one at a time.

Worthy

Your learning objectives must all contribute to accomplishing the underlying organizational goal. Responsible developers continually check their objectives against the organizational goal: "Why am I teaching this?"

There are six types of objectives

Some complex methodologies for writing objectives list hundreds of different types of objectives. I list six types of objectives—three primary and three secondary. Applied with sensitivity and common sense, they suffice 99% of the time.

Instructional intent can be expressed in the following format. This format consists of a standard preamble and one of six possible completions.

By experiencing this course, lesson or topic, the learner will:

**Primary objectives
(be able to ...)**

Secondary objectives

- ▶ **Create** or design an X that does Y.
- ▶ **Decide** X, given Y.
- ▶ **Do** procedure X to accomplish Y.

- ▶ **Know** X about Y
- ▶ Believe X.
- ▶ **Feel** X about Y.

Primary and secondary objectives

Objectives can be primary or secondary. Primary objectives are the ultimate reasons for learning while secondary objectives enable accomplishment of the primary objectives, even though they are seldom the targeted result.

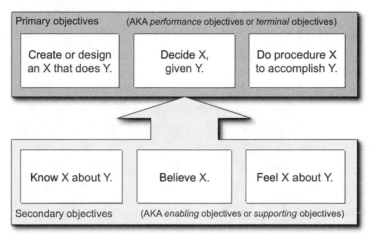

Both are important, but the primary objectives are the ones you must teach to accomplish your overall objective. Primary objectives are *performance* objectives in that they prescribe things people will be able to do as a result of your e-learning. As such, they are sometimes called *terminal* objectives. But there can also be *enabling* objectives, that is, things you teach so that learners can learn the terminal objectives. Secondary objectives are always enabling objectives. They are not the main goal, but may be essential, nonetheless, to accomplish the primary objectives.

So, if you write the *overall* objective for your e-learning and it looks like one of the secondary objectives here, reconsider. Ask yourself, why do you want someone to know, believe, or feel something? What will meeting such an objective accomplish? The answer to these questions pinpoints your primary objective.

Primary objectives state your goals

Primary objectives are the goals of your e-learning, that is, what the learner will be able to do. The following table lists the various forms of primary instructional objectives and provides examples of how they might be worded.

Type objective	When situation Z occurs, the learner will …	Examples
Create Synonyms: 　Build 　Design 　Draw 　Compose 　Synthesize 　Author 　Pen 　Conceive 　Form 　Formulate 　Invent	**Design or build an X that does Y.** Notes: ▶ Originality is required for a create objective, not merely building something by a rote procedure, for instance, painting an original scene but not painting-by-number. ▶ Creation does not have to be from scratch. Finding a new use for an ancient tool is a create intent. So is streamlining an established procedure. ▶ The thing created can be a physical object, a concept, or a plan. It does not have to be something commonly considered "creative." Any innovation qualifies.	… **specify** the layout of a city park that meets environmental, aesthetic, and logistical requirements. … **write** a program to export information from a common database to an XML format containing just the information specified. … **build** a 1/24-scale model of the proposed dwelling. … **adapt** a generic disaster-relief plan to a specific catastrophe.
Decide Synonyms: 　Choose 　Pick 　Select 　Rate 　Rank 　Prioritize 　Vote 　Resolve 　Judge 　Conclude 　Differentiate 　Discriminate 　Filter	**Decide Y.** Notes: Types of decisions include: ▶ Categorical (Yes/No, Go/No-go, Is/Is not, and Accept/Reject). ▶ Quantitative (How many? How much?). ▶ Selective (Which one?) A true decision requires some degree of judgment, not merely following an evaluation procedure.	… **pick** a course of treatment based on a physical examination of the patient and standard blood tests. … **decide** a strategy for dealing with a difficult co-worker based on the past behavior of the co-worker. … **order** a salad rather than a double cheeseburger. … **pick** team members based on what they can contribute rather than on familiarity, friendship, or superficial characteristics.

Type objective	When situation Z occurs, the learner will …	Examples
Do Synonyms: Perform Operate Act Construct Build Carry out Accomplish Arrange Complete Comply Execute Implement	**Do X to accomplish Y.** Notes: ▶ *Do* means performing a procedure without having to make decisions. ▶ Procedures can be physical, mental, or a combination. ▶ Define what support will be available during performance, for example, prompting, help on demand, or written instructions.	…once a month, **complete** the cleanup procedure to remove invalid e-mail addresses from the mailing list. … **mix** base and tint colors to match a sample provided by the customer. … **lift** heavy packages by flexing the knees rather than bending the back. … **apply** principles learned in Calculus 101 to problems encountered in Calculus 201.

Secondary objectives help accomplish goals

Secondary objectives teach something necessary to accomplish a primary objective. They state what the learner must know, believe, or feel.

Type objective	When situation Z occurs, the learner will …	Examples
Know Synonyms: Understand Recall Remember Appreciate Be informed Comprehend Remember Recite Cite	**Know X about Y.** Notes: *Knowing* can mean being able to: ▶ Recall facts and figures. ▶ Obtain information by online search or through a social network. ▶ Use one's mental model of how things work to answer questions. The mental model consists of connected assumptions and generalizations.	… **recall** the country codes for 99% of our international shipments. … **remember** calming words to use during disputes. … **identify** all bones in the human hand by name. … **identify** the last flight of the day to the customer's destination. … **cite** three reasons to use centrifugal pumps instead of positive-displacement pumps.

Type objective	When situation Z occurs, the learner will …	Examples

Believe
Synonyms:
    Have faith that
    Trust
    Rely on
    Accept
    Affirm
    Think that
    Be convinced of
    Expect
    Deem
    Maintain
    Presume
    Assume
	Believe X.
	Notes:
	▸ Believe objectives convince the learner that a claim is true, that something exists, or that an idea is important.
	▸ Believe and feel objectives often occur together. Believe is the intellectual part and feel is the emotional part.
		… **believe** that our company is the most reliable supplier in our market.
		… **believe** that they can accomplish their financial objectives through conservative investments.
		… **deem** mutual funds worthy of a place in their portfolios.
		… **believe** that risk-management techniques can reduce insurance premiums.

Feel
Synonyms:
    Sense
    Suffer
    Experience
    [emotion]
	Feel X about Y.
	Notes:
	To identify feel objectives, complete the following:
	▸ To succeed, learners must feel _____.
	▸ Or must not feel too much _____.
	Fill in the blanks with the appropriate emotions.
		… **feel** positively about our company's entire product line.
		… **remain** calm when confronted by an angry stranger.
		… **have** confidence that they can use our products to solve their own problems.
		… **feel** sympathy (rather than pity) for co-workers with disabilities.

Pick objectives by what you teach

You may not be used to thinking in terms of Create, Decide, Do, Know, Believe, and Feel. Perhaps your organization identifies learning needs in terms of knowledge, skills, and attitudes (KSAs); or as types of information, such as concepts, principles, facts, processes, and procedures. Translation is not difficult. The following sections show how.

Pick objectives for KSAs

You may be accustomed to writing objectives in terms of knowledge, skills, and attitudes (KSAs). If so, just remember that skills typically require Create or Do objectives. Knowledge requires, you guessed it, Know objectives. Attitudes occasion Decide objectives because attitudes reveal themselves in decisions people make. Because attitudes have their roots in people's beliefs and emotions, they may require Believe and Feel objectives.

Pick objectives for types of information

Some development methodologies work in terms of information types or subject areas, such as principles, procedures, processes, and facts. If you have classified your learning into these information types, you are halfway to objectives.

The following table lists objectives common for each information type.

Info type	Common objective
Fact	**Do**: Look up efficiently. **Know**: Recall a few critical facts. **Know**: Format of codes, names, etc. to aid in recalling and verifying. **Decide**: Apply the concept to make a decision.
Concept	**Know**: Add the concept to a mental model.
Process	**Decide**: How to improve a process. **Decide**: Assign people and objects to roles in the process. **Decide**: One's role in a process. **Decide**: Who to contact for process-related problems or questions. **Feel**: A valued part of a large endeavor. **Decide**: Diagnose problems. **Decide**: Predict results.
Procedure	Alternate between: **Decide**: What to do next. **Do**: Perform the next step.
System	**Know**: Form and refine a mental model. **Decide**: Predict outcomes of changes to the system.

Info type	Common objective
Principle	**Know**: Recall the principle. **Know**: Add it to the mental model. **Decide**: Whether it applies. **Do**: Apply the principle. **Decide**: Apply the principle to make a decision.
Rule	**Know**: Recall the rule. **Decide**: Recognize that it applies. **Decide**: Apply the rule to make a decision.
Attitude	**Decide**: What the attitude leads to. **Know**: Ignorance is the cause of the problem. **Believe**: Truth of claim, importance of decision, and effectiveness of action. **Feel**: Urgency to act, empowered to act, courageous enough to act.
Psychomotor skill	**Do**: Execute moves fluently. **Know**: Necessary moves to accomplish the goal. **Decide**: How to respond to change. **Feel**: Calm and undistracted.

Flesh out objectives

We've made a good start on defining objectives, but we have a bit more work to do. To flesh out our objectives, we need to add criteria we can use to determine whether learners have met the objectives.

Spell out the situation

We teach so that learners can apply what they learn, not merely accumulate knowledge. People apply learning in real-world situations. As part of the objective, we need to specify what those situations are. That way, designers can tailor the design to accomplish results in those situations.

Situation is a pretty broad term. It can include three main factors: events that *trigger* application of learning, *conditions* under which the learner must act, and *resources* the learner will need in order to apply learning.

Trigger. What events will trigger application of the learning? What must the learner recognize as a cue to act? Will the learner receive explicit prompts to apply learning? Or will the learner need to infer the need for action from subtle cues in the environment? Is this an action that is applied periodically or on a schedule?

Conditions. Under what conditions does the learner perform the action? In what environment does the learner act? Where does the action take place? How noisy is the environment? Is it especially hot or cold? How much room does the learner have? Is lighting adequate? Is the learner subject to frequent interruptions? (See p. 13 for a list of difficult conditions.)

Resources. What resources can the learner draw on: books, calculators, or access to the Web? What assistance will the learner have: supervisor to guide the learner or peers with whom to discuss problems?

Set criteria for success

What degree of success will learners accomplish? We like to think that all learners will be perfectly successful in accomplishing the intended results. Ironically, though, designing for a goal of perfect performance often leads to worse, not better, results. Thus, for each objective, we should realistically state how successful learners should be in applying what they learn.

Quantifying the degree of success is not easy, but we can adapt metrics such as these:

▶ Percent of learners who will accomplish the objective perfectly.

▶ Average error rate.

▶ Time required performing the task.

▶ Results produced in a specified period of time.

▶ Reduction in frequency of problems or increase in rate of favorable incidents.

Examples of complete learning objectives

Here are some examples of learning objectives from different courses:

Learners	Situation	Action	Criteria
Full-time foresters with less than five years' experience.	When asked to recommend a policy. They will have access to Web-based resources.	Objectively consider controlled burns as a means of forest management.	Novice foresters will recommend controlled burning with the same frequency as more experienced foresters.

Learners	Situation	Action	Criteria
Customer support technicians.	When answering customer complaints over the phone. Using a diagnostic procedure recalled from memory.	Correctly identify the cause of battery failures.	Reduce the current rate of misdiagnosis by 90%.
Individual investors.	Using Web-based resources during the course.	Develop a balanced financial plan to accomplish their individual objectives.	Over 90% will complete their plans.

Identify prerequisites

No project of any complexity will have just a single, simple learning objective. Whatever the top-level learning objective, it has prerequisites that you must identify. Such prerequisites specify the abilities, knowledge, beliefs, and feelings learners must possess before they can begin to accomplish the main objective. These prerequisites may have prerequisites of their own.

Spot related objectives

Starting with the top objective, we begin identifying prerequisite objectives.

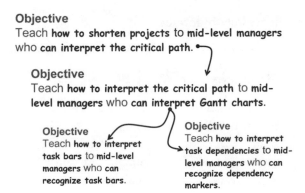

For example, let's look at the top objective for the course *Using Gantt Charts*. It is to teach how to shorten projects to mid-level managers who can interpret the critical path. Fine, but not all mid-level managers will already know how to interpret the critical path.

That means we need another lower-level objective to meet that prerequisite. This objective would require teaching how to interpret the critical path. It would be aimed at the same mid-level managers as before. This new objective has its own prerequisite, namely, the ability to interpret Gantt charts in general.

Interpreting Gantt charts in turn requires objectives on how to interpret task bars and how to interpret task dependencies. Both of these two new objectives are prerequisites of the prior objective.

Thus, objectives develop in a cascade downward from the top-level learning objective as we repeatedly ask what the learner must know before beginning an objective.

State objectives in shorthand

My formula for writing objectives is simple; even so, writing dozens of objectives can become tedious. Perhaps that is why many designers skip all that work and just begin developing content. Resist that urge. If you want to, you can streamline the process by writing objectives in a shorthand fashion.

To streamline the statement of an objective, state just what the learner will be able to do after accomplishing the objective. "Teach how to shorten projects to mid-level managers who can interpret the critical path" becomes just "shorten projects." Our next objective becomes just "interpret the critical path." And our final two objectives become just "interpret task bars" and "interpret task dependencies."

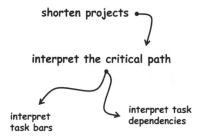

We can streamline the statement of objectives because the learners are typically similar throughout an entire course and because the prerequisite for a higher-level objective becomes the subject for the next objective down the cascade.

This shorthand works best when the objective is stated in the grammatical form that expresses it as a task the learner will be able to accomplish. The first part of this grammatical form is an active verb, such as "interpret" or "shorten." The second part is a phrase representing the direct object of the verb, that is, what the verb acts on. This format keeps the focus on performance.

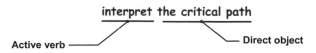

Here's a best practice for you: The top tools for cataloging your streamlined learning objectives are a whiteboard or Post-it™ notes because they make it easy for you to change your mind.

Hierarchy of learning objectives

Our cascade of learning objectives and their prerequisites naturally forms a tree-structure or hierarchy. For example, let's look at the analysis that was conducted for the *Using Gantt Charts* course. It started with the top-level objective, to teach how to shorten projects to mid-level managers who can interpret the critical path.

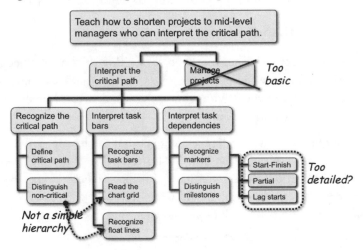

For that objective, I identified two prerequisites, namely the ability to interpret the critical path (which I mentioned earlier) and to manage projects generally. Interpreting the critical path had three prerequisites. It required the ability to recognize the critical path, interpret task bars, and interpret task dependencies. Recognizing the critical path required the ability to define the critical path and distinguish non-critical paths from critical paths. Interpreting task bars required the ability to recognize task bars, to read the chart grid, and to recognize float lines. Interpreting task dependencies required the ability to recognize dependency markers and to distinguish milestones from dependency markers. Recognizing markers required the ability to recognize three types of markers: start-finish, partial completion, and lagging starts. The actual analysis was a bit more complex than this, but essentially of the same structure.

Looking at this tidy hierarchy, it is tempting to proceed to the next step. We should not do so without dealing with some of the traps that often lurk at this stage. For one thing, some of the objectives may be too basic or too vast to fit within the scope of the project. For example, the objective of being able to manage projects is too elemental to fit in a course on using Gantt charts.

Another trap in such a neat hierarchy is that we may assume it represents all the prerequisite relationships. A closer look reveals that distinguishing non-critical from critical paths requires the ability to recognize float lines and to read the chart grid, which were earlier identified as prerequisites for interpreting task bars. The relationships among objectives are clearly not a simple hierarchy.

Scanning the lower-level objectives may also cause us to question whether some objectives are too detailed or esoteric to be included directly. We might consider omitting these objectives or putting them in reference materials. One suspect area covers the details about the different types of dependency markers.

One final trap is to automatically adopt this hierarchy as the structure for the course menu. Sometimes that is a good idea, but often it is not, especially if we feel that prerequisites should be taught first.

Identify what each objective requires

For each objective, identify the requirements for learning to take place, that is, its prerequisites.

To identify prerequisites for an objective, ask why learners may fail to accomplish the objective. Do they not recognize the need or misperceive the situation? Do they lack a crucial fact? Are they stumped on how to proceed, or are they afraid to take the next step? Or, are they just unmotivated or uninterested?

To state the problem as an objective, ask what the learner must be able to create, decide, or do and what the learner must know, believe, and feel.

For example, in a course on reducing workplace violence, one objective was that new supervisors be able to reduce disputes between subordinates.

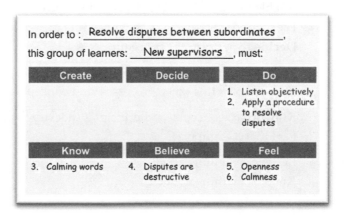

To meet the objective of resolving disputes between subordinates will require first meeting the six prerequisites listed.

List prerequisites

How do we quickly and systematically identify the prerequisites for a specific objective? There is no magic formula, but careful analysis of objectives will help. For example, we might identify component skills as prerequisites. Component skills are lower-level parts of a higher-level skill. For example, if a procedure has five steps, each step might be a component skill of that procedure.

Another category of prerequisites is definitions. Unless learners have the basic vocabulary of a field, they cannot learn the more advanced aspects of that field. Concepts may be needed when we want to go beyond rote learning and enable creative problem solving. Rules and regulations may be required to inform learners of the constraints on how they can apply their learning. Here are some common prerequisites for different types of objectives:

Type objective	Common prerequisites
Create an X that does Y.	**Do** procedure for planning or building. **Know** requirements for Y and rules governing the process. **Decide** approaches to take. **Feel** open to new ideas.
Decide X.	**Know** rules that govern the decision. **Know** what choices are available. **Know** the consequences of each choice. **Know** principles and concepts that can guide the decision. **Believe** that the decision is necessary. **Feel** positively toward the correct choice.
Do procedure X to accomplish Y.	Be able to **do** the individual steps of the procedure. **Feel** confident to perform the procedure. **Decide** to perform the procedure.
Know X about Y.	**Know** terms necessary to understand X. **Know** supporting facts, processes, and concepts.
Believe X.	**Know** facts, concepts, and principles that support X. **Feel** that X is important.
Feel X about Y.	**Believe** something about Y. **Know** something about Y.

Teach essential objectives

Instruction is only effective if it teaches the right things. For example, problems often occur when we teach low-level, explicit knowledge that learners already know, could figure out on their own, or will never apply. For instance, many courses on computer operations teach typing rather than the skills really needed to use the computer successfully.

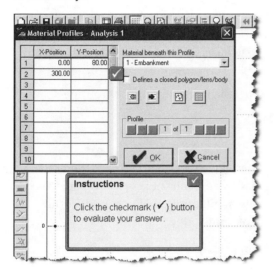

For example, this portion of a simulation requires learners to type numbers into the cells of a grid.

The problem with this approach is that it focuses attention on the task of typing in numbers. It encourages tunnel vision that distracts from the more important task of teaching *what* goes into the grid.

Typing skills are not the critical skill. The critical skill is entering the right pattern of data. This revision of the activity focuses attention on the relationships among values rather than merely typing numerals.

Created with Adobe Captivate.

How then do we identify which objectives are essential for effective learning?

Identify high-value objectives

Not all objectives are equally valuable. Some contribute more to ultimate success or go further in preventing failure than others. For example:

- ▶ A single low-level objective may be a prerequisite for many higher-level objectives.
- ▶ Some prerequisite objectives, once accomplished, render dependent objectives easy to accomplish.
- ▶ Some principles and concepts enable learners to infer a wide range of applications, for example a basic formula from which more complex formulas can be derived.
- ▶ Some objectives create schemas or mental models necessary for learners to organize new learning.
- ▶ Learn-to-learn objectives can obviate the need to teach vast amounts of routine material.

Eliminate unnecessary objectives

Just as some objectives are especially valuable, other objectives are of so little value that they do not justify the cost of accomplishing them. Question all "nice to know" objectives. Apply the "So what?" test. Ask where exactly learners will apply the proposed learning, especially if the objective is purely the possession of knowledge.

Consider omitting details the learner can infer from principles, look up in reference materials, or just ask others.

Question goals that try to turn total novices into subject-matter experts. Learners are seldom complete novices and rarely need to become full experts. Learners are usually motivated (or funded) to learn just enough to meet immediate needs.

Tip: Say "no" to *Know* objectives

For better e-learning, reduce the number of Know objectives. With information readily available online and onboard mobile devices, people seldom fail for a lack of knowledge. It is more likely that they are unable to apply their knowledge. Focus more on Create and Decide objectives to emphasize application of learning. And consider whether a lack of performance is due to the fact the learner does not believe what you are teaching or does not feel it is important. If so, increase the number of Believe and Feel objectives.

Next time you are tempted to write an objective using the word *know* or *understand*, stop and consider whether another objective might not work better.

Don't ignore *Feel* objectives

Emotion is necessary for behavioral change. We do not heed a warning unless it inspires at least a little fear in us.

Feel objectives are difficult. They are hard to define. Talking about them makes you sound like a second-rate, new-age, self-help guru. But Feel objectives can be crucial, especially in preventing failures, even in highly technical training. Often subject-matter experts and trainers fluent in a subject have no fear themselves, and hence fail to notice the degree to which learners fear they will fail and be embarrassed.

Language, even poetry, cannot precisely define emotions, but we can usually get close enough to state a workable objective. Start with these main families of emotions, remembering that some are simply differences of degree or polarity.

Family	Emotions
Affection	adoration, love, liking, indifference, apathy, dislike, contempt, loathing, hate, abhorrence
Happiness	ecstasy, euphoria, happiness, indifference, dissatisfaction, sadness, depressed, dejection, misery
Pride	pride, embarrassment, guilt, shame
Interest	curiosity, interest, disinterest, repulsion
Empowerment	empowerment, frustration, discouragement
Confidence	certainty, comfort, concern, unease, anxiety, worry, fear
Relationships	empathy, sympathy, gratitude, identity, envy, jealousy, hostility
Optimism	optimism, hope, fear, horror, depression
Surprise	awe, wonder, surprise, shock
Energy	energy, eagerness, lethargy
Responsibility	identity, responsibility, guilt

Consider defined curricula

When setting objectives for a course or curricula, consider whether someone has already defined the required body of knowledge or skills to be taught. For the area of your course or curriculum, requirements may be defined by:

▶ Government regulations.
▶ Certification or licensing procedures.
▶ Standard reference works.
▶ Professional associations.
▶ Standardized academic curricula.

Such definitions can save you months of research and debate in defining learning objectives for your project.

Stop before you go too far

Identifying prerequisites can easily get out of hand. At some point you have to stop adding objectives. Consider stopping when:

▶ You can't think of any requirements that learners do not already possess.

▶ Free, available resources adequately handle requirements.

▶ Requirements are handled by stated prerequisites for the course.

But not before the miracle occurs

Miracles do occur. Or at least what seems like a miracle occurs, in my experience, about 90% of the time when decomposing objectives. At first, decomposing objectives by prerequisites leads to an explosion of objectives. The number of objectives grows exponentially. For example, if each objective has three prerequisites, the numbers of objectives added at successive levels of decomposition are: 1, 3, 9, 27, 81, 243, … and so on.

At this point dismay sets in. Many, in despair, either quit early or abandon objectives altogether. Sorry to say, most people give up right at the point where things get better. If you, however, persist a bit further, the miracle occurs. Duplicate objectives start occurring. That is, you discover that several objects have the same prerequisite. And that meeting these prerequisites will make achieving higher-level prerequisites much easier.

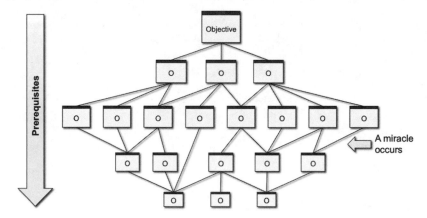

The newly discovered prerequisites may make meeting higher-level objectives trivial because, once learners have mastered these prerequisites, they can figure out high-level objectives on their own or just look up missing details online.

This miracle is so counter-intuitive that few believe it without proof and fewer still go deep enough to prove it to themselves. But it makes sense. The more you decompose objectives, the more you learn about the subject and the interconnections among its individual facts, formulas, and operations.

Perhaps the miracle is inherent in the structure of knowledge. Most scientific fields contain a few "laws" that explain vast realms of scientific data and give rise to many separate procedures, formulas, and processes.

Or, the miracle may just be an expression of the nature of nature. Our entire genetic code results from combinations of just four separate molecules. All matter is the result of combinations of a few subatomic particles. Combinations of just a few primary colors can replicate the wide gamut of colors we perceive.

Complexity emerging from underlying simplicity may be a natural law itself.

Wouldn't it be nice if there were a way to avoid all this work and just identify the essential prerequisite objectives directly? There is. It is called *Essentialism* and is described briefly on page 14 and in more detail in the Appendix, located in the back of this book.

Pick the approach to meet each objective

Once you have identified a preliminary set of objectives, you must now change direction a bit. Up to this point, you have considered only *what* you want to accomplish, not *how* you will accomplish it. You have not even decided whether e-learning is part of the solution—or even if learning is necessary.

Decide what you must actually teach

What must be learned, in the classic sense of the word? One of the first decisions you need to make about an objective is whether it requires learning or whether it can be met by some other means.

Certain objectives can be met only with learning. Learning is usually the best approach for objectives and content that is:

▶ Needed instantly and often, as for fluency of work.
▶ Needed under stress.
▶ Used for a lifetime.
▶ Constant and unchanging.
▶ Needed when there is no access to reference sources.
▶ Needed to enable effective search, social networking, and other means of meeting objectives.
▶ Needed to make sense of what we find by search or interaction with social networks.

Beware the baby-hammer syndrome: To a baby with a hammer, everything is a nail. Training departments and universities have a tendency to prescribe education to accomplish every objective. Just be sure to ask whether learning is the best way to accomplish the objective.

Choose how to meet objectives

As a designer, openly consider all the possible ways to meet objectives and pick the best solutions for your learners, your mission, and your situation. Possible solutions include standalone e-learning, games and simulations, virtual-classroom e-learning, physical-classroom learning, coaching, referring learners to existing learning materials, interacting with a social network, searching online resources, letting learners find solutions on their own, and changing external factors to make learning unnecessary. This is a long list; so let's consider each in detail.

Standalone e-learning

Conventional standalone e-learning leads learners individually through structured sequences of learning experiences chosen to accomplish specific learning objectives. In this form of learning, people interact with e-learning through a computer or mobile device. This is a proven, flexible approach. Let's consider where it fits in your mix of solutions.

Learners. Standalone e-learning can be designed to work for a wide range of learners. It is often the best solution for naïve, novice learners who prefer to learn by themselves and are willing to trust the authority of the e-learning. It does require a moderate level of self-motivation and technical skills though.

Subjects. Standalone e-learning has been adapted to a wide range of subjects. It excels in teaching broad, fundamental subjects of general applicability. It works best for established, explicit knowledge, rather than rapidly evolving tacit knowledge. Standalone e-learning has proven economical and effective in teaching common work skills. Though effective for all learning intents, standalone e-learning works especially well for Decide, Do, and Know objectives.

Situations. Standalone e-learning works well for providing economical long-term solutions to the need to educate many people in a wide range of subjects to a uniformly high standard of performance. It can also be designed to customize learning to the individual learner. The investment required for standalone e-learning is justified when the risks of failing to learn are high.

Requirements. Standalone e-learning requires adequate budget and time to research, design, develop, test, refine, and deploy the learning.

Games and simulations

Games and simulations (See Chapter 7) let learners discover knowledge, polish skills, and experience the consequences of a variety of behaviors. Games and simulations require effort, time, and money to develop, so we want to use them wisely, that is, where they are the best solution.

Learners. Games come in a vast variety to fit a wide range of learners from dependent to independent, novice to expert, self- to externally-disciplined. Games do require learners have enough technical skills and subject-matter knowledge to begin the game. And games work better for solitary learners, though team games are a possibility for social learners. Games are especially good for learners who need extra practice to master a subject.

Subjects. Games and simulations can handle a wide range of subjects. They excel at making abstract, general subjects accessible to learners who deal best with concrete, specific situations. Games work especially well in teaching the fundamental principles and rules of a field. They are, however, too expensive to teach vast subjects thoroughly or ones that require frequent revisions. They work much better for explicit than tacit knowledge. Games work well for Decide, Know, Do, and Believe objectives.

Situations. Games are good long-term solutions to educating many learners who need to fully master a specific area of a subject. Their cost is justified where the costs of failure are even higher.

Requirements. Plan to budget adequate time and money to develop games. Also take steps to introduce non-gamers to the game in ways that ensure their early success.

Virtual-classroom e-learning

Virtual-classroom courses (Chapter 10) structure learning on the model of a physical classroom. Scattered learners connect through an online meeting tool. An involved teacher may lecture, make assignments, and initiate discussions among learners directs activities.

Learners. The virtual classroom is good for learners who are familiar with and like the classroom model. It is a good solution if you must educate novice, dependent learners who need the external motivation provided by the teacher. The technical skills required are not many, and the analogy with a physical classroom helps overcome anxiety about a new form of learning.

Subjects. The virtual classroom works well to teach the same subjects as in the physical classroom, namely broad courses covering fundamental, general, abstract subjects. The virtual classroom is as flexible as the teacher conducting activities. Though the virtual classroom is better for established, explicit knowledge, a sensitive teacher can adapt interactions to teach tacit skills and emerging knowledge. Virtual classrooms are natural for teaching Know, Believe, and Do objectives.

Situations. The virtual-classroom works in situations where there is not time or budget enough to implement standalone e-learning, but experienced teachers are available.

Requirements. Virtual-classroom e-learning requires a virtual-classroom system or at least an online meeting tool. And it requires a teacher familiar with the subject, the system, and the type of learners enrolled.

Physical-classroom learning

Some learners, subjects, and situations are not suited for e-learning, but can still be handled by an old-fashioned physical classroom. Physical classroom activities include lectures, question-and-answer sessions, seminars, symposia, and other face-to-face activities.

Learners. The physical classroom may be the best choice for learners who lack technical skills, know little about the subject at hand, depend on external motivation, rely on the authority of experts to validate information, and require direct social interaction.

Subjects. The physical classroom works well to teach fundamental, general, abstract subjects. The physical classroom is as flexible as the teacher in charge. Though better for established, explicit knowledge, a skillful teacher can teach tacit skills and emerging knowledge. Physical classrooms are natural for teaching Know, Believe, Do, and sometimes Feel objectives. The physical classroom is necessary when close observation of the physical behavior, body language, facial expressions, and gestures of the learner is required.

Situations. The physical classroom may be the best alternative when there is not time to develop e-learning, and experienced teachers are available. And learners can afford the time and money required to travel to the site of the classroom. Where a quick solution is needed and travel costs can be avoided, the physical classroom is a good solution.

Requirements. The physical classroom requires a classroom, a teacher, and the ability to get learners into the classroom. It requires a budget to pay teachers and to compensate for time off the job while attending classroom learning, plus the travel costs of learners who must travel to the classroom.

Coaching

Instead of a formal learning program, the best solution may be to assign a coach, mentor, or advisor to each learner. Apprenticeship is one of the oldest and most effective ways of learning.

Learners. Coaching can help just about any type of learner, though not all learners accept coaching well. Coaching works best for naïve, dependent learners who respond to the authority and external discipline provided by the coach. Learners with minimal technical skills can receive coaching by phone or e-mail. Learners with deeper technical skills can engage in a virtual apprenticeship program (See "Distance apprenticeship program" in Chapter 9.).

Subjects. The range of subjects accessible through coaching depends mainly on the expertise and communications skills of the coach. Ironically, coaching works especially well with very fundamental subjects and very advanced ones. The coach can diagnose the problems facing the initial learner and quickly remove misconceptions. Being an expert, the coach is likewise adept at refining the learner's knowledge and behavior. Coaching works well for building tacit skills without written rules and principles. However, one-on-one coaching is not efficient enough to use for broad subjects or large numbers of learners. Use coaching for Create, Do, and Believe objectives that take advantage of the coach's ability to spur innovation, model behavior, and give authority and credibility to ideas.

Situations. Use coaching for special cases where a few learners each need to learn a different aspect of a subject or learn it to a different degree and standard of performance. Use it where the cost of individual failure is high and the coach can thoroughly evaluate the learner's abilities before the learner is put in harm's way.

Requirements. Coaching requires coaches who possess the necessary expertise and interpersonal communications skills.

Referring to learning resources

Instead of teaching an objective directly, you may choose to send learners to existing resources that can teach it for us. Such resources include other courses, podcasts, e-books, paper books, blogs, and other sources of well-researched and structured learning materials.

Learners. Referring learners to external resources can be risky for naïve, dependent learners who lack the self-discipline necessary to learn on their own, who have yet to acquire the fundamental knowledge necessary to understand the external materials, or who have no ability to access them electronically. Still, external resources can be useful for helping novices who need introductory or background knowledge and for advanced learners who want to go further into the subject.

Subjects. Use external resources for aspects of the main subject that lie outside the needs of mainstream learners. Use external resources to ensure all learners have necessary prerequisites, can pursue side interests, and are not limited by the narrow scope of the course. External resources are most reliable for established, explicit knowledge. Consider external resources for Decide, Do, and Know objectives.

Situations. Use external resources to quickly and inexpensively provide solutions for objectives relevant to only a minority of learners. Use them where you face large variations in the needs of learners and in their starting abilities. Do not use this approach, however, if the cost of failing to learn the objective is high or you lack faith in the external materials to accomplish the objective.

Requirements. This approach requires effective materials that will accomplish the objective for your learners. You must carefully locate, analyze, and even test these materials. You may also need to prepare an introduction or bridge from your course to the external materials (See "Integrate foreign modules" in Chapter 6.).

Searching online resources

Instead of providing the answer or providing specific resources, you can teach learners to find the answer for themselves. Sophisticated search engines and vast online resources mean that much of what learners need to know is only a few seconds away. Teaching facts, figures, and simple procedures makes less and less sense every day.

Learners. The search solution works best for moderately knowledgeable, independent learners who have the self-discipline and wariness to drill through layers of third-hand reports, partisan opinions, gossip, and outright deception to get to substantial, accurate information. Effective search requires generic search skills as well as skills searching within a particular document, database, or library. It also requires core knowledge of the vocabulary, principles, and structure of the field.

Subjects. Search works best for advanced learning in narrow areas of tacit knowledge. It is a way to deal with constantly changing details, such as research data, laws and regulations, and areas of rapid technical advancement. Use search to accomplish Decide, Do, Know, and Believe objectives.

Situations. Use search in areas where learners need information that is readily available online. Use it to avoid the costs of teaching people information they could more easily look up or that will quickly become obsolete. Use it to help learners become more self-reliant.

Requirements. A search approach requires that the information be online and readily accessible by learners. It may also require teaching learners generic search skills and enough of the subject so they can conduct effective searches on their own.

Interacting with a social network

Advances in collaboration software and the emergence of social networking have provided new ways for people to learn. One of the most important uses of social networking is to serve as a source of education, guidance, and information for learners. As such, it serves as a human performance-support mechanism. Learners, at any time, can ask their networks of friends, experts, and fellow learners. Answers are not limited to short text answers; they can include any appropriate media and can include ongoing conversations. For more, see Chapter 8.

Learners. Using a social network for learning is not for everyone. It works well for learners who are more social than solitary, who understand the principles and vocabulary necessary to interact productively, who have the self-discipline to keep conversations focused, and who question rather than blindly accept new information.

Subjects. Social networking is especially effective for refining existing skills. It can help learners find specific applications for general principles, see concrete examples of abstract ideas, acquire tacit knowledge lacking clear rules and formulas. Social networking is especially effective for rapidly emerging subjects where knowledge is provisional at best.

Also consider it as an element in any subject that is applied by a team rather than by individuals. Likewise, use it to refine skills of conversation, negotiation, and collaboration. Consider it for Create, Decide, Believe, and Feel objectives.

Situations. Use social networking to round out learning efforts. Use it to handle concerns and needs of individual learners, to provide learning needed by only a few, and to illustrate standards of performance. Social networking can be a solution when you lack time and budget to develop formal learning for just a few learners or topics. Social networking works best when it continues over long periods of time.

Requirements. A social-networking solution requires a social network that spans the needed expertise and includes individuals willing to share it. You may need to put in place tools to make collaboration natural and easy. You may also need to put in place policies that encourage sharing information across traditional boundaries. Effective social learning will also require time for learners to join groups, identify experts, build trust, and carry on conversations.

Letting learners find the solution on their own

Sometimes the best way to teach learners is to do nothing—well, not exactly *nothing*. Instead of directly trying to accomplish an objective, we challenge learners to accomplish the objective on their own. In this case, we do not specifically tell learners to conduct a search, refer to a social network, or consult specific materials.

Learners. It is no surprise that this approach does not work for all learners. Reserve it for moderately experienced, independent learners who have the self-discipline and inquisitive mind needed to pursue learning on their own. Use it for learners who relish the challenge of solving a mystery.

Subjects. Sending learners to find the solution on their own works for narrow areas of explicit subjects. Challenge learners to find concrete examples of abstract principles or specific applications of general knowledge. Use it especially for Do and Decide objectives.

Situations. Don't use this approach merely to cut your budget or to avoid the hard work of developing learning. Use it only when it is in the best interest of learners, for example, to initiate a culture of independent learning.

Requirements. Don't send learners to accomplish objectives on their own without a good chance of success. Make sure the resources learners need exist and are accessible to them. You may also need to provide a test learners can use to verify that they have met the objective.

Changing external factors

Learning and information are not the solution to all problems. Often the best way to meet an objective is to change factors outside the realm of learning. These may be organizational or business factors. They may involve changes to economics or technology.

For example, if the goal is to increase sales, an organization might train its sales force in new techniques—or it might just increase the sales commission.

Don't try to teach your way around a problem when a more direct solution exists. For example, consider changes such as these:

- ▶ Rewrite a contract.
- ▶ Change economic incentives.
- ▶ Streamline workflow procedures.
- ▶ Change personnel: hire, fire, transfer, or reclassify employees.
- ▶ Redesign the product or its user-interface.

Blending if necessary

If all objectives can be perfectly met by one approach, great! Your design and development task just got simpler. If not, you must either adapt one approach to handle objectives for which it is not ideal—or you must mix or blend approaches within a single course, lesson, or topic.

Strike a balance. A blend of more than a half-dozen approaches may seem chaotic to learners and frightening to your budget committee. Remember that all objectives are not equally important. Some must be taught perfectly—others, only competently. Even though an approach is not the best possible way to accomplish an objective, you can often apply your creativity and hard work to make it work adequately.

Decide the teaching sequence of your objectives

Once you have identified what objectives you must teach, you need to decide the order in which learners will accomplish these objectives. You can defer this decision until you have created learning objects, but only if your objects are designed with no assumptions about which objects learners will have taken earlier. Beware the as-shown-above-syndrome (p. 314).

One way to manage this decision is to make a preliminary strategic decision early in the design process and then to refine the decision on later design revisions. To that end, you can use the ideas here to decide a sequencing strategy and then those of online Chapter 12 to craft purpose-specific learning sequences.

In what order should you teach? To decide, let's return to the hierarchy of learning objectives. Three main sequences are possible.

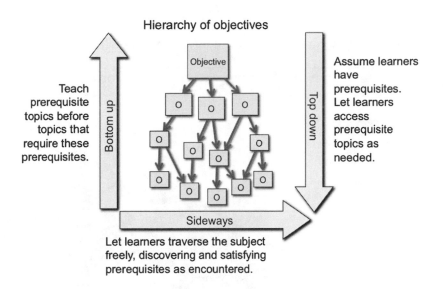

The most common sequence is *bottom up*. In a bottom-up sequence, we teach prerequisite objectives before objectives that require these prerequisites. It makes sense. Unless we teach the prerequisite first, learners could become confused or frustrated.

A second sequencing strategy is *top down*. In a top-down sequence, we start learners at the top objective, as if they have all the prerequisites. Learners who lack prerequisites can continue down the hierarchy to access the objects that teach prerequisites they lack.

The third sequencing strategy is *sideways*. Here we let learners traverse the subject freely, discovering and satisfying prerequisites as encountered.

These strategies, which are covered further in this section, are good general approaches. For more specific sequencing options, see online Chapter 12.

Example: Bottom-up sequencing

The course *Good Clinical Practice* had a bottom-up structure. This course dealt with a critical subject with life-or-death consequences. Its goal was to teach experienced medical researchers to follow regulations and ethical practices in conducting tests on human subjects, some of whom had died due to lapses by researchers.

The legal concerns were serious. The course was mandatory. Every learner was required to complete every page of the course. A sequential, bottom-up structure aided that goal. Let's look at the sequence of topics within a lesson on obtaining the informed consent of test subjects before conducting experiments on them.

The lesson starts with a definition of informed consent, as this is the basis of the whole lesson. Next, the lesson introduces the general principles of informed consent that will guide the researcher. Next are spelled out the specific elements of the document used to record informed consent. After that come details of the process through which the document goes to fully secure and document informed consent.

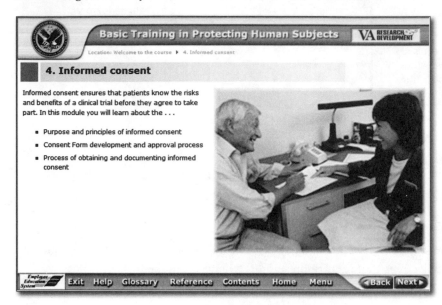

The structure of the course is made evident by the **Next** button in the lower right, suggesting a strongly recommended path through the course.

Built using Adobe Dreamweaver.

With all the background established, the lesson now provides specific details about obtaining consent from the test subject. Finally, it specifies the requirements the researcher must follow to document informed consent. The following pages provide a practice activity and a summary.

Did you notice how the lesson carefully begins with definitions, fundamental concepts, and contextual background before presenting the exact procedure the researcher must follow? That order is a classic example of the bottom-up sequence.

Example: Top-down sequencing

Let's look at an example of a top-down sequence. This example teaches operation of the *GALENA* Slope Stability Analysis computer program, which is used to analyze the stability of earthen dams, road cuts, surface mines, and other slopes.

After an introduction, the course starts with a preview of the entire process of using the program. As part of this preview, the learner can select a show-me demonstration (p. 74). The demonstration provides a narrated, over-the-shoulder look at the use of the program to analyze an earthen dam. The demonstration is complete. If that is all the learner needs, the learner can quit the training and begin using the program. If not, the learner can continue for more detailed instruction on how to perform each of the steps shown in the overview.

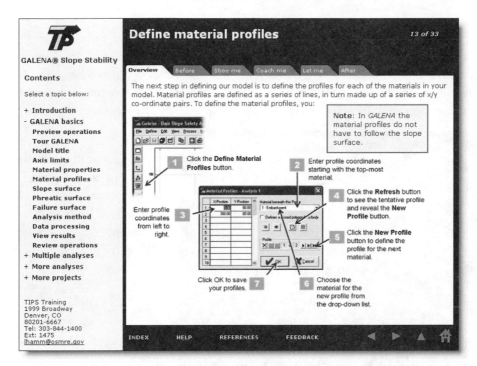

Tabbed interface built using Adobe Dreamweaver and custom JavaScript. Screens captured with TechSmith SnagIt. Illustrations created in Microsoft PowerPoint. Simulations built with Adobe Captivate.

For example, if the learner selects the Material profiles step, the lesson on how to define the cross section of a slope model appears. Note that this lesson also has a top down structure. The first tab presents an overview or summary of the required steps. If that is all the learner needs, the learner can continue with another lesson or begin using the program.

Within the lesson is a **Show me** tab containing a demonstration elaborating on the steps summarized in the overview.

For even more detailed instruction, the learner can click the **Coach me** tab and launch a coached simulation (p. 335) on how to perform the task of defining material profiles.

Even within this simulation, the structure is still top-down. (See page 387 to view the navigation within the simulation.) The learner proceeds through the simulation receiving no explicit instructions until needed. If the learner makes a mistake, the system displays an error message to correct the mistake. Another way the learner can receive instruction is to press the **Hint** button. The **Hint** button dispenses a suggestion to guide the learner's thinking toward discovery of the next step. Learners who are truly stumped can click the **Show how** button to get explicit instructions on how to proceed.

At the course, lesson, and simulation levels, learners are presented with prerequisite information only when they request it or demonstrate they need it. That is the essence of the top-down sequence.

Example: Sideways sequencing

The sideways sequence is most common in learning games and simulations. Here is an example. It is called *The Crimescene Game*. (See page 324 for more.) It teaches interviewing skills by having the learner simulate interviewing the witness to a crime. The learner conducts the interview by selecting from possible questions or responses.

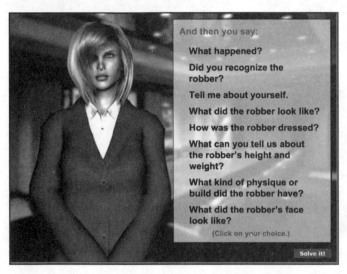

Once the learner completes the introduction to the game, a menu of possible paths appears. Here the learner can choose from a range of questions to ask the witness. The learner can pick them in any order.

Created using SmithMicro Poser and Microsoft PowerPoint. Converted for Web delivery using Articulate Presenter. View example at horton.com/eld/.

The menu and the paths that issue from it take the learner through the learning object's scenes. Within each scene, the learner can choose what follow-up questions to ask and how to respond to comments by the witness.

Let's say the learner asks, "How was the robber dressed?" The learner would receive some information and have a choice of whether to probe deeper or ask a different question. If the learner probes more deeply, more information is revealed.

At this point the learner might decide to ask a different question. That choice takes the learner back to the menu, where the learner chooses another question to ask. Thus the learner decides how to proceed through the interview.

Each learner will take a different path through the interview. The feedback each learner receives is thus unique, depending on the questions asked. By repeatedly playing the game, the learner eventually receives feedback to correct all the misconceptions he or she is prone to. This indeterminate path is what we mean by a sideways sequence.

Where would you use each sequencing strategy?

Where would you use each of these sequencing strategies in your e-learning? For what groups of learners, for what subjects, and for what objectives is each strategy appropriate?

Let's start with the *bottom-up* sequence. The prerequisites-first sequence is often necessary where safety is a concern. If missing information or misconceptions could endanger learners, we must make sure they receive such prerequisite information before encountering the need for it. Novices also benefit from a bottom-up structure because novices, by definition, lack extensive knowledge in a field. The bottom-up sequence is so common in school learning that we often use it for students whose model of learning is based on traditional schooling.

Now, how about the *top-down* sequence? The top-down sequence is often used for efficiency of learning. Learners encounter only the content they explicitly request or clearly need. Nobody wastes time covering material already mastered or not relevant.

The top-down sequence is also good for experts who already know much of a subject and can quickly identify gaps in their own knowledge and skills. Top-down sequencing is well suited for just-in-time learning where learners seek out just the nuggets of learning they need at the moment of need.

So where do we use the *sideways* order? The sideways order, because it is less predictable, can add excitement to the learning process. It is a good choice for discovery learning where learners must discover and integrate separate bits of knowledge. And it is good where you are teaching learners to learn on their own as they cope with a complex, dynamic situation—like many work environments today.

Create objects to accomplish objectives

Now that we have identified our prerequisites and narrowed them to the ones the course will directly accomplish, it is time to plan how we will accomplish those objectives. It is time to start specifying learning activities for each objective. And that leads us to learning objects.

What is a learning object?

What do we mean by the term *learning object*? Let's start with a simple definition:

> **A learning object is a chunk of electronic content that can be accessed individually and that completely accomplishes a single learning objective and can prove it.**

That's a mouthful, so let's look at it a bit at a time:

chunk of electronic content	A learning object is not an ephemeral concept but a concrete collection of electronic media. It contains text and graphics and perhaps animation, video, voice, music, and other media. It may also include pointers to other learning resources, such as documents and databases. Or it may recommend interacting with a coach, mentor, or social network.

can be accessed individually	Through a menu, search engine, or just a Next button, the learner can get to just this piece of content apart from other pieces. That is, this piece appears to the learner to be separate from other objects.
completely accomplishes a single learning objective	The key characteristic of a learning object is that it accomplishes a learning objective. The objective may be narrow or broad, abstract or concrete, lofty or mundane.
can prove it	The object contains the means to verify that the objective was met. This may be a simple test or a sophisticated simulation. A score may be recorded or not. In the end, though, the learner or the organization offering the object can tell whether the objective was met.

A simpler, although less precise definition, is this:

> **A learning object is a micro-course designed to be combined with other micro-courses.**

If a course is a unit of education that can be completed in some number of days or hours, then an object is a similar unit that can be completed in some number of minutes. An object is smaller, but still complete. An object may teach less than a course, but it teaches it equally well.

What a learning object is not

The term learning object is used quite loosely. The term is applied to many things that are not true learning objects. To understand what we mean by the term, let's focus on some of the things a learning object is *not*.

A learning object is not a shrink-wrapped product you can buy. Although many vendors use the term in referring to their content and tools, a learning object is much more than a single, simple product. It is more like a philosophy for developing and packaging reusable content.

Likewise, learning objects are not a proprietary tool or technology. They depend on tools and technology but are not the province of any particular vendor.

Some learning objects can contain other learning objects, which contain still other learning objects. This hierarchy means that learning objects can be entire courses, lessons, or just individual topics.

Because learning objects can contain a hierarchy of other learning objects, a learning object is not always a single file. At the bottom of this hierarchy each object may be a file or page, but clearly higher-level objects cannot be limited to single files.

The concept of a learning object is not always apparent to the learner. Nor should it be. Learners just want to acquire new abilities or knowledge. They do not care where one learning object leaves off and another begins. As long as they can navigate and access the learning they need, they are happy. Only designers and builders need concern themselves with the precise definition of learning objects.

Learning objects can serve multiple purposes. And an object-based development method can work for many different purposes. Learning objects can be used for training, for reference information, for quick-reference to facts, for job aids, and even for games and other forms of entertainment.

Turn objectives into learning objects

Each objective leads us to create a learning object that completely accomplishes the learning objective and can prove it.

The starting point for designing the object is the objective it is to accomplish. The objective statement makes a fine charter for the learning object. The objective is also the ending point and a constant reference when designing the object. Anything that does not contribute to accomplishing this objective should be omitted forthwith. Although the learner may not see the objective statement, every designer and developer should see it and work to accomplish it.

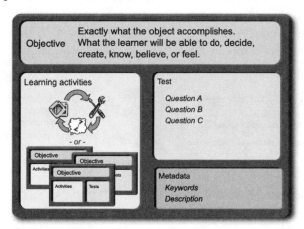

Once we have defined the objective, we can begin to specify the content necessary to meet that objective. There are two ways we can specify content. For a high-level learning object, we may specify sub-objects, that is, a structured sequence of learning objects for more specific objectives.

For low-level learning objects, we may specify learning activities that will directly accomplish the objective of the learning object. These learning activities may occasion a variety of learning experiences.

Tests are another part of the object. Tests verify that the learning objective was met. The test might be a simple self-check to let the learner decide whether to move on. Or, the test might be a formal exam with a recorded score. Our diagram shows tests as questions because that is the most common form of a test, especially for a cognitive subject. Just keep in mind that other types of tests are possible, such as simulations, games, and work assignments.

In addition to content, the learning object may require other components such as keywords to help learners search for the object and a description to appear in a course catalog. Although not directly part of the content, these components, called *metadata*, assist in meeting the goal by making the learning object easier to find, understand, and remember.

Create tests

Tests gauge accomplishment of the objective. They can range from small tasks that give the learner confidence to move to the next object all the way to formal tests used to legally certify the learner's skills. Chapter 5 will help you design effective tests.

A learning object requires both learning activities and tests. Most people create the learning activities first and then, if time permits, tack on a few multiple-choice test questions. A better approach is to create the tests as soon as you have defined the learning objective. It may seem illogical to create the test before creating the learning that the test measures, but the test is the best guide to designing learning activities. By developing tests first, you save time and money while making your testing and teaching more effective.

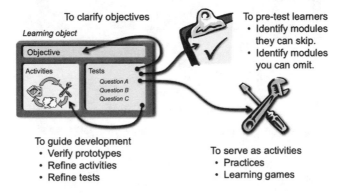

Tests clarify the objective. There is no clearer and more precise statement of a learning objective than a test question that measures whether that objective has been accomplished. If the test is valid, passing the test indicates accomplishing the objective. Rather than struggle through a complex methodology for expressing objectives, focus your efforts on specifying effective tests.

You can use the tests to pre-test learners. Such pre-tests will identify objects that learners can skip. More importantly, pre-tests used early in the development process can identify objects you can omit because the tests show learners already can meet the objectives.

Tests can often serve as the learning activities for the object. Tests can be designed as practices, learning games, simulations, or work assignments.

Tests can guide you in the development of content. Tests can verify prototypes for learning activities. If learners take the prototype and pass the test, the prototype is working. Tests can help refine learning activities by comparing the learning results from different designs or variations. Having tests available early gives time to refine the tests by sharpening the focus and removing ambiguity.

So, develop tests first and then the learning activities necessary to prepare for the tests.

Select learning activities

Activities are necessary to provoke learning experiences. Used in combination, simple learning activities can accomplish difficult learning objectives.

Learning activities exercise basic skills, thought processes, attitudes, and behaviors. But mere action is not a learning activity. People learn little by just clicking the mouse or chatting about vacation plans. People learn by considering, researching, analyzing, evaluating, organizing, synthesizing, discussing, testing, deciding, and applying ideas. Activities may use mouse clicks and tablet taps, but their goal is to provoke the exact mental experiences that lead to learning.

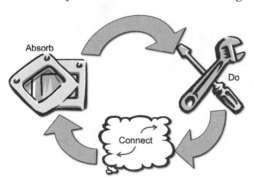

To accomplish learning objectives, we typically require three types of learning activities: *Absorb*, *Do*, and *Connect*. What are they and why do we need them?

Learners *absorb* knowledge, typically by reading text, watching an animation, or listening to narration. In an Absorb activity, the learner is physically passive, but mentally active.

Another type of learning activity has learners *do* something with what they are learning, for instance, practice a procedure, play a game, or answer questions. The learner practices, explores, and discovers.

The third type of learning activity has learners *connect* what they are learning to their work, their lives, or their prior learning. Connect activities "seal the deal," making it easier to apply learning when it is needed later.

These three activities are shown as a cycle starting with the Absorb activity. This is the most common sequence for cognitive subjects, but it is not a requirement and not always the best sequence. Different types of subjects and different instructional strategies will demand a different sequence.

Provoke proven learning experiences

Consider learning experiences in your life. Can you classify them as Absorb, Do, or Connect activities? Remember that Absorb activities typically have the learner read, watch, and listen. Do activities have the learner do something with knowledge, such as practice, explore, and discover. And Connect activities lead the learner to connect current learning to life, work, and prior learning.

Common types of learning experiences include asking questions, discovery activities, field trips, job aids, original work assignments, ponder activities, practice sessions, readings, research, stories told by the teacher, and stories told by the learner. Which are Absorb, which are Do, and which are Connect activities?

Here's how I classify them—which is important only in that this is how they appear in the rest of this book.

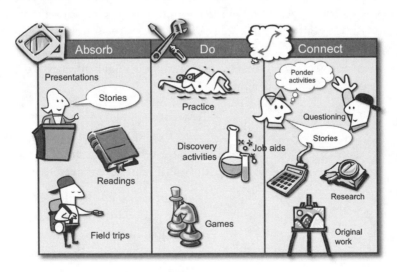

Absorb activities

In the Absorb column are activities in which the learner reads, listens, and watches.

Presentations lurk at the left edge of the Absorb column, because all the learner can do is look and listen. We hope the learner absorbs the information in the presentation actively.

Readings include activities for which the learner reads from online or paper documents, such as textbooks, research papers, or technical manuals.

Stories by the teacher or an expert are, likewise, absorbed by the learner.

Field trips are at the right edge of the Absorb column. Although the learner may be physically active on a field trip, the learner learns by absorbing information. In a field trip to an art museum, for example, the learner may learn by looking at paintings, reading their descriptions, and listening to a museum docent lecture about them. A field trip to a hands-on museum, such as the Exploratorium in San Francisco, however, would be more of a Do activity, as learning occurs through experiments and discovery.

Do activities

In the Do column we place activities where the learner actively exercises, explores, and discovers.

Practice activities fall squarely in this column. They allow learners to apply skills, knowledge, and attitudes and receive feedback on their efforts. They help learners refine and polish learning. Practice activities can range from simple drill-and-practice exercises to sophisticated guided-analysis activities.

Discovery activities are times for experimenting and exploring. Their goal is to lead learners to discover concepts, principles, and procedures for themselves.

Games and simulations let learners discover and practice new skills and strategies in a safe environment. Learners can gain insights and confidence as they solve realistic problems in an entertaining context.

Connect activities

Connect activities lead learners to link what they are learning to prior learning and to situations in which they will apply the current learning in subsequent courses or on the job.

Ponder activities ask learners to stop and think about the subject more broadly and deeply. They encourage learners to view the subject from a new perspective. They are typically used for connecting to what learners already know.

Questioning activities let learners obtain answers to their individual questions. They require learners to conceive and express questions, to consider answers, and to ask follow-up questions. They let learners fill gaps in their current learning.

Stories told by learners require learners to draw on their own experiences. They help learners connect the subject of learning to personal experiences.

Job aids are used on the job at the time when learning must be applied. As such, they help connect learning to work.

Research activities, where learners must identify learning resources on their own, are Connect activities, as they require accessing and interpreting outside resources.

Performing **original work** is the ultimate final exam. It fully connects learning to the life of the learner.

Can't wait to learn more about these activities? Here are some destinations for you:

Absorb activities (Chapter 2)	Do activities (Chapter 3)	Connect activities (Chapter 4)
Read, watch, and listen.	Exercise, experiment, and discover.	Link to prior learning, to work, and to life.
▶ Presentations and demos (p. 69). ▶ Readings (p. 93). ▶ Stories by the teacher (p. 105). ▶ Field trips (p. 112).	▶ Practice (p. 130). ▶ Discovery activities (p. 146). ▶ Games (p. 157).	▶ Ponder activities (p. 166). ▶ Questioning activities (p. 176). ▶ Stories by the learner (p. 184). ▶ Job aids (p. 187). ▶ Research (p. 196). ▶ Original work (p. 207)

Where did this list come from?

The activities we identified have been essential for learning in different eras, from different cultures, for different learners, on different subjects, and in different media. If the same technique was used three thousand years ago in Asia for face-to-face religious instruction and is used today in Canada for social learning in business management, then it is a very powerful and versatile technique indeed.

We have chosen these activities for this book because they are proven and flexible activities. When well designed and appropriately deployed, they work well. They can be adapted to work with any subject matter. Many can be used with the class as a whole, by small teams, by individuals monitored by the teacher, and by learners working alone.

Use these activities as a start

You may be wondering whether these kinds of activities are all you will ever use. No. The range of activities listed here are adequate to teach most subjects, but they should not limit your creativity in coining new kinds of activities or in adapting these activities to new media, new situations, and different objectives. Use the activities here as a starting point only.

Choose learning activities to accomplish the objective

It is one thing to know what types of learning experiences we need. It is another to list the exact learning activities we need to accomplish a specific learning objective.

Here's how we go about it. We start with the objective of our learning object. We consider the three types of essential activities we will need: Absorb, Do, and Connect. For each of these types, we need to describe the actual experience. And we need to specify the order in which each activity occurs. For example, let's specify learning activities for an objective from the *Using Gantt Charts* course.

Learning objective	
Teach how to interpret a Gantt chart to mid-level managers who recognize the individual symbols	
Activity	**Type**
Watch a narrated animation of a typical Gantt chart being constructed.	Absorb
Examine Gantt charts at work to see how they were constructed.	Connect
Construct a similar Gantt chart by dragging and dropping pieces into place.	Do and test

We start with an Absorb activity that has the learners watch a narrated animation of a typical Gantt chart being constructed. Next, we include a Connect activity that guides learners to examine Gantt charts in their environment to see how they were constructed. We close with a Do activity that requires the learners to construct a similar Gantt chart by dragging pieces into place. This Do activity serves as a test as well.

Notice that the order (Absorb, Connect, and Do) varies from the classic order. This is not unusual where it serves to increase motivation or streamline the flow of learning experiences.

Here you see the resulting learning object.

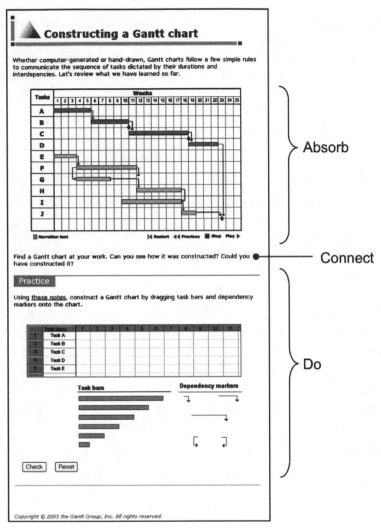

View example at horton.com/eld/.

At the top of the page is an animated presentation with voice-over narration. The animation shows the construction of a simple Gantt chart. Watching the animation is the Absorb activity.

Below the presentation is a ponder activity. It invites learners to find a Gantt chart in their work. It then asks whether they can figure out how it was constructed and whether they feel they could have constructed it. Answering this rhetorical question makes up the Connect activity.

At the bottom is a practice activity that lets the learner construct a Gantt chart by first popping up a description of the tasks of a project and then dragging symbols into place representing the project. This practice implements the Do activity.

More examples of learning activities to meet objectives

Here are several sample objectives and potential learning activities to accomplish them:

Objective	Learning activities
Identify creative uses of the chemical element niobium.	**Absorb**: Presentation on chemical properties. **Do**: Practice deciding whether to use niobium for specific goals. **Connect**: Identify some uses for niobium in your work.
Believe that employees must act to prevent bullying in the workplace.	**Absorb**: Presentation of three cases where employees ignored bullying, thinking it was solely management's role to prevent such behavior. **Do**: Identify places where employees could have intervened to stop escalating violence. **Connect**: Discuss with other employees instances of workplace bullying that learners have observed.
Decide whether a main bank can delegate to an association bank the authority to make loans.	**Absorb**: Watch and listen to a presentation of legal problems that resulted due to improper delegation. **Do**: Find rules concerning delegation in online policy manuals. **Do**: Decide in several scenarios whether the main bank properly delegated authority. **Connect**: Research policies at your own bank.

Notice that the last example has two Do activities. This is a common variation where an objective is broad or where deeper learning is required. Don't be afraid to vary the basic pattern for special cases.

1

Designing e-learning

Match activities to the type of objective

The following job aid ties the six types of objectives to common types of learning activities. Along the left are the main types of activities grouped into Absorb, Do, and Connect categories. In columns are the six types of objectives. A circle at the intersection of a type's column and an activity's row means that the activity is recommended for that type of learning objective. A black dot indicates a stronger recommendation.

Activities		Types of objectives					
		Create	Decide	Do	Know	Believe	Feel
Absorb	Presentation	○	○	○	●	●	●
	Readings	○	○	○	●	○	○
	Story by teacher					○	○
	Field trip	○			○	○	○
Do	Practice	●	●	●			
	Discovery		○		●	●	●
	Game		●			○	○
Connect	Ponder					○	○
	Questioning		○	●	○	○	○
	Story by learner		○				
	Research	○	●		●	●	
	Job aid	○	○	●			
	Original work	●		○			

How much of each?

I am often asked what proportion of time learners should spend on each type of activity. Common proportions of Absorb, Do, and Connect activities are 90-9-1. That is, learners spend 90% of their time absorbing, 9% doing, and only 1% connecting. There is no universally best mix, but 90-9-1 is *not* even a good mix, except perhaps for novices who need extensive Absorb before they can do anything meaningful. A better goal may be 40-50-10. That is learners spend 40% of their time absorbing, 50% doing, and 10% connecting.

Pick winning combinations of learning activities

Learning activities are seldom deployed individually. For effective e-learning, we must combine learning activities. To accomplish a learning objective, we typically combine Absorb, Do, and Connect activities. But what activities should we combine? Are some combinations better than others?

Yes, some groups of activities naturally reinforce one another. For instance, some that use related resources can be combined so that learners feel they are in a single integrated activity, rather than a sequence of separate activities. Let's look at some productive combinations.

▶ One traditional combination starts with a presentation supplying information, a practice session applying the information to simple problems, and finally an original-work activity that requires applying the information in realistic situations. Conceptual knowledge varies this pattern. It begins with a presentation or readings on the concept, followed by a question-and-answer session and then an opportunity to practice applying the concept.

▶ Stories told by the teacher are frequently followed by comparable stories told by learners. The story told by the teacher challenges learners to tell a corresponding story and models the kind of story they should tell.

▶ Another logical combination is a research activity in which learners find documents containing useful information followed by a reading activity where learners read the documents to extract information needed for a specific purpose.

▶ Original-work activities can take place with the assistance of a job aid to improve a learner's ability to perform work in the real world.

▶ Learning games and readings complement one another. The game motivates learners and establishes principles. Reading materials supply detailed information needed to win the game.

▶ Original work can be designed so that learners must perform research to gather needed information. This combination prepares learners to face work situations where they do not yet have the necessary information.

These combinations are but a few of the many productive mixes of learning activities. Use your creativity to think of even more combinations and sequences of learning activities that will accomplish your learning objectives.

Simplify activities

For some objectives, the Absorb, Do, or Connect part may be small and simple. For some activities, the only Absorb needed is reading the instructions. Likewise for a job aid, the only Absorb is reading from the job aid. After learners watch a demonstration (Absorb), you may invite them to try the same procedure (Do) with sample materials you provide, or with materials they provide (Connect). When searching on their own, the learner's reason for searching is all the connection they need. One of the most effective Connect activities is simply asking a rhetorical question, such as, "How would you use this." Connect activities can occur spontaneously when learners are invited to use available social media tools to discuss with their peers ways to apply learning. Advanced learners may be challenged to provide their own Do and Connect activities.

Cascade related activities

Where learners follow a defined path along a chain of prerequisites, activities can cascade from topic to topic. For example, the Do activity of one object may require applying (connecting) learning from the preceding object.

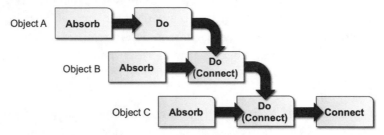

Objects early in the chain do not require explicit connect activities because that connection is provided by the next object in sequence.

Adapt the Absorb-Do-Connect scheme flexibly

Having a distinct set of Absorb, Do, and Connect activities per topic (objective) is a safe, sane way to proceed—but not the only way, especially where information is highly interconnected and tasks have many prerequisites. Here are some common variations:

▶ One long reading or viewing experience serves as the Absorb activity for a number of topics.

▶ One broad Do activity can consolidate skills acquired in multiple prerequisites.

▶ For search activities, Connect occurs first as the need to complete a task, Absorb occurs briefly at the end of the search, and Do occurs as the information is applied.

▶ In games, Absorb, Do, and Connect occur seamlessly as learners repeatedly confront a situation, look around to figure out what to do, and experience the consequences of their actions.

▶ In social learning, Absorb generally comes from independent research and reading, Do consists of sharing and shallow discussion, and Connect comes from deeper discussions on how to apply ideas.

▶ For work simulations, the Absorb activity comes in watching a demonstration of how to perform an activity, the Do activity occurs as learners are coached through a simulated attempt at a task, and the Connect activity occurs as learners attempt the task without assistance.

Consider ways that activities can be tightly integrated and blended seamlessly to produce a coherent learning experience.

Enable discovery

There is one more experience that is essential to learning. It is the ah-ha moment of discovery. The good news is that it does not require adding anything to the design, just checking to ensure that it occurs.

Where Absorb, Do, and Connect are activities, discovery is an event. It is the key moment in learning. It marks the realization of learning, resulting from Absorb, Do, or Connect activities.

Discovery has physical and emotional manifestations. The learner may exclaim or whisper, "Oh, I see, I get it!" "I can do this!" or some other equivalent of "Eureka!" Discovery is accompanied by an emotional change such as a burst of confidence or the sudden relief of tension. It may occasion awe at the power of a concept or the simplicity of a formula. It may manifest as fear at the danger revealed by a warning. Often it is evident by a smile or a slight laugh.

When does discovery occur? In a classic Absorb-Do-Connect sequence, discovery typically occurs at the end of the Connect activity. But that is not the only place discovery can occur. An especially effective Absorb activity can provoke discovery. Discoveries occur rapidly and continually throughout a game. And, as their name suggests, discovery activities are designed to provoke discovery.

In designing learning experiences, consider where you want discovery to occur. When testing your e-learning, watch learners to ensure that discovery indeed does occur.

Choose media

Once you have prescribed the activities necessary to accomplish the objective and the tests necessary to verify that accomplishment, you can turn to selecting and specifying the media necessary to implement the activities and tests. Each object may require a different mix of text, graphics, sound, voice, music, animation, and video.

Speak the natural language

Now that all media are technically possible, and most are economically practical, we need to exercise judgment to pick the media that most directly and effectively express the ideas we want to get across. That is, we must look for the natural language for the learning experience we want to create.

To identify the natural language, ask yourself, "What medium is essential to accomplish my objective?" That is, what medium could you *not* do without or swap for another medium? For example, in some cases we could replace voice with text and in other cases only voice would do. Sometimes we could use a series of static graphics rather than smooth-flowing animation, and sometimes not.

Let's look at some purposes and identify the one medium that you cannot do without.

Objective	Media	How employed
To teach airline pilots to recognize audible alarms	Sound	Match sounds to meanings
To convince sailors to seek treatment for drug problems	Video	Of grandfatherly admiral's plea
To explain to an engineer how a circuit works	Graphics	Simplified circuit diagram
To teach spoken English in China via mobile phones	Vision	Not much choice
To explain battlefield tactics to history students	Animation	Animated troop movements on maps

What medium would you require to teach airline pilots to recognize audible alarms? Since we are talking about audible alarms, sound is necessary. We might have learners practice matching the sound with its meaning. We might augment the sound with animation or video of the condition indicated by each alarm. However, without sound, we would have little chance of success. That's why we say sound is the natural language in this case.

What did the U.S. Navy require to convince sailors to seek drug treatment? In this situation, the thing that worked was a video of a grandfatherly admiral sincerely asking sailors to think of themselves and their shipmates.

Suppose your objective was to explain to an electrical engineer how a circuit works. Have you ever seen two engineers carry on a conversation without drawing pictures? In this case, a simplified circuit diagram would seem to be a requirement. Animating the diagram might help, but graphics are essential.

What about for teaching spoken English in China via mobile phones? The only difficulty with this one may be thinking it is a trick question. It is not. The subject matter and the assigned technology both make voice the essential medium. Sometimes it is just that easy!

What medium would you require to explain the tactics of a famous battle to history students? The best way to handle this may be to use animated maps on which learners see lines and symbols representing troop movements.

You may want to continue this analysis for some messages you must communicate as part of your e-learning. You can make it even more meaningful by selecting primary and secondary media for the various messages.

Trade off power and difficulty of media

In picking media, we must make tradeoffs among media in terms of the power and difficulty. Power represents the ability of media to communicate facts, explain concepts, and trigger emotions. Difficulty refers to the requirements of using the medium, that is, the network speed, storage space, tools, and skills necessary to create and deploy the medium. Let's see how media stack up.

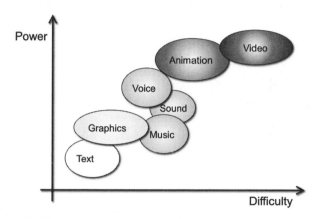

Text is displayed words. Text is easy. For many, however, text is not compelling, unless the author has the abilities of a Shakespeare.

More powerful and more difficult are graphics. Pictures can express 2- and 3-dimensional concepts and often include text. Even with drawing programs and clip art libraries, graphics are still more difficult to use than text.

Sound includes subject sound, background sound, and sound effects. Because of its effect on the imagination, sound can be extremely powerful, but it requires substantially more storage space and network speed than graphics. Few people have sound-editing skills.

Two types of sound deserve special consideration, especially as they occur in e-learning. One is voice. Spoken words have high power to express both logical concepts and emotional nuances. And, music has tremendous power to affect emotions, but little ability to convey cognitive concepts.

Animation, that is, moving drawings, adds motion to graphics. It is powerful because it can show change, even to conceptual subjects. Because it requires creating and showing multiple pictures, it is more difficult to create than static graphics. In the last few years, animation has gotten easier to create. Tools like Adobe Flash and SmithMicro Poser have made sophisticated animation practical. And, even office tools like PowerPoint include simple methods to animate content.

Video, that is, moving photographs, is at the upper right of our scale. Because video can include all the other media, it has great power. But because it requires dozens of photographs per second, its production and delivery costs are high. Video is getting much easier. Today, even mobile phones record video. And video editing tools come as part of most operating systems.

Though all media are possible, we still must consider creative and practical reasons for our choices.

THEN REDESIGN AGAIN AND AGAIN

Design of e-learning never follows a smooth and straight path. First you analyze your requirements and design your e-learning. Then you build it and test it. Oops! Better analyze the results and redesign a bit. Then you need to build in a few changes and test again. And so it goes.

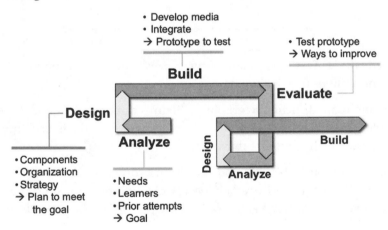

Effective development is more of a cycle than a straight path. It is iterative, empirical, and cumulative. That is it progresses through repeated cycles of discovery and accumulated improvements. Good development is cyclical, but that does not mean that designers run around in circles. They follow a disciplined development process repeatedly.

This process consists of four main activities. First designers analyze the situation, propose a solution, build it, and then evaluate the results. The results are seldom perfect, so they analyze again, design some more, build some more, and so on and on.

Let's look at what happens in each of the phases. In the analyze phase, what do designers analyze? They analyze needs of the organization. They analyze learners who will take the course. They also analyze prior attempts to identify ways to do things better this time. The result of the analysis is a goal for this cycle of development.

In the design phase, we specify components of the solution, organize these components into a coherent whole, and choose an effective strategy. The result of the design is a clear plan of how to meet the goal.

In the build phase, we develop media and integrate them into a prototype that we can test.

In the evaluation phase, we test the prototype to identify ways to improve our design.

Re-design but do not repeat

The design process proceeds in a cycle of analyze, design, build, and evaluate. The evaluation in one cycle becomes research for the analysis in the next cycle. Thus, design is a series—sometimes a seemingly endless series—of decisions. This essentially cyclical design process corkscrews along from high level to detailed issues while continually revisiting the same requirements over and over again.

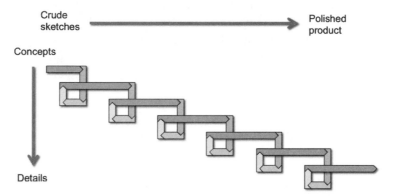

Not your sequential ADDIE process

If you are familiar with the ADDIE (Analyze, Design, Develop, Implement, and Evaluate) process, you may think we left out one of the phases. Not true. We just consolidated Develop and Implement into Build. Two reasons: One, since e-learning is delivered over networks, the implementation is a natural part of development. And two, since the process is iterative—as opposed to sequential—implementation does not lag development but goes on at the same time.

Make steady progress

The design process involves top-down design gated by testing at every level and tempered by a willingness to back up and start over where called for. At the beginning, you deal with high-level issues and work with a crude prototype, perhaps nothing more than a stack of sketches on index cards. At the end of the process, you are fine-tuning individual pixels of the final e-learning.

IN CLOSING ...

Summary

E-learning uses computer and network technologies to create learning experiences. Varieties of e-learning include standalone courses, learning games and simulations, mobile learning, social learning, and virtual-classroom courses.

The advantages of e-learning are not automatic nor are the disadvantages inevitable. Good design makes all the difference. Designing e-learning requires more than traditional instructional design.

Start with clear goals and objectives so you do not waste time and effort or just bore or distract learners. Systematically identify the prerequisites for each learning objective you must accomplish and decide how learners will achieve each prerequisite. Specify the learning activities to accomplish each objective. Determine what knowledge the learner must absorb, what the learner must do with the knowledge, and how the learner will connect the knowledge to work and life. Invest in good tests. Tests will (1) tell you how well your design is working, (2) help learners monitor their own progress, (3) show what content learners can skip and what content you can omit, and (4) make your objectives crystal clear.

Build your e-learning using iterative cycles of analysis, design, building, and evaluating. Start with big-picture issues and proceed to low-level details.

For more ...

The rest of this book will guide you in carrying out the steps shown in the overview provided in this chapter. For more on designing learning activities, flip to Chapters 2, 3, and 4. For help creating tests, go to Chapter 5. If you want to start designing learning objects, turn to Chapter 6. And, consult online Chapter 12 to learn how to design lessons (horton.com/eld/). For higher-level design issues affecting the course as a whole, view online Chapter 13 on strategic decisions (horton.com/eld/).

As far as instructional design is concerned, this chapter was just a crib sheet. For the complete book, pick up *Multimedia-Based Instructional Design* by William Lee and Diana Owens or *Principles of Instructional Design* by Robert Gagné. Or, search the Web for *e-learning and "instructional design"*.

2 Absorb-type activities

Presentations, demonstrations, stories, and field trips

Absorb activities inform and inspire. Absorb activities enable motivated learners to obtain crucial, up-to-date information they need to do their jobs or to further their learning. In Absorb activities learners read, listen, and watch. These activities may sound passive, but they can be an active component of learning.

ABOUT ABSORB ACTIVITIES

Of the three types of activities (Absorb, Do, and Connect), Absorb activities are the ones closest to pure information. Absorb activities usually consist of information and the actions learners take to extract and comprehend knowledge from that information. In Absorb activities, the learner may be physically passive yet mentally active—actively perceiving, processing, consolidating, considering, and judging the information.

In Absorb activities, it is the content (really the designer or teacher or writer of it) that is in control. The learner absorbs some of the knowledge offered by the content.

Common types of Absorb activities

Several types of Absorb activities have established themselves in conventional education and have made the leap to online learning. They are:

▶ **Presentations** during which learners watch or listen to a slide show, demonstration, podcast, or some other organized explanation (p. 69).

▶ **Readings** for which learners read online or paper documents (p. 93).

▶ **Stories by a teacher** in which learners listen to a story told by the teacher or some other expert or authority. The story is relevant to the subject of learning (p. 105).

▶ **Field trips** for which learners visit museums, historic sites, and other places to examine many relevant examples (p. 112).

When to feature Absorb activities

Where would we rely heavily on Absorb activities—not to the exclusion of all others—but for what they can offer as part of a complete design?

Because Absorb activities provide information efficiently, they are ideal when learners need a little information. They are especially helpful when just updating current knowledge. For example, the learner has used Version 6.0.2 of a software package for months and just needs to learn how to adapt to Version 6.0.3. Or, a long-standing regulation has undergone a slight revision.

Absorb activities are also an efficient way to extend current knowledge and skills. Learners who understand the fundamentals of a field can increase their knowledge by absorbing new details that elaborate a theory, concept, or principle. If learners have the trunk and limbs of a field, they can absorb branches and leaves.

Additionally, Absorb activities are good partners to other kinds of activities. Often they are used to prepare learners for a Do activity. The absorb part of the partnership orients the learner, sets the context, establishes vocabulary, introduces principles, and supplies instructions needed before the learner can engage in a highly interactive Do activity. Likewise, Absorb activities are a good follow-up to Do activities. For instance, a Do activity, such as a learning game, may lead learners to discover the main principles of a subject and evoke curiosity to learn more. After the game, learners may be ready to absorb the principles and theories that will help improve their game scores.

Absorb activities are best for highly motivated learners. They are not inherently interesting. However, they are highly efficient for individuals who can focus their attention and are motivated enough to expend the effort to learn from "mere information."

PRESENTATIONS

Presentations supply needed information in a clear, well-organized, logical sequence. They are analogous to a classroom lecture or an explanation by an expert.

Students learn by watching and listening to the presentation. Presentations may be experienced live in an online meeting or may be played back from a recording.

About presentations

Presentations convey information and demonstrate procedures and behavior in a straightforward (literally) flow of experiences.

When to use presentations

Presentations explain and demonstrate things to learners. They are commonly used to convey basic information, to demonstrate well-defined procedures, and to model human behaviors.

Presentations allow the designer to control the sequence of learning experiences. Use them where designers really *do* know the best way to teach certain material. Someone who has taught a course for ten years may know that certain explanations work better than others and that ideas must be introduced in a particular order to avoid confusion.

How presentations work

Presentations have a sequential structure. Most often they consist of an introduction, the body section, and a summary. The sequence is chosen to clarify the subject. Relatively uniform size segments occur at a regular pace.

Throughout this book I use little diagrams (such as the one that follows) to visually capture the flow of various activities. The little stick figures show what the learner or teacher is doing, and the rectangles more fully describe the type of activity in which they are engaged.

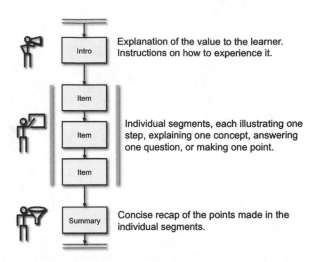

Although presentations may allow some optional topics, the primary pathway is linear—with the designer controlling the order of learning experiences. In recorded presentations, learners can control the pace of the presentation. And in live presentations, the learner may ask some questions, but the presenter determines the order.

Types of presentations

The types of presentations that are popular and effective in the classroom are popular and effective online. You may also want to model your presentation on one of these familiar forms:

▶ **Slide shows** are based on an effective business or classroom slide show. True, most such presentations are not effective, but they could be. And yours can be too. A good slide show makes each point on a single slide. Slides include informative graphics and just enough text to convey the main point. Many use recorded voice to narrate the slides (p. 71).

▶ **Physical demonstrations** show a person performing a physical procedure such as repairing a leaky faucet or lobbing a tennis ball. Physical demonstrations may be live or recorded as video (p. 72).

▶ **Software demonstrations** are an over-the-shoulders view of an expert performing a complex procedure with a computer program. We hear the expert's words and watch as the mouse clicks and typing appears (p. 74).

▶ **Informational films**, such as documentary films, have been used to educate, inform, and motivate people since the development of film. Although now the "film" is digital video, the information conveyed uses many of the same cinematic techniques (p. 80).

▶ **Dramas** show people in a fictional scene. You might use dramas to illustrate a successful interview or reveal team dynamics (p. 81).

▶ **Discussions**, such as interviews, debates, and panel presentations, are useful for revealing important information and opinions (p. 82).

If people can learn by watching and listening to something, it can be an effective online presentation. Recorded presentations are, thus, as varied as designers are clever. You can alter them by your choice and sequencing of topics, by use of different media, and by ways you share control over pacing and branching with the learner.

Slide shows

Classroom slide shows can be converted to online, recorded presentations. These are usually a series of linked slides or Web pages through which the learner advances, typically by jack-hammering a **Next** button or hyperlink.

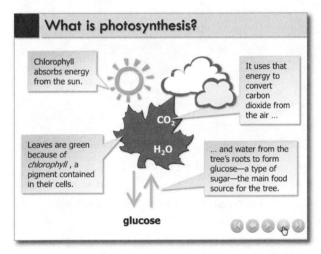

This slide from the middle of a slide presentation about why leaves change color in the fall, explains the process of photosynthesis. Animation shows the basic phases of photosynthesis and is synchronized with the text and voice-over narration.

Created in Microsoft PowerPoint and converted for Web delivery using iSpring Presenter. View example at horton.com/eld/.

Online slide shows may be created by narrating a classroom slide presentation and converting it to Web media. Tools for doing this include Articulate Presenter (www.articulate.com), Adobe Presenter (www.adobe.com), iSpring Presenter (www.ispringsolutions.com), and Impatica for PowerPoint (www.impatica.com). Or, you can record an online meeting during which you present slides.

Such sequences can be quite concise and graphical, especially when commentary is provided by voice-over narration. If sound is not a practical option, the commentary can be provided in text—after editing to reduce the amount of text, of course.

Slide shows rely primarily on text and graphics to tell their stories. They may also incorporate podcasts, informational films, dramas, demonstrations, and other forms of presentation.

Where to use slide shows

Since recorded presentations are much like a conventional slide show, they work well when presenting logically connected ideas, especially if expressed visually.

They may be the best choice economically and technically when you have proven slide presentations and the tools to quickly convert them for Web delivery.

Best practices for slide shows

- ▶ **Communicate visually**. Make graphics carry the load. Convert paragraphs to pictures, tables, and lists. Where you can, replace wordy bullet lists with illustrations or diagrams.

- ▶ **Narrate clearly**. Move excess text to voice-over narration. Make a transcript available by a button click so none of the text is lost.

- ▶ **Animate graphics**. Use motion and transitions to tell the story. Show how things move and evolve.

- ▶ **Build up the display** one object at a time to avoid overloading learners or creating a cluttered display. Add each item at the time when it is discussed. This will focus attention on the item and control how learners perceive the item.

Physical demonstrations

In a physical demonstration, learners see a person performing a procedure, such as repairing a device, kicking a soccer ball, or performing a dance move. The demonstration shows the right or wrong way to interact with a three-dimensional object. Such demonstrations are almost always conveyed as video.

Here is a physical demonstration from a course about using histograms. It shows how to view the histogram of a photograph just taken, evaluate the histogram, make adjustments to improve the photograph, and then re-take the photograph.

Where to use physical demonstrations

Use a physical demonstration to introduce a physical task you are teaching learners to perform. This could be a task they perform as part of their work, such as lifting heavy packages. Or, it could be a movement they make in dance, athletics, or performing arts.

Physical demonstrations can also be used to model human behavior, such as how to greet business associates of different cultures. Such demonstrations may involve gestures, body language, facial expressions, and tone of voice.

Best practices for physical demonstrations

▶ **Preview the action**. Start with an establishing shot showing the location of the action. Introduce the actor. State the purpose of the demonstration.

▶ **Use close-ups to show individual actions**. Because the video may have to appear in a small window, do not waste pixels.

▶ **Move smoothly and slowly**. The video may be played at a lower frame rate than conventional television, so actions may appear jerky. And fast motions may be missed altogether. For steps that must be performed quickly, show the individual steps slowly and then combine them at normal speed.

▶ **Keep the demonstration short**. Show a single action or phase of a task. If you have to teach a complex task, divide it into its component actions. Teach them, and then teach how to combine the actions.

▶ **Let learners control the demonstration**. For recorded demonstrations, give learners playback buttons to let them re-start the demo, fast forward it, play it backwards, and play it in slow motion.

Software demonstrations

Software demonstrations of late have become a category in their own right. A software demonstration, or *show-me* activity, lets learners watch a clear sequence of actions. These actions are explained by commentary provided as displayed text, spoken narration, or both. Software demonstrations can be performed live in an online meeting or recorded for playback by learners.

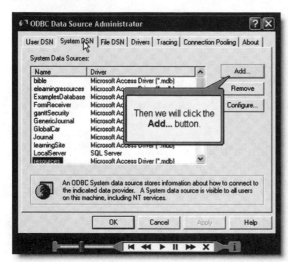

Demonstrations are good for how-to procedures like the one shown in this example—creating a system data source name.

Built in Adobe Captivate. View example at horton.com/eld/.

Software demonstrations are not the same as software simulations (p. 335). In *demonstrations*, the learner watches and listens as someone else operates the software. In software *simulations*, the learner performs the operations.

You can create a software demonstration by starting a recording program, performing the demonstration, and editing the recording. Such recordings capture the motions and clicks of the learner's mouse, text entered from the keyboard, and other actions visible on the screen. They record this action to a format that can be edited and then converted for Web delivery. Camtasia (www.techsmith.com) and Captivate (www.adobe.com) are a couple of popular tools for creating software demonstrations.

Software demonstrations are frequently used in standalone e-learning. However, do not forget to make use of live demonstrations in online class meetings, as shown in the next example:

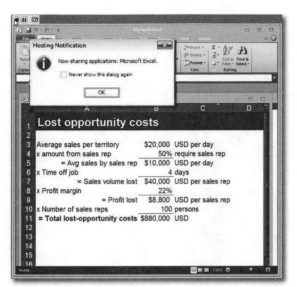

Here, the teacher discusses how to calculate lost opportunity costs. Rather than simply show a static spreadsheet and tell learners how to arrive at the values shown, the teacher demonstrates how the spreadsheet works by sharing the Excel application. The learner sees the spreadsheet just as it appears on the teacher's computer.

Microsoft Excel window shared using Elluminate.

As learners watch the teacher conduct the demo, they experience an Absorb activity. The teacher may then call on a student to perform a similar procedure. For that student, it is now a Do activity. For the other students watching, however, it is still an Absorb activity.

Where to use software demonstrations

Use software demonstrations to introduce computer procedures. They are effective in introducing the navigation scheme of a Web site, learning portal, or other electronic document to new learners. Software demonstrations are a good first step in teaching people to use an unfamiliar feature in a computer program.

Software demonstrations are seldom sufficient by themselves to teach absolute novices to use the software, but they can prepare the novice for a software simulation (p. 335) during which the novice attempts to perform the procedure demonstrated. For experienced learners, the demo may be adequate to teach a new procedure, especially if the learners follow along in the actual program.

This lack of interactivity is the strength and weakness of a demonstration—it requires little skill or motivation on the part of the learner. Learners who can play a YouTube video can watch a demonstration.

Scenario demonstrations

Several types or genres of software demonstrations are possible. One popular type shows a scenario involving use of a program to accomplish a particular piece of work.

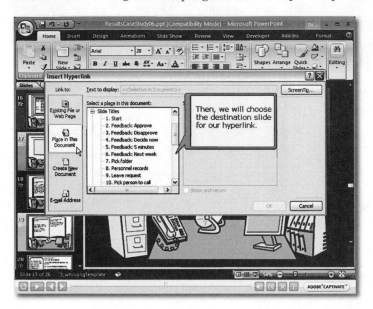

This example starts with the goal of adding a hyperlink to an object on a PowerPoint slide so that the presenter can click the hotspot to display an additional graphic.

Built in Adobe Captivate. View example at horton.com/eld/.

Use a scenario demonstration to show a practical result the learner can achieve with the software. Pick an example that is realistic and meaningful. A scenario can also be used to motivate further learning. It prepares the learner to engage in a coach-me simulation (p. 386).

Narrate the scenario demonstration in the first or third person to make clear that the learner is watching someone else perform the task. The first-person narration might say: "Here's how I performed the task." The third-person narration would say something like: "Here's how an experienced user might perform the task." In a scenario demonstration, tell learners what they are seeing rather than how they are to do it.

User-interface tours

The user-interface tour is a demonstration that introduces users to parts of the screen they will need to interact with to operate a computer program. The user-interface tour helps orient and entice learners. It answer's questions such as:

▶ What's there?
▶ What can the program do?
▶ What do these icons mean?

This example points out the main areas of a timer application and provides generous commentary about them.

Built in Adobe Captivate. View example at horton.com/eld/.

The user-interface tour covers the main areas of the interface and shows features crucial to its use. It provides a clear overview of the interface without excessive particulars. The successful user-interface tour avoids providing too much detail too soon. It may, however, offer links to demonstrations of specific features. That way, learners can choose how much detail to see.

Feature demonstrations

Another very common type of software demonstration is the feature demonstration. It shows an important part of a computer program, such as a complex command or a valuable capability.

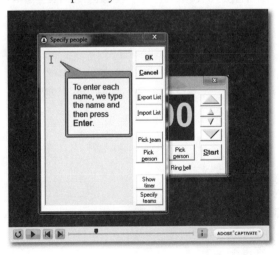

This example demonstrates the capability within the countdown timer to add names of people to a list, and have a random name displayed at the end of the countdown.

Built in Adobe Captivate. View example at horton.com/eld/.

2

Absorb-type activities

Use feature demonstrations to show a simple way to use an individual capability of a computer program, to perform a task that many users perform frequently, to concentrate on a single command or tool, or to explain an individual dialog box where the learner may need to take several actions.

Because the feature demonstration provides details on specific parts of a program, it is a good complement to the user-interface tour, which provides an overview.

Make software demonstrations flow smoothly

What are the human experiences in effective show-me demonstrations? Some patterns and sequences have proven themselves.

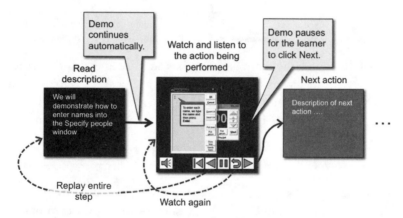

One pattern starts with the learner reading a description of what will be shown. Next the learner watches the described action being performed and at the same time listens to a narration describing the action. Then the demonstration waits for the learner to click Next to go to the next step in the procedure, click Replay to watch and listen again, or click Previous to view the entire step with description again. This pattern works because it breaks the task into a sequence of steps that alternate between reading and listening and watching.

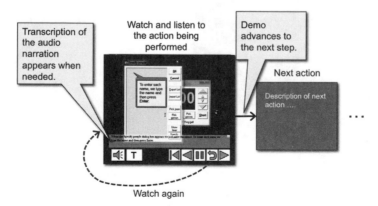

Some variations are common for this pattern. For simple tasks, where there is little risk the learner will misunderstand a step, we often advance to the next step without requiring the learner to click a button. In this case, make sure the learner can click a Pause button to stop the playback.

It is also common to omit the step of reading the description. If you do so, make sure those who cannot hear the voice can still get the information provided by the text, perhaps by displaying an optional transcript of the voice.

Another successful variation for show-me demonstrations begins with the learner reading (and perhaps listening to) the description. Then, the learner watches the action being performed (without any narration) before clicking a Next button to begin the cycle for the next step in the task. This pattern previews the action in text and voice and then lets the learner concentrate on watching the action. It works best if the text description can remain displayed during and after the demonstration shows the action. That way the learner can refer back to the description after watching it being performed.

Best practices for software demonstrations

▶ **Introduce the demonstration**. At the beginning tell learners what they will gain, what software is involved, and what the demonstration will cover. A few words of text and a sentence or two of narration are usually sufficient.

▶ **Keep demonstrations simple and to the point**. In each demonstration, illustrate just one way to perform one task. Do not clutter the demonstration with too many alternatives, shortcuts, and exceptions.

▶ **Make clear this is a demonstration, *not* a simulation**. If you say, "Click the **OK** button," some of your learners will try to do so. Tell learners just to watch.

▶ **Follow the demonstration with a simulation**. After showing learners how to perform the procedure, let them practice it in a simulation (p. 335).

▶ **Invite learners to follow along**. If the procedure is not dangerous, invite learners to start up the software and try to follow along. Remind learners to pause the presentation when it is time for them to attempt a step or two.

▶ **Provide a low-bandwidth alternative**. If the video-with-voice format of your demo is too large for all learners, provide an alternative version with static pictures and a transcript of the narration.

Informational films

Since the invention of motion pictures, the documentary film has presented factual information in a visual narrative. In the context of e-learning, the technology of film has been replaced with digital video.

This example of a documentary film shows the aftermath of the 1906 San Francisco earthquake. The film by the Thomas Edison Company shows a panorama from the east side of 4th Street near Natoma, just south of Market. This is just one example of many such historical films available from the U.S. Library of Congress (memory.loc.gov).

It is far beyond the scope of this book to tell you how to design, author, direct, and produce such films. For a starting point, pick up *Communicating Ideas with Film, Video, and Multimedia: A Practical Guide to Information Motion-Media* by Marty Shelton.

Where to use informational films

Use the informational film to explain a subject in a definite logical order, especially where the subject is visual but may be difficult for the learner to imagine.

Use it to present a logical narrative for which the order of images and experiences is important, for example to convey cause-and-effect relationships or to follow a chronological sequence. You might use it to show the chain of discoveries that led to a particular invention or to walk a chemical engineer through the processes and pipelines of a refinery. Use it when the motion of three-dimensional objects is especially important, such as when explaining how birds fly or fish swim.

Creating an informational film from scratch is complex and expensive, so you may want to reserve this form for critical, high-budget projects. Or, you may want to reuse an existing documentary film.

Best practices for informational films

▶ **Borrow if you can**. Designing, authoring, shooting, editing, and publishing a documentary film is expensive and a lot of work. (I know first-hand. I wrote and edited a short documentary called *Flights of Fantasy* about ultra-light airplanes and the interesting people who fly them.) If possible, re-use an existing documentary film. Supplement it with materials to adapt it to your purposes. You may need to provide a docking module (p. 315) to introduce the film to your learners.

▶ **Get permission.** Before you publish e-learning with someone else's video in it, make sure you have permission in writing.

▶ **Design for the small screen.** To reduce download times and to make the video play smoothly, keep the video window small. To make things clear in such a small window, always start with an establishing shot to give an overview and then proceed through a series of close-ups that reveal details. Periodically zoom back to re-establish the location.

▶ **Beware the bandwidth monster.** Good informational films feature motion and present interesting details—just the kind of video that is hard to compress. So try several compression schemes to find the best for your material. Offer several versions so learners can pick one appropriate for their connection speed. For those with slow connections, provide a sequence of still pictures accompanied by the text of the narration or dialog.

Dramas

In a drama, learners watch a fictional scene among people, for example to illustrate a successful interview or reveal team dynamics. Dramas can be conveyed in video, a combination of still pictures and voice, or by just voice alone. A drama is the fictional counterpart to the informational film.

Sam: Don't blame this on Lisa. It's not her job to fix your mess.

This example by Global Compliance (www.globalcompliance.com) from a course on preventing workplace violence shows a physical confrontation between two employees as witnessed by a passive third employee. It demonstrates how bullying and intimidation take place in the workplace.

Where to use dramas

Dramas are good to illustrate desirable and undesirable human behaviors and styles of interaction. I have used them for teaching lawful hiring, ethical behavior, and interviewing skills. Dramas can also be used to re-enact historic events, such as scientific discoveries or political discussions. Dramas may be useful to prepare learners for multi-person role-playing activities and simulations.

Best practices for dramas

▶ **Write credible dialog**. The way people speak in successful movies and television series is quite different from the way people talk in the real world and even more different from the way people write. Aim for dialog that is credible and clear. Hire a good fiction writer. At least read your dialog aloud and revise, revise, revise until it sounds right.

▶ **Hire good actors**. Recruit players who can put emotion into their voices and whose body language and gestures reinforce what they are saying. If you cannot afford professional actors, use still photos. Pose your players carefully before you snap the shutter.

▶ **Don't forget the drama**. If the sequence is totally predictable, there is no drama—and hence no curiosity. Keep the learner wondering how things will work out. Avoid stereotypical characters and situations.

▶ **Tell a story**. When we see people interacting, we expect a story with an introduction of characters, a crisis, and a resolution for good or ill. The story can be that simple.

Discussion presentations

We watch events wherein people interact, and we learn from what they say and do. The interplay among human beings is inherently interesting and provides a natural contrivance for revealing important information and opinions. People can be shown interacting as part of a live online meeting or they can be recorded interacting so learners can play back the recording. Most such events are shown in video, but audio recordings of discussions are sometimes useful as well.

Fieldworker David Taylor interviews Anne Murphy about c. 1918 photo of workers and managers at Newberger's Towel Factory, Paterson. From memory.loc.gov.

This example, from the U.S. Library of Congress, shows an interview of a retired factory worker about working conditions and procedures.

To see more examples of discussion-type presentations, search the Web for these words: *panel discussion video*.

Where to use discussion presentations

Use discussions when a speech would be too boring or might challenge the learner's opinions too directly. Many would rather watch a debate and make up their own minds than to listen to an expert state an opinion.

One of the best reasons to use this form is that it helps elicit valuable information and opinions from experts in a form that learners find interesting. In a speech, the expert drones on in a nervous monotone; in an interview, the expert enthusiastically responds to friendly provocation from the interviewer.

Forms of discussion presentations

Here are just a few forms where people interact in ways that reveal ideas, opinions, and information:

▶ News interviews.
▶ Talk-show interviews.
▶ Debates.
▶ Panel discussions.
▶ Mock trials.

Best practices for discussion presentations

▶ **Record the interaction with multiple cameras.** Then you can cut from person to person without having to swish back and forth across the scene, making viewers seasick.

▶ **Light the scene well**. Use adequate lighting and keep the lighting even throughout the scene (flat lighting) as is done for most TV interview shows.

▶ **Use close-ups of people**. Get in close enough so that the learner can see the emotions of the speaker as illustrated in gestures and facial expressions.

▶ **Don't use it if it does not work**. Sometimes discussions go flat. Panelists can just say, "I agree." Debates can expose too much rancor and not enough information. If your event flops, throw away the recording and pretend it never happened.

▶ **Take care with borrowed presentations**. To show a discussion, you may need legal permission from all the individual participants. And such presentations have a relatively short life on the Web. So, you will need to obtain a copy and make it available to your learners.

Best practices for presentations

Now here are some suggestions for better presentations, regardless of the form.

Give learners control

Give learners control over how they experience the presentation.

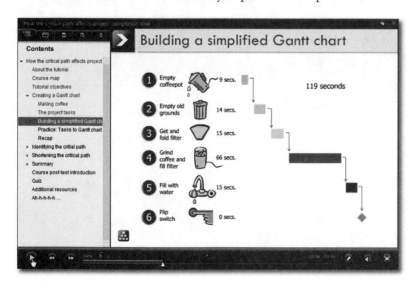

How the critical path affects project completion time shows learners how to recognize and shorten the critical path. The buttons at the bottom of the window let learners control the pace of the presentation.

Built using Microsoft PowerPoint and iSpring Presenter. View example at horton.com/eld/.

2

Absorb-type activities

Let learners read the narration as well as listen to it. Some learners may be deaf, dyslexic, or listening in a language other than their first. Reading along while listening will help comprehension. Also, some learners may work in open cubicles, making it difficult to turn up the volume of the computer audio. Sometimes learners just need to check a fact, so let them print a transcript of the narration, too. Being able to print the narration makes reviewing the material much easier.

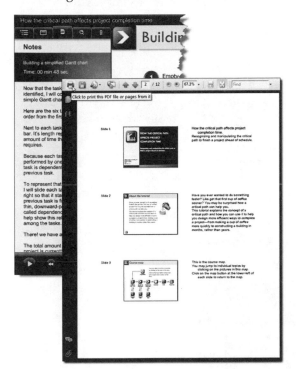

In *How the critical path affects project completion time* the learner can choose to view the Notes (transcript) panel instead of the Contents panel.

There is also a link to a print-ready Adobe PDF handout showing each slide with the transcript alongside.

Presentation built using Microsoft PowerPoint and iSpring Presenter. Handout created using Microsoft Word and Adobe Acrobat. View example at horton.com/eld/.

Supply examples, examples, examples

Many lectures have too much theory and not enough concrete, specific, realistic examples. Remember, not everyone can reason from general concepts to particular applications, or at least not without the help of examples that they can understand and apply.

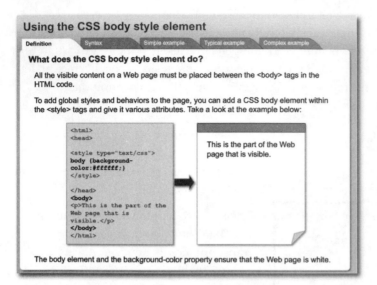

The topic shown here is from a course on Cascading Style Sheets (CSS). For such practical, but abstract subjects, include at least three examples of key points.

The topic starts with a definition. The Syntax tab contains the abstract format of the style element and main attributes.

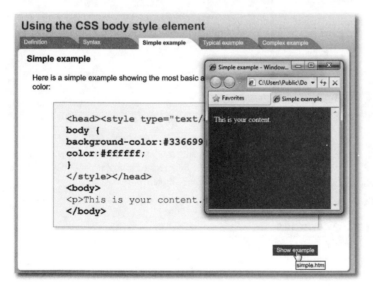

The first example shows the most simple and useful attributes to add to the body style. It gives learners something they can easily understand and apply immediately.

The **Show example** button launches a browser window that shows how this fragment of code displays.

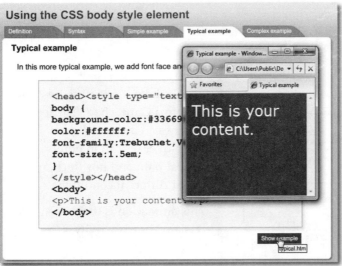

The second example is the most common case. It shows features most learners will use frequently.

Like the simple example, it contains a button to launch a page so learners can see the results of changes made to the code.

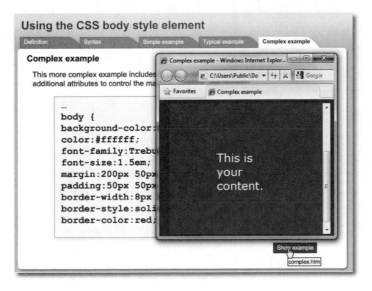

The final example is quite a bit more complex. It shows additional attributes that the advanced learner may find useful.

Created in Microsoft PowerPoint and converted for Web delivery using iSpring Presenter. View example at horton.com/eld/.

2

Absorb-type activities

Provide immediate practice

Combine presentation with practice. At the end of a presentation, include a chance for learners to demonstrate what they have learned.

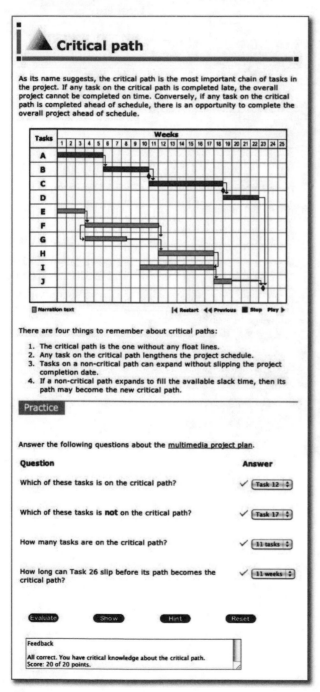

This topic from *Using Gantt Charts* teaches how to identify the critical path in a Gantt chart. The learner watches an animated chart as voice-over narration points out the critical path and how it changes under different conditions.

This animation is the presentation. It is an Absorb activity.

Also in the topic, learners can immediately confirm their understanding of the concepts presented. Scrolling down they encounter a practice activity in which they answer several multiple-choice questions that verify understanding of the most important and the most often misunderstood concepts.

This practice is a Do activity. It is seldom wrong to follow a substantial Absorb activity with a Do activity to verify understanding.

Built using Adobe Dreamweaver, JavaScript, and Flash. View example at horton.com/eld/.

In the e-learning I have taken, far too many of the presentations went on too long and covered too many concepts. By the time I had an opportunity to practice what I had learned, I had forgotten what I had learned.

Augment presentations

An especially effective presentation can serve as the core of a topic or lesson. To turn a presentation into a more comprehensive learning experience, consider augmenting it with navigation controls to allow learners to move back and forth in the presentation.

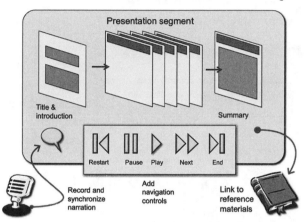

You may also need to add an introduction with instructions for playing the presentation, access to more detailed reference information, a summary, and a practice activity or test.

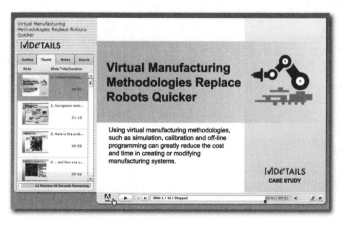

Here is an example of a simple slide presentation that was augmented to create a complete e-learning topic. It is a case study that demonstrates how virtual manufacturing processes, such as simulation, can shorten the time it takes to replace manufacturing robots.

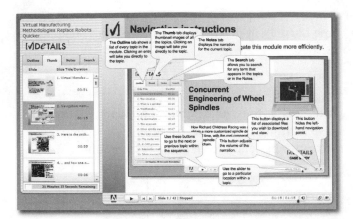

A brief introduction acquaints learners with the navigation controls and viewing aids.

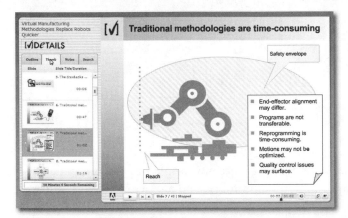

Here we see a single slide from the presentation. The displayed text summarizes the voice narration.

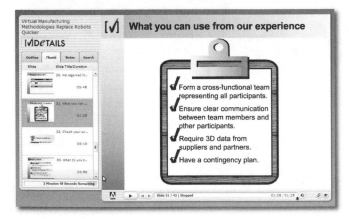

The summary recaps the main points we want the learner to retain from the presentation. Because this summary was created separately from the presentation, it can emphasize things especially important for this particular use of the presentation.

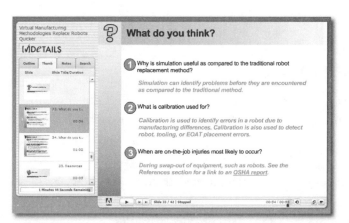

The augmented presentation includes a simple test to help learners gauge their knowledge.

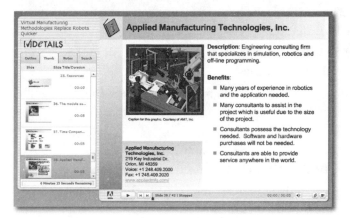

Because the presentation provides only an overview of the subject, it includes links to more detailed industry information.

Created in Microsoft PowerPoint and converted for Web delivery using Adobe Presenter.

And a few more best practices

Here are some suggestions that come from my own experiences designing presentations:

Pick the best mix of media to express your ideas to your learners. If you are explaining to recent college graduates how things move, animation and video are logical choices. If you are discussing abstract concepts with experienced practitioners in a field, voice may be adequate.

Keep learners active. Combine presentations with Do activities so learners are not physically or mentally passive for too long. For example, alternate a presentation that teaches a concept with an activity that lets the learner apply the concept.

Borrow. Excellent presentations on many subjects already exist on the Web. Consider linking to one of these available recorded presentations. Make clear that someone else provides the material; otherwise, learners may be confused by differences in the appearance of the materials. Also make sure the provider of the materials has no

2

Absorb-type activities

objections to your use of the materials. Provide a docking module (p. 315) to the borrowed material.

Extend presentation activities

We can increase the reach and power of presentation activities by combining them with other types of activities and by adapting them for social learning and for mobile learning.

Combine presentations with other activities

Like all activities, presentations gain power when combined with complementary activities. Here are some tested combinations:

▶ Follow hardware and software demonstrations with practice activities (p. 130) to let learners apply what you demonstrated. Have learners repeat the demonstration on their own or complete a coached simulation.

▶ Use discovery activities (p. 146) to help learners notice principles and slide shows and informational films to expand on these principles.

▶ Begin games (p. 157) with a short slide show to teach the rules and user-interface of the game. Make available an informational film or slide show to teach concepts needed to win the game.

▶ Supplement presentations with readings (p. 93) to reveal details only hinted at in the presentation and to satisfy curiosity about a subject aroused by the presentation.

▶ Immediately follow the presentation with a Q&A session (p. 562) or group discussion so learners can fill in gaps and satisfy aroused curiosity.

▶ Precede the main presentation with a separate presentation or reading introducing the concepts, principles, objects, or people seen in the presentation. Use the pre-presentation to supply prerequisites for the main presentation.

▶ Follow the presentation with a quiz-show game (p. 331) asking questions about the presentation. Require both recall and inference.

▶ Practice applying principles, rules, and concepts of the presentation in games (p. 323), role-playing activities (p. 476), and original work (p. 207). Or have learners summarize the presentation as a job-aid (p. 187).

Design presentation activities for social learning

Have social learners:

▶ **Present through social media**. For instance, embed the recorded presentation in a blog, podcast, or forum so discussion naturally follows.

▶ **Provide feedback** during the presentation through a back channel.

▶ **Control the presentation as a group**. Let the group pause for discussion and decide where to go next in non-linear presentations and tours.

▶ **Create presentations**. For example, have each learner provide one slide for a slide show. Discuss and revise individual contributions.

▶ **Comment and discuss the presentation**. Have learners restate key points, summarize or outline the presentation, publish notes taken during the presentation, rate the value of the presentation, point out flaws and gaps, suggest applications, offer corrections, assess validity and credibility, draw conclusions, and suggest better ideas and alternative interpretations.

▶ **Link the presentation to related resources** that go deeper, offer contrary views, better express the same ideas, reveal the research or other basis for ideas, extend with visuals and other media, locate items on maps and satellite views, and supply external commentary.

▶ **Edit and annotate the presentation**. Embed comments pointing out errors, updating content, and linking to supporting evidence and related resources. Highlight key points. Add new pathways and cut down to the essentials.

Design presentation activities for mobile learning

Have mobile learners:

▶ **Originate and record the content** for presentations from remote locations, as do news programs.

▶ **Experience presentations in the locale where they will apply learning**, such as a construction site, archaeological dig, or speaker's podium.

▶ **Capture real-world content for others to absorb**. Capture speeches and lectures, presentations, physical and software demonstrations, workflow procedures, dramatic situations, debates and discussions, and walkthroughs of buildings and public spaces.

READINGS

Sometimes the best e-learning is a good book … or a good e-book.

Reading is not dead. Far from it. E-learning can effectively incorporate reading assignments. We can direct learners to individual documents or make entire libraries available to them.

About reading activities

Reading activities direct learners to electronic or paper documents that are well researched, organized, and written. By reading these documents, learners gain important information and inspiration.

Printed documents may seem so very 20th Century. Their displays just sit there. They lack play buttons and offer limited interactivity. Yet, it is this stability that gives them their value in this increasingly ultra-dynamic, hyper-interactive world. Written documents do not squirm, shift, twitch, flicker, or misinterpret the reader's subtle intentions. They present information in a precise visual organization and a predictable sequence.

Ironically, reading may be a more active learning experience than some learning games, especially as the learner skims, peruses, reads, imagines, compares, re-reads, jots notes, makes bookmarks, and reflects.

When to use reading activities

Use reading activities to present complex and difficult information in a stable form for careful study by the learner. Use reading activities when:

▶ Learners need deeper knowledge on a subject.

▶ You do not have time to develop more interactive materials and well-written documents are readily available.

▶ Learners are skillful readers and motivated enough to read on their own.

Reading activities are an important part of a new definition of learning. Instead of teaching people to memorize and then recall information, today we teach them how to find, read, and understand information when they need it. What you "know" includes all the things you can recall—along with all the things you can find in online libraries, on the Internet, and through social networks. For more on implementing this new style of learning, look at research (p. 196) and job-aid (p. 187) activities and skim Chapter 8 on social learning.

Types of readings

Reading activities for e-learning typically provide access to readings in three ways:

▶ Individual documents.

▶ Libraries of documents to select from.

▶ Predefined searches to find Internet resources.

How reading activities work

The procedure for reading activities is quite simple. First the learner obtains the document and then reads it.

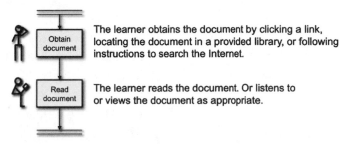

Obtaining the document should be simple, swift, and reliable—unless this step is part of a research activity (p. 196).

Assign individual documents

The simplest form of reading activity assigns a single, specific document. The learner typically clicks a link to obtain the document and then reads it either online or after printing it out.

Consider many types of documents

Many different types of documents can be useful in e-learning. Here is a short list to start you thinking.

- Textbooks.
- Popular books.
- Manuals.
- Handbooks.
- Reports.

- Regulations.
- Brochures.
- Data sheets.
- Specifications.
- Diaries and journals.

- Scholarly papers.
- Trade journals.
- Magazines.
- Newspapers.
- Blogs.

Include standard references

Many fields of study have standard reference works that make a valuable addition to your e-learning.

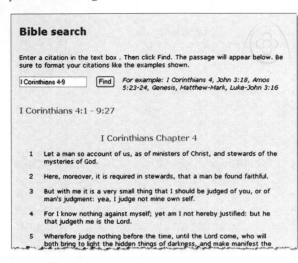

A project for church congregations provided access to one reference work particularly important to them. Learners could find Biblical passages by typing in the citation in conventional form, including ranges.

Built using Adobe Dreamweaver and Active Server Pages.

Standard reference works include:

▶ Textbooks for conventional courses in the field.

▶ Professional handbooks used by practitioners.

▶ Laws and regulations governing the field.

▶ Classical literature that may be the subject of study.

▶ Scripture that is the basis for values and policies.

▶ Biographies of key figures in a field.

▶ Historical reviews of a field.

▶ Collected works of important researchers or artists.

Pick file formats for documents

If you are making documents available for learners, consider how you will convert conventional documents to Web-accessible media. Several formats are quite common in e-learning.

Format	Advantages	Disadvantages
HTML	Can be displayed in browser with no plug-ins.	Only for simple formats. Otherwise the conversion efforts are complex.
Adobe Acrobat Portable Document Format (PDF)	Faithful to original format, even if complex. Works for any document you can print.	Requires learners to have the Acrobat Reader software.
Microsoft Word or Rich Text Format (RTF)	Can be opened by Word and other word processors for editing.	Requires learners to have a word processor or download a viewer. You cannot control what learners do with your document.

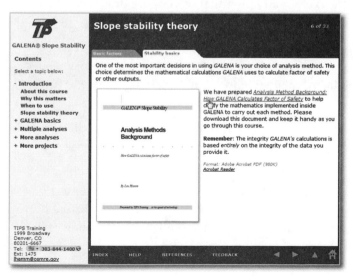

I find Adobe's Acrobat Portable Document Format (PDF) an attractive format for documents and handouts the learner may need to read. PDF provides a high-fidelity image of the original document—as it would appear printed. In fact, this is the strength of PDF: It can be used for any computer document that can be printed. And creating a PDF file is little more difficult than printing a document.

Built using Adobe Dreamweaver and Adobe Acrobat Professional.

2

Absorb-type activities

PDF does, however, require learners to download and install the free Acrobat Reader. For technically sophisticated learners, this task is not a serious barrier. But not all learners are technically sophisticated … or blessed with an attentive information technology department to install the reader for them.

The advantage of PDF is that documents are 99% faithful to their original format, including graphics. PDF files are not as compact as HTML, but still relatively compact, especially compared to straight, graphical formats.

There is an easy test to determine whether you should use PDF. If the document is long, intricately formatted, and will be read from a printout, use PDF so that the learner gets a legible and precisely formatted copy.

Create an online library

Sending learners off to the library for a bit of reading is a tradition in education—one that e-learning designers can well capitalize on by integrating libraries into e-learning courses.

We can make reading assignments much quicker, more reliable, and less frustrating by providing learners with a well-organized and cataloged library of learning resources. Rather than assign specific works to read, we can provide a library of relevant material for learners to select from.

One advantage of this approach is that the reading activity does not fail if a single source of information is removed from the Web or an individual server goes down. Another advantage is the ease of combining research and reading activities.

The basic idea of libraries has not changed much since ancient Alexandria. It has not needed to. Libraries make knowledge accessible by collecting the best and most needed works, labeling them, organizing them, cataloging them, and enabling people to find them on their own. And Web-based libraries keep longer hours.

Design your library not as a monumental shrine to dusty books, but as an inviting portal to self-education. Make the library practical, helpful, and fun. Tailor it to the needs and tastes of learners.

Such a library can be as simple as a page of hyperlinks to valuable resources or as rich as a vast database of thousands or millions of resources. The key to a successful virtual library, though, is not the breadth of content, but that the content is well organized and easily accessible.

What will your library offer that public search engines do not already offer? The one thing you can probably offer is the application of your knowledge in a field, so that learners using your library get better answers to their questions in less time than they can with any search engine.

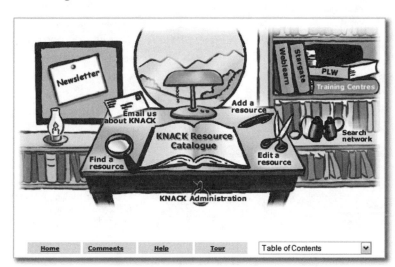

Here is an example of the learner-interface for an online library.

Built using Adobe Dreamweaver and Active Server Pages.

Be sure to verify the quality of your resources. Include the *best* resources on a subject, not *all* the resources on a subject. Remember, one of the goals of the librarian is to reduce information overload.

Design your library to serve multiple purposes. It can be the basis for a variety of research activities (p. 196). One library can serve the needs of multiple courses. And, a library can be a valuable information source in its own right.

Rely on Internet resources

In a sense, the whole Web is like a library ... after an earthquake. The Web contains the equivalent of trillions of pages of information, but finding the one you want requires a lot of rooting around in disorganized piles. You want to spare your learners that effort. So a third way to direct learners to specific Internet readings is to link to them directly or trigger specific Internet searches.

Link to Internet resources

One of the simplest ways to use the Web is to link directly to documents useful to your learners. To see the document, learners just click on the link.

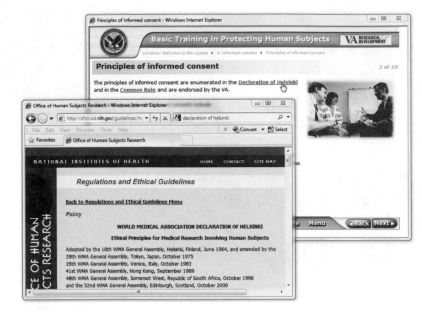

This course on medical ethics and procedures links to regulations and guidelines defining correct behavior for learners of this course.

Designed by William Horton Consulting. Built by William Horton Consulting and VA Research and Development.

Trigger a search

Provide specific search terms learners can enter into a search engine. Or, provide a link that triggers a Web search on a search engine and display the results to your learners. This removes the trouble of typing in the search terms and the risk of typing them wrong.

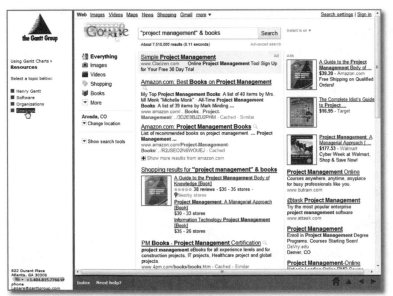

This example shows a Google search page triggered from a "Readings" entry in the course table of contents.

Course built with Adobe Dreamweaver. Searches are performed by Google under license.

The advantage of this procedure is clear. You do not have to maintain the list of reading materials. The individual providers do that, and the search engine finds them for you. The list never goes stale.

Before you do this, however, make sure you have permission from the search engine to display their results in your course.

Sources of useful documents

Even if 99.999% of the content on the Web were trash, there would still be enough valuable reading material to supply millions of e-learning courses. Here are some places to look for readings for your activities and courses:

scholar.google.com	Searches scholarly literature such as papers, articles, books, abstracts, and journals.
print.google.com	Google Book Search searches the full text of books to find items of interest. It can display images of full pages and links to places where you can buy or borrow the book.
www.gutenberg.org	Project Gutenberg makes available over 17,000 free electronic books you can download.
books24x7.com	For a fee, SkillSoft provides access to the complete online versions of popular scientific, technology, and business books.

Best practices for reading activities

Reading activities can be boring and pointless or engaging and enlightening. Opt for the latter.

Grow your library gradually

Grow your library smoothly and surely. Start with a Course Resource page. As it grows to several scrolling zones, put a menu in front of it. As it increases beyond a few hundred resources, incorporate a database to hold the individual records. As you begin offering more and more kinds of resources and services, consider migrating to a true knowledge-management system. Start simple and adopt technology only as you need it.

Publish a usage policy

Make clear what learners can do with the documents you provide them. Specify what rights learners have to read, share, copy, reuse, and modify the documents. Some items may be ones you own, while others are ones you have rights to display only. Still others may be resources you do not possess but provide links to.

One practical solution is to include a blanket rule that is quite restrictive and to flag items for which learners have additional rights.

Simplify obtaining documents

For freely available electronic documents, you can just link to the document. But how should you handle documents not available online; or, documents that charge a fee?

- ▶ Link to the publisher's sales site where learners can order a copy or purchase access.
- ▶ Link to Amazon (www.amazon.com), Barnes & Noble (bn.com), or some other online bookstore where learners can order a copy.
- ▶ Set up your own bookstore and sell the item yourself. This is easier than it sounds. Amazon or another seller will handle the technology and billing for you.
- ▶ Buy limited electronic rights and make them available to just your learners.
- ▶ Provide the document in several formats so learners can pick the one that works best for them.

Feature active examples

One of the most valuable forms of online resources is a library of examples that learners can actually manipulate and use.

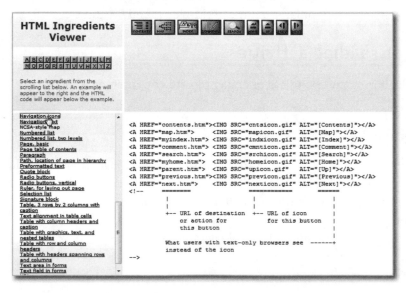

The collection shown here offers HTML ingredients that can be used in Web pages to create tables, headings, bullet lists, and so forth.

Built using Adobe Dreamweaver and JavaScript. View example at horton.com/eld/.

Here's how it works. The learner clicks a letter button to scroll through the list of examples to the ones with names beginning with that letter. The learner then picks an example in the list. The example appears formatted at the upper right and as HTML at the lower right.

The learner can then copy the HTML to an authoring program. Embedded comments guide learners in modifying the example to suit their purposes. Because such examples can be modified and used by learners, we call them active examples.

Use active examples for:

▶ Programming code.

▶ HTML, XML, and other tagging languages.

▶ Templates used to create slides, documents, etc.

▶ Forms to print out and fill in.

Extend reading activities

We can increase the reach and power of reading activities by combining them with other types of activities and by adapting them for social learning and for mobile learning.

Combine readings with other activities

Merge your library and museum

Build and manage a library and a museum (p. 119) as one operation. They are separate institutions in the physical world only because they warehouse different kinds of objects: paintings and sculpture in art museums, books in libraries. Online, all objects are just bits.

The missions of libraries and museums are complementary. Museums contain unique original two- and three-dimensional objects and provide tiny plaques of commentary on them. Libraries provide extensive commentary on everything imaginable but only low-fidelity reproductions of objects of interest. Sounds like an ideal merger.

You may still want to maintain separate learner interfaces for the library and museum—at least until patrons seem ready to accept a merger. Behind the interface, the two institutions can share a common Web server, database, and access mechanisms.

Teach learners to use your library

▶ Create a guided tour (p. 113) of the library to show learners around. Focus on items related to your course.

▶ Conduct scavenger hunts (p. 198) to familiarize learners with the organization and search mechanisms of the library.

▶ Assign guided research activities (p. 200) that get learners in the habit of using library resources.

Integrate readings into other activities

▶ Supplement presentations (p. 69) with readings that provide more depth and detail.

▶ Attach readings to games (p. 157) to provide the principles needed to win the game and to help learners who find the high degree of interactivity required in computer games a bit intimidating.

▶ Use library-based materials throughout e-learning. Get in the habit of beginning each lesson with links to alternative ways of learning the subject and ending it with links to ways of learning more on the subject.

Use other activities to motivate reading

Activity	How it motivates reading
Game	Tests recall of facts, principles, and concepts from the reading.
Software simulation	Require learners to look up details in the manual or online help.
Scavenger hunt	Searching the document reveals content of interest to learners.

Use other activities to supplement readings

▶ Use a presentation to provide an overview and prerequisites needed to read productively.

▶ Use guided research to enable learners to go deeper into the subject of the readings.

▶ Have learners conduct research to identify additional reading materials.

Design reading activities for social learning

Have social learners:

▶ **Create and share readings** to educate other learners. Individual learners can, for example, write a short essay or section of a larger work, document a step or phase in a procedure, or profile one character in a novel or play.

▶ **Comment on and discuss readings**. Invite learners to rate, review, summarize, restate, generalize, suggest alternatives, and propose applications of ideas of the readings.

▶ **Link readings to related resources** that go deeper, offer contrary views, better express the same ideas, or put the readings in context.

▶ **Edit and annotate the document** to highlight key points, embed comments, update facts and figures, flag errors, and spell out jargon.

▶ **Engage in micro-learning** in which the teacher, an expert, or learners in rotation post a daily nugget of learning in the field of inquiry, for instance a surprising fact or figure, person of interest in the field, admirable piece of work, or tool. The posting includes a link to a page, video, or podcast that elaborates on the subject of the initial post. Learners are invited to comment on the post.

Design reading activities for mobile learning

Have mobile learners:

▶ Play an audio version of the readings, either by accessing an "audiobook" version or by using text-to-speech synthesis to generate a spoken version.

▶ Record readings for others. Use the device's screen as a teleprompter.

▶ Access readings to confirm and learn about real-world discoveries.

STORIES BY A TEACHER

Can you remember a classroom course during which the teacher used stories to help make the point? Can you remember such courses in which the most memorable parts were the stories?

Now, can you think of an online course that includes such stories? One of the ironies is that stories are often what learners remember best but what designers leave out when converting classroom courses to e-learning.

About sharing stories

Storytelling activities relate individual human experiences. They make information real and personal.

Types of storytelling activities

There are two types of storytelling activities. One involves stories told by the teacher and the other involves stories told by the learner. Both types of stories can be told live or played back from a recording. We often combine stories by the teacher with an invitation for learners to share similar stories. This combined activity is called *story-sharing*.

When the teacher or designer tells a story, it is an Absorb activity. When the learner tells a story, it is a Connect activity. Stories told by the teacher are covered here; stories by learners are in Chapter 4.

For stories by the teacher, the "teacher" who tells the story can be any expert, authority, guru, or pundit with a valuable story to share. The storyteller does not have to be the designated teacher, professor, or instructor. The storyteller can even be another learner. The important thing is not who tells the story but that the learners listen and the story teaches.

How story-sharing works

After a brief introduction, the learner listens to a story told by the teacher or another authority. Then the learner may be given the opportunity to tell a comparable story. The whole activity then ends with a brief recap of the points made in the story.

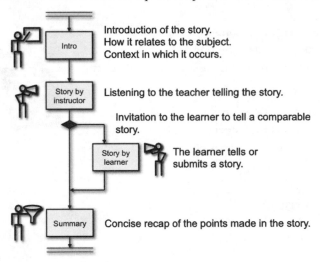

When to tell stories to learners

Use stories by a teacher to directly relate what you are teaching to the experiences of learners. Tell stories to:

▶ Demonstrate the applicability or importance of what is being taught.
▶ Give concrete instances of the subject matter.
▶ Humanize a subject by showing its effects on people the learner cares about.
▶ Encourage and motivate learners to overcome difficulties.

Tell stories that apply to learners

Tell stories to learners in a way that encourages them to think how the stories apply to their lives.

Example of a story by a teacher

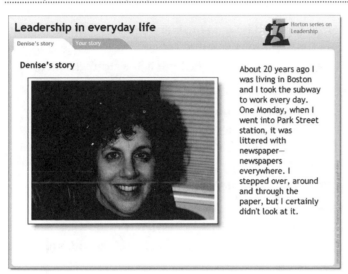

The example shown here comes from a course on leadership. We see a picture of Denise who tells a story about leading by example.

Created in Microsoft PowerPoint and converted for Web delivery using Articulate Presenter. View example at horton.com/eld/.

Here is what she says:

> About 20 years ago I was living in Boston and I took the subway to work every day.
>
> One Monday, when I went into Park Street station, it was littered with newspaper— newspapers everywhere. I stepped over, around, and through the paper, but I certainly didn't look at it.
>
> Standing not too far from me, waiting for his train, was a middle-aged man. He was looking around at the mess and then looked down at his feet. He bent down, picked up some of the newspaper and took it to the trash. He did this a few times until his train arrived.
>
> After his train was gone and the station had quieted down a bit, a young woman on the platform bent down and picked up some newspaper at her feet and took it to the trash. Then a young man did the same thing. Finally, we were all in the act. By the time my train arrived, the station looked pretty good—and the trashcans were full.
>
> You know, I wonder if that man had any idea I would be telling this story 20 years later, or that he had had such an effect on my life? But I think it illustrates something about leadership that we tend to forget. That is, leadership is not just what prime ministers and CEOs do, but leadership is how we lead our lives every day and how we affect other people.

Every time I play this story in a classroom, students cease fidgeting and whispering and give it their rapt attention. Such is the power of stories.

Types of stories

Just about any kind of human story can be used effectively in e-learning—provided it is relevant to the subject and appropriate for the learners. Here are some that have proven themselves over the past few millennia:

Hero stories

Hero stories, sometimes called "war stories," tell how an ordinary person with whom the learner can identify overcame obstacles like those facing the learner. The hero triumphed by applying knowledge and behaving correctly. Usually the hero is the storyteller. The story told by Denise is a hero story.

The hero story is as old as storytelling. From prehistoric campfires to the latest scientific conferences, hero stories have been told. Such hero stories follow a familiar pattern: First we meet the hero and learn about the setting. Then the hero encounters a challenge and is stymied by its difficulty. The hero then finds or develops strength that enables the hero to overcome the difficulty. The hero profits from the experience.

The hero story is good for giving learners courage to take on difficult tasks and for suggesting how the subject they are studying will help them overcome difficulties. Such stories are popular in business, politics, religion, warfare, and other complex human endeavors for which learners need encouragement to apply what they are learning.

The hero stories are also good for motivating learning of difficult material. Use them to illustrate how applying the subject of learning saved the day.

Love stories

Love stories concern the wooing and winning and the happy ever after of two people. Love stories might seem an odd thing to include in e-learning. However, love stories are not just the province of Shakespeare and Jane Austin. They are not limited to Hollywood romantic comedies. Love stories can tell how a sales representative won the affections and purchase orders of a reluctant customer. It can tell how a scientific theory won, lost, and then regained favor among the scientific community.

The structure of the love story is amazingly consistent: A meets B. A pursues B, but B resists. A wins B. A and B break up because of a silly mistake by A or the treachery of a rival. A and B get back together and live happily ever after.

Use love stories to illustrate the importance and difficulty of winning loyalty, trust, respect, and commitment. Use them to point out the fragility of human relationships.

Disaster stories

Disaster stories vividly convey the negative consequences of failure to apply knowledge or to behave correctly.

About five times a year, TV viewers in the United States are treated to a disaster miniseries. Although the disasters change from earthquakes to tidal waves to meteors to hurricanes, the plot is exactly the same: The hero predicts disaster. Arrogant superiors ignore the hero. Disaster occurs. The hero saves masses of people. Arrogant superiors perish. The hero then saves his or her family.

Although this pattern is too melodramatic for our purposes, it does suggest some elements to include, such as ignored warnings or bad behavior leading to a disaster. For e-learning, we make clear that application of the knowledge and skills we are teaching could have prevented the disaster.

A Pilot's Guide to Ground Icing, a course for professional pilots, begins with a story about how a plane crashed upon takeoff, killing five on board—all because the crew ignored the potential adverse effects of ground icing (aircrafticing.grc.nasa.gov/courses.html). The *GALENA Slope Stability Analysis* course begins with stories and statistics of the damage caused by slope failures.

Tragedies

Like the disaster story, the tragedy is a precautionary tale. It focuses on the actions of an individual, rather than on public consequences.

The pattern of the tragedy is well established. From Oedipus to Lear to the hubris of Wall Street egos, we hear the same story. The pattern is this: The hero does good works, but a flaw leads to disaster. The hero regrets the flaw. Sometimes the hero recovers and sometimes not. For e-learning, the flaw that afflicts the hero is usually ignorance of the knowledge we will convey or the lack of the skill we will teach.

Tragedies are common in sales training. Their gist is "I didn't learn an essential knowledge or skill and lost a big sale as a result." Such stories are very effective because the personal confession of an authority figure the learner respects reduces resistance from the learner's ego. "If it could happen to you, I guess it could happen to me."

Use tragedies in much the same way you would use a disaster story, but use them for subjects that are applied by the individual learner.

Discovery stories

The discovery story relates how the storyteller gained valuable insights. It is similar to the hero story except that the point is in the storyteller's experiences and what they taught. Such stories emphasize the scientific breakthroughs, personal insights, new perspectives, or altered attitudes that resulted from unexpected experiences.

The pattern is this: The hero starts out to accomplish a task. The hero encounters difficulties and is stymied. The hero becomes frustrated or encouraged. The hero makes a discovery more important than the original task.

Use discovery stories to teach the importance of learning by discovery and the need to be open to new experiences. They are a good way to introduce a principle or concept that the learner might not immediately accept. The discovery story puts the idea into context and immediately demonstrates its value. It makes the idea real and arouses curiosity about it.

And many, many more

As you read novels and short stories, as you watch movies and TV, take note of the stories you experience. Note their plots and consider whether you can use them as a basis for a story in your e-learning.

Oh, by the way, these same types of stories work for stories told by learners.

Best practices for stories by a teacher

The effectiveness of a story-sharing activity depends on the story and how it is told. Here are some guidelines to improve stories told by teachers and those by learners too.

Tell effective stories

What makes a good story for e-learning? There is no magic formula, but effective stories do seem to share some characteristics.

▶ **The story is credible**. It may be a composite of several experiences or even a parable, but it sounds and feels true to learners.

▶ **The story is important**. It makes a valuable point and is apt to the subject at hand. It directly helps accomplish the learning objective.

▶ **The story is short and focused**. Everything in the story contributes to its objective. In e-learning, stories should be about one-third or one-half the length of a story told in the classroom.

▶ **The story is dramatic**. The result is not clear until the end. And learners want to know how the story ends.

▶ **We care about the characters**. We have a hero we can identify with, a victim we can sympathize with, a villain we can despise, and others who make us feel joy, fear, or anger. The worst reaction to a story is "Who cares?"

▶ **The storyteller cares**. The story is told with emotion. The storyteller's feelings for events and characters are not hidden. The voice is well modulated and rhythmical.

▶ **The moral is clear**. The learner does not have to ask, "What was the point?" The point of the story is abundantly clear. Or the storyteller states it explicitly. Sometimes both. You can record multiple morals and then reuse the same story for different purposes.

Polish the telling

Tell the story well. Perfection is not the goal, but credibility and clarity are.

▶ **Coach storytellers** to put enthusiasm and emotion into their voices. Rehearse the telling. Remember, the goal is to sound credible, not professional.

▶ **Aim for sincerity**. A professional narrator can sound too perfect. Better a few *uhs* and *ahs* in a credible voice than a perfectly polished enunciation.

▶ **Require good voice quality**. Record and edit the voice carefully. If emotion is an important component of the story, you will require higher audio quality than if you were just relating facts.

▶ **Do not settle for the first take**. To get a good recording from a hesitant storyteller, have the storyteller repeatedly tell the story. Use whatever ruse works, such as "Sorry, I forgot to push the Record button." With each telling the story gets shorter and more to the point. Usually the third version is the best one.

Develop the story

Go beyond a bare-bones telling of a simple story.

▶ **Show the face of the storyteller**. Video is not necessary, but a good quality photo will help the listener imagine the person. You might even show a series of three repeating photographs, each dissolving into the next. Many viewers will remember it as video.

▶ **Illustrate the story**. Add newspaper clippings and other materials to flesh out the story. The story can thus become part of a larger case study.

▶ **Spread a single complex story throughout a lesson**. Tell the story in episodes, arousing curiosity and building suspense.

Extend stories by a teacher

We can increase the reach and power of stories by combining them with other types of activities and by adapting them for social learning and for mobile learning.

Combine stories by a teacher with other activities

Storytelling by itself is seldom sufficient to accomplish an ambitious learning objective. Consider some combinations that ally the story with other activities.

▶ Follow the experience of listening to a story with an invitation to tell a comparable story (p. 184).

▶ Interleave stories with presentations (p. 69) and readings (p. 93) on an abstract subject. The stories remind learners of the practical application and value of the abstract information.

▶ Precede any difficult activity with a story that illustrates the value of overcoming obstacles and the value of what will be learned.

▶ Use a story to launch a research activity (p. 196), wherein the learner gathers background information about the teller of the story or the related event.

▶ Give learners opportunities to apply the moral of the story in a game or simulation.

▶ Incorporate stories (p. 105) into case studies (p. 152) and role-playing activities (p. 476). The storyteller can be a key figure in the case under study or an imaginary character in the role-playing scenario. Story-telling activities can flesh out a role-playing activity when you do not have enough learners to fill all the roles.

Design stories-by-a-teacher activities for social learning

Have social learners:

▶ Capture and share stories by experts and authorities within their professional networks.

▶ Comment on stories as they are being told via a back channel (p. 469).

▶ Discuss the story: What did the main character do right or wrong? What was the moral? How can we apply the moral?

▶ Contribute related stories: "Reminds me of the time …."

Design stories-by-a-teacher activities for mobile learning

Have mobile learners:

▶ Listen to stories told by experts in the field. The expert can tell the story in a context relevant to the story, perhaps even the one where the story occurred.

▶ Capture and share stories by experts in the field.

FIELD TRIPS

Online field trips take learners on educational excursions to places where they can observe concrete examples of what they are learning. In conventional education, a geology student might take a hike through a canyon to examine various rock layers, or an art student might visit a museum to see the paintings. In e-learning, the same students might tour an online representation of the canyon or search exhibits in a virtual museum.

About field trips

Field trips take us to educational examples and intriguing displays. The essential aspect of the field trip is not walking from example to example, but in examining the examples and seeing relationships among them. Field trips let us visit museums, parks, battlefields, historic neighborhoods, zoos and greenhouses, archaeological digs, manufacturing plants, and ancient ruins.

When to use field trips

Get learners out of the virtual classroom. Send them on a virtual field trip. Use them whenever you would recommend a real field trip, but schedule and budget say no. Use field trips to:

▶ Show how concepts taught in the course are applied (or misapplied) in the real world.

▶ Provide access to many concrete examples.

▶ Reveal examples in context.

▶ Orient learners in a new environment or system.

▶ Encourage discovery of trends and patterns.

Types of field trips

There are two main types of online field trips:

▶ **Guided tours**, which are perused in a predetermined order. Guided tours take us to physically separated examples. Guided tours can be self-directed or instructor-led and can be conducted live or played back from a recording.

▶ **Museums** (p. 119), in which the learner decides where to go next. Museums collect examples in one place. In museums, learners can compare examples and discover relationships.

Guided tours

The guided tour orients the learner in a virtual or real environment. The guided tour can be used to lead learners through an online representation of a real environment, such as teaching the layout of equipment in the bay of an ambulance, the twists and turns of a river channel, or the sequence of rock strata in a mountain range.

Another popular guided tour introduces an interactive computer system, such as a computer application, a Web site, or an e-learning course. It does not teach how to operate the software, but does give an overview of its structure and a preview of its capabilities.

Example of a guided tour

The following guided tour introduces a repository of learning resources. The learner can embark on the tour from any page by clicking a **Tour** button (at the bottom of the main window). Clicking the **Tour** button displays the first stop on the tour and opens a separate tour window that guides the learner through the tour. The learner clicks on the **Next** button to advance to the next stop. Here are the second, third, and forth stops:

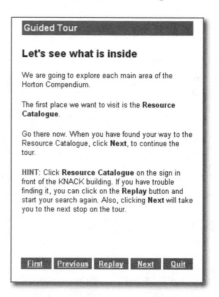

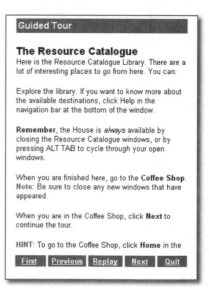

Built using Adobe Dreamweaver and Active Server Pages. Graphics
created with Adobe Photoshop.

Notice that the tour describes the stop and suggests exploring it—like going ashore from a
cruise ship. The learner can always rejoin the tour by clicking on the **Replay** button, which
resets the underlying window to the current stop in the tour. Other buttons also give the
learner choices. **Previous** lets the learner return to the previous stop, and **First** restarts the
whole tour from the beginning.

At the end of the tour, learners are returned to the point where the tour started and are
given a brief summary of what they saw.

How guided tours work

Typically, the learner starts the tour by clicking on a button or link in a Web site,
computer program, or e-learning course. This action pops up the tour window.

The learner begins the tour in earnest after a brief introduction, which states the purpose
and subject of the tour.

At each stop on the tour, pertinent features of an exhibit, object, or location are pointed
out. In some tours, advancing to the next stop automatically displays the item discussed
at that stop of the tour. In others, the learner receives instructions on how to navigate to
find the next stop.

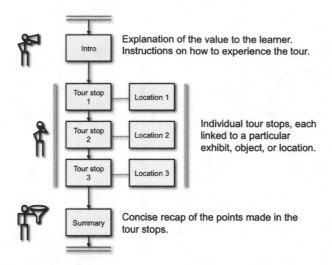

At the end of the tour, the learner sees a summary of the highlights of the tour.

When to use a guided tour

Use guided tours to orient learners in an environment, building, Web site, computer program, or e-learning course. Provide a quick guided tour for those who:

▶ **Need to see the big picture before getting lost in the details**. Use the guided tour to walk learners through a complex procedure before asking them to perform it on their own.

▶ **Just want an overview**. For example, sales representatives need to know enough to demonstrate a product and its advantages, but do not have time to learn to operate it.

▶ **Will be involved with a product but will not be operating it**. These might include managers of the operators, prospective buyers of a product, and product reviewers too lazy to actually use the product.

Use guided tours to help people explore a place they cannot visit in person. The place visited can be a real locale or an imaginary one. Use guided tours when the locale is:

▶ **Too far away**. To travel to the real locale would be expensive and time consuming.

▶ **Too spread out**. A field trip can include stops in Mobile, Moscow, Montreal, Mumbai, Monte Carlo, and Metropolis. The only airfare is a mouse click.

▶ **Too dangerous**. Nuclear radiation, fragmentation grenades, and cosmic rays cannot penetrate the computer screen.

▶ **Imaginary**. How about taking learners to a place where impossible theories are real and alternate realities predominate?

Variations of guided tours

Adapt guided tours to your style of e-learning and your technology.

Personal travel diaries

A simpler form of a guided tour resembles a personal travel diary illustrated with snapshots. Such tours can present an individual's experience of a subject in a direct and interesting way.

This example introduces learners to the geology of the Rocky Mountain region. It recounts an automobile trip northward along the Peak-to-Peak highway in Colorado. Each stop consists of an annotated photograph of a vista or road cut.

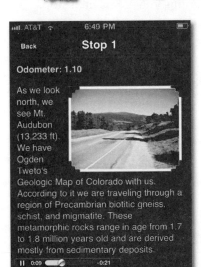

If a tour involves movement through physical locations, you may want to design the guided tour so learners can take it along. That way, learners can recreate the tour and experience it for themselves.

This version of the Peak-to-Peak tour was designed to play on a mobile device. And learners could choose to listen to a recording of the displayed text.

Both examples built with Adobe Dreamweaver.
View examples at horton.com/eld/.

Web tours in an online meeting

In online meetings, you can conduct guided tours of Web sites and other electronic media using Web tours or application sharing (p. 438). On such tours, learners watch the locations visited by the teacher. In others, the teacher takes learners to a location where they can explore on their own.

Tours of imaginary worlds

Let learners explore virtual locales. Provide tours of imaginary worlds and of physical objects they could not tour in reality. Here are some examples of imaginary tours.

▶ **The human body**. Swim through arteries. Use the diaphragm for a trampoline. Tickle the funny bone.

▶ **An imaginary town** with exactly one example of every architectural style, kind of like Greenfield Village (www.hfmgv.org/village), but more so.

▶ **A cave** through all the major kinds of rocks found on earth.

▶ **The atom**. Scuba dive thorough electron clouds and touch down on the nucleus.

For a menu, create a schematic map or scene containing all the features you need to display.

Best practices for guided tours

A good tour leaves learners excited, satisfied, and confident to navigate on their own.

Let learners explore objects of interest. Let learners click on an object to enlarge it or to display commentary about it. Let learners select among various viewpoints at a stop. Clearly flag activities, that is, places where the tourist can do more than just look and read.

Narrate stops well. Tell learners what they should notice on the tour. Otherwise, they may flail or become distracted by all the pretty pictures. For each stop, explain what the scene shows. What are the names of the objects shown? From what direction is the scene viewed? What in particular is significant about the objects shown in this stop? If technical conditions permit, consider providing the narration by an authoritative voice as well as in text.

Show spatial relationships. If the spatial relationships among objects on the tour are important, help learners see the relationships. Overlap the stops so that the next stop is visible at the edge of the current stop. Show both stops on a you-are-here map. And be sure to include an overview map showing all the stops in the guided tour.

Encourage learners to explore on their own. Have learners explore the sights at each stop. Suggest things to click on. Map out a side trip or two. Let learners pick or design their own tours. Provide an overview map and gallery from which learners can pick destinations in any order they choose.

Make side excursions safe. If there is any danger that learners will wander too far afield, include a **Rejoin tour** button to rescue them. Or, start digressions away from the tour in a separate window so that the main tour window remains on the screen.

Anchor each stop with a visual. For each stop, display a compelling visual image. It should be attractive, but it is more important that it clearly communicate the main idea of the stop.

Keep the tour focused. A tour is not a tutorial, a Help facility, or an instruction manual. A tour provides a broad overview of how the pieces fit together.

Virtual museums

A museum is an organized collection of exhibits gathered in one place. Exhibits consist of informative objects, such as paintings by van Gogh or the skeleton of a T-Rex, annotated with relevant facts. A virtual museum is much the same, except that the place where objects are gathered is not a building made of granite and marble but an online space viewed through a browser.

A virtual museum is much like a guided tour except that the learner decides how to navigate the museum. Virtual museums are also called *Web-based museums*, *e-museums*, *virtual galleries*, *online museums*, and *online galleries*. Virtual museums have been used to showcase objects as diverse as human organs, paintings by a second-grade class, and airsickness bags.

Example of a museum

Here you see a small museum of minerals. It contains pictures of minerals and information about them. A learner can pick a mineral by appearance or by name to jump to the exhibit of that mineral.

Built using Adobe Dreamweaver and Active Server Pages.

2

Absorb-type activities

The individual exhibit shows a single mineral. It also provides technical details about the mineral, along with a brief description of it.

The **Next** and **Previous** buttons take the visitor forward and backward through all the minerals in the museum. The **Fast Forward** button starts advancing through the exhibits at a rate of about six seconds per exhibit. This is called *autoscanning* (See online Chapter 15 for more about navigation.). The **Stop** button stops on the current exhibit. Paging through the exhibits is useful if the visitor can recognize a mineral, but does not know what it is called.

Clicking on the **Search** button lets the visitor search for minerals that meet specified characteristics.

How virtual museums work

Virtual museums let learners create their own tours and displays. The learner specifies what kinds of exhibits are desired, and the museum makes them available.

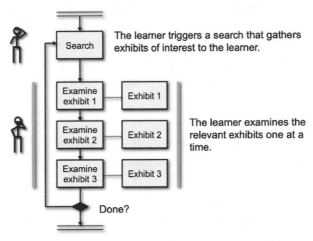

After examining the gathered examples, the learner may quit or continue with another search.

When to create a virtual museum

Museums organize large numbers of separate objects into meaningful collections. Museums are useful to:

▶ **Provide** access to many concrete instances of objects from a field being studied.

▶ **Enable** learners to discover patterns and trends among separate objects and instances.

▶ **Make available** the artifacts of a field of endeavor—or of an organization engaged in that endeavor.

On university campuses, learned professors lecture about subjects that their listeners cannot visualize. Abstractions remain clouds, gently blowing away. A museum of concrete instances of what the professor is talking about would bring the abstractions back to earth.

Every day busy companies with crowded offices and cramped disk drives archive their history with the Delete key. Years later, their leaders wonder why employees have no sense of the tradition or heritage of the great company they work for. A museum is a great way to preserve and organize the artifacts of an organization's formative years and epic struggles. I am not suggesting you exhibit the hairdos worn in 1983 by the current CEO or video clips of embarrassing incidents at last year's Christmas party. No, the best use of the virtual museum will be to display how the organization got where it is today and why certain traditions exist.

Best practices for virtual museums

Think about your last visit to an art museum. Close your eyes and imagine yourself walking through one of the galleries. What do you see? Fine art, for sure, but what about the people you see? Do you see a shushing teacher herding a gaggle of giggling third-graders? Do art students from the local university languidly sketch the exhibits between trips to the espresso bar? Do parents with children in tow sidestep around the perimeter of the room, dutifully reading the plaques of every painting? Museums are places where many different kinds of people can learn many different things in many different ways. Here are a few suggestions to enable just as many kinds of learning in your virtual museums.

Put learners in control. Let learners choose the exhibits they want to see. Guide them through the collection, but let them decide which exhibits to view and which objects to study in detail.

Give private tours. A virtual museum has no fixed floor plan, no permanent arrangement of exhibits, no limitations on available space. The use of search engines and databases makes it possible for learners to have an experience custom-tailored to their individual needs. Here are some ways to custom-tailor the display.

▶ Display just the subset of interest to the individual learner.

▶ Arrange the exhibits to reveal trends and patterns of interest to the learner.

▶ Generate custom maps and menus that reveal what the learner is interested in learning.

Let learners make their own tours. Let learners search the museum for exactly what they want to see right now. Do not force them to plod through the whole Louvre if all they want to see is the Mona Lisa. Here are some ways to make it easier for visitors to find the exhibits they want to see:

▶ **Catalog**. Index the whole museum. Provide a conventional alphabetical index listing each object in the museum by its name and by what it illustrates.

▶ **Menus**. Provide several menus that let learners search by whatever characteristics are important to them. For example, a corporate history museum might contain menus organized by time period, by current product line, by underlying technology or market, and by the person in charge.

▶ **Visual gallery**. Let learners pick objects by scanning thumbnail images of all objects on exhibit. Also let them graze the display by having it automatically advance from item to item at a rate of about one per second until the learner says, "Stop, that's the one I want."

▶ **Linked keywords**. Assign keywords to each exhibited item to describe it. Let learners search for items indexed with a particular keyword. Also display the keywords on each exhibit. Make them links so that clicking on one displays a list of other items indexed with that same keyword.

▶ **Search by characteristics**. Include a search engine that lets learners find exhibits by specifying detailed characteristics of the item sought.

If many paths through the museum are possible, suggest a simple one. Or, provide a tour (p. 113) conducted by a docent.

Integrate museums into e-learning

Wandering a virtual museum on your own may be a pleasant way to while away an afternoon, but it is not automatically a learning experience. Here are some tips to increase the learning that takes place in the galleries of your museum and to make the museum a part of your overall e-learning efforts.

▶ **Create a learner's tour of the museum**, pointing out the galleries and exhibits of interest to learners in your course. The guided tour can teach learners to search and navigate the museum on their own.

▶ **Create research activities** that require learners to find information and examples in a museum. Give learners tasks that, for example, require them to search a virtual museum for exhibits of a particular type and discover how they are related. Scavenger hunt activities (p. 198) are especially good ways to motivate searching in a museum.

▶ **Craft guided-research activities** (p. 200) that use the museum's assets as resources.

▶ **Organize specialized tours** through exhibits to reveal patterns and trends you are teaching.

▶ **Assign learners tasks** to find relevant objects of personal interest.

▶ **Combine a museum with a presentation** (p. 69) **or reading** (p. 93) so the museum provides concrete instances of the theory presented in the reading or presentation. Or the presentation or reading provides more background and details about individual museum exhibits.

Best practices for field trips

Whether you are using guided tours, museums, or some other form of field trip, you need to make sure it advances learning. Here are a few suggestions.

Require learning

Require specific learning outcomes. Make the field trip more than a vacation away from the responsibilities of learning. Give learners specific assignments they must accomplish on the field trip—objects they must find, patterns they must notice, or principles they must infer.

Include a variety of media

Enrich your museum with other media as well. Here are some candidates.

- ▶ **Scanned documents**. Print advertisements, covers of annual reports, articles of incorporation, the first stock certificate, and critical patents.

- ▶ **Video clips of important events**. Speeches, technical presentations, product demonstrations, experiments, product tests, award presentations, and TV commercials.

- ▶ **Audio recordings**. Speeches, presentations, and jingles from commercials.

- ▶ **Virtual reality.** Models of prominent or proposed buildings, walkarounds of important objects, and conceptual models of a field of research.

Tell what is important

Highlight the aspect of the exhibit that is important for the learner to notice. Learners may discover the important point on their own. Or they may not. Why take chances? In our online collection of good examples of e-learning, we include a list of important features to notice.

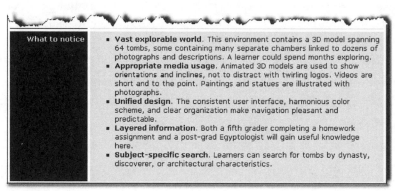

Annotate exhibits thoroughly

Label items you exhibit. Provide concise but thorough details for each item on exhibit. Here is a checklist of the kinds of details people may want to know. No individual item will need all these details, but this checklist will make sure you consider all possibilities.

- ▶ **Name**. Include both official and unofficial names. Include the formal, legal, scientific name of an object along with its informal common name.

- ▶ **Description**. What is the object? What does it exemplify? Why is the object on exhibit here? What is important about it?

- ▶ **ID number**. What is the product number, model number, or serial number of the item?

- ▶ **Dimensions**. What are the object's height, width, depth, weight, area, and volume?

- ▶ **Creator**. Who is responsible for creating this object? List the lead designer, artist, and project manager. Link to their biographies, if available.

- **Date**. When was the object manufactured, completed, or discovered? If you cannot give a specific date, consider specifying a time span, historic era, or geological period.

- **Medium**. Of what materials is the object constructed? What are its important components?

- **Owner**. Who owns the actual object? Who holds copyright on its design?

- **History**. How and when was the object conceived, created, and modified? What is its provenance?

- **Classification**. Does the object fit into a defined taxonomic scheme? Does it fit a standard industry category? Does it illustrate an artistic or design movement?

- **Rating**. How does this object compare to comparable objects, as rated by the curator of the museum, by an industrial rating agency, or by museum patrons?

- **Sales**. If the object is a product, how many were sold and for how much money?

- **Price**. If the object is for sale, what is its price?

- **Keywords**. How is the object indexed? Link each keyword to other objects indexed with the same keyword.

- **Links to details**. Link the annotation of the object to more complete materials about it.

Let learners choose what to download

Guided tours and museums can contain a lot of large graphics and multimedia. This is appropriate to their mission. What is not appropriate is to fail to warn learners before starting a lengthy download. Here are some common-sense courtesies to practice.

- **Preview the object**. Describe the object in words or display a small thumbnail image. Then let the learner decide to download it.

- **Specify the size** of the download.

- **Consider providing both high- and low-bandwidth versions**. For example, for a photograph, you might provide a large JPEG image optimized for quality, along with a smaller version optimized for maximum compression.

Let learners inspect items in detail

Let learners enlarge photographs to inspect items of interest. Make the image of an exhibit into an image-map with each object linked to its enlargement. Or, overlay the illustration with a grid of rectangular areas, each triggering the display of an enlargement of that area.

Extend field-trip activities

We can increase the reach and power of field-trip activities by combining them with other types of activities and by adapting them for social learning and for mobile learning.

Combine field trips with other activities

▶ Provide a short presentation (p. 69) to preview the field trip by telling learners what they will experience on the field trip.

▶ Offer a presentation on the subject area of the trip. Teach principles and terminology necessary to recognize and understand items encountered on the field trip.

▶ Have learners try to find the next location on their own. This makes the field trip more like a game and encourages independent learning.

▶ Have learners use search to find places on the field trip.

▶ Add a scavenger hunt (p. 198) to encourage learners to find important information during the field trip.

Design field-trip activities for social learning

Have social learners:

▶ Take a field trip as a group. At each stop, the group discusses discoveries and where to go next.

▶ Create tours by adding pathways to existing online field trips. Or create new field trips among online materials.

▶ Create field trips of physical locations. Learners can capture photos or video of sites within the location and record voice narration of the tour. They may also capture GPS tracks to display on maps or to enable others to take the physical tour.

▶ Ask questions, make comments, get advice, report problems, report discoveries, and ponder their discoveries while on the field trip.

▶ Enhance tours with personal commentary, suggested paths, and links to related resources.

Design field-trip activities for mobile learning

Have mobile learners:

▶ Visit a physical site, such as an art museum, rock quarry, archaeological dig, historic neighborhood, battlefield, or other location where they can see relevant examples.

▶ Read commentary for a physical field trip triggered by GPS, bar code, or RFID (p. 510).

▶ Access commentary and background information, even if only from Wikipedia.

IN CLOSING ...

Summary

Absorb activities provide information to learners. In Absorb activities, learners read, listen, and watch. In well-designed Absorb activities, learners also consider, select, combine, judge, and process information. Absorb activities come in several forms. Here is where you might use each:

Presentations	To provide information or to introduce a subject. Presentations are especially useful where you can organize information in a clear and logical sequence.
Readings	To enable learners to pursue subjects in greater detail. Readings make good use of existing documents to broaden the scope of e-learning and to let learners customize learning to their individual interests.
Stories by a teacher	To show the human dimension of a subject by showing how it affected the life of the teacher, and expert, or someone else respected by the learner. Stories told by the teacher are Absorb activities; stories by the learner are Connect activities.
Field trips	To let learners experience a variety of real-world examples the way they might on a physical field trip or visit to a well-stocked museum.

Pick Absorb activities to accomplish objectives

The following job aid ties the six types of learning objectives to common types of Absorb activities. Along the left are the main types of Absorb activities grouped into categories. In columns are the types of learning objectives. A circle at the intersection of a type's column and an activity's row means that the activity is recommended for that type of objective. A black dot indicates a stronger recommendation.

Absorb activities		Types of objectives					
		Create	Decide	Do	Know	Believe	Feel
Presentation	Slide show	○	○	○	●	●	●
	Physical demo	●	○	●		○	
	Software demo	●	○	●		○	
	Informational film	○	○	○	●	●	●
	Discussion		●			○	●
	Story by teacher	○	○		●	●	●
Reading	Assigned docs.	○	●	●		○	○
	From library	○	○	○	○	○	○
	From Internet	●	○	○	○	○	○
Field trip	Guided tour				○	○	○
	Virtual tour				○	○	○
	Online museum	●	○		○		

For each learning objective, first identify its type. Then find the column that matches the type. Scan down the column looking for black dots. For each black dot, consider using the Absorb activity listed at the left of that row. If none of the black dots work for you, try the open circles. If none of the open circles work, get creative. With enough creativity, you can use any technique to teach any subject.

For more ...

To learn more about any of the Absorb activities described here; search the Web for the name of the activity. If necessary, include words like *online, virtual,* and *e-learning* to bias the results toward electronic versions of the activities.

The next two chapters suggest even more activities to include in your e-learning. The next chapter on Do activities will help you find more active partners for your Absorb activities.

On horton.com, we have made available a wide variety of materials on producing online documents and information. Help yourself.

3 Do-type activities

Practice, discovery, and playing games

If Absorb activities are the nouns, then Do activities are the verbs of learning. They put people in action. They elevate learning from passive reading and watching to active seeking, selecting, and creating knowledge. Doing begets learning.

ABOUT DO ACTIVITIES

While Absorb activities provide information, Do activities transform that information into knowledge and skills. In Do activities, learners discover, parse, decode, analyze, verify, combine, organize, discuss, debate, evaluate, condense, refine, elaborate, and, most importantly, apply knowledge.

Common types of Do activities

Do activities include a variety of forms that exercise learning:

▶ **Practice activities** (p. 130) give learners experience applying information, knowledge, and skills. They include drill-and-practice, hands-on, guided-analysis, and teamwork activities.

▶ **Discovery activities** (p. 146) lead learners to make discoveries. They include virtual laboratories, case studies, and role-playing activities.

▶ **Games and simulations** (p. 157) have learners attempt tasks in safe environments and learn from the feedback they receive. These activities include quiz show games, word games, jigsaw puzzles, adventure games, software simulations, device simulations, personal-response simulations, mathematical simulations, and environmental simulations.

When to feature Do activities

Where should we rely most on Do activities? Do activities require active imagination to concoct and extensive testing to perfect. When is this cost and effort justified? Feature Do activities to:

▶ Provide safe, encouraging practice to prepare learners to apply learning in the real world.

▶ Motivate learners by activating curiosity for material learners might otherwise consider boring.

▶ Prepare for Absorb activities by showing learners how little they know about the subject and making clear the value of information they are to absorb.

▶ Enable learning by exploration and discovery.

As a rule, learners should spend 50% of their time in Do activities (90% would be better; but 50% will do just fine).

PRACTICE ACTIVITIES

Practice helps learners strengthen and refine skills, knowledge, and attitudes by applying them and receiving feedback. Practice tasks do not teach new information. They give learners an opportunity to exercise newly acquired abilities.

About practice activities

Practice activities are like classroom sessions in which students are encouraged to apply what they have just heard the teacher talk about or what they have just read in a book.

When to use practice activities

You have probably heard that practice makes perfect. Practice certainly does refine skills and streamline performance. Use practice activities in e-learning to:

▶ Prepare learners to apply skills, knowledge, and attitudes in real situations.

▶ Teach learners to adapt general, abstract knowledge to specific, concrete situations.

▶ Automate skills and consolidate separate bits of learning so that application is faster and more fluent.

▶ Build confidence in the ability to apply learning.

▶ Verify the ability to apply low-level skills or knowledge before moving on to more complex items.

Types of practice activities

Practice activities range from simple, mechanical activities to complex, analytical activities.

▶ **Drill-and-practice activities** (p. 132) are the repeated application of a series of similar, simple tasks. They help learners automate skills and improve fluidity of application.

▶ **Hands-on activities** (p. 133) allow learners to perform tasks with real tools but with guidance. They teach real tasks and help learners apply theory.

▶ **Guided-analysis activities** (p. 137) lead learners through an analysis task with step-by-step instructions. They strengthen a learner's ability to perform a complex cognitive task.

Practice activities performed by a team are covered in Chapter 8 on social learning.

How practice activities work

Practice activities have a recurring 3-step sequence. First the teacher or the computer assigns the practice task to the learner, explaining it in adequate detail for the learner to begin the task immediately. The learner performs the task and receives feedback from the teacher or the computer.

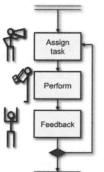

Teacher or the computer assigns a task for the learner to perform.

The learner performs the task.

The teacher or the computer evaluates the learner's performance and provides feedback.

Done? Many repetitions for drill and practice. Linear steps for guided analysis.

The cycle may recur for another step in a procedure or for a slightly more advanced objective.

Drill-and-practice activities

Drill-and-practice activities repeatedly exercise a simple or small area of knowledge. They are like the flash cards used to teach multiplication or a foreign language vocabulary.

A drill-and-practice activity starts with an introduction that welcomes learners and explains how the activity works. Then learners repeatedly solve problems and receive feedback on their solutions. At the end, learners may review what they have learned and try applying it in a more realistic situation.

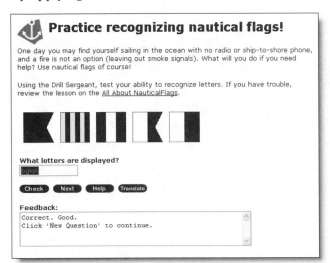

This drill and practice teaches learners to recognize nautical flags and associate them with letters of the alphabet. Learners view a grouping of flags and then enter the equivalent letters.

Built using Adobe Dreamweaver and JavaScript. View example at horton.com/eld/.

When to use drill and practice

Educational theorists of late have so thoroughly condemned drill and practice that it is easy to believe that this method has no use whatsoever. However, drill and practice is very useful in helping people memorize facts that they must be able to recall reliably without hesitation. Some examples include:

▶ Foreign language vocabulary.

▶ Sign language.

▶ Symbols, emblems, and signs used in a profession.

▶ Spelling, grammar, and punctuation rules.

▶ Syntax of a programming language.

Drill-and-practice activities are also useful to automate procedures learners must perform fluidly without much conscious thought. Basic movements in sports and dance fall into this category, as do all emergency procedures that must be performed under noisy, confusing situations.

Use drill and practice to help people learn the simple rules and procedures that they must apply unconsciously as part of higher-level activities.

Varieties of drill-and-practice activities

Online drill-and-practice activities come in several varieties.

▶ **Auto-generated problems.** Use the computer to generate unique problems for the learner to solve. See page 272 for an example of how this might be done.

▶ **Increasing challenge**. Start with a simple problem to establish a baseline of acceptable performance. Then ratchet up the difficulty of practices. Offer more complex and difficult problems. Give learners less time to solve problems. Add distracters or noise.

▶ **Database of problems**. Draw individual problems from a fully developed repository of problems. Problems can be chosen at random or sequenced by prerequisites and paced by the learner's demonstrated abilities. Such an approach works well for subjects with simple recurring tasks, such as learning the grammar and syntax of a language.

Best practices for drill and practice

When designing a drill-and-practice activity:

▶ **Combine drill and practice with other learning activities** to teach how the rote knowledge exercised in the drill and practice can be applied. Drill and practice is seldom sufficient in itself.

▶ **Increase the difficulty level as the learner progresses**. Give more complex problems or require faster responses.

▶ **Give learners lots of problems to solve**. Let learners decide when to quit. If possible, design the activity so that it can generate an infinite number of new problems. That way the material is always fresh.

Hands-on activities

Hands-on activities give learners a small piece of real work to perform. In a hands-on activity, the learner completes a task outside the lesson, such as performing a calculation with an on-screen calculator, filling in a form, or operating a piece of machinery.

The hands-on activity guides learners through the real-life task and provides feedback on their success. The teacher or computer assigns a task and gives detailed instructions. Learners perform the procedure, checking each step as performed. After a review of the procedure, learners repeatedly perform the task on their own.

Converting numbers

Learn to convert numbers from decimal to hexadecimal and octal forms.

In this hands-on activity you learn to use the Windows 7 system calculator to convert decimal numbers to their hexadecimal and octal equivalents.

When you are ready, click:

This example teaches the use of the Windows system calculator to convert decimal numbers to their hexadecimal and octal equivalents.

The activity begins with an introduction explaining what the learner will accomplish. The window is small so that the rest of the screen is available for performing the hands-on activity.

Starting the calculator   ◄◄ ◄ ►

To begin:

1. Open the calculator program.
2. Verify that you have started the calculator correctly by answering the following question:

The menu (just below the word "Calculator") contains three items. Which is the first one?

[Edit]

[Help]

[View]

I need help opening the calculator

Learners must perform a step and answer a question. To answer the question, they must successfully complete the step. The answer requires observing something not visible until the step is completed.

Requiring an indicator of success makes this a *gatekeeper* task, that is, one that requires performance of a prerequisite task before the learner can advance. A correct answer reveals the next step in the procedure.

To start the calculator   ◄◄ ◄ ►

Need a little help starting the calculator? No problem. Here's how:

From the Start menu select:

Programs ›› Accessories ›› Calculator

To verify that you have started the calculator correctly, answer the following question:

The menu (just below the word "Calculator") contains three items. Which is the first one?

[Edit]

[Help]

[View]

Learners who cannot perform the step successfully can click "I need help opening the calculator" to get more detailed instructions—as shown here.

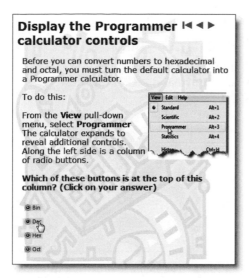

If learners make a mistake, they receive help getting back on track. For example, learners who click on **Dec**, rather than the correct answer **Hex**, see the next page.

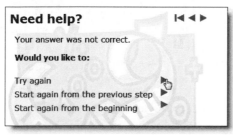

Here, learners have three choices: to try again, to go back a step, or to start from the beginning.

For simple steps, where errors occur almost exclusively from inattention and carelessness, let learners go back and try again.

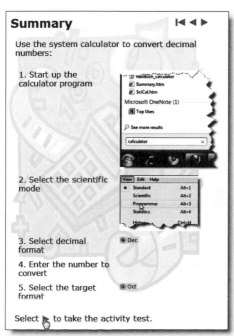

After completing the activity, learners see a summary. It serves as a review as well as a job aid. Learners may bookmark or print the summary.

Make sure the summary is compact enough to print to a single page of paper. Or provide a button to jump to a special printable version.

Test — Convert numbers ⏮ ◀

Demonstrate your ability to convert numbers to hex and octal

Convert the decimal numbers in the left column to their hexadecimal and octal equivalents. Enter the converted numbers in the slots provided and select **Evaluate**.

Decimal		Hexadecimal		Octal
546	✓	222	✓	1042
4556	✓	11CC	✓	10714
10,298	✓	283A	✓	24072

(Evaluate) (Reset) (Show)

Finally, learners test their ability to perform the procedure on their own.

This test requires repeated application of the procedure to confirm and lock in the newly acquired skill.

Built using Adobe Dreamweaver and JavaScript. View example at horton.com/eld/.

When to use hands-on activities

Use hands-on activities to teach hands-on tasks. Although not especially effective in teaching abstract knowledge, hands-on activities can provide a pleasant descent from the stratospheric heights of conceptual thought common in many courses. They are powerful stimuli for learning practical skills.

Variations of hands-on activities

If performing the task for real is too dangerous or daunting to the learner, provide a simulation that mimics the look and feel of the real system (p. 336). Application sharing (p. 438) can also be used for hands-on activities. The teacher might start an application and then call on a learner to demonstrate a task for the rest of the class. For the learner performing the task, this is a hands-on activity.

Best practices for hands-on activities

Use gatekeeper tasks. To control advancement to the next step, ask questions about things learners can only observe by successfully performing the current step. Such questions can focus attention on important parts of the task and on those parts of the scene that will be important in subsequent steps.

Print out instructions. If learners must perform the activity away from the computer, let them print out the instructions and any other materials they may need. If they must record data, give them a paper form on which to write the data.

Require evidence. Have learners submit digital photographs of the results of any hands-on activity that produces visible results. One way to monitor learning of computer skills is to require learners to e-mail screen snapshots of the results.

Guided-analysis activities

Many designers limit practice activities to rote procedures and almost manual tasks. Practice is even more important for intellectual tasks that require sensitive application of adaptive procedures.

Guided-analysis activities step learners through the process of analyzing a complex situation. Guided analysis answers one of the most important questions ever asked: "So what?" Guided analysis helps learners to separate useful from useless information and to infer general principles and conclusions from separate, confusing, concrete instances. It teaches learners how to turn data into information—and even knowledge.

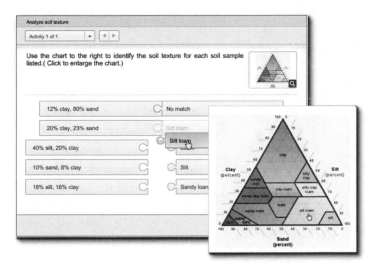

This example guides forestry professionals in classifying soil textures based on the proportions of sand, loam, and silt in the soil. Learners can enlarge the diagram and use it to answer the questions.

Built with iSpring Presenter. View example at horton.com/eld/.

In guided analysis, the learner follows a procedure to gather and analyze data. After several cycles of gathering and analyzing, the learner may abstract a principle revealed by the analysis and test it by analyzing new data. The learner may have to revise the principle until it reliably predicts results.

When to use guided analysis

The primary use of guided analysis is in teaching formal analysis techniques. The technique may involve calculating or estimating mathematical values. Or it may involve sorting, classifying, or ranking items according to defined procedures.

A secondary use is teaching principles *revealed* by the analysis of data. In this case, guided analysis exposes a trend or pattern that learners might not otherwise notice or believe. If exposing a trend or principle is primary, use a discovery activity instead.

Ways to guide analysis

One way to guide analysis is to have the learner apply a specific formula or procedure. Here are a few more methods of analysis. Each focuses the learner's attention and thought on a different aspect of the data.

Compare and contrast

Evaluating complex data is … well, complex. One way of simplifying it is to guide learners in comparing alternatives. The easiest way to do this in e-learning is to have learners create a side-by-side comparison.

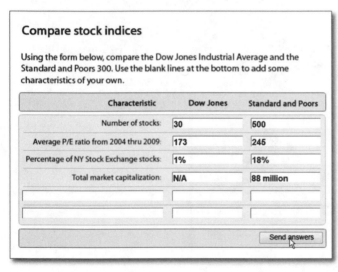

In this example, learners compare two major indexes of the stock markets in the United States.

The form draws attention to critical differences between the two indexes. It requires learners to juxtapose contrasting facts so differences are inescapable.

To encourage independent thought, the form includes blank rows where learners can compare the two indexes according to characteristics learners select.

Built using Adobe Captivate. View example at horton.com/eld/.

Classify items

Much learning in science and business involves classifying items into established categories. To classify items, learners assign real-world or net-available objects to established categories.

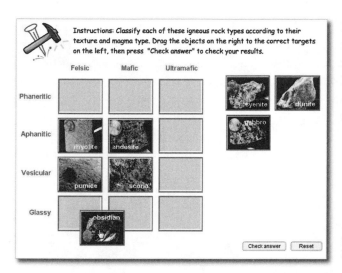

In this example, learners classify igneous rocks by their texture and magma type. To classify the rocks listed to the right, the learner drags each rock into a box in the appropriate row and column.

Built using Adobe Flash. View example at horton.com/eld/.

There are several ways to have learners assign items to categories. You can have learners:

- ▶ Pick categories from a drop-down list beside each item to be classified.
- ▶ Select from a pick-one list of categories the item could belong to.
- ▶ Select from a pick-multiple list to identify members of a category.
- ▶ Match items in one list with categories in another.
- ▶ Drag items to their categories or categories to their members.

Outline items

Most technical and business fields rely on hierarchical organization. Having learners outline items requires them to put individual items into a hierarchical scheme. This kind of guided analysis teaches general organizing skills as well as particular organizational schemes.

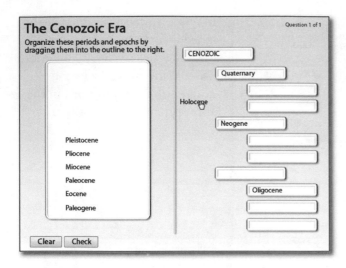

The Cenozoic Era

Organize these periods and epochs by dragging them into the outline to the right.

Question 1 of 1

CENOZOIC

Quaternary

Holocene

Neogene

Pleistocene
Pliocene
Miocene
Paleocene
Eocene
Paleogene

Oligocene

Clear   Check

This example of guided analysis asks learners to organize the geologic periods and epochs of the Cenozoic Era into an indented list—the correct epoch indented beneath the correct period. To do so, learners drag a name from the left-side area and drop it into its correct place in the hierarchy to the right.

Built using Adobe Captivate. View example at horton.com/eld/.

In a field without clear, well-defined categories, this activity may still be valuable, although quite complex. Allow enough time for learners to change their minds several times. Or make it a team activity. The discussions of the team can provoke a lot of thinking about categories and classification schemes.

Re-create famous examples

Have learners re-create a famous example from the area of study. Examples learners can re-create include:

- Paintings and photographs.
- Scenes from famous films and plays.
- Writings.
- Music compositions.
- Architectural drawings.
- Scientific experiments.

Have learners start by reproducing the example exactly as done originally. Then have them try slight variations. Next they can reproduce the example, but in the style of another example. Finally, they can try to create examples entirely in their own styles.

Here learners are challenged to re-create a famous poster they have studied. They have all the pieces and must rearrange them by dragging pieces around, resizing them, and flipping them vertically and horizontally.

To see another example, visit www.wildlifeart.org/Rungius/ home.html.

Built using Adobe Flash and Adobe Dreamweaver. View example at horton.com/eld/.

Best practices for guided analysis

Focus on techniques or principles

Do not forget what you are teaching. If you are teaching the analysis technique, emphasize the technique. Lavish attention on each step. If, however, you are using the analysis to reveal principles that are the real subject, then focus attention on the principles and keep the analysis simple. If the principles are primary, consider a discovery activity (p. 146) instead.

Spend time analyzing, not collecting, data

Eliminate unnecessary steps that may distract from what you are teaching. If finding the data is not part of the activity, provide it or link directly to it. If calculations are complex, provide a calculator (p. 192).

If gathering data is part of what you are teaching, combine the guided-analysis activity with a research activity (p. 196).

Specify a format for answers

You could let learners submit answers in any format they chose. However, structuring the response can focus attention on the idea being taught and away from irrelevant details. It can also simplify evaluation by the teacher and perhaps permit automatic evaluation and scoring by the computer.

The most direct way to structure an answer is to require the learner to fill in a form. The form below requires the learner to express and defend opinions.

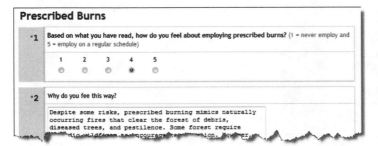

It simplifies and focuses the process by defining each issue as a scale between two extreme positions.

It simplifies answering by letting the learner pick a point along the scale. It includes five points so learners realize they have a range of responses. The text area requires learners to defend their positions. Its size strongly encourages them to be brief.

Label to guide analysis

Vague prompts lead to vague answers. Text-input areas are especially difficult because they provide few constraints or hints as to the form of the answer. To help learners stay on track, label and size the field in a way that implies the form of the answer.

Label a text input area with either a simple question or an incomplete statement that the learner is to complete. Phrase the label so that it requires analysis to write a response.

> In the cases studied, buy-back marketing plans failed when ….
> Harassment complaints are most likely when ….
> The three main causes of brake-rotor failure are ….
> Editors should use Smart Blur rather than Gaussian Blur when ….

As a rule, make text-response areas about 25 to 50% larger than the size of the response you want. Most people will fill one-half to three-fourths of the available area. Do not require learners to enter more than one answer in a field. If an activity has three questions, provide three text boxes, one for each question.

Prompt higher-level thinking

If learners must make judgments about objects, products, or ideas, they will need practice. Often activities that ask learners to critique an item draw vacuous responses like "Just great" or "It sucks."

To provoke deeper responses, ask questions like these:

▶ What are the advantages of this item?

▶ What is wrong with this item?

▶ How can this item be improved?

▶ How can this error be corrected?

▶ What would be the results of performing this action?

▶ What are the categories of these items?

▶ What are the critical characteristics of this item?

▶ What conclusions can you draw?

▶ What evidence can you offer?

▶ What follows from a principle?

▶ What is the pattern in these incidents?

▶ How does your opinion differ from those of others?

▶ How could you apply this principle?

Best practices for practice activities

Now here are a few best practices for better practice activities, regardless of type.

Let learners decide how much to practice

In general, adults learn more effectively and efficiently when they decide how much to practice. Novices may need more practice to develop basic skills. Advanced learners may need only to refresh or refine their skills. Some with learning disabilities may benefit from extensive practice.

This means you may need to create many practice activities and to suggest a minimum number for learners to complete or a target score to achieve, such as "Practice till you achieve 85% correct" or "Try to earn 1,200 points."

Require the right skills

Ensure that learners apply the skills, knowledge, and attitudes that you are teaching. Minimize irrelevant requirements to complete the practice, such as:

▶ Purely mechanical tasks that are not part of the real task, such as typing things that could be clicked.

▶ Gathering materials and downloading many sample files. Gather all the materials into one Web page or one downloadable file.

▶ Unnecessary mathematical calculations. Provide a calculator (p. 192) or pick numbers that simplify the math.

Provide authentic challenge

Do not oversimplify practice. You may want to start with simple activities to introduce concepts and build confidence, but do not stop until learners confront realistically difficult tasks.

For example, in the *Using Gantt Charts* course, learners were required to interpret Gantt charts. Practice activities required them to deal with charts in a variety of formats and at a realistic level of detail, such as the ones shown here:

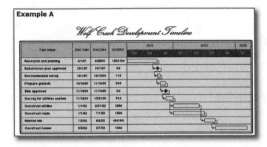

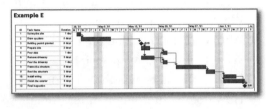

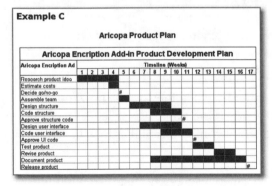

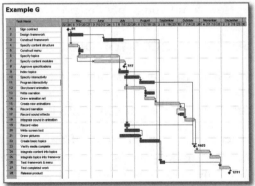

Extend practice activities

We can increase the reach and power of practice activities by combining them with other types of activities and by adapting them for social learning and for mobile learning.

Combine practice with other activities

Practice activities can augment almost every other kind of activity, especially Absorb activities. Here are some especially useful combinations.

▶ Combine presentations (p. 69) and readings (p. 93) with practice sessions to let learners refine their ability to apply what was presented.

▶ Precede games (p. 157) with practice sessions to help learners develop the simple skills that the game requires them to integrate and apply at a higher level.

▶ Combine research (p. 196) and readings (p. 93) with guided analysis (p. 137). Have learners conduct research to identify documents to read. Use guided analysis to help them make use of what they read.

▶ Precede and follow practice with a Q&A session. Before the practice, learners have questions about the instructions for the practice. Afterwards, they want to know how well they did and how to improve their technique.

Design practice activities for social learning

Have social learners:

▶ Get advice and feedback from experts, fellow learners, or their extended social network. Advice can include new techniques or alternative strategies to try. Feedback can range from simple ratings to structured critiques.

▶ Practice as a team. Learners can subdivide work and combine results or the team can collaboratively make each decision by brainstorming, discussing, and then voting. (See page 468 for some suggestions.)

▶ Share insights, discoveries, successful strategies, and applications.

▶ Analyze practice. Have learners compare experiences; discuss results; draw conclusions; and generalize to devise a theory, principle, formula or rule.

▶ Compete on criteria of speed, accuracy, quality, or style of work. Competition can make practice more like a game.

Design practice activities for mobile learning

Have mobile learners:

▶ Practice with real-world objects, people, and situations. View notable examples to analyze or imitate.

▶ Submit a photo, video clip, or audio recording of physical performance for evaluation or to prove accomplishment of an assigned task.

▶ Receive feedback from a remote coach, mentor, or judge.

▶ Practice skills in real-world situations, for example, speaking a foreign language while on vacation. Fill in knowledge gaps that prevent fluent performance, for example, by accessing a foreign-language dictionary.

DISCOVERY ACTIVITIES

Much of what we learn is by discovery. We conduct experiments or just try things out. We explore. We delve into things that arouse our curiosity. We systematically investigate subjects, and sometimes we just poke about. We prod and probe and provoke, just to see what will happen. We scrutinize and examine. We inspect and study situations to see what they can teach us. For many people, this is how most practical knowledge is acquired.

About discovery activities

Discovery activities do not present ideas, but lead learners to discover ideas on their own. They transform trial-and-error into trail-and-aha learning.

When to use discovery activities

Discovery learning is an alternative to presentation-based teaching. Use discovery learning:

▶ **For exploratory learning**. Some people learn by being told or shown, but many must discover skills and knowledge for themselves—especially those who are skeptical, concrete thinkers, or creative.

▶ **To reveal principles**. Experiments guide learners to discover principles, trends, and relationships for themselves. Many learners give more credibility to concepts they discover for themselves and tend to remember them longer.

▶ **To stimulate curiosity about a subject**. Discoveries can focus attention on a subject and motivate learners to seek explanations for what they discover.

Types of discovery activities

Two main kinds of discovery activities are especially useful in e-learning.

▶ **Virtual laboratories** (p. 147), where learners interact with a system to discover principles and refine thinking. Virtual laboratories are useful for hard knowledge.

▶ **Case studies** (p. 152), where learners analyze a complex, real event or situation to understand its underlying causes and concepts. They then draw conclusions, abstract principles, or make recommendations.

3

Do-type activities

Additional discovery activities, such as role-playing scenarios, are discussed in Chapter 8 on social learning starting on page 476.

How discovery activities work

Discovery activities guide learners in conducting experiments and analyzing situations so that learners can observe and record their findings.

The teacher or the computer prepares learners by giving instructions on how to perform an analysis or experiment and by assigning specific questions to answer. Learners perform the assigned activity and record results or observations.

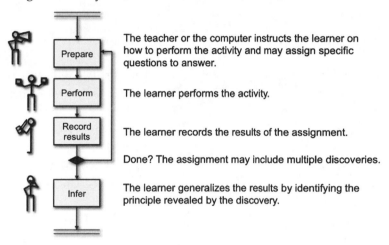

Prepare — The teacher or the computer instructs the learner on how to perform the activity and may assign specific questions to answer.

Perform — The learner performs the activity.

Record results — The learner records the results of the assignment.

Done? The assignment may include multiple discoveries.

Infer — The learner generalizes the results by identifying the principle revealed by the discovery.

This basic cycle of performing activities to answer questions may be repeated several times before the learner generalizes results to an overarching principle or summarizes them as a procedure or formula.

Virtual-laboratory activities

A virtual laboratory provides an on-screen simulator or calculator that learners can use to test ideas and observe results.

The learner gets the assignment, learns to operate the laboratory equipment, and then embarks on a series of experiments, carefully recording the results of each. After the last experiment, the learner generalizes what has been learned.

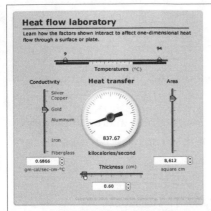

Here, mechanical designers conduct experiments to learn how heat flow depends on factors such as temperature, area, thickness, and thermal conductivity.

Lab built using Microsoft Excel and SAP Crystal Dashboard Design. Embedded in PowerPoint and converted for Web delivery using Adobe Presenter. View example at horton.com/eld/.

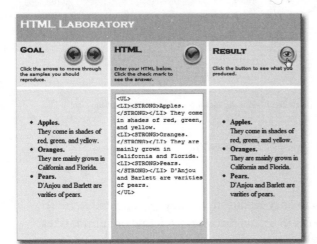

This virtual laboratory teaches HTML. Learners can use the arrow buttons to advance through a series of progressively more challenging goals shown at the left. Learners enter HTML in the text-entry area in the middle. Clicking the button in the Result panel processes the learner's HTML and shows what it produces.

Built using Adobe Dreamweaver and custom JavaScript. View example at horton.com/eld/.

The learner can compare the result to the goal and adjust accordingly. Learners who are stumped can click the check mark above the HTML area to see the solution for the currently displayed goal.

Over the decades, learners have consumed forests of grid paper drawing charts and graphs to detect trends and patterns in numerical data. Learners can now plot data right in their Web browsers by clicking and dragging.

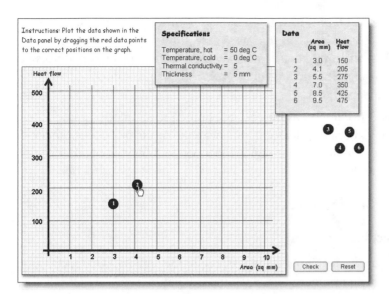

This example provides measurement data and allows the learner to plot it by dragging dots into place on the virtual graph paper. Doing so reveals a simple relationship between area and heat flow, which makes even the most dull-witted learner shout "Eureka!"

Built using Adobe Flash. View example at horton.com/eld/.

Plotting data points is tedious and teaches nothing by itself. So why not just show the graph with the points already plotted? The act of plotting the data forces learners to more actively process it, and more active processing leads to deeper learning. Just make sure that learners discover the relationship hidden in the data. Provide a hint or draw the trend line on the graph, if necessary.

When to use virtual laboratories

In a virtual laboratory, learners can try all kinds of experiments without risk of damaging equipment or injuring themselves, fellow learners, or lab technicians. They can also conduct experiments not possible in even the most generously funded real laboratory. Use virtual laboratories:

▶ **Instead of real laboratories**. You can use virtual laboratories to replace real laboratories. Once built, virtual laboratories have no additional costs for supplies, maintenance of equipment, or replacement of broken parts. Learners do not have to drive (or fly?) to the laboratory. Virtual laboratories are never crowded, never closed, and never broken. They never blow up.

▶ **To prepare learners to use real laboratories**. Virtual laboratories prepare learners for efficient work in real labs. Virtual labs can start as simple, limited representations of the real lab. As learners master simple experiments, the lab can reveal more controls and variables so that, in the end, the virtual lab has the same richness and range of experimentation as the real laboratory.

▶ **For abstract experiments**. Virtual laboratories are not limited to simulating real laboratories. With a virtual laboratory, learners can swap the orbits of planets, tinker with the global economy, or crossbreed a piranha and a panda. Use virtual laboratories to let learners experiment with concepts of any scale and any level of abstraction.

Best practices for virtual laboratories

Focus on what you are teaching

Focus your efforts on what you are teaching. If the purpose of the activity is to teach someone to use real laboratory equipment, then make the simulation richly detailed.

If the purpose of the laboratory experiment is to teach principles, design the activity to make discovering the principles efficient and reliable. Do not let operating laboratory equipment get in the way of learning. Make sure that every click and each pixel contribute to the goal, rather than just adding busy work. Just because the real-world lab equipment requires a lengthy calibration process does not mean that your virtual laboratory need include the same inconvenience.

Challenge learners' assumptions

Design experiments to challenge what learners believe to be true. Such a strategy can correct misconceptions and lead to exciting discoveries. Have learners state their perceptions or beliefs. Then have them conduct an experiment to learn how their ideas compare to reality.

Prescribe experiments

Do not just give learners a laboratory and assume they will make up their own experiments. Assign experiments to perform. The best format for such an assignment is a set of questions that laboratory experiments can answer. Before receiving the questions, the learners may not care about the subject, but the questions challenge them to prove that their initial guesses are right.

3

Allow independent experiments too

Let learners conduct their own experiments. In designing virtual labs, allow imitation, then innovation. Here is an example of what I mean.

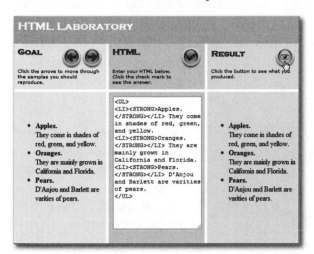

When I created the HTML Laboratory, I stocked it with goals for the learner to achieve. This was imitation.

What I didn't foresee was that many learners would try out variations of the goals I set.

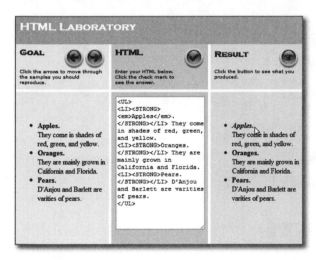

For instance, a learner might want to italicize the word **Apple**. So the learner typed in the additional code and clicked the Result arrow. Voila, the word *Apple* is now both bold and italicized. That's innovation.

Built using Adobe Dreamweaver and custom JavaScript. View example at horton.com/eld/.

By letting learners conduct their own experiments, I added value to this laboratory and made it more active.

Reuse your virtual laboratories

Developing a simulated laboratory is a lot of work. Consider whether you can use the same laboratory in multiple activities or even in multiple courses.

Case studies

Schools have used case studies since—well, since there were schools. Case studies provide relevant, meaningful experiences in which learners can discover and abstract useful concepts and principles.

Case studies can be the basis for a reading activity, if we just wanted learners to absorb information from the study. However, case studies make fine discovery activities when learners must actively apply analytical and problem-solving skills to the events cited in the case study.

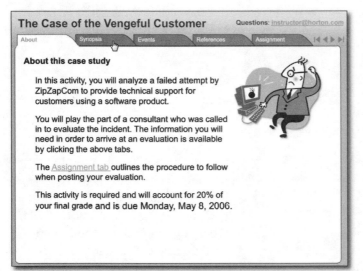

In this example, learners are asked to analyze a failed attempt to provide technical support for customers of a software product. Here you see the introduction.

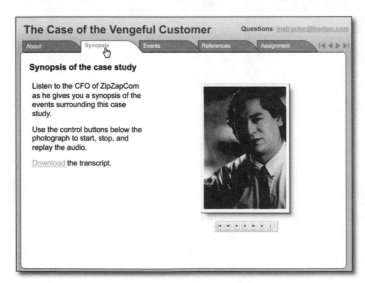

Here is the synopsis of the case study. It is narrated by the CFO. A transcript is available for learners to follow along. Notice the other tabs that contain a chronicle of events, reference documents, and the assignment.

Created in Microsoft PowerPoint and converted for Web delivery using iSpring Presenter. View example at horton.com/eld/.

In a case study, learners are given a comprehensive example to study. The case can be a real-world event, process, or system. Learners are also given materials that describe or perhaps even simulate the case. After working with these materials, learners attempt to answer questions about the case or to generalize the principles revealed by the case.

In e-learning, case studies differ from classroom case studies in the variety of material available through the Internet, in the use of interactive multimedia presentations, and in the multiple perspectives possible through collaboration. E-learning case studies can include a richer mix of materials for learners to examine and can more realistically mimic real-world cases.

When to use case studies

Case studies teach abstract, general principles from specific, concrete particulars. As such, they mimic the way most people learn most of what they know: by observing and analyzing their own experiences. Case studies are good for teaching complex knowledge that cannot be reduced to a simple formula. They are especially good for teaching the judgment skills necessary to deal with complex, contradictory situations common in real life.

Variations of case studies

Case studies can take many forms. Here are some of my favorites:

Instructor-led case studies

The teacher welcomes participants and introduces the case to study. The teacher then assigns a list of questions to answer and provides access to material describing the case. Learners individually study the case materials and post their answers to a discussion forum where they review and critique each other's answers. Learners continue to refine their answers until time runs out. Then learners post lists of the principles, trends, heuristics, and guidelines they inferred from the case. Finally, learners generalize their findings and specify how this knowledge can be applied to future cases in the real world. The teacher grades participants based on whether they identified the correct principles without oversimplifying the situation.

Virtual field trips

The case study can be presented as a virtual field trip (p. 112) that allows learners to observe objects and events as they actually occurred. Learners can navigate a locale by clicking links that jump from page to page. They can traverse a series of events by moving along a timeline. Along the way, learners are asked questions and make observations. As a recap, learners generalize their findings and specify how this knowledge can be applied to situations they may encounter in the future.

Observe-and-comment activities

Learners may observe a video or animation sequence (or just read a narrative) of people interacting. Such a scene may be organized as a drama presentation (p. 81). Learners can view the sequence as many times as they wish. Then they comment about what they have seen, answering such questions as:

▶ **What happened?** What did the people do? What did they think? How did they feel? What did the people gain or lose? What did they learn?

▶ **What does it mean?** What does the experience mean to you? How does it apply to your real-world experiences?

▶ **What will you do?** What have you learned? How will you think or act differently in the future? How will you apply what you have learned?

Mini-case studies

You can provide realistic, real-world experience by presenting a series of concise but complete examples. The formula is simple: Start with a statement of the situation. Introduce any characters, objects, or organizations of importance. Spell out crucial relationships among them. Then alternate questions and answers about the situation. Questions should require the learner to carefully examine the situation, infer facts not stated, apply principles, and deduce conclusions.

As a follow-up, pose additional questions to learners. Have them submit their answers to a discussion forum (p. 425). Or challenge learners to make up their own case studies and submit them to a discussion forum for use and critique by other learners.

Reaction papers

Have learners express their reactions after carefully examining a work in the field of study. The work can be a simple example, a report, or a physical artifact. To structure the activity, give learners a form to fill in. Include areas for them to enter:

▶ **Personal goals**. What do you hope to gain by examining the work?

▶ **Summary**. What does the work say? What does it mean to all those who come in contact with it?

▶ **Reaction**. What is significant about the work for you? What does your own background and experience tell you about it?

▶ **Utility**. How can you apply what you learned in this activity to your own work?

Best practices for case studies

Provide a rich mixture of case materials

Traditionally, case studies have used just paper memos, transcripts of interviews, and sometimes videotapes. Today case studies can include a much wider variety of materials. Some of the materials you can use include these:

▶ Conventional business documents, such as reports, contracts, instruction manuals, e-mail messages, memos, and letters.

▶ Blueprints, drawings, and specifications of products and systems.

▶ Patents, depositions, rulings, and other legal documents.

▶ Spreadsheets of numerical data.

▶ Charts, graphs, diagrams, and other technical and business graphics.

▶ Video or audio interviews.

▶ Simulations of an actual system.

Where possible, include live documents, such as word processing and spreadsheet files, that the learner can experiment with.

Guide study of the case

Prompt discovery of the important principles illustrated by the case study. Give specific guidance that will make good use of learners' time. Tell learners:

▶ **What the case study shows**. Do not be too specific. Just explain how the case relates to the subject under discussion.

▶ **What to notice**. What are the important features? Where should learners focus attention? Again, do not be too specific. Just give some clues as to where to start their examination of the case.

▶ **Questions to answer.** The answers form the deliverable for the activity. They direct learners' searches and control what discoveries they are likely to make on their own.

▶ **What to think about**. Ask questions that guide learners to think about how this case relates to others or to the subject of the lesson or course.

Best practices for discovery activities

Resist the urge to lecture

Not that you would, but many designers find it difficult to let go of control. In discovery activities, we have to trust that learners will discover the trends, principles, and concepts we are teaching. And, we have to design the activities so that learners actually *do* make the intended discoveries. Plus, we have to test and refine and test and refine even more. Designing discovery activities is like teaching by remote control.

Provoke experiments and interaction

In team activities, it is not unusual to wait for minutes or hours for action to begin because everyone is waiting for someone else to take the lead. In a new environment like a computer-mediated scenario, people may hesitate to take action. To overcome this reluctance, start with a specific trigger event that requires a response from all learners.

Include a synthesizing activity

Just performing experiments or reading case studies can leave learners with a lot of information but little knowledge. Include a synthesizing activity that requires learners to consolidate observations into a coherent theory. One simple way is to ask learners to summarize what they learned into a formula or a concise set of best practices.

Balance realism and complexity

Make the activity realistic enough that learners recognize it and can see similarities to their own situations. But do not become so obsessed with realism that you leave out the learning experiences or make the situation so specific that learners cannot map it to their situations.

Extend discovery activities

We can increase the reach and power of discovery activities by combining them with other types of activities and by adapting them for social learning and for mobile learning.

Combine discovery with other activities

Discovery activities combine productively with other types of e-learning activities.

- ▶ Start with a brief presentation (p. 69) introducing an area of study, raising issues to explore, or providing explicit instructions. Have learners conduct experiments (p. 147) to discover key principles and arouse curiosity. Follow up with a discussion activity (p. 484) to extend the principles, satisfy curiosity, and consolidate separate discoveries into a coherent theory.

- ▶ Include optional virtual-laboratory activities (p. 147) when teaching any subject where learners may doubt what you are teaching unless they discover it for themselves.

- ▶ Incorporate stories (p. 105) into case studies (p. 152). The storyteller can be a key figure in the case under study.

- ▶ Have learners apply discoveries in practice activities (p. 130) or simulations (p. 323).

Design discovery activities for social learning

Have social learners:

▶ Collaboratively form hypotheses, plan an experiment, interpret results, and draw conclusions.

▶ Individually pursue different experiments and then consolidate results.

▶ Share and discuss individual discoveries.

Design discovery activities for mobile learning

Have mobile learners:

▶ Discover by conducting physical experiments, gathering real-world data, or exploring physical environments.

▶ Use mobile devices to record data, for example, sensor readings, latitude-longitude coordinates, field notes, photos, audio clips, and video sequences.

▶ Access online resources to identify objects and characteristics, such as rocks and minerals, animal and plant species, architectural styles, sculptures, paintings, and people.

▶ Use GPS coordinates to locate valuable real-world examples, to develop navigation skills, and to enable learners to converge on others' discoveries.

GAMES AND SIMULATIONS

Games and simulations turn learning into play—meaningful, productive play.

Games and simulations can be superb Do activities. They can also be tests, lessons, and entire courses. The design of learning games and simulations is the subject of Chapter 7.

This chapter discusses how to use games specifically for individual Do activities.

Use games as single activities

Games for individual learning activities differ from those used for entertainment and from those used for larger units of learning. These differences stem from differences of goal, scale, and economics.

Base the game on a single objective

Each topic accomplishes a single objective, and each activity contributes to accomplishment of that objective. Design the game activity to contribute directly to the single objective of its topic. Use the type of objective as a guide in selecting the type of game. For example:

Type objective	Type game for a Do activity
Create	Simulation that requires creating a simple instance, for example, by assembling component pieces.
Decide	Simulation where learners make a decision and immediately experience the consequences of that decision.
Do	Simulation where learners practice a realistic task, perhaps with coaching.
Know	Quiz-show or other question-based game.
Believe	Game providing "evidence in experience" so that learners discover rules, principles, and concepts for themselves.
Feel	Game or simulation with emotion-provoking situations.

Clarify the purpose

Games serve two purposes: to provide practice of a skill or to provoke discovery of knowledge. Before developing the game, decide which purpose is primary and communicate that purpose clearly to everyone involved in development of the game.

Make learning to play the game easy and quick

To learn from a game, learners must first learn to play the game. Time spent learning to play the game is time not spent learning from the game. If learning to play the game takes too long, learning is inefficient and frustrating. To minimize time wasted in learning to play the game:

▶ **Base the game on just a few, simple rules**. Spell out the rules clearly. Make them accessible so learners can begin play before memorizing the rules.

▶ **Use a familiar model**. Base the learning activity on a game learners already know how to play or on a situation learners have experienced repeatedly.

▶ **Use the same type game throughout the entire course**. Or for each Do activity, use different segments of an ongoing game. Require learners to acquire game-playing skills only once.

Scale the game to work as an activity

Many learning games are just too complex and extensive to work as a single activity. Pick a simple game and limit the scope of the game so it exercises or tests accomplishment of a single objective. Here are some suggested size limits:

▶ Branching simulation of up to five jumps.
▶ Quiz-show game with up to 25 questions.
▶ Word puzzle with 30-40 clues.
▶ Jigsaw puzzle with 25-50 pieces.
▶ Personal-response simulation for three to five decisions.
▶ Math or financial simulation for a single calculation involving five to ten variables.

Or use segments of a larger game

Another solution for scaling games to work as activities is to use individual segments of an ongoing game. For example, a whole course could use a work simulation covering the whole job. Each lesson could consist of the simulation of a single complex task or job duty. The simulation of each step of the procedure or phase of the task could be a separate activity.

Likewise, a whole-product simulation could be divided into simulations highlighting each capability or distinct use of the product.

For another example, consider an extensive interpersonal simulation. Each group of related decisions represents a separate Do activity that contributes to learning a part of the subject and, at the same time, gates progress through the overall simulation. Each episode or mission within the game serves as a separate activity.

Keep game activities consistent

If you use games throughout an entire course, keep the games consistent from activity to activity. You do not have to limit a course to just one type of game, but using too many types of games can confuse learners and deplete your budget. Games are often too complex and expensive to develop for just one activity.

Consider using types of games that can be played over and over again without getting stale, for example quiz-show games, word games, and task simulations where different questions, clues, and job goals make each game or simulation a fresh challenge.

Where possible, build individual game activities from a common template that ensures consistency in the display, rules, and operation of the individual games. Templates for common types of games are relatively inexpensive. And, even if you are developing your own games, creating templates first can still save time and money.

Use the same type game for testing

Because games can serve as Do activities and as tests, it makes sense to use the same basic game for the test—with some differences.

	Game for the Do activity	Game for the test
Purpose	To provide practice or to provoke discovery.	To measure accomplishment of the objective.
Task	For initial learning, the problem or task assigned the learner may be simpler and easier than ones faced in real life. For more advanced learning, the problems are authentically difficult.	As difficult as those faced in real life.
Coaching?	Yes.	No.
Resources	Any that will help to learn in the game.	Only those available in real life.
Time limit	No.	Yes, if speed of performance is critical in real situations.
Retries	Unlimited.	Limited, depending on the costs of real-world failure.
Scored?	No.	Yes, if other test activities are scored.

Extend game activities

We can increase the reach and power of games and simulations by combining them with other types of activities and by adapting them for social learning and for mobile learning.

Combine games with other activities

► Have learners view a presentation on concepts before playing the game and read materials afterwards to explore issues more deeply.

► Provide a presentation, readings, or job-aids as a source of answers in quiz-show games and word games.

► Include practice activities that require the learners to do for real what was simulated in a game.

► Have learners hypothesize underlying formulas, rules, principles, or processes. Then require learners to plan future actions based on findings.

Design game activities for social learning

Have social learners:

▶ Engage in multi-player games that require communication, coordination, and teamwork. For example, conduct a role-playing activity as a game.

▶ Brainstorm, discuss, and vote on moves.

▶ Create and share simple games and puzzles. Provide templates to simplify creating the game.

▶ Share successful and unsuccessful strategies, discoveries, and insights.

▶ Contribute questions to a pool used in quiz-show games.

▶ Play the game as an individual but get advice from fellow learners, experts, or an extended social network.

Design game activities for mobile learning

Have mobile learners:

▶ Play physical games and board games—educational ones, that is.

▶ Solve puzzles that require gathering information at different locations.

▶ Visit real locations to see what the finished puzzle should look like, for example, a jigsaw puzzle on architecture.

▶ Perform instructed actions on an actual device with feedback provided by the mobile device.

▶ Discuss game play to try to identify underlying rules, processes, or principles.

IN CLOSING ...

Summary

Do activities are the path between information and knowledge, between explanations and skills. They put brains into action, exploring, discovering, practicing, refining, and perfecting knowledge and skills. Learners should spend at least half their time in meaningful Do activities. Do activities include:

▶ **Practice activities** that exercise and refine a wide range of skills from simple mechanical skills to complex analytical or interpersonal skills.

▶ **Discovery activities** that use exploration and experimentation to lead learners to discover new concepts, principles, and facts for themselves.

▶ **Games and simulations** that let learners discover new knowledge, try out their growing skills, and monitor their progress—all while having fun.

Pick Do activities to accomplish learning objectives

The following job aid ties the six types of objectives to common types of Do activities. Along the left are the main types of activities grouped into Practice, Discovery, and Games and simulations. In columns are the six types of objectives. A circle at the intersection of a type's column and an activity's row means that the activity is recommended for that type objective. A black dot indicates a stronger recommendation.

Do activities		Types of objectives					
		Create	Decide	Do	Know	Believe	Feel
Practice	Drill-and-practice			●			
	Hands-on			●			
	Guided analysis		●			○	
Discovery	Virtual lab		○		○	○	
	Case study	○	○		●	●	○
Games and simulations	Quiz show	●			●		
	Word puzzle				●	○	○
	Jigsaw puzzle	●		●	●		
	Branching scenario		●	○	○	●	○
	Task simulation		●	●			
	Personal response sim		●	○		●	●
	Environmental sim	○	●			●	●
	Role-playing sim	○	○	○	○	●	●

For more ...

Do activities are often scored. That turns them into tests. Check out Chapter 5 for more ideas on tests. Some Connect activities require doing things. Perhaps some of them could serve as Do activities as well. Look at Chapter 4 for some ideas.

To find more on Do activities, search the Web for combinations of these terms: *e-learning, interactivity, game, simulation, practice, case study*.

4 Connect-type activities

Linking learning to life, work, and future learning

Connect activities help learners close the gap between learning and the rest of their lives. They prepare learners to apply learning in situations they encounter at work, in later learning efforts, and in their personal lives. If Absorb activities are the nouns and Do activities the verbs, then Connect activities are the conjunctions of learning.

ABOUT CONNECT ACTIVITIES

Connect activities integrate what we are learning with what we know. Often simple and subtle, Connect activities are regularly neglected by designers who leave learners to make connections on their own.

Connect activities bridge gaps. They do not so much add new knowledge and skills as tie together previously learned skills and knowledge. In doing so, they add higher-level knowledge and skills. To know whether an activity is a Connect activity; we have to ask the purpose of the activity. If the purpose is primarily to teach something new, it is a Do or an Absorb activity. If the purpose is to link to something already known or prompt application of learning, it is a Connect activity.

Common types of Connect activities

Connect activities range from simple stop-and-think questions to complex real-world work assignments. Here are types of Connect activities that have proven themselves in classroom and online learning:

- ▶ **Ponder activities** (p. 166) require learners to think deeply and broadly about a subject. They require learners to answer rhetorical questions, meditate about the subject, identify examples, evaluate examples, summarize learning, and brainstorm ideas.

- ▶ **Questioning activities** (p. 176) let learners fill in gaps and resolved confusion by asking questions of teachers, experts, and fellow learners.

- ▶ **Stories by learners** (p. 184) require learners to recall events from their own lives.

- ▶ **Job aids** (p. 187) are tools that help learners apply learning to real-world tasks. They include glossaries, calculators, and e-consultants.

- ▶ **Research activities** (p. 196) require learners to discover and use their own sources of information. These include scavenger hunts and guided research.

- ▶ **Original work** (p. 207) requires learners to perform genuine work and submit it for critique.

When to feature Connect activities

Learners often fail to apply what they learn. For example, a manager passes a course on how to interview people of different cultures. Six months later she botches an employment interview of a shy Iranian woman wearing a traditional head scarf. A math student may get an A in introductory calculus but later a D in advanced calculus. Why? He did not apply the concepts from the introductory course to the advanced course, which assumes the introductory material as a prerequisite.

If you are familiar with Donald Kirkpatrick's four-level evaluation model, you know the importance of application. Application is right there on level 3, called *behavior*. It asks whether learners apply what they actually learned (level 2) to their subsequent behavior. Unless application occurs, intended organizational results (level 4) never occur.

By the way, if you are not familiar with Donald's model, you should be. Add *Evaluating Training Programs* by Donald and his son to your Amazon shopping cart. And be sure to read Chapter 11 (wink, wink).

Connect activities aim squarely at increasing application of learning. So use Connect activities when:

▶ **Application is crucial**. The success of individuals, organizations, or societies depends on learners applying skills and knowledge. Every day people die because safety instructions are ignored. Economies sag because their workers are not competitive in a global economy.

▶ **Application is not adequate**. Perhaps learning is applied but not in enough depth or by enough people. For example, many companies hire expensive management consultants to teach their employees subjects like Six Sigma or TQM. Six months later the posters are peeling off the walls and the slogan-embossed pencils have been ground down to the nibs, and the only lasting result is a few additional coffee mugs in the break room. The teaching may have been great, but there was scant application.

▶ **You teach a general subject**. Broad principles and concepts can be applied in varied situations. You cannot include enough examples and custom activities to prepare learners to apply the learning in every possible situation they may encounter. For example, a course on business writing might be applied by an engineer to write a technical specification or by a marketing manager to write a sales proposal.

▶ **Learners doubt applicability of material**. College students apply binge learning to pass courses they are required to take but for which they see no practical value. Two weeks after the end of the term, they have forgotten most of what they learned. Much compliance training in industry fares no better. Learners get their tickets punched and go on just as if nothing happened. Why? They never saw how what they were learning applied to their lives.

▶ **Learners cannot make connections by themselves**. Sometimes it takes extraordinary efforts to see the connection between abstract subjects and daily life. This "in the clouds" stigma plagues mathematics, science, philosophy, and dozens of other subjects. Many learners lack the experience, motivation, or creativity to make connections on their own.

Connect activities can solve these problems without a lot of extra effort. As a rule, they require only about 10% of learners' time. Sometimes a rhetorical question may be all you need.

PONDER ACTIVITIES

Ponder activities require learners to think deeply and broadly about what they are learning. They focus attention on the subject and invite learners to adopt a new perspective regarding the subject.

About ponder activities

Ponder activities are simple learning experiences that prompt the learner to examine ideas from a new perspective. They say:

> Stop and think about it!
> Zoom back and see the big picture.
> Look at it from a different angle.

Ponder activities are like classroom activities during which the teacher performs an out-of-the-ordinary activity to break the routine and to get learners to look at the subject afresh.

When to use ponder activities

Use ponder activities when you need learners to think about a subject in a new way. Use them to:

▶ Encourage broader and deeper thought about a subject.

▶ Make learners aware of how ideas and values apply in their lives.

▶ Reduce tunnel vision resulting from stress or anxiety.

▶ Trigger conceptual breakthroughs by getting learners to integrate separate ideas in new ways.

Types of ponder activities

Ponder activities come in several flavors. Here's a list of types and what they do.

▶ **Rhetorical questions** (p. 167) ask thought-provoking questions to direct attention to an aspect of the subject.

▶ **Meditations** (p. 168) promote a relaxed, open consideration of the subject.

▶ **Cite-example activities** (p. 171) require learners to identify real-world instances of a concept or category.

▶ **Evaluations** (p. 172) ask learners to judge the importance or value of an item under study.

▶ **Summary activities** (p. 174) require learners to identify and recap important principles, concepts, facts, tips, and other items of learning.

In social learning, brainstorming (p. 472) also provides a Connect activity where learners collect suggestions from a group of learners.

How ponder activities work

Ponder activities are usually simple one-shot experiences without any sequence. If they involve more than a couple of steps, they are probably part of another type of activity. The utter simplicity of ponder activities makes it easy to integrate them into other more complex activities. We often interleave ponder activities with Do and Absorb activities without the learner noticing the Connect activity as a separate event—especially if it is a simple form such as a rhetorical question.

Rhetorical questions

Rhetorical questions provoke thought. They may not require a visible response from learners, but they do require learners to think deeply in order to answer the question for themselves. We sometimes call them *stop-and-think* questions.

In the *Using Gantt Charts* course, I included these questions in one topic:

> Find a Gantt chart at your work. Can you see how it was constructed? Could you have constructed it?

There were no checkboxes for learners to click and no text boxes for learners to type in their answers. Thinking about the answers was enough.

When to use rhetorical questions

Use a rhetorical question as a simple way to get learners to think about a subject. For example, when:

▶ Real-world examples abound and you only need to direct learners' attention to them.

▶ All you need to do is to get the learners to think about an aspect of the subject.

▶ You lack time, space, or energy to do more.

Best practices for rhetorical questions

You can ask rhetorical questions about any topic you teach, such as a policy, procedure, principle, concept, attitude, or value. So how do you ask good rhetorical questions?

Ask stop-and-think questions. Teachers since Socrates have peppered students with rhetorical questions designed to direct their thoughts to aspects of a subject. Here are some proven thought-starters:

▶ Why do you think this is so? Why did this happen?

▶ What other results could you expect?

▶ Where will this idea apply? Where will it not apply?

▶ How can you apply this idea?

▶ How important is this idea to you?

▶ How consistent is this idea with other things you know?

Make questions personal. Feature the second person singular: "How will **you** …?" "Why do **you** …?" Get learners to think about their own experiences, knowledge, attitudes, and values.

Require thought about the subject and the learner's world. Just asking questions about the subject makes the question seem like a test. So put the question in the learner's context. "In the work that you do, what is the best way to …?"

Require some action if necessary. "Find an example of this idea and then answer these questions about it ….."

Trigger thought about when, where, how, and why to apply learning. Ask questions learners would have to answer before applying learning for real. "How often will you apply this idea?"

Meditation activities

The word meditation may conjure the image of someone sitting cross-legged, repeatedly chanting "om." Although such forms of meditation might provoke a relaxed state appropriate for learning or lead to mystical insights—that is not what I have in mind by a meditation activity. Meditation involves a relaxed consideration of a subject with a mind open to insights that may occur.

Meditation activities are not tightly focused. The big picture and content are more important than interior details. Meditation activities may involve more than cognitive aspects of a subject. They may delve into emotional meanings and implications for the learner's values and attitudes. Meditations may use non-verbal and non-explicit media such as music and abstract graphics.

Example of a meditation activity

On one project, I needed to broaden the concept of vision from just a "vision statement" to something involving the feelings of the group and how those feelings guide the group's actions.

A secondary purpose was to help the learners—the vision committee for a Christian church congregation, who have other jobs, demanding families, and busy lives—to let go of their daily concerns long enough to work together in this course.

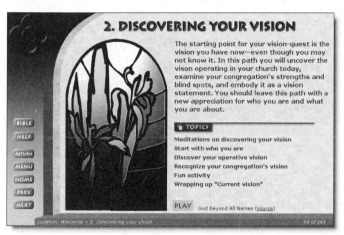

To accomplish these objectives, I began each lesson with meditation activities. The lesson started with a page featuring a stained-glass window. On each window was a different flower from the Christian Bible. The purpose was to draw learners out of their noisy world by letting them look at a beautiful image.

The choice of a window was not accidental. The window reinforced the message that vision looks outward and colors how the organization sees the larger community of which it is a part.

To further help learners disengage from daily concerns, the page included a button to play music associated with spiritual values.

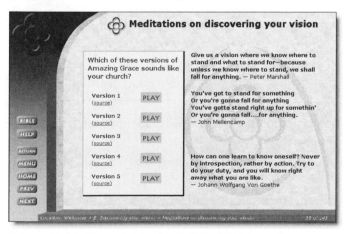

The second page of the lesson included meditative activities designed to further the contemplative mood necessary to work as a team to discover a common vision. The main activity on this page presented different styles of music and challenged participants to pick one that reflected their vision.

Built using Adobe Dreamweaver and Active Server Pages

This activity provoked lively discussion as learners asked each other, "Why do you feel that way?"

Rounding out the meditation were quotations from sources sacred and common—again reinforcing the point that an organization's vision connects it to the surrounding world rather than isolating it.

When to use meditation activities

Meditation activities are especially valuable for subjects that may trigger emotional resistance, for example, leadership style, negotiation, ethical behavior, politics, and dealing with angry people. They are also good when discussing basic human values or teaching aspects of spirituality.

Use meditation activities to:

▶ **Relax tense learners**. Help them disengage from outside concerns that could interfere with their learning.

▶ **Broaden the focus and emphasize context**. Get learners to step back and see how a subject fits into a broader scheme.

▶ **Involve other sensory modalities and "intelligences"**—for variety, sure, but in a purposeful way that learners will find natural and sponsors will pay for.

▶ **Prepare for work requiring openness and creativity**. Meditative activities can disengage critical and analytical modes of thinking when they might interfere.

▶ **Encourage holistic thinking**. Help learners resolve conflicts and inconsistencies between what they are learning and what they believe.

I have also used meditation activities to reduce tension in "hard" subjects such as law and computer programming by reminding learners how these subjects fit into the larger universe of human endeavors.

More kinds of meditation activities

Here are some more simple meditation activities:

▶ **Coloring**. Learners must pick colors for a symbol and justify the implications of their choices.

▶ **Symbolizing**. Search a clip-art library for all the different ways to represent a group, concept, value, or principle. Justify the choice.

▶ **Chanting**. Repeatedly say the name of a concept or organization to sense its hidden associations.

▶ **Deep watching**. Experience a video segment normally, then with the sound turned off, then with only the sound, then in slow motion, and finally speeded up.

▶ **Meaning quest**. Search the Web to collect or compare quotations on a subject or definitions of a term.

► **Deja viewing**. Identify ancient analogies to modern technologies and recent historical events.

Best practices for meditation activities

Meditation activities are subtle and benefit from sensitive design.

► **Have a good reason for the activity**. Many designers throw in colorful artwork or music for no good reason. Your reason for a meditation activity may be intellectual, emotional, or spiritual—but not just decorative.

► **Clarify your purpose**. What do you want the activity to achieve? Excitement or a calm, receptive mind? Are you trying to make a subtle point? Or is your goal to get learners to put aside a bias or prejudice?

► **Explain the reason for the activity** lest learners think you are being "weird for weird's sake."

► **Vary the type of meditation activity**. Different learners will respond to different types of activities. Use different media. Consider music, symbolic graphics, animation, and video.

Cite-example activities

Challenge learners to identify instances of a concept or category you have described and illustrated. Such an activity connects the concept or category with things the learner is already familiar with or can easily find in the world.

This activity requires learners to identify existing examples, not to create original examples. Creating original examples is part of the Original work activity (p. 207).

A course on information architecture challenged learners to find examples of Web sites organized according to different principles.

Built using Adobe Dreamweaver and Active Server Pages.

In the *Using Gantt Charts* course, I introduced dependency markers and then challenged learners to cite examples.

> Can you think of some examples of this kind of dependency relationship on projects you have worked on?

That's right. Sometimes a rhetorical question is all you need.

When to have learners identify examples

Requiring learners to identify examples achieves several educational goals, such as:

▶ Rounding out the definition of a term or category.

▶ Making a concept more concrete and specific.

▶ Verifying that students can correctly apply terms and categories.

▶ Proving the applicability of learning.

The response of one student to such an activity shows its value: "Wow. This stuff really exists. I never knew."

Best practices for cite-example activities

▶ **Require searching to find examples**. Require learners to do more than pick from lists you provide. To simplify the search, give learners a starting point. If extensive searching is required, combine the cite-example activity with a research activity (p. 196).

▶ **Simplify submitting examples**. Let learners submit by entering Web addresses of the examples; by uploading or e-mailing a photograph, sound recording, or video clip; or by giving directions on how to find the example, such as providing its GPS coordinates. In an online meeting, have learners identify examples by entering them in chat (p. 418) or describing them orally by audio-conferencing (p. 420).

▶ **Specify the type of examples sought**. Clearly define the category or concept for which examples are sought. Show a few examples as models of the type examples learners should identify. Also specify any quality standards ("legibly formatted"), required characteristics ("at least three levels deep"), or technical limitations ("1 MB max").

▶ **Encourage personal examples**. Ask learners to look for examples in their own experiences, work, personal life, and prior education.

Evaluation activities

Require learners to rate the importance of items of learning. Learners must judge from their personal perspective, such as in the context of a project in which the items of learning might be applied.

Pick access methods

For a real or imaginary online document you are creating, choose which access methods you would recommend. To the right is a list of the access methods we discussed in this lesson.

First, write the goal of your document. Then type 5 to 7 of the most important access methods you will employ.

Goal of the course:

Access methods (from most to least important):

[Enter] [Compare] [See all]

Click **Enter** to add this decision to your journal. Click **Compare** to see what other learners have chosen for their courses. Click **See all** to review the decision you have made so far.

Available methods
Autoscanning
Bookmarks
Context sensitivity
Full-text search
Grazing
Guided tour
History list
Home topic
Index
Keyword search
Map
Menu structure
Natural language search
Picture gallery
Table of contents

This example required learners to rate the utility of various access methods for an online document or Web site they were creating.

Built using Adobe Dreamweaver and Active Server Pages.

An evaluation activity can be used as a whole-class activity as well. In an online meeting you can have the class vote on the value for each item. Let them re-vote after considering the opinions of others.

When to use evaluation activities

Asking learners to rate the importance of ideas they have been taught challenges them to critically examine those ideas from a personal perspective. Such re-examination is valuable to:

▶ Get learners to start winnowing the ideas they will actually apply.

▶ Force reconsideration of individual items and their practical advantages and disadvantages.

▶ Replace rote rule-following with sensitive judgments.

Best practices for evaluation activities

▶ **Personalize ratings**. Remind learners to evaluate items from their unique individual perspective. Ask them "How important or valuable is this idea *to you*?"

▶ **Set a context for evaluation**. State the area for which importance is rated. Use phrases like "in the work you do" and "in your math courses."

▶ **Require criteria.** Have learners state the criteria they used to judge the idea. "Rate the importance from 1 to 10 and explain how you arrived at that number."

▶ **Require precision**. Avoid vague ratings like "good and bad." Require a numeric rating along a scale or require learners to rate the relative importance of a group of ideas.

Summary activities

Summary activities ask learners to recap what they have learned. Learners must review a subject area, select what is important, organize the selection logically, and express it clearly in their own words.

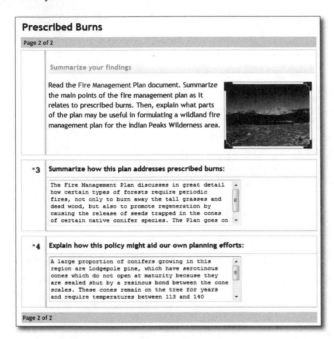

This example challenges learners to summarize a document and how the ideas of the document apply to their work.

Built using Moodle.

When to use summary activities

Summarizing prior learning has several effects on learning. It:

▶ Prepares learners to apply learning by having them rehearse recalling needed information.

▶ Prepares learners to teach or inform others, such as members of their team or study group.

▶ Triggers a systematic, personal review of an area of learning.

These activities let you monitor learners' level of understanding. Do learners recall the main points? Are the points logically integrated and prioritized? Have learners translated learning into their own vocabulary?

Best practices for summary activities

Simplify creating the summary. A blank text area is not always the best way for learners to express a summary. For some subjects, you may want to have learners draw a picture and submit it by e-mail or post it to a discussion forum. For other subjects, you may want to structure the form of the summary. You could, for example, let learners construct a summary by selecting and sequencing statements from a list.

Clarify what to summarize. Have learners summarize a specific lesson, topic, or activity. Have learners summarize specific learning experiences—books, articles, presentations, regulations, or other documents.

Assign summary activities to a group. Have learners compare separate summaries and then consolidate them. First, each learner individually creates a summary and posts it to a discussion forum (p. 425). Then, as a group, the class discusses the summaries either in an online meeting or on the forum. Together they identify points to include in the master summary and how these points should be organized.

Set a context for the summary. Rather than have learners write a conventional academic summary, consider requiring a format that they might need to produce in the real world or in an ongoing scenario, such as one of these:

▶ Press release.
▶ Advertisement.
▶ Poster.
▶ Block diagram or organization chart.
▶ Book jacket and blurb.
▶ Headline and first few paragraphs of a newspaper story.
▶ Storyboard for a 60-second TV news spot.
▶ 20-second sound bite.
▶ Review or synopsis.

Extend ponder activities

We can increase the reach and power of ponder activities by combining them with other types of activities and by adapting them for social learning and for mobile learning.

Combine ponder activities with other activities

Ponder activities are simple Connect activities that bond well with other activities.

▶ Combine ponder activities with research activities (p. 196) so learners can explore the significance of what their research revealed.

▶ After a presentation (p. 69), have learners summarize the presentation, evaluate its importance, and cite examples to illustrate its principles.

▶ Sprinkle rhetorical questions throughout other activities, especially Absorb activities.

▶ Follow Absorb and Do activities with a ponder activity that requires learners to identify and reflect upon what they learned.

Design ponder activities for social learning

Have social learners:

▶ Provoke others to ponder, by asking stop-and-think questions, attempting to stump the group, and by continually asking "Why?"

▶ Share cited examples, summaries, job-aids, application techniques, and other results of ponder activities. Learners can use blogs, podcasts, tweets, or social bookmarking to share results of pondering.

▶ Ponder as a group, for example, by brainstorming ways to apply learning.

▶ Compare, evaluate, and consolidate the work of other learners.

Design ponder activities for mobile learning

Have mobile learners:

▶ Navigate to objects and environments that cause learners to ponder. Select ones that evoke feelings of awe or grandeur, for example, monuments, public spaces, works of art, and construction projects.

▶ Travel to a peaceful environment in which to meditate.

▶ Use the calendar function to trigger rhetorical questions or other ponder activities.

▶ Use audio to lead meditation, free association, and imagination.

▶ Find examples and applications of learning in the real world.

▶ Evaluate real-world work, such as the quality of a construction job.

QUESTIONING ACTIVITIES

Asking and answering questions is fundamental to education and training—and to any endeavor involving more than one person. Asking and answering questions is inherently a Connect activity. It emerges from the individual's recent learning and background experiences. Personal curiosity is the spark that initiates the question. Asking and answering questions is almost always social as it often involves interacting with fellow learners, teachers, experts, co-workers, and friends.

Though a simple activity, questioning triggers powerful learning processes. Questioning requires learners to conceive and express a question and then attend to and reflect on the answer. Questioning activities may also present learners the chance to answer questions, thus exercising their ability to integrate and apply learning.

As a formal activity, asking and answering questions is new to this edition. In the first edition, I considered it a natural sidecar experience in activities like presentations, readings, and research. After all, I reasoned, questioning is a human experience, not an explicit activity. That was a mistake. We e-learning designers are a literal-minded lot. Some readers, assuming it was not important, omitted the questioning part of other activities. This section should correct my mistake.

Questioning activities can range from simple, spontaneous actions by learners to carefully choreographed online meetings. As a designer, you must decide which form best accomplishes your learning objectives.

Why use questioning activities?

Questioning activities help individuals integrate new learning. Include such activities where learners need to:

▶ **Fill in gaps**, either in the overall picture or between theory and application.

▶ **Get unstuck**. By asking questions, learners can get suggestions of new techniques to try or even acquire a new viewpoint for interpreting facts.

▶ **Connect learning to a personal situation**. Learners can answer the all-important question: "What's in it for me?"

▶ **Learn to learn** by asking questions. Skillful questioning is not just a learning skill; it is a survival skill. Practice asking and answering questions can teach what, when, whom, and how to ask.

▶ **Verify truth**. A quick question can relieve doubt or remove a misconception. It can quickly validate (or not) a belief, suspicion, or claim.

Keep in mind that questioning activities deal primarily with knowledge. Such activities may, therefore, be a core part of *know* and *believe* objectives and a secondary part of others.

As designers, we can also employ questioning activities to assess learners and learning. The level of learning is often revealed by the sophistication of questions asked by learners.

Encourage learners to ask the right people

The quality of an answer usually depends upon the expertise of the answerer. Design questioning activities and processes so that questions naturally go to those who can best answer them. Let's consider the candidates:

▶ **Fellow learners**. Cohorts of the learner are best at answering simple, routine questions, but not advanced questions. Questions directed to fellow learners should fall within the objectives of the course and within the expertise of fellow learners. In a general education course, adult learners can draw on a life of experience as a learner and perhaps some experience as a teacher to answer questions. However, in a course on complex new financial regulations, questions might better be answered by an expert.

Fellow learners can answer questions that the teacher answered before or questions on material already covered in class. For everyday questions, asking fellow learners is a logical first step.

▶ **Teachers**. Teachers and instructors should be prepared to handle ordinary subject-matter questions within the scope of course objectives. They should also handle administrative questions. However, do not let ready access to the teacher encourage learners to forego the hard work of conducting research and discussing issues with fellow learners. Put in place policies that reward self-reliance and protect the teacher from an overwhelming workload.

▶ **Subject-matter experts**. Use SMEs to answer advanced subject-specific questions, especially ones that go beyond the formal objectives of the course. Use SMEs for questions beyond the expertise or professional credibility of the teacher. Take care not to overwhelm SMEs with trivial questions that could be answered by the teacher, by fellow learners, or by a well-phrased Internet search.

▶ **Panel of experts**. Schedule a panel or symposium (p. 413) to discuss very advanced questions, especially controversial and complex ones that need discussion rather than a one-shot answer. Respect the time and expertise of the experts. Have learners prepare and refine questions in advance.

▶ **Help desk**. Refer technical questions to a small group of outside experts on call to answer such questions. If this type service exists for your field, gain access for your learners. Otherwise, create a service, modeling it on a customer-support hotline or a library's reference desk.

▶ **Fans, friends, and followers**. For general questions, or just to get another opinion, learners may turn to their professional or personal social networks. Avoid this option for advanced questions or issues of safety. Encourage learners, if using public social networks, to target specific groups with the needed expertise rather than broadcasting questions to anyone and everyone.

▶ **Search service**. Google and other search engines are, in-effect, question-answering machines. They try to match a search query to content that matches that query. They are a good way to answer questions about specific products, people, places, and organizations. A search service is especially good to verify facts and figures and to gather opinions.

To control who answers which questions, put in place mechanisms that naturally route questions to the right person. Give clear instructions to learners on how to get answers to their questions. Design specific activities, such as question-and-answer sessions or online panels, where teachers and experts are available to answer and discuss questions. Set up online office hours for teachers. Provide directories of e-mail addresses and other contact points for designated experts. Build incentives into grading criteria.

Encourage good questions

Encourage learners to ask good questions by using policies, procedures, prompts, and grading criteria. But what is a good question? Let's consider some common-sense criteria. A good question is:

▶ **Original and non-trivial**. The answer cannot be found in the course materials or a FAQ file. The question has not already been asked. And the answer is not easily found with a simple Internet search.

▶ **Simply structured**. Many questioners are so eager to ask questions that they jam several questions together, making the question hard to understand and requiring the answerer to untangle them. In my experience, when learners jam multiple questions together, only the last question in the bundle gets answered.

▶ **Clearly expressed**. Good questions are easy to understand. They take the grammatical form of a question, use proper terminology from the field, and follow conventions of standard business language. If the question is spoken, the words are understandable. If poor audio quality or a speaker's thick accent renders questions (or answers) incomprehensible, provide a text channel for asking questions.

▶ **Sincere**. Rather than asking a genuine question, some learners may use the occasion to make a statement. Watch out for these non-questions:

- **Spam questions**. The learner precedes the question with a recital of credentials and accomplishments. The purpose is often self-promotion. Or, perhaps the learner feels the expert is patronizing the class and not taking questions seriously.

- **Aren't-I-smart questions**. These are questions asked to impress the teacher, expert, or fellow learners. They usually involve esoteric matters expressed in jargon of the field.

- **Putting words in the mouth of the expert**. Sometimes learners will ask questions in a way designed to elicit a specific answer. "Don't you believe that …?" Often this is a sign that the learner is trying to use the expert to convince someone else.

▶ **Just contextual enough**. A good question provides just enough details to enable a specific, applicable answer. Learners must strike a balance between supplying every possible detail and requiring the answerer to interrogate the questioner before answering. This is a difficult criterion because the learner may not know what is relevant. Give novices more leeway than experienced practitioners.

▶ **Helpful to the learning effort**. Good questions build on current learning. They help other learners by supplying important knowledge and by triggering even more advanced questions.

▶ **Open-ended**. Except for quick questions to verify understanding, questions should not have simple yes/no answers. They should elicit more than a simple fact or figure.

▶ **Answerable by the target**. A good question falls squarely in the area of expertise of the person called on to answer it. Mistakes include asking a low-level functionary about organizational policy or asking a highly technical question of a sales representative. Publish credentials of experts available to answer questions. Encourage learners to match their question to the person best able to answer it. Remember, you do not want to embarrass experts by requiring them to say, "I don't know."

Insist on good answers

Almost as important as good questions are good answers. Encourage the kind of question-answering behaviors that fully answer questions and that set a model for learners when they answer questions. A good answer:

▶ **Resolves uncertainty**. It directly answers the question, or it provides a way the learner can do so. Enabling learners to answer their own questions may be a better goal than a quick reply.

▶ **Avoids ambiguity**. Before answering a question, an expert should resolve any ambiguity, for example by asking, "Do you mean ____ or ____?" One good approach is to paraphrase the question and require confirmation, for example, "OK. As I understand it, you want to know _____, right?" This technique is necessary if the question is not expressed in correct, standard terminology or if the questioner speaks with a thick accent. The answerer might also ask some other learner to rephrase the question.

▶ **Is understandable**. The answer should use terminology already understood by learners. It should follow rules of grammar and syntax. If spoken, the answer should be pronounced clearly.

▶ **Is polite**. A silly question is no excuse to embarrass or humiliate the questioner. The answerer should never respond by giving a sarcastic or snide reply, by criticizing the question as unworthy, or by ignoring the question ("Next question!"). What seems to be a silly question can reveal valuable information about the current state of learning, such as simple but profound misunderstandings, learners who lack prerequisites, or creative interpretations of facts that the expert did not anticipate.

▶ **Verifies understanding**. A good answer will provide a way for learners to confirm satisfaction: "Does that answer your question?" "Anything else?" Or the expert may pose a question or test to verify deep understanding: "So, what would happen if _____?"

▶ **Encourages further learning**. A good answer may mention resources for additional learning: "If you want to go deeper into this issue, search through the blog postings by _____."

Best practices in questioning activities

In addition to good questions and good answers, questioning activities can benefit from procedures honed by practical experience.

▶ **Plan and explain the activity well**. For a formal question-and-answer session, set a clear goal and communicate the goal and procedures to learners. State the purpose and the type questions appropriate. For any experts involved, list their credentials and areas of expertise. Reveal any limits, such as time period, restrictions on quotations, and taboo topics.

▶ **Have learners try to find answers on their own**. Encourage learners to conduct research before asking questions. Make sure they learn common terminology of the field and what is commonly known in the field. Before asking external experts, require learners to ask fellow learners.

▶ **Formulate questions deliberately**. Encourage learners to conceive and express questions carefully. Allow time to think, express, and revise questions. Encourage learners to write and edit their questions first. Have learners submit questions by e-mail before a meeting. Within a meeting, pause long enough for attendees to edit questions before pasting them into the chat window.

▶ **Moderate questions in an online meeting**. Have the meeting moderator consolidate duplicate questions, generalize similar questions, and filter out improper questions before submitting them to the expert or teacher.

▶ **Answer private questions privately**. Require learners to ask private questions outside the general discussion. Candidates for private questions are ones that involve restricted information, that are of interest to no one else, or that potentially could embarrass the questioner or anyone else.

▶ **Summarize in a FAQ file**. Periodically, sweep common and important questions and their answers to a frequently-asked questions file and make it available to all learners.

Mechanism for asking questions

E-learning tools and technologies offer rich possibilities for asking and answering questions. Here is a list of common mechanisms:

▶ **E-mail** messages to the teacher or an expert.

▶ **Phone** calls to the teacher, a designated expert, or fellow learners—during agreed upon hours.

▶ **Text messages** to the phones of the teacher, experts, or fellow learners.

▶ **Chat session** during an online meeting. The online meeting tool that hosts the meeting may provide the chat capability.

▶ **Audio- or video-conferences** as part of an online meeting. The online meeting tool that hosts the meeting may provide these capabilities. These capabilities are valuable where questions and answers rely on tone of voice, gesture, body language, or facial expressions.

▶ **Comments** to a discussion forum, blog, or micro-blog. These can be useful for contacting experts and professional groups.

See "Social capabilities of software" in Chapter 8 for details on these technical capabilities.

Enable questioning at the right time

Let learners ask questions at the best time to promote learning. Often the best time is right when the question occurs. Some questions, however, may best be asked as part of a scheduled event or at specific times when an expert will be available.

Spontaneous questioning

Learners can ask spontaneous questions at any time, such as when the question occurs, while performing a practice activity, or while listening to a presentation. The value of an immediate answer is obvious. But, the cost may be high if teachers are expected to check e-mail and text messages every fifteen minutes throughout the night.

Fully supporting spontaneous questioning may require routing questions to a discussion forum and setting realistic expectations about the timing of replies.

As a formal part of an event

Several kinds of learning events include a formal question-and-answer session. Opportunities to ask questions may occur immediately after a presentation or as part of a symposium or class meeting. Consider how you can use chat or the conferencing capabilities in an online meeting tool to add Q&A sessions to your curriculum.

During specific times

Questioning may occur at fixed times, such as during "office hours" kept by a teacher. Restricting questioning to specific time periods is also common where outside experts agree to take questions. Such sessions typically use phone, chat, or the conferencing capabilities in an online meeting tool.

Assess learners and learning

Like all other types of activities, questioning activities provide evidence of learning that can be used to assess learners and to evaluate learning efforts. For instance, you can assess learners by how well they find their own answers, help answer others' questions, and exhibit good questioning technique.

In assessing learners, be careful not to discourage asking good questions. If learners feel they could lose grade points by asking bad questions, they will refrain from doing so. On the other hand, if they know they can gain points, learners will ask questions. Just be on the lookout for questions contrived to win points—shallow questions or questions that are not on topic.

One successful approach is to offer bonus points for questions and answers deemed especially valuable. The bonus points may be given based on ratings by fellow learners, experts, and teachers on such criteria as insightfulness, expression, and completeness.

Extend questioning activities

We can increase the reach and power of question-and-answer activities by combining them with other types of activities and by adapting them for social learning and for mobile learning.

Combine questioning activities with other activities

▶ Immediately follow presentations (p. 69) or readings (p. 93) with a Q&A (p. 562) session so learners can fill in gaps and avoid misunderstandings.

▶ Enable questioning after a Do activity to satisfy curiosity aroused by the activity and to resolve issues it may raise.

▶ Publish a transcript of the Q&A session as a FAQ file or other reading.

▶ Enable learners to ask questions at decision points within other activities, especially within research activities (p. 196), games and simulations (Chapter 7), and practice activities (p. 130).

Design questioning activities for social learning

Have social learners:

▶ Nominate, discuss, refine, and then ask questions.

▶ As a group, ask questions of an expert or the teacher. First, the group researches the expert and the expert's area of expertise. The group also nominates, discusses, consolidates, and refines a list of questions. The group extends the list by adding potential follow-up questions.

▶ Answer questions posed by fellow learners or experts.

▶ Pose questions in their blog, podcast, or micro-blog feed which others can answer by comments or replies. Likewise, answer questions posed by others.

Design questioning activities for mobile learning

Have mobile learners:

▶ Ask questions when and where they occur. This will require making answers available 24x7 through access to a help desk, classmates on a social network, or discussion forums.

▶ Ask questions triggered by real-world experiences.

▶ Use phone, texting, video-chat and other device capabilities to ask and answer questions.

STORIES BY LEARNERS

Learners can listen to stories as an Absorb activity—or they can tell their own stories as a Connect activity. Because storytelling emanates from the personal experiences of the storyteller, it is superb for connecting learning to those experiences.

In storytelling activities, learners tell stories relevant to the subject they are studying. This activity is the mirror image of listening to stories. Because the process of telling stories is similar, regardless of who tells the story, the advice for stories by teachers (p. 105) will apply to stories by learners, too.

Have learners tell stories

Encourage learners to share their own stories that connect the subject they are learning with their own experiences.

In this activity from a course on leadership, learners are invited to share a story about an event that taught them the importance of leadership in daily life.

Not only are learners able to contribute text stories, they can also include pictures and video. They can even link to an audio recording.

This example was hosted on Tumblr.com

In an online meeting where learners can speak, invite them to tell their own stories. The invitation to tell a story adds the element of reflection and encourages learners to think about what has been said and how it applies to their own situations. The process of composing an analogous story connects the events to the learners' lives. It also verifies learning. If learners tell appropriate stories, you know they got the point of the story you told. And letting learners tell stories is a great way to gather new stories.

Good stories are hard to tell

Learners may find it hard to come up with relevant stories if they are young, have led a sheltered life, or have limited professional experience. Someone who has lived on three continents and is nearing retirement from their seventh career will have more stories to tell than someone just entering college in the town in which they were raised. In addition, learners from a different society, studying in a second language, may find they need to translate their story both culturally *and* linguistically.

For many learners, their best stories may be uncomfortable to tell. The stories may recount events that caused them shame, anger, sadness, or other painful emotions. Good stories often reveal the storyteller as vulnerable or foolish. Though learners may find it hard to tell effective stories, with enough time and encouragement, just about everybody can tell meaningful stories.

Evaluate storytelling fairly

Stories by learners are personal and unique. How then can we tell if the storytelling activity contributes to learning? Let's look at some simple criteria for stories by learners.

Is the story relevant to the topic? Does the story make a point that contributes to ongoing learning? That is, does the story offer an example of a principle or concept being taught? Or does it present a counter example to sharpen distinctions? Listeners should immediately and clearly see how the story applies to what they are learning.

Is the story complete? Does the learner's story present everything needed to get the point of the story. Effective stories provide complete information, namely the setting, characters, conflict, resolution, and moral.

Does the moral follow from the events? Does the point of the story emerge naturally and logically from the sequence of events related in the story? Does the story make roughly the same point to all listeners?

Do not penalize awkwardness. Do not penalize learners for moderate awkwardness in telling the story. Unless you are teaching the subject of storytelling or acting, the style of delivery is secondary to the content and point of the story. Do not criticize learners for a thick accent, minor grammatical slips, mispronunciations, slight stutters, or an occasional "uh" or "ah".

Best practices for storytelling activities

Because telling stories is hard, most of the following best practices aim to help and encourage learners to tell meaningful stories.

Make storytelling optional. Elicit and encourage, but do not demand, stories.

Make telling stories easier for learners. Give learners time to think of a story. Announce storytelling activities well in advance. Let learners submit stories when they are ready, for example by posting a text message or voice-recording to the course discussion forum. Let learners write their stories rather than speak them aloud. Some learners may be self-conscious about their speaking voice but comfortable writing and editing text. Let learners tell someone else's story if they cannot think of one of their own stories. Require them to identify the source of any borrowed story.

Suggest a simple structure for their stories. For example, suggest that stories have these five elements:

- ▶ Setting: When and where does the story occur?
- ▶ Characters: Who is involved?
- ▶ Conflict: What difficulty had to be overcome?
- ▶ Resolution: How did things work out?
- ▶ Moral: What is the point of the story?

Model good storytelling. Let the best storytellers go first so others have an example to emulate and time to recall a story.

Simplify submitting stories. If learners cannot communicate by audio in a meeting, do not ask them to type their stories into chat. Unless they are super typists, the process is so painful it will become its own disaster story. Instead, invite them to contribute their stories to a discussion forum (p. 425).

Extend storytelling activities

We can increase the reach and power of stories by learners by combining them with other types of activities and by adapting them for social learning and for mobile learning.

Combine storytelling with other activities

Have learners:

- ▶ Tell stories that echo the point made in case studies (p. 152), dramas (p. 81), games (p. 323), role-playing activities (p. 476), or stories told by the teacher or an expert (p. 105).
- ▶ Tell stories that contradict the point made by other activities.
- ▶ Research (p. 196) to find a story that makes a specific point.

Design storytelling activities for social learning

Have social learners:

▶ Present a story to the group, discuss it with the group, and refine it.

▶ Publish stories as blog or podcast entries.

▶ String together tweets or other short messages to tell a coherent story.

▶ Pick the best learner-told story to become part of the official course.

▶ Group others' stories by the point they make, by similarity of characters, or by style of language.

▶ Have learners suggest alternative morals for a story.

Design storytelling activities for mobile learning

Have mobile learners:

▶ Record their story in an environment where they feel comfortable or the environment that best illustrates the story.

▶ Show where the story took place and introduce some of the characters.

▶ Reenact the story as a drama.

JOB AIDS

Job aids help learners apply knowledge and skills to real-world tasks they encounter on the job—or anywhere else in life. Job aids are not formal education, but they can shape the need for learning and in some cases can substitute for formal learning. We lump them with Connect activities because they prepare and encourage learners to apply learning on the job.

About job aids

Job aids are as much a category of tool as a specific learning activity. The term *job aid* covers a lot of ground, from a recipe on an index card to an elaborate electronic performance support system. The idea of a job aid is to provide help to someone performing a task right when and where they need it.

When to use job aids

Use job aids as part of your e-learning efforts when:

▶ The subject is too complex for learners to recall all the important details.

▶ Tasks are critical or have negative side effects if not performed exactly as specified.

▶ Rote memorization would distract from learning more important principles and concepts.

▶ A job aid can replace unnecessary training and education.

For a lot of performance problems, a job aid is the perfect solution. Yet many training departments have developed whole courses when a job aid would have solved the problem for 1% of the cost. Why? They are training departments, not job-aid departments. Before you develop a course, consider whether a job aid is a better idea.

Types of job aids

Job aids are as varied as the jobs they aid. Here are some job aids that have made the transition to e-learning. Because the last three make special use of electronic media, they are described in more detail later.

▶ **Checklists** record the essential steps in a procedure or components of a system. Format the checklist for printing. For online checklists, use checkboxes so learners can keep track of items completed.

▶ **Reference summaries** recap crucial information in a field. They are sometimes called a *crib sheet* or *cheat sheet*. One common form is the pocket-sized card listing commands in a computer program or their keyboard shortcuts.

▶ **Glossaries** (p. 188) define the key terms, abbreviations, and symbols of a field.

▶ **Calculators** (p. 192) perform mathematical calculations for learners, thus eliminating the need to memorize formulas or consult complex tables.

▶ **E-consultants** (p. 193) dispense advice on complex situations. They can range from simple if-then tables to full expert systems.

How job aids work

There is no real flow, as job aids are used by themselves or as a part of a Do activity. When the need arises, the learner obtains the job aid and follows its advice. Obtaining the job aid may involve downloading it from a Web site or just reaching in a pocket for a creased and stained page printed out six months ago.

Glossaries

Learning a new subject often requires acquiring a new vocabulary. A glossary lets us look up the meaning of terms as we encounter them. A good glossary can define terms, spell out abbreviations, and save us the embarrassment of mispronouncing the shibboleths of our chosen professions.

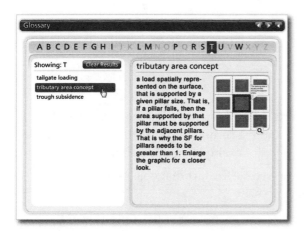

In this example from a course on surface deformation in mining, the definition for *tributary area concept* includes not only text, but also a graphic (that can be enlarged), which illustrates the concept.

Built using Articulate Engage.

In addition to the definitions, a glossary can include:

▶ Illustrations or links to pop-up illustrations.

▶ Synonyms and other related words, each linked to its definition.

▶ Pronunciation, both spelled out in text and linked to an audio file.

▶ Part of speech of this word, for example, noun or adjective.

▶ Usage notes to help learners use the term appropriately.

When to create a glossary

Glossaries are almost mandatory in e-learning that contains terminology unfamiliar to learners or that aims to teach correct use of terminology. A glossary makes strange words familiar and guides learners in their use. Consider creating a glossary for subjects when:

▶ Practitioners use many specialized terms and abbreviations. Every complex endeavor is subject to the Tower-of-Babel effect.

▶ Correct use of terminology is crucial to success. Misusing terms can cause legal penalties or just severe embarrassment.

▶ People of different specialties (and hence different vocabularies) must collaborate. An architect may use a technical term for something that a general contractor refers to by its common name and the construction worker calls by yet another term.

▶ Specialists and non-specialists must work together. Often reports written by a specialist must be typed and edited by those not versed in the esoteric terminology of the specialist's field.

Before you create e-learning on the concepts and principles of a field, consider whether a glossary would meet your requirements.

4

Connect-type activities

Best practices for glossaries

Glossaries are relatively easy to create. Effective glossaries, though, require close attention to linguistic and technical issues.

Use the classic formula for definitions

The classic form for a definition has two parts. The first part (called the *genus*) tells the general category to which the term belongs, and the second part (called the *differentia*) tells how it differs from other items in the category. For example, in this definition:

> **chromostereopsis** – illusion of depth caused by the fact that objects of different colors come into focus at different distances.

The genus is "illusion of depth," and the differentia is the rest of the definition. OK, it's an old-fashioned way of writing definitions and the terms are from a dead language, but the formula is easy to follow and leads to definitions that are easy for learners to understand.

Clarify when the term applies

Provide general definitions before specific ones. For each specific definition, begin with the area in which this definition applies.

> **filter** – a device or process to limit what is included. In camera-work, a sheet of material in front of the lens that restricts which colors of light reach the film or sensor. In photo-editing, any process that systematically alters the recorded image, such as blurring, sharpening, or tinting.

Notice how this glossary entry includes a general definition and two specialized definitions differentiated by the context in which they apply.

Phrase definitions for clarity

If the definition refers to something besides the term, make the definition a complete sentence. For example:

> **linked list** – a data structure in which each member stores an item of data and a pointer to the next member in the list. In double-linked lists, each member contains pointers to both the previous and next member in the list.

Do not use the term within its own definition.

 No   ☺ **Yes**

☹ No	☺ Yes
display control panel – a control panel where you can control the display of your computer's monitor.	**display control panel** – a utility for changing the size, number of colors, and other characteristics of the image shown on your computer's monitor.

Separate the term and its definition

Format the term and definition so they are clearly separate. This is crucial for multi-word terms.

 No   **Yes**

peep-hole effect misinterpretations caused by receiving information without being aware of the context in which it applies.	**peep-hole effect** misinterpretations caused by receiving information without being aware of the context in which it applies.

Cover a particular field

Design your glossary so it covers an entire field of study, not just the terms needed for a single course. That way you can offer your glossary as a separate product and your glossary can support multiple courses. Do focus on a specific area of knowledge. A glossary is not a replacement for a general-purpose dictionary. There are already plenty of general-purpose dictionaries on the Web. And don't forget to clearly label the field your glossary covers.

Evolve your glossary

Start simply and make your glossary more sophisticated as you increase its size and functions.

1. Start with a simple, single-page list of terms and definitions. Or just link terms in your text to their definitions in a separate window.

2. If the list of terms gets longer than 5 or 6 scrolling zones, add letter buttons at the top of the page to scroll directly to the first term beginning with each letter.

3. As the list grows beyond a size that will load quickly, break it into separate pages, one for each letter or group of letters.

4. If your glossary grows beyond a couple of hundred terms, or if it needs frequent revision, consider storing the terms, definitions, and other data in a database and generating each definition in response to a request from the learner.

5. Add advanced search features. For example, let learners search for terms whose definitions contain specific words. Or let learners look up terms by how they are pronounced.

Borrow a glossary

Before you start your glossary project, check to see whether someone else already publishes a glossary for your field. Glossaries exist for most technical and business subjects, and most are free. If a glossary is on the Web, link to it.

4

Connect-type activities

Link related definitions

If the definition of one term includes words defined elsewhere in the glossary, consider linking each of these terms to its definition. This is especially important in a field in which novices would have trouble understanding definitions otherwise.

Calculators

One popular job aid is a job-specific numerical calculator. Such a job aid lets workers compute numbers directly, rather than having to recall formulas, perform calculations, or look up answers in complex tables. On-screen calculators may also eliminate the need to teach complex formulas.

Case study of an online calculator

Let's consider a case study of just such a calculator. Photographers frequently need to calculate camera settings for a particular shot. Such calculations involve relationships among aperture or f-stop, shutter speed, film speed or ISO, and exposure value.

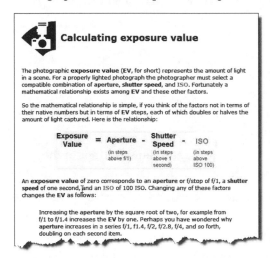

Photographers could calculate the desired values from formulas they have memorized.

A better approach might be to make the calculator run on a mobile device so photographers could slip it into a pocket or camera bag.

Build in Adobe Dreamweaver. View example at horton.com/eld/.

On-screen calculators remove unnecessary barriers to successfully applying what the learners know about a subject.

Best practices for calculators

Incorporate such calculators into your e-learning to relieve learners of the tedium of manual calculations.

▶ **Link to publicly available calculators**. Do not waste time replicating existing calculators. If calculations in your subject are simple, just tell learners how to use a standard calculator.

▶ **Make entering numbers easy**. Let learners input numbers by mouse or keyboard.

▶ **Use calculators to promote your e-learning**. Put the course emblem or department logo on the calculator. Include a link to launch an e-learning course on the concepts and principles supported by the calculator. Give away calculators freely. Demonstrate them in classroom courses.

▶ **Test and refine your calculators**. Make sure they cover the real-world situations your learners encounter. Survey practitioners to learn the range of values the calculator should handle.

E-consultants

E-consultants give advice. An e-consultant is a form that the learner fills in to describe a problem—a virtual interview. When the learner clicks the **OK** or **Submit** button, the form analyzes the learner's answers and recommends actions to take.

This e-consultant helps employees determine whether they can ethically accept gifts, favors, and entertainment.

First, the employee is asked what kind of gift is being considered. In this instance, the employee thinks it may be classified as cash or an equivalent. Not sure, the employee reads an explanation and determines it is cash. So, the employee chooses "Yes". The e-consultant advises the employee that accepting cash is unethical and what steps the employee should take.

Built in PowerPoint and converted to Flash with iSpring Presenter.

The e-consultant is used at the time a problem arises. It asks a series of questions, as if conducting an interview. Then it dispenses advice based on an organization's policies and procedures.

E-consultants are sometimes called soft-skills calculators because they deal with situations too complex to be reduced to a single, simple mathematical formula. Use them when a situation has a lot of conditions mixed with irregularities and exceptions.

When to use e-consultants

E-consultants work well for any complex decision that can be divided into separate decisions and governed by a moderately complex set of rules. These include management decisions, such as go/no-go decisions on a project or selecting among alternative suppliers; technical decisions, such as selecting among design strategies; or, any kind of problem-solving activity, such as diagnosing problems or recommending further tests.

Best practices for e-consultants

▶ **Do not try to handle every situation**. Cover the most common and most critical ones. It is better to create a job aid that lets 90% of people solve 90% of the problems than to create one that solves 95% of the problems but only 50% can use.

▶ **Refer learners to human advisors** and other sources of information. Link to e-mail addresses and give phone numbers of people who can help analyze the problem and recommend solutions.

▶ **Phrase questions simply** so someone under the stress of making a critical decision can understand them. The people most in need of advice may be the ones least able to understand complex questions.

Best practices for job aids

Designing job aids is not difficult so long as you keep in mind that they are first and foremost tools for use in the work environment.

Design for how the job aid will be used. If a job aid will be used to guide a learner in performing a procedure on the computer screen, keep it compact so it does not cover up too much of the learner's work area. If the job aid guides a procedure done away from the computer, design it for printing out.

Keep job aids compact and concise. As a rule, design the job aid so it fits in a single scrolling zone of the browser at its default size, or on a single piece of paper, if it will be printed out.

If printing out, format for paper. If a job aid will be printed out, make sure it prints on a single sheet of paper. Consider formatting the printable version in Adobe Acrobat PDF format so that you can control the layout more precisely than with HTML. And remember to allow for differences between A4 and U.S. paper sizes.

Make job aids stand alone. A job aid should work outside the context of your e-learning and should not require extensive training to use.

Do not make job aids into tutorials. A job aid is not a training tool. Making it into one destroys the unique value it has as a job aid. Use job aids to supplement and complement training, but not as training.

Use job aids to simplify e-learning. Just as job aids simplify work, so too can they simplify taking e-learning. Use calculators to relieve learners of having to make tedious calculations. Use reference summaries and task-specific instructions to guide them in using tools within your e-learning.

Replace courses with job aids. Do not develop a course if all people need is a job aid. Do not teach formulas if a calculator eliminates the need to learn the formulas. Do not teach concepts and terms if a glossary is what people really need. Instead, teach how to use the job aid and you may not need to teach the theory, concepts, procedures, principles, and other details encapsulated by the job aid.

Do not short-circuit learning. If you really need to teach a concept or procedure, do not give learners a job aid that obviates learning the concept or procedure. At least teach the concept or procedure first, and then let learners have the job aid.

Use job aids as mementos. Give learners job aids that they can continue using after your e-learning. These mementos will remind them of what they learned and where they learned it. Put your logo onto the job aid. Link it to your Web site.

Extend job aids

We can increase the reach and power of job aids by combining them with other types of activities and by adapting them for social learning and for mobile learning.

Combine job aids with other activities

▶ Include job aids where they will simplify other activities. Design activities to encourage learners to begin using job aids. Use reference summaries to summarize key points from a presentation (p. 69) or reading activity (p. 93). Include calculators in practice (p. 130) and guided-analysis activities (p. 137) that require performing calculations as part of the activity. Combine practice activities with reference summaries and checklists.

▶ Satisfy the curiosity aroused by a job aid. Link the job aid to instruction manuals that cover more situations and to presentations (p. 69) or readings (p. 93) that spell out underlying concepts and deal with exceptions to the rule.

▶ Look for more opportunities to use job aids in practice activities (p. 130), original-work activities (p. 207), games (p. 323), or guided analysis (p. 137).

Design job-aid activities for social learning

Have social learners:

▶ Collectively brainstorm, prototype, and refine a new job aid.

▶ Prepare a glossary, reference summary, or other job aid as a wiki, in which the group reviews, discusses, and refines entries.

▶ As a group, use a job aid to perform a complex task. At each decision point, the group discusses proper application of the job aid.

▶ Access a human job aid: coach, mentor, friend, or an entire social network.

Design job-aid activities for mobile learning

Have mobile learners:

▶ Access job aids from a mobile device. Ensure that the job aid displays quickly and legibly.

▶ Locate and load job-aid apps onto the mobile device. Available job aids include subject-specific handbooks, manuals, calculators, data recorders, and augmented-reality displays.

▶ Use publically available information sources, such as Google and Wikipedia, as job aids.

▶ Capture wall posters, Post-it™ notes, warning labels, and other job-aids built into machines and environments.

RESEARCH ACTIVITIES

Research connects learners to the whole world of knowledge by teaching them to learn on their own. In our complex world, research is a basic skill. Rote memorization of facts will not do. There is too much to learn, and what is accurate and applicable today is erroneous and inappropriate tomorrow.

About research activities

Research activities teach learners to gather, analyze, and report on information. Because they involve information, research could qualify as an Absorb activity. Because they require performing actions to gather information, they could be considered Do activities. I have classified them as Connect activities because the most valuable effect of research is to connect learners with the universe of knowledge on which they must draw to lead successful lives.

Technologies that let us instantly access large bodies of information have called into question the very definition of what it means to know something.

> The verb to know used to mean, having information stored in one's memory. It now means the process of having access to information and knowing how to use it. – Herbert Simon, Nobel Laureate

This view shifts the mission of education from putting facts in people's heads to giving people the tools they need to learn what they need when they need it, that is, conduct research. The editor of the *Harvard Business Review* put it even more bluntly:

> It's not what you know, it's how fast you can access all the things you don't know. And if you get that time down to a few seconds, then you effectively know everything. – Thomas Stewart, *The Wealth of Knowledge*

The ability to find information when needed is now basic education.

Types of research activities

Research is often a natural part of other types of activities, such as readings or discovery activities. Two main types of research are learning activities in their own right.

▶ **Scavenger hunts** (p. 198) challenge learners to identify reliable sources of information to answer questions and enable tasks.

▶ **Guided research** (p. 200) requires learners to consult various sources of information and opinions on a topic and then summarize their findings.

Although similar, these two forms differ in their purposes. Scavenger hunts teach learners to find reliable sources of information, whereas guided research teaches learners to draw conclusions from information.

How research activities work

In research activities, the learner considers a question or assignment, gathers data, and then uses the data to answer questions or solve a problem.

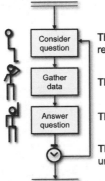

The learner reads and understands a question that requires research.

The learner conducts research to gather data.

The learner applies the data to answer the question.

The learner continues researching and answering questions until all questions are answered or time runs out.

Scavenger hunts

Scavenger hunts send learners out on a quest for answers and sources of reliable information on the Web or corporate and campus intranets.

The scavenger-hunt activity specifies the questions to be answered. It may specify additional information the learner must submit, such as the location where the answer was found, the method used to find it, the reason why it is the correct answer, conclusions drawn from the answer, and the category into which it fits.

The activity may recommend sources of information, or learners may be on their own to locate sources. Using these sources, learners answer the specific questions posed by the activity. Relying on the answer to the specific questions and on sources identified earlier, learners may answer a more general or abstract question. Submissions may be automatically scored or graded by a teacher.

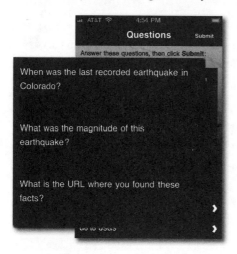

This example, designed to run on a mobile device, asks learners when the last recorded earthquake occurred in Colorado and its magnitude. Learners are also prompted to enter the URL of the page where the answer can be found.

To simplify search, the activity includes a link to the U.S. Geological Survey Web site, the official source for such information.

After locating the answer on the Web site, learners return to the **Questions** page to enter the answer and where it was found.

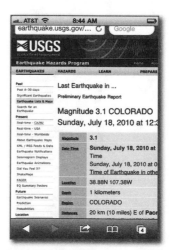

Built using Adobe Dreamweaver.
View example at horton.com/eld/.

ENDRUN Ethics Scavenger Hunt

Answer the following question and state where in the Endrun Code of Ethics the answer is found.

ENDRUN Code of Ethics

What is an approved gift for customers?

Answer | Where found
Display | Houston Ballet tickets. ▼ | Section 1.3 ▼
Check

You got the answer right but must have guessed because you got the location wrong. Next time you are in a gift-giving mood, check out Section 1.2 first.

Built using Adobe Flash. View example at horton.com/eld/.

Here, a learner practices resolving ethical concerns by answering a question on how to behave ethically in a common situation. The learner consults online information, in this case, a code of conduct, and then selects the answer from a drop-down list. In addition, the learner must specify where in the reference document the answer was found. Feedback guides the learner in more effective searches.

Learning a rapidly advancing body of knowledge requires learning how to keep current with changes in the field. For instance, programmers must have access to the latest information on a programming language, database technologies, and the various code libraries they use daily in their projects. Such information is quite volatile because producers are frequently releasing new versions of their tools as well as the inevitable patches, bug fixes, and work-arounds. With such volatility, printed documentation and classroom training cannot keep up. The programmer who relies on the tools and documentation that came in the box is left behind.

When to use scavenger hunts

Use scavenger hunts to teach learners to find their own sources of reliable information. This is especially valuable in fields in which the best, most up-to-date, most accurate information is found only online. In such fields, knowing where to find information is an essential skill in its own right. Use scavenger hunts to teach learners to:

▶ Find information on the Internet or intranet.

▶ Navigate a large reference document, such as a specification or technical manual.

▶ Retrieve information from a database.

Best practices for scavenger hunts

Keep the activity simple. Scavenger hunts do not have to be complex. They can be as simple as a list of five to ten short questions that learners can answer by consulting Web resources.

Show the value of information. To emphasize the importance of data gathered in the scavenger hunt, have learners use that data in calculations or in making decisions.

Focus on the goal of the activity. Emphasize that merely answering the question is not enough. The goal of the scavenger hunt is to identify reliable sources of information for use in the future. Require learners to identify the sources of their answers and to judge the accuracy of information provided by those sources.

Simplify scoring. To automate scoring, let learners pick from lists of pre-identified locations. If learners must type in locations, match them to a list of acceptable locations. Submissions with unmatched locations are routed to a human evaluator. If the location is OK, it is added to the list.

Challenge learners. To give the scavenger hunt more of a game flavor, add a countdown timer that imposes a visible time limit on searches.

Guided research

As its name suggests, guided-research activities coach learners on how to perform research in their subject-area. Learners are assigned a research topic. The topic may be a complex question or a series of simple questions. Learners, individually or in teams, gather the information necessary to answer the questions. Learners evaluate the information they have gathered, select relevant facts, and organize them. A teacher or facilitator may then grade reports prepared by learners based on the extensiveness of the research, accuracy of the facts, and logic of the organization.

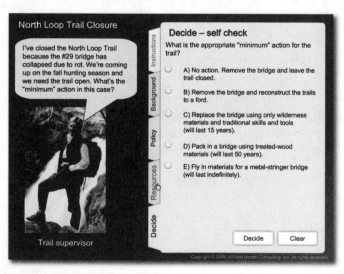

In this course for wilderness managers, learners start with the decision that needs to be made. If they understand the implications, they can make the decision right away. If not, learners can choose to review and explore supporting materials to help them make their decision.

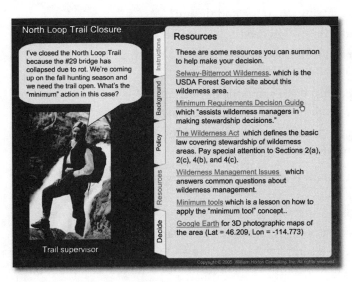

One of the tabs learners can choose is the **Resources** tab. It provides links to useful documents, job aids, and general information.

Created in Microsoft PowerPoint and converted for Web delivery using Adobe Presenter. View example at horton.com/eld/.

When to use guided research

Because guided research works well with individuals, teams, and entire classes, make it a staple of instructor-led e-learning. Use it to teach learners how to conduct informal research on a subject, especially if learners will frequently need to prepare reports summarizing their research efforts.

Although locating information and analyzing it are a part of guided research, these tasks are not the primary focus. Use guided research when you want to teach learners to evaluate, select, and organize information. To teach just information-gathering, use a scavenger hunt (p. 198). To teach analysis, use a guided-analysis activity (p. 137).

Variations of guided research

You can adapt guided-research activities for many different kinds of e-learning and for different class sizes—even classes of one. Here are some ideas on how to adapt guided research to your needs:

Personal perspectives

Rather than have each learner perform the same research task, pick a complex subject and assign each learner a different perspective to research. For example, a course on project management could research the case of the Swedish ship, *Vasa*, which sank on its way out of Stockholm Harbor on its maiden voyage in 1628. Perspectives to research would be:

▶ **Engineering**. What design flaws caused the ship to capsize and sink? Was naval engineering advanced enough at the time to have prevented the failure?

▶ **Managerial**. How did the management process of designing and building the ship contribute to its failure?

▶ **Social**. What social pressures contributed to the bad design?

▶ **Legal**. What were the civil and criminal proceedings that followed?

▶ **Historical**. How did Swedish history influence the design of the ship? How did the failure affect events afterward?

▶ **Aesthetic**. What features of the ship were symbolic or decorative? What was the role of aesthetics in design at that time? Did aesthetics contribute to the failure?

▶ **Scientific**. Why were the remains found virtually intact? How was the ship recovered and preserved? What did scientists learn by restoring it?

Learners can consider the research of all the different perspectives to augment their own.

Scrapbook

One popular form of guided research is the scrapbook. Here learners gather and organize knowledge on a subject. They create a scrapbook by cutting and pasting (not linking) resources. Learners can later post their scrapbooks to a forum for others to comment on.

Give learners instructions such as these:

> Visit the resources listed below. Collect text, pictures, statistics, bits of multimedia, and quotations important to your role and assignment. Assemble the pieces into a scrapbook, annotated with brief explanations of what they mean and why you selected them.
> Prepare a table of contents showing the logical organization of the materials you have collected.

Day in the life

Have learners research a current, historical, or fictional character and then write about what this person experiences on a typical day. Pick a person who has contributed to the subject matter of the course or who is an exemplary practitioner in the field. Or pick an ordinary person typical of a social class or profession.

Self-derived best practices

One form of research for practical subjects is to request learners to spot, analyze, and express best practices in examples of excellent work in the field of study. Here is how this activity might work:

▶ Start by presenting sources of dozens, or even hundreds, of examples of excellent work for learners to peruse. You can pick them yourself or select museum exhibits, award winners, or items frequently cited by experts.

▶ Next, direct learners to specific aspects of the examples. You may list characteristics to notice or ask specific questions about the examples. Or you might give learners specific categories in which to compare the examples.

▶ Then, ask learners to pick the best example in the category and state why it is the best. Instruct learners to repeat the process in another category.

▶ Finally, ask learners to generalize what the best examples have in common.

Criteria for comparison should ask questions an expert would ask but not be weighted to suggest an answer. You may want to include a worksheet to guide analysis and structure the activity.

Ongoing research

For a research project, require learners to keep and periodically submit logs of their research activities. The teacher can identify additional sources, suggest more efficient techniques, and challenge questionable resources. Once a week, require learners working as a team to submit a brief summary of their findings.

Best practices for guided research

Assist learners in locating reliable sources of information. Provide links or search terms that will reveal answers to some questions, but not all. Require learners to find analogous resources. Guide the research.

Emphasize the importance of evaluating, selecting, and organizing facts. Make guided research more than simply recording information found at the end of a Web search. Require learners to judge the accuracy of what they find, select the best evidence, and combine it into a coherent argument or explanation.

Use probing questions to guide research. Ask questions that require combining information from multiple sources. Require learners to sort out contradictory information or to separate fact from opinion. Ask why and how, not just when and what.

Best practices for research activities

Design to connect

Ensure that research activities connect learners to life and prior learning.

- ▶ Emphasize locating sources of information and the process of analyzing data, not just the results that answer individual questions.
- ▶ Offer learners a selection of information sources to choose from and require them to consult multiple sources.
- ▶ Require analysis and synthesis to teach learners to apply what they gathered through research.

Use the Web as a source of material

Both kinds of research activities benefit from the vast library of resources available on the Web. Amidst the sex shops, bigot-blogs, and watch-me Webcams are a treasure of case studies, reports, books, manuals, historical documents, databases, dictionaries, news, music, images, and cataloged data on every subject imaginable. Much of it is free. Before you start shoving material online for use in research activities, consider whether your time might be better spent designing an activity that relies on available Web resources.

Starting points for research. There are thousands of Web sites that can direct you to useful sources of information. Some of these Web sites are maintained by search engines, some by government agencies, some by universities, and some by communities of passionate amateurs. Here are some of these sources to consider as a starting point. Don't recognize the URLs? Well, check them out.

- ▶ **wikipedia.com** for articles on a vast variety of subjects.
- ▶ **dictionary.reference.com** for definitions of words.
- ▶ **urbandictionary.com** for the meaning of the latest slang and jargon.
- ▶ **etymonline.com** for the history of words and phrases we use.
- ▶ **earth.google.com** for 3D views of everywhere in the world (no kidding).
- ▶ **scholar.google.com** for scholarly papers and books.
- ▶ **images.google.com** for pictures of just about anything you can imagine.
- ▶ **books.google.com** for access to the text of millions of books.
- ▶ **uspto.gov** for thousands of patents describing a myriad of devices and methods.
- ▶ **sec.gov** for information on companies publicly traded in the USA.

Product literature and documentation. Today the Web sites for most companies provide detailed operating instructions, marketing literature, repair procedures, reference manuals, technical specifications, and documentation for their products and services. Use these materials in e-learning that involves selecting, operating, designing, evaluating, manufacturing, or recycling such products. Go to the company's Web site and click on **Products** or **Support** to start finding such resources.

Magazines and journals. Even paper-based magazines, trade journals, and scholarly journals now make articles, abstracts, and back issues available over the Web. Some charge for access to complete articles or back issues, but most provide free access to summaries of current articles.

Professional associations. If more than a few people perform a job activity, there is probably a professional organization with a Web site from which learners can get useful information regarding the principles, ethics, standards, job categories, skill requirements, and other aspects of the job. Of special interest to us designers of learning will be Web sites of user-groups for the products we routinely use. One sterling example of the valuable resources available on such sites is the National Association of Photoshop Professionals (www.photoshopuser.com).

Most professional association sites reveal their full riches only to members of the association. You may want to encourage learners to join. Or, you may need to restrict yourself to the freely available resources.

Government agencies. Increasingly, government agencies are making their collections of regulations, artwork, and scientific data available over the Internet. For example, NASA makes available 3D Landsat and Shuttle Radar imagery for the whole planet (worldwind.arc.nasa.gov). The U.S. Library of Congress (www.loc.gov) offers free access to maps, photographs, video clips, and librarians. The European Union On-Line (europa.eu) provides information on governance of the European Union. The United Nations provides similar information (www.un.org).

News networks and newspapers. Almost all major news-reporting organizations have Web sites that provide up-to-the-moment and archived articles and video clips on politics, technology, business, science, nature, entertainment, education, sports, medicine, travel, and law. Here are just a few to get you started:

▶ news.bbc.co.uk

▶ www.cnn.com

▶ www.wsj.com

▶ www.msnbc.com

▶ nytimes.com

▶ ft.com

Keep in mind that each of these organizations has its own perspective. Several have multiple divisions. For example, the *Financial Times* has separate Web sites for the UK, the U.S., Europe, and Asia.

Discussion forums and newsgroups. If more than a thousand people worldwide are interested in a subject, you can bet there is a discussion forum or newsgroup on the subject. Such online discussions provide a great resource to introduce learners to subjects as they are practiced in their field of study. They can also be a way to introduce learners to the petty bickering, narcissistic self-promotion, bombastic pontificating, and personal invective common out in the real world.

Have learners access a forum or newsgroup, lurk for a while, then join in the conversation, and finally report on what they have learned. Suggest that learners report on what the real function of the group appears to be. For what kinds of questions is it a good source? For which kinds is it not an effective source? Is its function primarily scholarly, job-related, or social?

Direct observation sites. Live Webinars have shown babies being born, hearts being bypassed, and sex being had. But not all sights on the Web are so spectacular. Some have solid educational value. NASA has a Web site called SkyView, where professionals and amateurs alike can view any astronomical body or phenomenon (skyview.gsfc.nasa.gov). Webcams let us view live images of the Ocean Tank at the New England Aquarium (www.neaq.org), various views of the USS Intrepid Museum (www.earthcam.com), or a volcano smoldering (www.fs.fed.us/gpnf/volcanocams/msh/). If you want learners to see it, just type the subject and the word *Webcam* into a search engine and see what's out there.

Extend research activities

We can increase the reach and power of research activities by combining them with other types of activities and by adapting them for social learning and for mobile learning.

Combine research with other activities

▶ Combine guided analysis (p. 137) and guided research to teach learners to identify sources of information, to extract facts from them, and to analyze the facts in detail.

▶ Follow presentations (p. 69) or readings (p. 93) with research activities to teach learners how to learn more on their own.

▶ Have learners conduct research to locate materials for reading activities (p. 93).

▶ Recommend presentations or readings to verify research findings or to round out discoveries.

Design research activities for social learning

Have social learners:

▶ Conduct research as a group. The group plans the effort, subdivides the task, conducts research separately, discusses findings, and draws conclusions.

▶ Share tips on research technique, sources of information, and results, especially if unexpected or hard to explain.

▶ Construct a scrapbook or wiki summarizing a broad research effort. Each learner originates one or more entries, and the group discusses and refines the entries.

▶ Investigate myths, urban legends, and conspiracy theories in their field of study. As a group, identify a questionable claim, decide how to prove or disprove it, conduct the test, discuss results, and publish conclusions and evidence.

Design research activities for mobile learning

Have mobile learners:

▶ Use mobile-devices to guide learners in accessing physical research sources, such as a reference library, museum, or newspaper morgue.

▶ Enable learners to conduct online research at the time and place at which they will apply knowledge.

▶ Gather information in a physical environment with commentary and clues located by GPS, bar-codes, or RFID chips (p. 510).

▶ Use photography, audio-recording, and video-recording to capture real-world evidence.

ORIGINAL-WORK ACTIVITIES

Original-work activities are the ultimate final exam—they require learners to apply learning to their own work. Learners must solve a real-world problem and submit their solutions for critique by a teacher or by fellow learners.

About original-work activities

Original-work activities encourage learners to begin applying learning to current projects.

When to use original-work activities

Original-work activities let you and your learners verify that they can apply learning to real work or future studies. Use original-work activities to:

▶ Verify that learners can apply what you are teaching.

▶ Ensure integration and synthesis of separate areas of learning.

▶ To serve as a final exam or practicum.

Types of original-work activities

There are several ways learners can perform original-work activities. The ones listed here represent different approaches you can take to conduct an original-work activity. You can combine some of these approaches quite productively.

▶ **Decision activities** (p. 208) require learners to submit decisions made at critical junctures in a real project.

▶ **Work-document activities** (p. 208) require learners to create a document that would be a part of actual work, such as filling in a form, creating a slide presentation, or writing a specification.

▶ **Journal activities** (p. 210) provide a way for learners to collect decisions into an ongoing document that they can review and take away at the end of the e-learning.

In social learning, comparison activities (p. 480) and group-critique activities (p. 481) provide additional original-work activities.

How original-work activities work

Original-work activities are a two-step process: First the learner creates original work and then the teacher or fellow learners critique it.

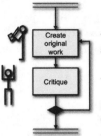

The learner creates an original piece of work as assigned.

The teacher or fellow learners critique the work.

Done? The learner may create additional pieces of original work or may revise a submission.

Decision activities

Invite learners to make decisions for real projects and to submit their decisions for critique. The decision may take the form of a small component of work.

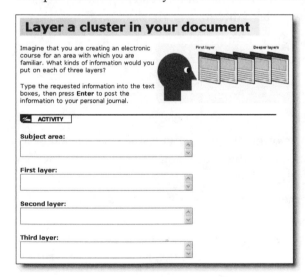

This example asks learners to make decisions on layering information for a project. Learners can choose a subject from their own work or studies. And that's what makes it original work.

Such a decision activity is simple and easier to evaluate for a teacher who may not know all the particulars of the learner's field of work.

Built using Adobe Dreamweaver.

Work-document activities

Much work and study requires producing official documents or giving presentations. One form of original-work activity requires learners to submit a real document from their work.

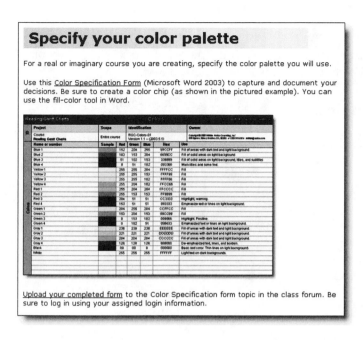

This example requires learners to specify colors for a Web site they are designing. They create their specification using a form downloaded as part of the activity.

Built using Adobe Dreamweaver and Microsoft Word.

Think about the work activities the learner engages in. What are the products of those activities? Any of these work products could be the basis of an original-work activity. For example, consider the work of a social worker and resulting documents.

Interviewing people	Recording, transcript, or report of the interview.
Recording data	Form filled in to record the data.
Recommending actions	Report with supporting documents.

Consider the wide variety of work products you can have learners submit:

- ▶ Writings.
- ▶ Plans.
- ▶ Procedures.
- ▶ Policies.
- ▶ Spreadsheets.
- ▶ Photographs.

- ▶ Reports.
- ▶ Designs.
- ▶ Sketches.
- ▶ Slide presentations.
- ▶ 3D models.
- ▶ Storyboard.

- ▶ Advertisements.
- ▶ Musical compositions.
- ▶ Video clips.
- ▶ Animation sequences.
- ▶ Audition tapes.
- ▶ Business letter.

Journal activities

Original work is ongoing. A journal activity can collect the pieces of work in a workbook, database, or discussion forum, where it can be reviewed and updated.

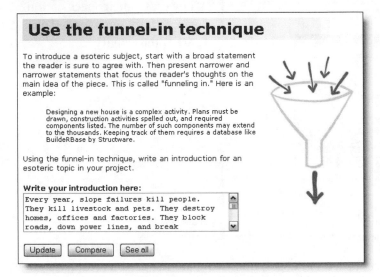

This example shows a journal activity. Each individual activity like this is written to a database. Once entered, the learner can revise it by making changes and clicking the **Update** button.

Clicking the **See all** button reveals the entire journal.

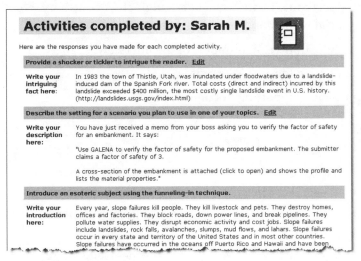

Here is the entire journal, displaying all the learner's entries so far. Each entry has an **Edit** button the learner can click to make changes to the entry.

Built using Adobe Dreamweaver and Active Server Pages

Journal activities are good after a learner has completed a significant piece of work. The Journal then contains the completed work, along with a clear trail of its creation and refinement. The journal activity is like the decision activity repeated over and over again for all the key decisions of an entire project.

Best practices for original-work activities

Specify criteria for critiques

Provide objective criteria for critics to use. Focus the critique on the work, not the person who created it. Make clear that personal criticisms are not helpful. Have learners suggest criteria for evaluation of their work. You may want to go so far as to provide a form to structure the critique.

If you were a venture capitalist with money to invest, how likely would you be to invest in the proposed business?

○ Not at all   ○ Unlikely   ○ Maybe   ● Likely   ○ Certainly

What was the main strength of the proposed business plan?

The main strength of the proposal was the realistic income
and expense projection for the next 5 years.

What was the best thing about how the business idea was presented?

Although the subject is serious, the style of the writing
was simple and easy to read. I also liked the concise
Executive Summary at the very beginning.

How could the presentation be improved?

I would have liked to see more details regarding staffing
requirements.

Here is a form eliciting a critique of a business plan.

Built using Adobe Dreamweaver.

Offer helpful comments

The teacher can promote helpful comments by offering some as an example. If learners seem reluctant to criticize the work of others, the teacher can start the process and establish a pattern of helpful comments. Two kinds of helpful comments include questions that require the learners to rethink their work and suggestions for improvement. Neither directly criticizes the work or the learner who submitted it.

Use revision features of word processors

If the whole class uses the same word processing program, you can have learners prepare a detailed, precisely formatted document in the word processor. Learners can use the revision features of the word processor to insert their comments into the body of the document.

Clarify what learners must submit

▶ Give learners a form to fill in or a template. For example, if learners must prepare presentations, give them a slide file with necessary slides containing placeholders for the kind of information you require.

▶ Remind learners to remove personal, proprietary, or secret information before submitting their work.

▶ Require learners to provide the context against which their work is to be evaluated, for example, the goals it is to accomplish.

Extend original-work activities

We can increase the reach and power of original-work activities by combining them with other types of activities and by adapting them for social learning and for mobile learning.

Combine original work with other activities

▶ Have learners conduct research (p. 196) so they can perform original work up to professional standards, so they can compare their work to that of experts, and so they know criteria to use in critiquing the work of others.

▶ Assign original-work activities that require learners to assemble their own libraries of reference materials (p. 98) and create their own job aids (p. 187).

▶ Have learners integrate presentations (p. 69) or readings (p. 93) into the original work.

▶ Prepare learners for original work by having them perform an analogous task in a simulation (p. 323).

▶ Supply a job aid for use in original work.

Design original-work activities for social learning

Have social learners:

▶ Produce a single piece of original work as a group. The group will need to discuss the work, analyze tasks required, subdivide the tasks, work separately on their assigned tasks, and then integrate their individual results into one work product.

▶ Work on individual original-work activities; but, periodically discuss their work with others in their group, receive advice from group members, and compare their work to that of others in the group.

▶ Call on the group for advice, critique, and inspiration throughout the work process.

Design original-work activities for mobile learning

Have mobile learners:

▶ Create real-world artifacts that are then evaluated by on-site experts.

▶ Record and communicate their decisions using media on a mobile device.

▶ Submit a photo, video clip, or audio recording of results.

▶ Use the mobile device to access instructions, plans, standards, job aids, or other documents needed in original work.

IN CLOSING ...

Summary

Connect activities ensure that people can apply what they learned. They do not usually teach knowledge and skills, but make existing knowledge and skills more useful. Connect activities range from a simple stop-and-think question to a full-scale work project. To design effective Connect activities; start with a clear idea of what you want to connect.

To connect this	To this	Use this type Connect activity
Individual principles, concepts, and other bits of learning.	The learner's work or studies.	Ponder activities, such as identifying examples.
Critical bits of information.	Gaps in the learner's current understanding.	Questioning activities.
Major themes in your e-learning.	The learner's life.	Stories told by the learner.
Procedures and policies.	The learner's professional work.	Job aids and original-work activities.
Limited information in your course.	The larger body of knowledge in a field.	Research activities.
Current information.	New information that the learner will encounter.	Research activities.

Pick Connect activities to accomplish learning objectives

This job aid ties the six types of learning objectives to common types of Connect activities. Along the left are the main types of activities. In columns are the six types of objectives. A circle at the intersection of a type's column and an activity's row means that the activity is recommended for that type objective. A black dot indicates a stronger recommendation.

4

Connect-type activities

Connect activities		Types of objectives					
		Create	Decide	Do	Know	Believe	Feel
Ponder	Rhetorical question		○			○	○
	Meditation	○				○	●
	Cite-example	○			○	●	
	Evaluation		○			○	
	Summary			○	○		
	Questioning		○	○	●	○	
	Stories by learners					●	●
Job aids	Glossaries				○		
	Calculators		○				
	E-consultant	○	●				
Research	Scavenger hunt	●	○		●	●	
	Guided research	○	●		○	●	
Original work	Decision		●	○			
	Work document	●	○	●	○		
	Journal	○	●	○	○	○	

For more …

Because the primary purpose of Connect activities is to ensure that learners apply what they learn, search the Web for combinations of these words: *education, training, learning, transfer, performance,* and *application.*

Connect activities seldom work alone. Be sure to consider Do activities (Chapter 3) and Absorb activities (Chapter 2) as partners.

Social learning activities easily serve to connect learners to co-workers, to work, and to experts. See Chapter 8 for ideas on how to use social learning for Connect activities.

5 Tests

Assessing learning

Educational experts underrate them. Instructional designers disregard them. Course authors overlook them. Learners fear them. We may cloak them as games or puzzles. We may put off writing them until there is not time enough to do them well. Whether we call them *tests, assessments, quizzes, drills, examinations, competence monitors,* or *demonstrations of mastery*, they, nonetheless, remain essential for gauging a learner's progress. And they represent an opportunity for clever designers to engage learners and provide objective feedback.

In my not-so-humble opinion, creating effective tests does more to improve effectiveness of e-learning than anything other than defining clear objectives—which creating tests also does.

What exactly is a test? Any activity that indicates how well learners meet learning objectives is a test. Any activity that provides feedback on performance of an objective can serve as a test.

DECIDE WHY YOU ARE TESTING

Before you begin writing test questions, make sure a test is warranted. Unless your reasons for testing are clear, your tests will fail.

When are formal tests needed?

Tests are difficult to create and administer. Often informal practice activities may be sufficient to teach a subject. In *Tests That Work*, Odin Westgaard lists three conditions for using formal tests with recorded scores:

▶ Learners require specific skills, knowledge, and attitudes.

▶ You do not know whether learners possess those skills, knowledge, or attitudes.

▶ A test is the best way to provide that assessment.

Otherwise, use some other kind of activity, such as an unscored practice activity or a survey.

Why are you testing?

Before deciding to test, list your goals. Here are some reasons for testing. Some are good, and some are not.

☺ Good reasons	☹ Bad reasons
▶ Let learners gauge progress toward their goals.	▶ Fulfill the stereotype that all e-learning courses have tests and all tests are unpleasant.
▶ Emphasize what is important and thereby motivate learners to focus on it.	▶ Reinforce the teacher's power over learners. Pay attention or else.
▶ Let learners apply what they have been learning—and thereby learn it more deeply.	▶ Torture learners. Training is supposed to be painful. Tests can ensure that it is.
▶ Monitor success of parts of the e-learning so that the teacher and designers can improve it.	▶ Artificially bolster learners' self-esteem by giving them easy tests with gushingly positive feedback.
▶ Certify that learners have mastered certain knowledge or skills as part of a legal or licensing requirement.	▶ Use a testing tool you paid a lot of money for.
▶ Diagnose learners' skills and knowledge so they can skip unnecessary learning.	▶ You can't think of any other way to add interactivity.

Consider testing carefully. Contradictions lurk within these lists. What learners want to learn may not square with what teachers want to teach. Knowledge required for certification may not be sufficient to actually do a job.

If sorting through this long list is too complex, let me simplify it. The reasons for testing usually boil down to a choice between teaching and measuring performance. Ask yourself, "Am I more interested in using tests to enhance learning or to accurately measure learners' abilities?" Although these two goals are not opposites, achieving each requires compromises in the other.

There is also a valuable side effect of creating tests. A test question is a concrete, specific statement of what the learner must do to meet the learning objective. Creating test questions precisely defines and clarifies learning objectives.

What do you hope to accomplish?

Consider your purpose for testing when you decide how to test, whether to record scores, and what feedback to give learners.

Purpose for testing	How to test	Record scores?	Feedback
Measure the progress of learners.	At the end of each topic, lesson, and course.	Yes.	Numeric, at end of test.
Help learners measure their own progress.	Frequent short tests.	No.	Descriptive and numeric.
Certify learners' knowledge.	Proctored, legally defensible tests.	Yes.	Pass-fail or overall score. May also provide scores for sub-components so learners can study and try again.
Certify learners' skills.	Observed accomplishment of prescribed tasks.	Yes.	Pass-fail or overall score. May also provide scores for sub-components so learners can study and try again.
Motivate learning.	Informal pre-tests.	No.	Recommended areas of study.

Purpose for testing	How to test	Record scores?	Feedback
Exercise independent-learning skills	"Open-book" test where learners can find answers in available resources.	No.	Recommended search targets and strategies.
Teach new knowledge and skills.	Informal, frequent, before presentation of content.	No.	Presentation of just the content that testing indicates the learner needs.
Diagnose learners' skills and knowledge.	Comprehensive test.	Yes.	Complete profile of what learners already know and need to learn.
Measure the effectiveness of learning modules.	Comparison of test scores between different modules and between modules before and after revisions of pre- and post-tests.	Yes.	--

What do you want to measure?

To design a test, you must know exactly what you want to measure. This is not a problem if you followed the procedure in Chapter 1, because you already know the specific learning objectives for your course, lessons, and topics. Review the learning objective for the unit of content covered by the test. Chapter 6 on topics contains some advice on tests appropriate for specific types of learning objectives (p. 299).

Watch out for the "as-shown-above syndrome (p. 314)." Learners do not always start at the beginning of the e-learning and proceed straight through to the end. Learners may jump into the middle of a topic in the middle of a lesson in the middle of the e-learning. Many consider this their right. They will consider you unfair if you test them on material not found in the section supposedly covered by the test—or in a clearly identified prerequisite section.

Once you have decided why you are testing and what you hope to measure, you can make tactical decisions on what kind of test to use. Let's look closer at the decisions you must make.

MEASURE ACCOMPLISHMENT OF OBJECTIVES

To design a test, we must decide how to test for a specific learning objective. We start with the learning objective. In this example the objective was: **To interpret dependency markers in a Gantt chart.**

Objective:	To interpret dependency markers in a Gantt chart.
Discriminating task (What can those who meet the objective do that those who do not meet the objective cannot do?)	Identify dependency relationships among the tasks of a project shown in a Gantt chart and interpret dependency markers to determine which tasks affect or depend on another task.
Test activity (How learners prove they meet the objective.)	Examine a real-world Gantt chart and answer five pick-one questions, such as what task depends on a particular task or what tasks must be completed before a task can begin.
Resources (Media and technology.)	▶ Graphic showing a real Gantt chart. ▶ Pick-one test.

The first step is to pick what is called a "discriminating task." To do so, we ask, "What can those who meet the objective do that those who do not meet the objective cannot do?" In our case, the discriminating task was:

> **Identify dependency relationships among the tasks of a project shown in a Gantt chart and interpret dependency markers to determine which tasks affect or depend on another task.**

The next step is to translate this discriminating task into a test activity. The test activity is how learners prove that they meet the objective. The test activity specifies how in e-learning we are going to simulate the real-world discriminating task. For our case, the test activity was:

> **Examine a real-world Gantt chart and answer five pick-one questions, such as what task depends on a particular task or what tasks must be completed before a task can begin.**

Finally, we list the resources we will need to create the test activity. These requirements are the media we must create and the technology we must deploy. In this case the list was short and simple. We needed a graphic showing a real Gantt chart and a testing tool to create a pick-one test.

By deciding how to test, we extend and clarify the learning objective. Our specified test activity now serves as our standard of performance to evaluate the learning objective.

SELECT THE RIGHT TYPE OF "QUESTION"

Any activity that can be scored by a computer or human can be a test question. For that reason, there are an unlimited number of test questions possible. In this section, we restrict ourselves to the types that are especially common in e-learning.

Throughout this chapter, I use the term *test question* rather than *test item*, even though some test items are not literally questions. Good test items at least imply a question. Anyway, it helps to think of test items as questions put to the learner.

Consider the type question you need

Before you decide to use a multiple-choice or matching-list question, take a moment to consider what kind of information you are trying to gather and what you are willing to do in order to get this information.

Subjective or objective?

Questions can be subjective or objective. *Subjective* test questions require human judgment to evaluate. They are sometimes called *open-response* questions because the exact form of the response is up to the learner. A composition question is an example of a subjective test question. Subjective questions are good for subjects without clear categories and ones that require finesse and judgment. Subjective questions usually require a human being to evaluate the answer and provide feedback.

Objective questions are ones with clear standards for correctness. They are sometimes called *closed-response* questions because the learner must select an answer from choices provided by the designer. For instance, multiple-choice questions are objective. Objective questions are good for mature subjects with established categories and well-accepted practices and principles. Objective questions can require subtle and sophisticated judgment, but they work best for questions with right-wrong answers. A computer easily scores objective questions.

Scored by computer or human?

Some types of test questions are easily scored by the computer. For example, multiple-choice, sequence, and matching item questions can be completely scored by the computer—as can simple fill-in-the-blank questions. Computer-scored questions make up in immediacy of feedback what they may lack in subtlety of evaluation.

More complex questions, such as text-entry questions that take more than a word or two, may require human evaluation. Human evaluation can better handle questions asking for subtle judgments, complex reasoning, and expressions of attitude. They do, however, require a human evaluator with the time, skills, and sensitivity to evaluate answers. Feedback comes only after a delay for scoring.

Common types of test questions

You can use a variety of test questions. This section introduces the most popular types. It is weighted heavily toward simple ones that can be created by a variety of simple tools and that can be scored by the computer.

Type question	Example	Use to measure the learner's ability to:
True/false (p. 222)	Does granite contain biotite? ○ Yes ○ No	Make categorical, either-or judgments.
Pick-one (p. 225)	Your best customer want to cut heating costs. What feature of the ThermoKAV would you disable? ○ Instant-on ○ Heat boost ○ Precision thermostat ○ Humidifier option ○ Particulate filter	Recognize the one correct answer in a list. To identify a member of a category or assign an item to a category.
Pick-multiple (p. 228)	**Practice your understanding** Practice developing information products. Which of the following statements describing the process of developing information are true and which are false?	Recognize multiple correct answers in a list. To recognize characteristics that apply to an object or concept.
Fill-in-the-blanks (p. 231)	Question 1: In the storage shed plan, how many calendar days does it take to frame the structure (Task 8)? [7]	Recall names, numbers, and other specific facts.
Matching-list (p. 234)	What chemical is responsible for each color in autumn leaves? Click a color and then the chemical that creates this color. Red, Green, Orange, Purple, Yellow → Chlorophyll, Phosphate, Anthocyanin, Carotenoids, Protein	Identifying associations between items in two lists, as between events and their causes or terms and their definitions.
Sequence (p. 235)	Rank these minerals by their hardness on the Mohs scale. Put the hardest mineral at the top and the softest at the bottom. You have three tries to get it right.	Identify the order of items in a sequence, such as chronological order or a ranking scheme.

Type question	Example	Use to measure the learner's ability to:
Composition (p. 237)	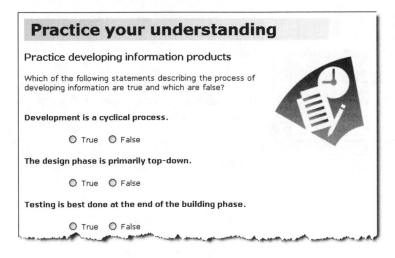	Create an original explanation, story, sketch, or other piece of work.
Performance (p. 240)		Perform a step of a procedure, typically in a simulation.

True/false questions

True/false questions require learners to decide between two alternatives, typically saying whether a statement is true or false.

Practice your understanding

Practice developing information products

Which of the following statements describing the process of developing information are true and which are false?

Development is a cyclical process.

    ○ True   ○ False

The design phase is primarily top-down.

    ○ True   ○ False

Testing is best done at the end of the building phase.

    ○ True   ○ False

Here are examples of true/false questions from a course on information architecture.

When to use true/false questions

Use true/false questions to test learners' abilities to make definite judgments. True/false questions require learners to make a binary decision:

- ▶ Is a statement right or wrong?
- ▶ Will a procedure work or not?
- ▶ Is a procedure safe or unsafe?
- ▶ Does an example comply with standards?

▶ Should you approve or reject a proposal?

▶ Which of two alternatives should I pick?

Before using a true/false question, consider other types of questions as well. True/false questions are restricted to simple cases and may encourage guessing. However, a well-designed true/false question that requires the same thought processes as the real-world activity is more accurate and valuable than a three-dimensional, immersive simulation that invokes only the decision-making skills of a twitch-and-splat videogame. And true/false questions are simple enough that learners can answer them quickly.

Questions need not have yes/no or true/false answers. Any mutually exclusive alternatives will do. Phrase the answer as a binary choice if that is more natural.

Watch out for cases in which the choices are not mutually exclusive or there really are more than two choices possible. Here is such a case:

Earth's atmosphere contains:

    ○ nitrogen   ○ carbon dioxide

The atmosphere of earth contains more gases than the two listed here. Although the percentage of nitrogen is more than that of other gases, the atmosphere does contain trace amounts of carbon dioxide.

Note: If your testing tool does not provide an explicit true/false test or if it does not let you change the labels for answers, use a pick-one question with just two answers. Or use a pick-multiple question that requires a series of related true/false judgments by asking, "Which of the following statements are true?" and then making each statement a choice.

Require thought

To make true/false tests effective, design them so they require thought rather than guessing.

▶ Ask more than one true/false question on a subject. The odds of getting them all right by guessing diminish with each additional question.

▶ For each subject, phrase true/false questions in different ways so that sometimes the right answer is false and other times it is true.

▶ Analyze your true/false questions to ensure about the same number are true as false.

▶ Phrase the question in neutral terms so you do not imply an answer.

Phrase the question to fit the answers

Make the question simple and straightforward. Do not ask what the learner *thinks* or *believes* unless that is what you are testing.

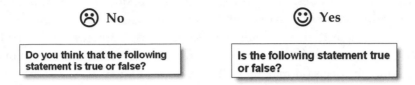

Often a statement followed by true/false radio buttons provides sufficient instructions.

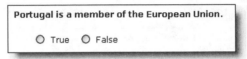

In true/false questions, phrase the question and answers so that the answers match the form of the question. Do not ask a yes/no question and then label the answers true/false.

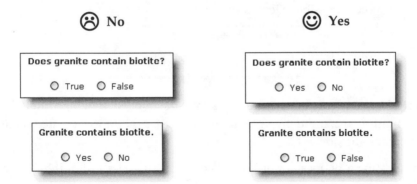

Discourage guessing

Many learners guess on a true/false question, figuring they have a 50-50 chance of being right. Unless you are teaching a course in probability or gambling, you should discourage such behavior. You can discourage guessing in several ways:

▶ **Penalize guessing**. In scoring true/false questions, give 1 point for right answers, 0 points for unanswered questions, and –1 point for wrong answers. Thus guessing is no better or worse than not answering.

▶ **Require higher scores**. Statistics to the rescue! The odds of getting 5 of 10 true/false questions right by guessing are 50%. But the odds of getting 80% correct are only about 5%.

▶ **Ask more questions**. Increase the number of true/false questions to 20 and the odds of getting 80% right by guessing drop to less than 1%.

Consider alternative forms for true/false questions

Most true/false questions are formatted as a pair of radio buttons, but any form that clearly implies a choice between opposites or between just two alternatives will do.

Graphical alternatives

Here are some graphical alternatives that have been used, with appropriate labels, in true/false questions:

Pick-multiple test

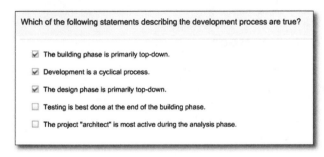

A series of related true/false questions can be converted to a single pick-multiple question, such as in this example.

Pick-one questions

Multiple-choice questions display a list of answers for learners to choose from. There are two main types of multiple-choice questions: *pick-one* and *pick-multiple*. Pick-one questions ask the learner to pick just one answer from the list. Only one answer is correct.

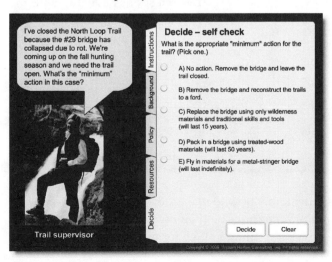

In this example from a course on wilderness management, learners are presented a scenario and asked the correct action to take in order to remedy the problem while complying with specific regulations.

Created in Microsoft PowerPoint. Test added using Adobe Presenter. Topic converted for Web delivery using Adobe Presenter. View example at horton.com/eld/.

When to use pick-one questions

Use the pick-one format for questions that have one right answer. They work well for activities that require people to assign items to well-defined categories, for instance:

- ▶ **Rating along a scale**. Ranking loan applications by degree of risk.
- ▶ **Recognizing a member of a specific category**. Picking the plant that is a member of a particular species.
- ▶ **Recognizing the main cause of a problem**. Diagnosing the most common cause of a flat tire.
- ▶ **Picking superlatives:** Picking the best, worst, greatest, least, highest, or lowest member of a group.
- ▶ **Selecting the best course of action.** Learners must weigh tradeoffs to choose among plausible actions.

Consider alternative forms for pick-one questions

Traditionally, pick-one questions present their answers as radio buttons and pick-multiple questions as checkboxes. Even if you need variety, do not reverse these forms. That would confuse learners. Instead, consider an alternative form.

Selection lists for multiple pick-one questions

If you want to ask several pick-one questions about a subject or if space is tight on the page, consider using a series of selection lists.

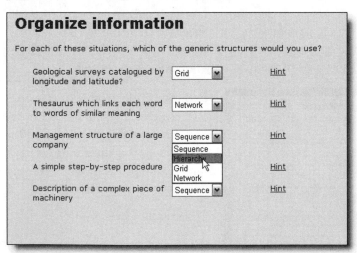

In this example, the selection-list format works especially well since all the questions have the same set of possible answers.

Built using HTML and custom JavaScript. View example at horton.com/eld/.

It does, however, mean that learners must know how to make a choice in a selection list. Most people figure out checkboxes and radio buttons on their own. Operating a selection list should be a problem only for the novices at filling in Web forms.

Click-in-picture questions for visual choices

If you want to let learners select among visual alternatives, you can present the choices as pictures and have learners indicate their choices by pointing and clicking. Because such questions are used primarily for visual subjects, they are treated as a separate type of question called a "click-in-picture" question.

Click-in-picture questions ask the learner to select an object or area in a picture by pointing to it with the mouse and clicking the mouse button. They are a visual equivalent of the pick-one question.

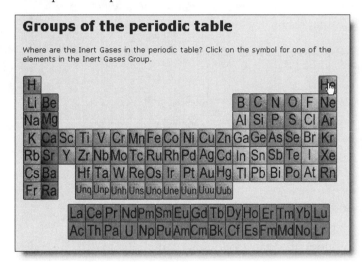

Here, learners are asked to identify a class of chemical elements by clicking an area in the periodic table.

Built using HTML and custom JavaScript. View example at horton.com/eld/.

Use click-in-picture tests to measure visual recognition of objects or areas. Use them to ask questions such as these:

What button would you press to trigger an emergency shutdown?

Who in this picture is not wearing required safety gear?

What country is home to our company's largest factory?

Click on the flag of the province where Mandarin Chinese is the official language.

Use click-in-picture questions instead of text pick-one questions when it is more important that learners know where something is or what it looks like than what it is called.

For click-in-picture questions, use clear images and write clear instructions.

▶ **Explain what learners are to select**. An area? An object? A point on a scale?

▶ **Make targets visually distinct**. Make them visually separate objects or areas with distinct borders.

▶ **Make targets large enough** so that learners with only average eye-hand coordination can quickly select them. The exact size depends on the device and the method of selection. A 20-by-20-pixel target may be fine when selecting with a mouse on a desktop computer with a low-cost monitor. But, such a target is way too small when viewed on an ultra-high-resolution screen of a smart phone where the learner selects by tapping things with a stubby finger. Follow the user-interface guidelines for the device learners will use to take tests.

▶ **Show the scene the way it would appear in the real world**, if simulating real-world activities, such as pushing buttons on a control panel.

Select along a scale for value judgments

To ask learners to express a relative value, you can request that learners select along a well-understood scale. For example, in a chemistry lesson you might ask:

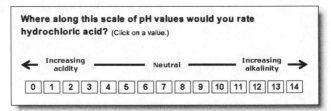

The learner can select a position along the scale by:

▶ Clicking on the scale.

▶ Moving a sliding icon to a position along the scale.

▶ Entering a number corresponding to a position along the scale.

▶ Selecting from defined positions along the scale (as in this example).

For scales where the learner must pick a position, include an odd-number of choices. This provides a neutral position so learners are not forced into a position. The neutral position removes the implication that the learner must make an either-or choice. And the neutral choice makes the question appear more objective.

Keep scale intervals equal and meaningful. It is usually OK to round numbers if that is how learners are accustomed to seeing the scale.

Pick-multiple questions

Pick-multiple questions let the learner pick one or more answers from a list of possible answers.

In the storage shed plan, what tasks depend directly on Task 7: Pour the driveway? (Pick all the apply.)

☐ Task 4: Prepare site
☐ Task 5: Pour slab
☐ Task 6 Remove driveway
☐ Task 8: Frame the structure
☐ Task 9: Roof the structure.

In this example, the learner can pick all answers that are correct.

When to use pick-multiple questions

Pick-multiple questions can be more sophisticated than pick-one or true/false questions. Use pick-multiple questions for asking questions with more than one right answer. Also use them for questions that require making a series of related judgments. For instance:

▶ Picking items that meet a criterion.

▶ Deciding when a rule applies.

▶ Making a quick series of yes-no decisions.

▶ Picking examples or non-examples of a principle.

Use a pick-multiple question to discourage guessing. The odds of guessing correctly are much less when the learner must select a specific combination of items.

Type question	Odds of guessing correctly
True/false	1:2
Pick 1 of 4	1:4
Pick 1 of 5	1:5
Pick multiple of 4	1:16
Pick multiple of 5	1:32

Each additional answer in the pick-multiple list reduces the odds of guessing the correct combination by half.

Pick-multiple questions are a compact way to ask several related true/false questions.

What are the characteristics of fluorite?
(Select all true statements.)

☐ Fluorite is colorless in its pure state.
☐ Fluroite has a hardness of 5 to 5.5 on the Mohs scale.
☐ The United States is the world's largest commercial producer of fluorite.
☐ Fluorite has a monoclinic crystal structure.
☐ The formula for pure fluorite is CaF_2.

This example asks five true/false questions. The point value of this question would of course be higher than five individual true/false questions to reflect the difficulty of getting all of them right.

Consider alternative forms for pick-multiple questions

Here are some alternatives that you may want to try:

Graphical pick-multiple questions

Let learners select items by clicking on them in a picture.

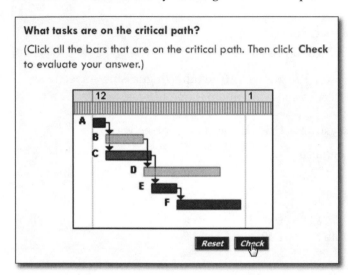

This example has learners select multiple bars on a chart to answer the question. Selected bars are highlighted.

Created in Microsoft PowerPoint and converted for Web delivery using iSpring Presenter. View example at horton.com/eld/.

Use click-in-picture tests to measure visual recognition of objects or areas. Use them to ask questions such as these:

> In what countries on this map does our company have sales offices?
> What items are allowed in carry-on luggage?
> What elements in the periodic table were discovered by Marie Curie?

Use graphical pick-multiple questions when it is more important that learners know where objects and areas are or what they look like.

Use clear images and write clear instructions.

▶ **Explain exactly what learners are to select**. Areas, objects, a range along a scale? Refer to the graphic ("on the map").

▶ **Make targets visually distinct**. Make them visually separate objects or areas with distinct borders.

▶ **Make targets large enough** so that learners with only average eye-hand coordination can quickly select them. Make targets at least 20-by-20 pixels as a minimum size.

If your tool does not offer a pick-multiple question

If your testing tool does not include a pick-multiple test question, you may be able to ask the same type question as a series of true/false questions. Each choice of the pick-multiple question becomes a true/false question.

Fill-in-the-blanks questions

Fill-in-the-blanks questions require learners to type in the answer to a question. Typically, these are short answers to very specific questions.

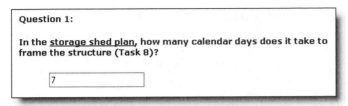

In this example, learners type in the number of days.

Fill-in-the-blanks questions require learners to supply missing words or numbers. The blank can occur within a sentence or at the end of a question. Multiple blanks can be sprinkled through a paragraph of text or across a table.

When to use fill-in-the-blanks questions

Use fill-in-the-blanks questions to verify that learners have truly learned the names of things. Use them to test recall of:

- ▶ Technical or business terms.
- ▶ Part numbers.
- ▶ Abbreviations.
- ▶ Commands and statements in a programming language.
- ▶ Vocabulary in a foreign language.

How to design a fill-in-the-blanks question

The most difficult aspect of designing fill-in-the-blanks questions is phrasing the question so that the computer can evaluate the answer.

- ▶ Make sure the context provides enough clues so that the learner can fill in the blank. Ensure that the introduction and context make clear exactly what is requested. One way to do this is to put the blank after a clearly phrased question rather than within a vague statement. Test your questions.

- ▶ Phrase the question to limit the number of correct answers. If possible, write the question so only one answer is correct.

- ▶ Phrase the question so that the answer can be evaluated based on the presence or absence of specific words or phrases, but not on the exact order or syntax of the answer.

- ▶ Accept synonyms (other words with the same meaning), grammatical variants, and common misspellings. Watch out for differences between British and American and Canadian and Australian English.

▶ Tell learners how to phrase their answers. Give an example of a properly phrased answer. Make clear whether the answer is to be text or numbers or mixed.

▶ If the question is complex, break it into separate questions, each with a simple answer. Do not ask two questions to be answered in one input box.

▶ Tell the learner the length, format, required parts, and other constraints on a free-form input. If you do not state a length, most learners will assume they can fill the input box.

Although automatic scoring of free-form text is not practical in most cases, you can write your question so that the completeness can be evaluated. For example, if you ask learners to compare various gemstones, the system could scan the learner's answer for the names of gemstones ("ruby," "diamond," "opal," and so forth) and for characteristics ("color," "hardness," and so forth).

Where possible, validate the form of the input right on the page before evaluating whether it is the correct answer or not. By "validate" I mean check for small mistakes that do not indicate subject-matter knowledge. For example, suppose you ask for a number. An engineer would probably not enter "One hundred ten," but you cannot be sure. A validation check examines the input to determine whether it is a number or text. If the input is not a number, the validation check throws up a caution and invites the learner to correct the form of the input.

Cloze questions

Questions with multiple blanks are sometimes called *cloze* questions. Such questions have been used for hundreds of years and are a staple of education.

Here is a classic example used to test knowledge of French grammar, syntax, and spelling.

Cloze questions work just like the paper workbooks in which students have to write their answers. With the e-learning version, learners fill in their answers by typing or by picking from selection lists.

As you can see, a cloze question is really just a tightly integrated series of fill-in-the-blanks or multiple-choice questions.

This function returns the screen coordinates for an object on a Web page, taking into account the location of the Web page, the scrolling zone, and the HTML container the object is inside of. Complete this function by selecting the appropriate Internet Explorer 5 properties from the select lists.

```
function agtGetCoordinates(theObject, XorY) {
    var parentElement = theObject
    var offsetsX = 0
    var offsetsY = 0
    while (parentElement. [tagName ▼] != "BODY") {
        parentElement = parentElement.offsetParent
        offsetsX += parentElement. [offsetLeft ▼] + parentElement.clientLeft
        offsetsY += parentElement. [offsetTop ▼] + parentElement.clientTop
    }
    elementX = window. [screenLeft ▼] + theObject. [Pick one ▼]
        + document.body. [Pick one ▼] + offsets      Pick one
                                                      tagName
    elementY = window. [Pick one ▼] + theObject.     offsetLeft
                                                      clientLeft
        + document.body. [Pick one ▼] + offsets      offsetTop
                                                      clientTop
    XorY = XorY.toLowerCase()                         screenLeft
    if (XorY == "x") {                                screenTop
        return elementX                               scrollLeft
    } else {                                          scrollTop
        return elementY
    }
}
```

This example uses selection lists from which learners pick words in a programming language to complete a function.

Built in HTML and custom JavaScript. View example at horton.com/eld/.

When to use cloze questions

Use cloze questions to measure learners' ability to apply knowledge within the context of a specific problem. Learners use a partial answer to figure out the complete answer. Use cloze questions:

▶ **To test incremental knowledge**. Learners know part of a subject and apply what they know to infer answers.

▶ **Where context matters**. Learners infer the correct answer from surrounding text or code.

▶ **To measure ability to apply verbal knowledge in context.** Learners guess the right words from the words that come before it and the words that follow it.

▶ **To ask complex questions.** Learners answer questions with multiple interrelated parts.

▶ **To provide scaffolding**. The context provides the support learners need early in learning a subject. Learners need not have mastered the knowledge supplied by the context.

How to design cloze questions

Make filling in the blanks simple and predictable so learners focus on answering the question.

▶ **Introduce the context**. Explain where the incomplete sample comes from and what it attempts to accomplish. For example, "Here is a paragraph from a Russian tour guide suggesting sights to see on your first day in St. Petersburg."

▶ **Explain the goal**. Tell learners what criteria they should use to fill in the blanks. For example, "Pick words that turn the paragraph into a concise summary of …."

▶ **Use a selection list** to let learners pick among several plausible alternatives if there are too many possible right answers.

Matching-list questions

Matching-list questions require learners to specify which items in one list correspond to items in another.

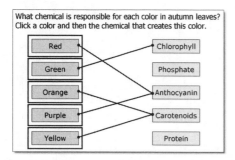

In this example, the learner chooses chemicals responsible for the respective colors of autumn leaves.

Created in Microsoft PowerPoint and converted for Web delivery with iSpring Presenter. View example at horton.com/eld/.

The lists need not be formatted as stacked lists of words. You can require learners to move icons or images to corresponding locations on the screen.

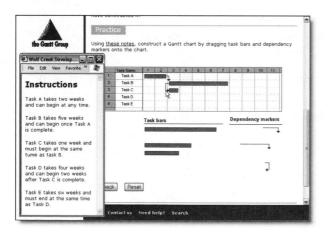

In this example, learners must drag elements of a Gantt chart into place to represent relationships among tasks of a project. Such drag-and-drop questions test the ability to assign items to the correct category or to arrange the parts of a system into a whole.

Built using Adobe Dreamweaver. View example at horton.com/eld/.

When to use matching-list questions

Use matching-list questions to measure knowledge of the relationships among concepts, objects, and components.

Use them to match:	With:
Questions	Answers
Terms	Definitions
Pictures	Captions
People	Titles or accomplishments
Tools	Their uses
Diseases	Symptoms or cures
Parts of one whole	Locations within the whole
Items	Their categories, their rankings along a scale, or their opposites

How to design matching-list questions

Make matching easy so that learners can focus their attention on the relationships between items in the two lists.

▶ **Write list items clearly**. Use familiar terms or provide a glossary for the learner to look up terms.

▶ **Keep the lists short so that they both fit in the same display.** If they do not fit, give the learner a button to jump back and forth. Generally seven items are plenty.

▶ **Do not mix categories within a list.** Include only comparable items in each list.

▶ **Let learners indicate matches simply.** Rather than having them type the letter or number of the matching item, let them select it from a list of choices, drag it from one list to another, or draw lines between items.

▶ **Eliminate the "process-of-elimination" effect** by including more items in one list than the other, by letting one item match more than one item in the other list, or by letting learners choose "None" if an item has no match in the opposite list. In instructions, tell learners of these possibilities.

Sequence-type questions

Sequence-type questions ask learners to put items into a sequence from beginning to end by some rule or according to some principle. Learners are presented with a list of items in an incorrect order. They must move the items to put the items into the right relative positions within the list.

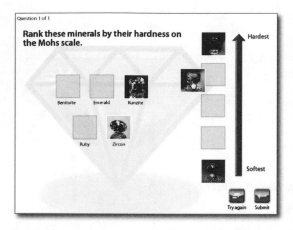

This example asks learners about the relative hardness of five minerals. Learners drag pictures of the minerals into the appropriate slot before clicking the **Submit** button to see which items are in their correct positions.

Built using Adobe Captivate. View example at horton.com/eld/.

When to use sequence-type questions

Use sequence-type questions to measure learners' ability to put items into a meaningful order. They ask learners to make judgments about the relationships among items in the list. Use sequence-type questions to test a learners' ability to sequence:

- ▶ Historical events by date.
- ▶ Steps of a procedure by order performed.
- ▶ Phases of a process by the order in which they occur.
- ▶ Logical arguments in inductive or deductive order.
- ▶ Innovations by a chain of dependencies.
- ▶ Rankings of value.
- ▶ Properties of objects, such as size, weight, or importance.
- ▶ Remedies by probability of success.
- ▶ Diagnoses of symptoms by probability.

Sequence-type questions are also valuable in polling, especially for subjective questions, such as value.

Communicate the desired sequence clearly

Make the sequence activity clear, simple, and fair.

- ▶ **Do not use sequence-type questions if there is more than one right sequence**. Even if your scoring procedure would accept all correct answers, learners may still feel the question is unfair. In general, avoid sequence-type questions when the sequence is subjective.
- ▶ **Use only distinct items familiar to learners**. Do not require learners to guess what items mean or conduct research during the test.

▶ **Specify the criterion for the sequence**. For instance, specify ("in chronological order"). Also specify the direction of the sequence ("from earliest to latest dates").

▶ **Specify only one criterion for the sequence**. Avoid complex criteria, such as "by primary and secondary constituents" or "by technology and then by year developed."

Score fairly

Ensure fair scoring of sequence-type questions. Simple scoring can be a problem. The nature of the sequencing task means that one item out of place can render the answer incorrect, even though the learner knew the relative positions of all other items.

Such strict scoring may be appropriate if the question is about steps in an emergency procedure. In other cases, it may unfairly penalize the almost-right answer. Some solutions:

▶ Give partial scores for items near their correct location.

▶ Score each item individually so the ones in correct final position win some points.

▶ Use sequence-type test questions for practice when scores are not recorded.

Consider alternative forms for sequence-type questions

If your testing tool does not provide a sequence-type question (and many don't), consider asking the question in some other form:

▶ Use a matching-list question to match items with their positions in the sequence.

▶ Number the items in a list and have learners enter the numbers of the items into a fill-in-the-blanks question.

Composition questions

Composition questions ask learners to write an essay, draw a picture, or write a song. They ask for an original analysis, opinion, or other piece of work. Composition questions are just scored original-work activities (p. 207). By far, the most common form is the essay question, but other media can be submitted as well.

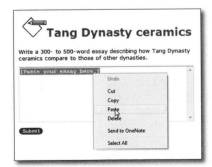

This example asks for a free-form answer that learners can prepare in a text-editor and then paste into the text box.

Built using plain old HTML.

Composition questions are most commonly used in instructor-led e-learning. They ask subjective or open-response questions. They require human evaluation.

When to use composition questions

Use composition questions to evaluate complex knowledge, higher-order skills, and creativity. Typical uses include questions that require learners to:

▶ Synthesize an original solution to a problem.

▶ Recognize and express complex or subtle relationships.

▶ Analyze a complex object or situation.

▶ Form and justify an opinion by weighing evidence.

▶ Resolve conflicting opinions and contrary evidence.

Do not use composition questions when answering them would place too much of a physical burden on learners. For example, entering long amounts of text on a mobile device without a keyboard would prompt learners to be unnaturally brief, to use extreme abbreviations, or just to skip the question altogether. Better to substitute another type of question that can be answered more easily.

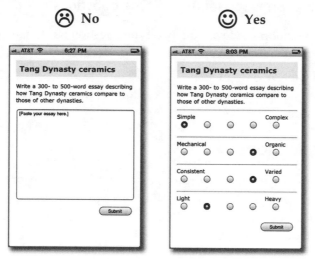

Built using Adobe Dreamweaver.

Designing composition questions

▶ **Require breadth and depth in answers.** Ask questions that require considering more than one aspect of the subject and going beyond surface details.

▶ **Require original thinking.** Do not reward "parroting" material from the course, teacher, textbook, or other sources.

▶ **Disallow copy-and-paste responses.** Do not let learners include the words or works of others as answers, except as clearly identified quotations or examples. And require an original explanation of why the item was included and how it supports the learner's original answer.

▶ **Let learners respond in the medium of their choice.** If the subject is writing, it makes sense to require a written response. However, if the subject is business, let learners submit their answers as a voice recording, a PowerPoint slide, or a video clip.

▶ **Be specific.** Do not say "List a solution" when you mean "Explain the least-expensive solution." Precise questions filter out trivial or obscure answers. Mention any constraints on the answer. Tell learners the requirements for a good answer.

▶ **Guide responses.** Give learners a model or template for structuring their response. The problem with many open-response questions is that they are too open.

▶ **Limit the number of composition questions.** They are tiring. After about a half-dozen such questions, all you are measuring is stamina.

Scoring composition questions

Write specific scoring guidelines (commonly called *rubrics*) to guide teachers in scoring answers and providing feedback. In such scoring guidelines, specify objective requirements for an acceptable answer:

▶ Characteristics of the answer. Length. Format.

▶ Items it must include. Facts it must mention. Media it must use.

▶ Relationships among items.

▶ Conclusions the learner should draw.

▶ Recommendations the learner should make.

Here is part of a rubric for an assignment in a management course. It helps the facilitator evaluate learners' responses.

Assignment 2.2	Grading criteria
■ If the learners list the skills and talents needed to build, promote, and *deploy*, make sure they include a. technical support b. subject-matter experts c. facilitators d. administrators These positions are clearly listed in Table 10-1 of Leading E-learning. Failure to do so indicates that they are not looking beyond the development phase and have lost sight of the fact that this plan includes deployment. ■ If learners recommend staffing levels, they need to justify their numbers. AND make sure that this section is consistent with the previous section on skills needed. ■ For outsourcing, make sure they justify why or why not. Why should e-learning be or not be a core competence?	If learners identify and address all three points—the missing skills, justify their staffing recommendations, and make a persuasive argument about whether to outsource or not— they get an A. If the writing is clear and well-structures, give them an A+. If they identify and address two out of the three issues, give them somewhere between an A- and a B-. If they identify address only one of the three issues, give them a C. If they take a whole different approach, make sure they explain it. You will have to make a judgment call whether the new approach will work or not. You need to be careful about not stifling their creativity. Add or subtract points either way to reflect the quality of their answers. If you feel that the learners just got off to a bad start, you can be a bit more lenient in the grading. Quite frankly, it is a judgment call.

List examples of ways the learner may answer the question. Include both right and wrong answers, along with the feedback each should trigger. List signs of common mistakes, such as incorrect statements or items often omitted.

Writing such rubrics is basic instructional design—and it is hard work. It is essential if someone other than the author of the course will score the composition. This is true whether the course is offered in a classroom, online, or by some other method. Such objective guidelines are especially important in e-learning because anxious learners may be hypersensitive to test scores and they may expect computer-like objectivity in every aspect of the course.

Alternative forms for composition questions

Essay questions are not the only possible form of a composition question. Consider including a button to let learners record a voice answer or upload a recorded audio file. Or, include a similar button to upload an answer from a video camera. Another option is to require learners to create their compositions using a template you supply. You might have them download, fill in, and submit a PowerPoint or Word template with placeholders for required elements of the composition.

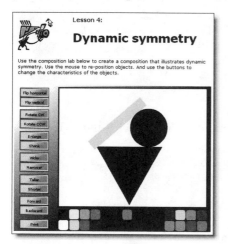

In this example, the learner must drag and drop and flip and flop shapes to create an abstract visual composition that meets a design goal.

To see another example, visit www.wildlifeart.org/Rungius/ home.html.

Built using Adobe Flash and Dreamweaver. View example at horton.com/eld/.

Performance questions

Performance questions require the learner to perform actual work. Each step of the work that can be scored individually serves as a separate test question.

5

Tests

In this test, the learner performs the steps to create a system data source name in a simulation. Each step of the simulation is scored. Because the learner did not perform this step correctly, a message is displayed telling the learner that no points were scored for that step and telling the learner how to proceed to the next step.

Built using Adobe Captivate. View example at horton.com/eld/.

Performance questions measure learners' abilities to perform complex activities. If learners accomplish the assigned task in the performance test, they pass and can presumably perform the real activity.

When to use performance questions

Performance questions help us test whether someone can perform a task. When should you use them?

▶ You are testing the ability to perform a procedure rather than abstract knowledge about a subject.

▶ The procedure is complex; requiring learners to make decisions, not merely follow a sequence of steps.

▶ The speed of performing the task is important to its success.

▶ You are qualifying people to perform a task in the real world.

Performance questions are not limited to tasks that are performed on the computer. You can use "gatekeeper tasks" (p. 136) as performance questions to verify that learners have successfully performed a step in a non-computer task.

Performance test questions that require simulation can be expensive and time-consuming to develop—typically 100 times the cost of a simple multiple-choice test question. Often they are worth the expense, but not always. Use simulations for performance questions when:

▶ Other types of test questions cannot adequately measure performance.

▶ Having learners perform the task on a real system could be dangerous.

▶ Using a simulation simplifies scoring the activity and integrating it with other types of test questions.

How to design performance questions

Simplify the test. A performance test should measure ability to perform a task, but not teach that task. Do not expose the learners to more choices and options than necessary to test for the target objective.

State the goal clearly. Tell learners exactly what they must accomplish to pass the test. Spell out any restrictions. Must they accomplish the goal using a particular method or feature? How long can they take?

Explain the question. Make sure learners know how to answer performance questions. If they must operate a simulation, tell them what buttons they can press, what knobs they can turn, and what switches they can flip.

Reveal the limits. No performance question or test is a perfect copy of the real-world task. How does the test differ from the real world? What are the limits on actions learners can take? If using a simulator, tell learners what dangerous aspects of the real system are harmless in the simulator and what features and capabilities are turned off.

Spell out scoring rules. If the test is not graded pass/fail, spell out the criteria for awarding points. Are learners rewarded for the quantity of work accomplished? Are they penalized for the amount of time they took, the number of actions used, or minor mistakes made along the way?

Pick type question by type objective

The following job aid will help you pick the type of question to use in testing for each type of learning objective. Along the left are listed the types of learning objectives. Across the top are the types of test questions. Circles indicate recommended types of questions to use for each type of learning objective. Black dots represent stronger recommendations.

Types of learning objectives	Types of questions							
	True/false	Pick one	Pick multiple	Fill in the blanks	Matching list	Sequence	Composition	Performance
Create an X that does Y.							●	○
Decide Y.	○	●	○		○	○		●
Do procedure X to accomplish Y.						○		●
Know X about Y.		○	●	○	○			
Believe X.	○					○	○	●
Feel X about Y.	○					○	○	○

WRITE EFFECTIVE QUESTIONS

To test learning, you must translate your learning objectives into test questions. Nowhere is precise, clear language more necessary. Questions are effective only if all learners understand them and can answer them the way you intended.

Follow the standard question format

Although many different types of test questions are possible, they share a common anatomy. Here is a typical test question with its parts labeled.

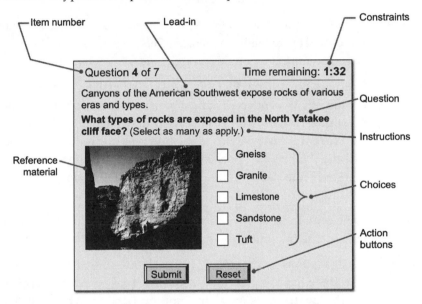

Let's look at the parts of a typical question and how to design them.

Part	Description
Item number	Indicates the place of this question in sequence. For long tests and timed tests, the number helps learners budget their time. It gives them a sense of progress as they move through the test.
Lead-in	Provides background information or context for the actual question. Use a lead-in to keep the actual question simple. A lead-in can be necessary if questions appear in random order or are chosen from a pool. The lead-in makes the question more independent of other questions.

Part	Description
Question	The question is the specific sentence the learner must respond to. Usually it is phrased simply as a question. For more on questions, look through the rest of this chapter, especially the segment starting on page 244.
Instructions	Instructions tell the learner the procedure for answering the question and any limits on how the question may be answered, for example, how many items should be selected or how many words can be entered. Learn more about instructions starting on page 246.
Choices	True/false, pick-one, and pick-multiple questions have learners select their answer from a list of choices. See the segment starting on page 255 for advice on designing choices for test questions.
Action buttons	Learners must signal that they are ready for their answers to be evaluated. Most often clicking a button such as **Submit**, **Evaluate**, or **Next question** does this. The learner may have other buttons to erase the current answer, return to the previous question, or exit the test. The exact labels are not as important as picking words that communicate clearly to the learners what will happen when they click the button.
Constraints	Time remaining or any other limitations on how the learner can answer the question.
Feedback	Feedback may be presented after each question or at the end of the test. If feedback is presented with each question, it may appear in an area below the question or in a pop-up window. The feedback can range from "Correct" or "Incorrect" to complete explanations of the answer and links back to related content. For aiding learning, meaningful feedback is crucial. See the section starting on page 263 for advice on giving feedback.

Ask questions simply and directly

Simple questions are easier to understand, to answer, and to score. Direct questions seem more objective and fair to learners.

Phrase questions precisely and clearly

Unless learners can understand the question, they cannot answer it. The difference between a clear and an unclear question may be just a single word or punctuation mark.

Take a little extra time to make sure your questions ask what you want them to.

Use the simplest language possible. Tests put learners under stress. Those learners may have varying language skills. Some may be taking the test in a second language or may suffer from reading difficulties such as dyslexia. Use of language not understood by all can even pose a legal problem if it penalizes certain groups relative to others.

Phrase questions as questions

If possible, phrase the test question as a simple, standard question. Use the canonical question format:

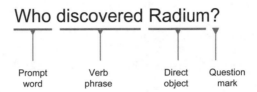

This is the form familiar to young children and new speakers of English. (If you are writing questions in another language, just use the standard format for questions in that language.)

The prompt word alerts the learner immediately that this is a question, and the question mark confirms it. No question about it: this is a question.

The prompt word announces that this is a question and specifies the type of answer requested. We are all familiar with Rudyard Kipling's six honest serving men: what, who, when, where, why, and how. Use them like this:

Use	To ask for
What	An object, process, or event.
Who	A person or a group.
When	A time, date, or place in sequence.
Where	A location.
Why	A reason, cause, or justification.
How	A procedure or process.

These are sufficient for 90% of the questions we ask. And no, I didn't forget *which* …. *Which* is usually inferior to *what* in asking test questions. Do not ask "Which of the following is …?" when you could ask "What is …?"

Put background information before the question

Do not supply new information in a question. For complex questions, supply background information in a lead-in to the question. Phrase the lead-in as simple declarative sentences.

No   Yes

> How is the tropical disease known as dengue (breakbone fever or dandy fever) and characterized by acute fever, chill, headaches, muscular and joint pain, and skin eruption, transmitted?

> Dengue is a tropical disease. It is also known as breakbone fever and dandy fever. Its symptoms include acute fever, chill, headaches, muscular and joint pain, and skin eruption. **How is dengue transmitted?**

Sometimes after moving the background information to the lead-in, you discover it is not necessary. Then delete it. Many times, however, background information is necessary to clarify the context of the question or fully identify a term in the question.

Include instructions on how to answer

If learners might not know how to indicate their answers, put instructions immediately after the question proper. For example:

> What chemicals are responsible for leaf colors? (Drag each chemical over the color it produces.)

Where might such instructions be necessary?

▶ In pick-multiple questions to tell learners they can pick more than one answer.

▶ If not picking any answer is an option.

▶ In a drag-and-drop activity wherein learners might not know that objects are movable.

▶ In fill-in-the-blanks or essay questions when spelling, punctuation, and capitalization matter.

Ask yourself whether 95% of your learners will figure out how to answer the question without any instructions. If not, add instructions.

Instructions are crucial for performance questions because they tell learners precisely what they must do to "answer" the question.

Phrase questions and answers simply

To ask questions that all learners will interpret exactly as you intended, just use language as simply and directly as possible.

KISS—Keep It Simple for Students

The challenge in a test should be answering the questions, not interpreting them. Tricky wording is a special problem for anxious and impatient readers—especially ones reading in a second language.

Here are some recommendations for keeping it simple:

▶ Stick to simple sentences. Avoid complex sentences with embedded clauses.

▶ Use standard spelling and punctuation. Begin each choice with a capital letter and end it with a period.

▶ Use common terms familiar to the learner. Provide a glossary for any technical terms you must use.

▶ Use blank space to distinguish questions, instructions, choices, and action buttons.

▶ Keep questions short; say no more than 10 or 12 words. Include only necessary words.

▶ Phrase choices so they match answers the learner may recall when reading the question.

▶ Keep choices short—a single line if possible.

▶ In negative test questions, emphasize the word **NOT** or its equivalent.

Remove ambiguity

Take special care to avoid ambiguous language in questions and answers. Some common problems include these:

▶ **Ambiguous terms**, such as "can not," which could mean "possibly not" or "not possible."

▶ **Fancy words** that not all learners will recognize. If a simpler word works, use it. Do not try to show off your vocabulary.

▶ **Double negatives**, such as "When should you not reject …?" If possible, ask the question in the positive sense, such as "When should you accept …?" At least untangle the logic. If you can ask a question in a positive form, do so. If you cannot, keep the form simple and emphasize the negative word.

▶ **Indefinite questions**, such as "Do you think that 3 + 5 is 7?" Is the question about mathematics or opinion? Take special care with phrases like "Does it seem that …?" or "Does it appear that …?"

▶ **Unrecognized humor.** Learners may take a humorous comment literally or be annoyed by your casual attitude to what to them is a nerve-wracking experience.

▶ **Metaphors, irony, or other figures of speech** that are unfamiliar to learners. Many such expressions are specific to a particular culture or language. Consider this question: "What military commander pulled a hail Mary on the day after Christmas 1776?" Answering depends on knowledge of a sports metaphor based on the name of a prayer.

Ask just one question at a time

Phrase questions so that only one answer is required. Do not ask or imply a second question, as does this shameful example:

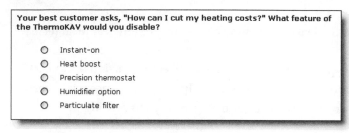

This example asks two questions. The first asks how to cut heating costs and the second asks what component wastes energy.

Rephrase the question to something like this:

Your best customer wants to cut heating costs. What feature of the ThermoKAV would you disable?

○ Instant-on
○ Heat boost
○ Precision thermostat
○ Humidifier option
○ Particulate filter

Now the example asks a single question.

One form of compound question is useful, but it must be designed with care. This is the what-and-why question. It asks learners to pick an answer and the reason why it is the best answer.

You are photographing an automobile race. What exposure mode should you select?

○ Shutter-priority mode so you can avoid motion blur.
○ Aperture-priority mode so you can control the depth of field.
○ Aperture-priority mode so you can capture more saturated colors.
○ Programmed mode because it is the most flexible.
○ Shutter-priority mode so glints do not fool the light meter.

This example asks not only for the correct choice but for the correct reason as well.

Use this form for subjects where the real-world answer to questions often is "It depends." Phrase the question clearly, and make sure every choice has both the what and why parts. Set up a pattern among choices and stick to the pattern.

Emphasize important words

In phrasing questions, emphasize small crucial words on which the meaning of the question depends—words that could cause the learner to misinterpret the question if not read correctly. Here is an example:

> What item is not an example of romdibulation?

Usually the most critical words are reversing or constraining words: *not, only, just, one, first, last,* and so forth. Emphasize the word, but not by underlining it, as learners are likely to interpret underlined words as hypertext links.

Ask application-related questions

Phrase your questions so that they resemble the kinds of decisions learners will have to make when applying the knowledge and skills you are teaching. Phrase questions so they re-create what would actually occur on a job. Here are some suggestions:

Set the scene

Set the scene using questions that might come from a customer, the boss, a subordinate, an angry co-worker, or a friend.

 No

> What are the three methods of peer mediation identified by Professor Morty Cerebrum?

 Yes

> John, a co-worker, bursts into your office. He collapses into your guest chair and mutters, "I'm either going to quit or throw my simpering weasel of a boss out the window!"
>
> How do you respond?

If you cannot imagine the question being asked in the real world, then why are you asking it in a test?

To ensure you are asking more application-related questions:

▶ Base your questions on performance objectives rather than enabling objectives (p. 19).

▶ Put the learner into the question. Present a situation and ask, "What would you do?"

▶ Ask questions that are more life-like in what they require the learner to decide or do, even if this means asking fewer questions.

▶ Establish a realistic scenario, introduce a problem, and then ask several questions about that problem.

Ask in the mode of application

Test-writers tend to ask questions verbally. This may be OK for learners who are verbal, but it is not fair for those with limited language skills. Nor is it accurate for tasks performed visually or physically.

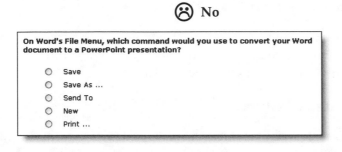

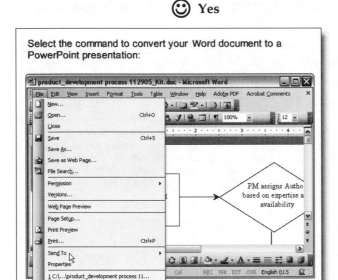

The pick-one question above uses words to ask for knowledge about a task performed visually and kinetically. The simulation mimics the real situation and requires exactly the same abilities, as does the real task.

Match the type of test question to the way knowledge and skills will be applied after learning:

How applied	Type test question
Verbally	Text questions, such as pick-multiple, pick-one, or fill-in-the-blank. (p. 225 to 234)
By locating something	Click-in-picture question (p. 227).
Software task	Simulation of performing the task. (p. 335)
Physical task	Performing the task and then answering a *gatekeeper* question about the results (p. 136).
Making yes-no decisions	True/false question based on information used to make the decision. (p. 222)

Base questions on a scenario

To make testing more engaging and more predictive of real-world performance, base questions on a scenario. Make the scenario a situation that learners expect to face and that requires what you are teaching. This example, from a food-safety course, requires the learner to decide what to do with a cooked turkey that was left cooling on a kitchen table.

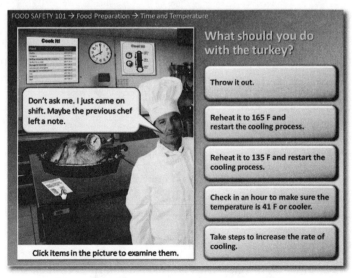

The learner can get information from the scene, for example, by clicking on the chef. Not all information will be helpful—just like in the real world. The learner can examine a note left by a previous chef. Such a note may reveal critical details not immediately obvious. The learner can also examine wall posters. These represent job-aids commonly available in commercial kitchens. The learner can also examine the clock to get the time or the thermometer to get the current temperature of the turkey.

By examining the scene, the learner gets enough information to make a choice. Wrong choices give corrective feedback. Correct choices confirm the learner's decision.

What does it take to make a scenario-based question? First, the scenario must require learners solve a practical problem. The problem is based on a specific situation rather than a general or abstract condition. The scenario may include human characters who may advise the learner. These characters may also add challenge by misleading or distracting the learner. The learner may have access to general reference materials that would be available in the real scenario.

The point is that the learner must investigate scenario-specific details because the correct choice depends on these details. As a result, the learner cannot simply answer based on general principles but must apply the principles to the specific details of the scenario.

Creating a scenario-based question is more work, but learners appreciate the authentic challenge and sponsors appreciate the accurate prediction of future job performance.

Avoid common mistakes

Inexperienced test-writers often write questions they later regret. Let's review some common mistakes and see how to avoid them.

Prevent obsolescence

Avoid questions whose answers may change over time. In rapidly changing fields, new developments or a new version of software can change the answer to such questions.

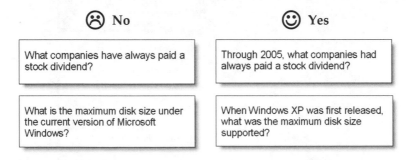

Be careful when asking absolute questions

Absolute questions assume rigid categories with razor-sharp boundaries. Beware questions like these:

Are _____ ever _____?
Is _____ always _____?
Are all _____ _____?

A single exception changes the answer. Learners can be quite clever in tracking down that one obscure, minor, nearly unknown exception you forgot about.

Avoid absolute words in questions and answers. Absolute words include *all*, *every*, *entirely*, *everybody*, *completely*, *altogether*, *always*, *exactly*, *no*, *none*, *never*, and *nobody*. Also take care with extreme words such as *most*, *almost*, *nearly*, *barely*, and *hardly*.

Avoid "all of the above" and "none of the above"

Take special care with answers of the form "all of the above" or "none of the above."

> **PDQ Corporation offers hourly employees which of these benefits?**
>
> ☐ Medical
> ☐ Prescription
> ☐ Dental
> ☐ Optical
> ☐ None of the above
> ☐ All of the above

Do you see the Escheresque logic in this question? Right. For "All of the above" to be true, "None of the above" must also be true. But if "None of the above" is true, then "All of the above" cannot be true. No combination of answers is logically possible.

In pick-one questions, an "all of the above" choice violates the form of the question, suddenly shifting from pick-one to pick-multiple. "All of the above" is also grammatically inconsistent with the form of the question. Instead of including an "all of the above" choice, simply change the style of the question to a pick-multiple.

In general, forego "none of the above" and "all of the above" as choices. But if you do use "none of the above" and "all of the above" answers:

▶ Always make "None of the above" the last choice.

▶ Do not use these choices just to fill out a list of choices. Try to think of more plausible answers.

▶ Remember to turn off the randomize-answers feature of your test tool as it could put these choices anywhere in the list.

Do not repeat phrases from the text

In phrasing questions, paraphrase rather than repeat exact phrases from the course materials, textbook, or reference materials. Savvy learners, taking an online test, can just type distinct phrases from the question into a search engine and wait for the results to pop up. There are two exceptions, but they are rare: You are teaching use of a search service or you want to search rather than memorize.

How to cheat on an online test (or how to prevent cheating)

Many online tests require no subject-matter knowledge, only a dollop of technical savvy and a dab of curiosity. Here is our guide on how to cheat on an online test—or things to prevent in online tests you create.

▶ **Pick the choice that differs from others** in length, tone, specificity, or grammar. Unskilled test writers have trouble designing incorrect choices that resemble the correct choice.

▶ **Mouse around** to see what appears in status messages and tool-tips. Developers find these features helpful in debugging tests, but they sometimes forget to disable the features in the final version of the test.

▶ **Scan the whole display**, including window titles and all small print. If the text does not give away the answer, it may make the question ambiguous, which learners can use to protest their grade.

▶ **Use the browser command "View Source"** to examine the underlying HTML code. Often the code may contain comments that indicate which choice is correct or what answer is expected.

▶ **Look for absolute words** like *all*, *always*, *every*, *any*, and *never*. Complex situations are seldom as absolute as test designers think.

▶ If questions are scored equally, **answer easy questions first**, for example, true-false and pick-one questions. Scoring should reflect the difficulty of answering, but inexperienced designers often lack the confidence or knowledge to assign appropriate weights to test questions.

▶ **If in doubt, pick "All of the above."** Unskilled designers tend to include this choice where it applies and omit it where it does not.

▶ With A-B-C-D choices **pick C**. With A-B-C-D-E choices, **pick C or D**. Why? Because that's where amateur test-designers put the answers.

Think back on tests you have taken. Can you list some more ways to get a better grade on a test without studying? Just make sure these techniques do not work for the tests you design.

To create many questions, specify patterns first

If you must create many test questions, consider specifying patterns to guide writing individual questions. Here is an example of patterns for test questions in a suite of courses on sales skills. Each paragraph specifies the pattern for a family of questions.

How do you respond to *{repeat customer, new customer, product reviewer, educator}* **who requests** *{customary pricing, discount pricing, free sample, loaner unit, technical information, etc.}*?

What products [pick from list] are most/least **appropriate for [purposes, customers, situations]?**

What are acceptable/unacceptable **ways to** *{install, set up, start up, operate, shut down, transport}* **[product]?**

What is the *{profit, revenue, sales commission, etc.}* **for the sale of [number] units of [product] at [percent] discount?**

The bold, black text appears "as is" in the question. The other pieces of text are placeholders for text that varies from question to question.

The italic words in curly braces are choices. One will be used for each question.

The light gray items separated by forward slashes are alternatives. One question uses the first alternative and another question uses the second one.

The bold gray words in square brackets are instructions on how to pick words for the actual question. Typically words in square brackets name a category, such as products, from which individual items can be picked for each variation on the question.

A simple specification like this one can prescribe hundreds of consistently phrased but unique questions. Use such patterns when you have to create many different questions or when test questions are written by subject-matter experts or others without specific training in writing test questions.

Make answering meaningful

Some tests encourage learners to guess rather than think about the answer. By listing incorrect answers, multiple-choice tests may cause learners to remember the wrong answers rather than the right ones. To avoid these problems, encourage learners to think carefully about their answers. Make sure learners understand all their choices in pick-multiple, pick-one, and true/false questions.

Make all choices plausible

Make all answers equally plausible to someone who has not yet learned the subject. Make each choice a natural response to the question. To test the plausibility of each choice, read aloud the question, immediately followed by the answer. To be plausible, all choices should be equivalent in length, grammar and syntax, complexity, specificity, and scope.

Keep all answers about the same length

Make all answers approximately the same length. Or at least make sure that the longest answer is not always the right one. Guess which of these answers is right:

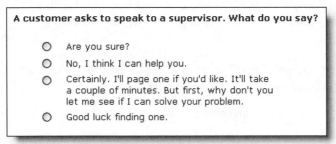

A customer asks to speak to a supervisor. What do you say?

○ Are you sure?

○ No, I think I can help you.

○ Certainly. I'll page one if you'd like. It'll take a couple of minutes. But first, why don't you let me see if I can solve your problem.

○ Good luck finding one.

Make all choices grammatically equivalent

Make all choices grammatically similar. Double-check that each answer is compatible with the question, especially if the answers are offered as potential completions of a lead-in phrase.

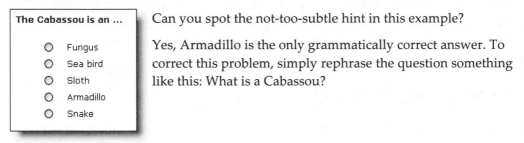

The Cabassou is an ...

○ Fungus
○ Sea bird
○ Sloth
○ Armadillo
○ Snake

Can you spot the not-too-subtle hint in this example?

Yes, Armadillo is the only grammatically correct answer. To correct this problem, simply rephrase the question something like this: What is a Cabassou?

Make choices parallel

Phrase all answers at the same level of abstraction, generality, and degree of common usage.

What are the colors of the standard BX-1000 snowboard?
○ Red and green
○ Blue and yellow
○ Pink and purple
○ Crazy Carmine and Yowzah Yellow
○ Gray and blue

Can you guess the right answer to this question?

All the colors are common ones—except those in the correct answer.

Simplify selecting answers

Reduce the effort required to indicate the correct answer. Minimize the amount of typing and the degree of eye-hand coordination required.

▶ Let learners choose the answers in multiple-choice tests by clicking on the items. Clicking on the text should have the same effect as clicking on the associated radio button or checkbox.

▶ If multiple-choice answers are presented visually, let learners answer by clicking on the pictures.

▶ Do not number choices that learners select by clicking on them. Numbers or letters before a choice imply that the learner selects by typing the number or letter.

○ A. True

○ B. False

Unfortunately, some test-creation tools insist on numbering all answers.

Keep choices concise

Do not repeat words in each answer that could be put in the question.

What are the differences between hornblende and biotite?
☐ Although both biotite and hornblende can be black in color and both occur in granite, only hornblende contains sodium.
☐ Although both biotite and hornblende can be black in color and both occur in granite, hornblende crystals are triclinic and those of biotite are monoclinic.
☐ Although both biotite and hornblende can be black in color and both occur in granite, hornblende is harder than biotite.
☐ Although both biotite and hornblende can be black in color and both occur in granite, biotite cleaves in one dimension while hornblende cleaves in two dimensions.

In this example, notice how much text is repeated in each question.

> **What are the differences between hornblende and biotite?**
>
> ☐ Only hornblende contains sodium.
>
> ☐ Hornblende crystals are triclinic and those of biotite are monoclinic.
>
> ☐ Hornblende is harder than biotite.
>
> ☐ Biotite cleaves in one dimension while hornblende cleaves in two dimensions.

Now notice how much easier it is to compare the answers when the repeated information is removed.

Put choices in a meaningful order

List choices in an order that helps learners find the correct answer. For example:

If choices:	List choices in this order:
Are numbers.	From least to greatest.
Are events.	Chronological order.
Vary by a common characteristic.	Increases or decrease in that characteristic.
Have no inherent order.	Alphabetical or random order.

Express choices simply

Keep the noise out of your questions by expressing choices simply and directly. Do not require mental efforts just to untangle the question or choices.

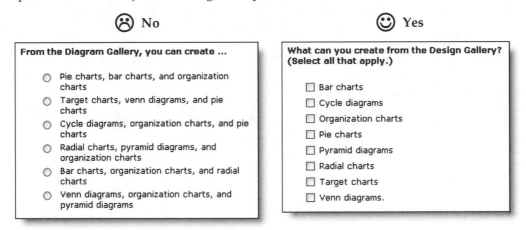

Beware of compound choices, of irrelevant details in questions and answers, and of words or symbols unfamiliar to learners.

Challenge test-takers

Good test questions require learners to think deeply about the subject matter in order to arrive at an answer. However, many questions do not appropriately challenge learners. Some designers fear scaring or offending voluntary learners. Others fear damaging the

5

mythically fragile self-esteem of learners. Many problems occur when good designers carelessly give away the answer to the question.

Require learning

In a too-easy test, little subject knowledge is required to pass the test, just a keen eye, a logical mind, and a bit of luck. Let's take a look at a too-easy test.

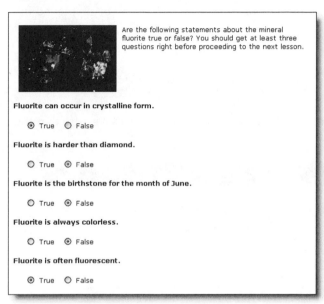

Notice that the first and fourth questions can be answered by looking at the picture. The second compares the mineral to the one other mineral whose hardness most people are familiar with. Most people could answer the third question by recalling that June is the month when many people get married and diamonds are used for engagement rings. The last question can be answered by connecting *Fluorite* to the similar word *fluorescent*.

Because only three correct answers were required, learners need little more than luck and cleverness to pass the test.

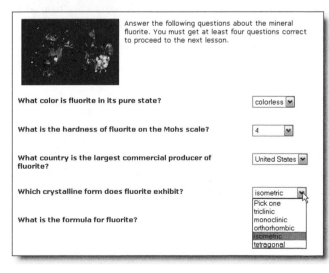

This example shows a test that actually requires knowledge of the subject matter.

Here the questions are harder. There are more choices per question. And the passing score eliminates guessing as a reasonable strategy.

Both bad and good tests were built using Adobe Dreamweaver and custom JavaScript. View examples at horton.com/eld/.

Supply enough plausible choices so that the answers are not too easy to pick out. Provide at least three plausible alternatives similar enough that the learner has to read them carefully and think deeply.

Do not give away the answer

Do not reveal the answer in a window title, file name, message, or URL. If tests involve scripts or external files, make sure that the URL or file name, which may be displayed in the browser's status bar, does not give away the answer. Suppose the learner points to a potential answer and the status bar shows one of these messages:

 or

If the question asks which picture shows a Gothic Revival style house, make sure that the title of the pop-up window is not:

Likewise, be careful if the answers are evaluated by scripts in the same Web page in which learners enter their answers. Technically astute learners could view the source of the file and read the scripts to see which answer is right.

Vary your pattern

Vary the position of the correct answer in a list of choices. Amateur test designers are less likely to make the first or last answer the correct one. Skillful test-takers who need to guess will pick the third of four choices. For five choices, they opt for the third or fourth. Not a sure thing, but it does put the odds in their favor. So analyze your answers to make sure the correct answer occurs throughout the range of answers. Or, use a tool that can shuffle answers so that each time the question appears, the answers are in a different order.

COMBINE QUESTIONS EFFECTIVELY

To create an effective test, you may combine test questions written separately at different times, perhaps by different test-writers. Your test may need to include questions to test multiple learning objectives or a high-level objective. What must you, as a designer, think about as you compose a multi-question test?

Ask enough questions

Include enough test questions to accurately gauge learners' understanding in the subject. Consider the number of learning objectives the test must cover. For a single, simple objective, three well-designed pick-one questions may be adequate. More complex objectives will require more test questions and more sophisticated test questions.

Also consider the purpose of your testing. To give learners a general indication of how well they are doing, you need fewer questions than you would to legally certify that learners can perform a dangerous task.

Don't forget to consider how what you are teaching will be applied. If your subject will be applied in widely varying situations, you may need a wider variety of test questions to accurately predict learners' ability to apply learning. You cannot cover every situation, but you can ask questions that span the range of application.

Make sure one question does not answer another

In a series of test questions, one question may ask about a subject mentioned in another. Often one of the questions provides unintended information that indicates the answer to the other.

What does the Fraud-D-Techt feature do?

- ○ Informs customers of bank holidays
- ○ Spots fraudulent transactions
- ○ Verifies checks are completely filled in
- ○ Maintains anti-virus software on the bank's servers

What feature spots fraudulent transactions?

- ○ Check-o-matique
- ○ Detectafraud
- ○ Fraud-D-Techt
- ○ SecureTrans

Can you guess the answers to these two questions?

Notice how the first question provides a clue for the second question, which provides a clue for the first question.

Make questions independent. Answering one question should not affect a learner's ability to answer subsequent questions. Make sure that the wording of one question and its answers do not imply the answers to subsequent questions.

Sequence test questions effectively

Most tests consist of a sequence of questions. Consider how separate questions are best combined for a comprehensive test.

Ask multiple questions about one scenario. For complex subjects, create a series of test questions based on the same situation, scenario, or description. Make it easy for the learner to refer to the original explanation. Either display the scenario in a separate frame or window from the questions or link back to the original explanation from each question. Repeat salient facts in each question.

Ramp up the difficulty. Let learners warm up on simple questions. Learners who cannot answer any of the first three questions are likely to despair and not sincerely try later ones. Or, they may spend so much of their time on the initial difficult questions that they do not get to the easy ones within the time limit of the test. Vary the difficulty of test questions so that no one completely fails and yet few get a perfect score. Start with the simpler questions. In that way, learners taste success and are motivated to continue trying.

Keep the sequence short. Few people like long tests. Four or five questions make a nice pop quiz. A dozen are enough for almost any sequence. A test containing more than 15 questions is a police interrogation. If you feel these limits are too restrictive, break your test into multiple short tests and sprinkle them among the presentation of material.

Enable navigation. If practical, let learners skip back and forth among the questions, answering the ones they can and skipping over the ones they cannot. Either put all the questions onto the same Web page or include navigation buttons to skip among the pages of a test. Make sure that skipping over a question does not lock in an answer until the time limit expires.

Vary the form of questions and answers

To keep a series of questions from becoming monotonous, vary the style and phraseology of the questions and answers.

- ▶ **Mix different forms of questions**: pick-multiple, fill-in-the-blanks, matching list, performance. Mix different media. Ask questions visually and verbally.
- ▶ **Design each question to test for a different common misconception**. Ask different kinds of questions, such as what, when, why, where, and how.
- ▶ **Vary the form of questions**. Ask learners to pick the right answer. Then the one wrong answer. Then the best answer. Ask which of a list of statements do apply, then which do not apply.
- ▶ **Vary the position of the correct answer** in multiple-choice lists. However, if several questions have the same list of answers, do not vary the order of the answers.

▶ **Arrange test questions in a predictable pattern.** For example: pick-one, pick-one, pick-one, pick-multiple, pick-one, pick-one, pick-one, pick-multiple, and so on. Learners should concentrate on the questions, not their format.

Such purposeful variety makes testing more robust. The results do not depend on learners' verbal skills or ability to answer one kind of question.

GIVE SIGNIFICANT FEEDBACK

After learners answer a question, they crave feedback. Did I get the right answer? No? Why not? What's wrong with my answer? What did I misunderstand? How can I correct my misunderstanding? Provide such feedback.

Report test scores simply

As soon as possible, tell learners how well they did on the test. For example:

Congratulations. You passed.	or	Sorry. You failed.
Your score: 85. Passing score: 75.		Your score: 66. Passing score: 75.
Continue with the next lesson.		Review the summary and retake the test.

Relieve the anxiety and let the celebration or remediation begin. Report scores simply and directly. Tell learners three things: their scores, the passing score, and the effect of their scores. Learners then know how well they did and what they should do next.

Provide complete information

Tests can teach too. Feedback on test questions can correct misunderstandings and augment knowledge. For each answer, consider including:

▶ **The question**. Repeat or re-display the question. If questions are numbered, include the question number.

▶ **Right/wrong flag**. Avoid vagueness. Do not say "Almost" or "Not quite" but simply "Wrong" or "Incorrect."

▶ **The correct answer**. Do not make learners repeatedly answer a question hoping they guess the right answer. A five-choice pick-multiple question can be answered 32 ways. That's a lot of guessing.

▶ **The learner's answer**. Learners may not have entered what they thought they did.

▶ **Why the correct answer is right** (and, if necessary, why the learner's answer is wrong).

▶ **Link to the original presentation** or a remedial one on this subject. Also include instructions on how to resume after reviewing the material.

Score Card

Score: 110 of 230

Question 1:

Correct. You use InStrRev to return the first place within a string that another string occurs, from the end of the string. 50 of 50 points.

Question 2:

Incorrect. The Mid function returns a specific portion of its input text string. 0 of 25 points.

Question 3:

Correct. The filter property limits the file types shown in the Open File dialog box. 25 of 25 points.

Question 4:

Incorrect. You should review these text manipulation functions again. You got 2 of 6 right. 10 of 30 points.

Here is a simple example of helpful feedback. It annotates the learner's answer to provide the necessary feedback.

Briefly acknowledge right answers. Tell learners they were right. Be enthusiastic, but do not be effusive. For positive feedback, all you need to say is "Correct," "Right," or "Yes." Anything more would interrupt the learner's momentum.

If your primary goal is teaching rather than measurement, you may want to ignore this advice and supplement the feedback for right answers. You may want to tell the learner why the right answer was right (the learner may have guessed).

For right answers, you can challenge learners to think about how they got the right answer and to consider other methods.

> Right. How did you get your answer? Did you calculate it in your head? The math was pretty simple. What would you do for a more complex case?

The feedback for a correct answer can teach additional information. You already have the attention of a happy, receptive learner. Use it.

Question 4: **Correct**. Summarizing the customer's complaint shows that you were listening to her. It is also a good way to get her to agree to your interpretation of the problem before you continue.

Notice how this example adds related information?

Keep the feedback brief, or the learner will not read it. Most of the time learners are satisfied to know they got the question right.

Gently correct wrong answers

For an incorrect answer, gently but clearly point out the problem. Help learners overcome their misconceptions.

Use a neutral term

For negative feedback, use a neutral term, such as "incorrect" without any exclamation points, please. You can also use "sorry" or "not quite," although these may seem a bit patronizing. Do not say, "WRONG!!!" or "Gotcha" or "I don't think so."

Tell why answers are wrong

Tell learners why their answers were wrong. For pick-multiple questions, make clear why each choice was right or wrong.

> The correct answers are Doyle and Scribner.
>
> Doyle and Scribner are both common methods of measuring the lumber volume of trees. Cordage is a measure of the volume of cut wood and is used for pulpwood. IDN and Wocon are just made-up terms and have nothing to do with forestry.

Do not embarrass or insult the learner

Do not shout at people if they get something wrong—no flashing headlines or embarrassing noises.

> **You ...**
>
> # Failed
>
> ... the test.
>
> You got 6 of 10 questions correct. This is **NOT** an acceptable score. To pass you must get at least 7 of 10 questions correct.
>
> Perhaps you did not pay attention while taking the lesson or did not have the prerequisite knowledge to take this lesson or this course.
>
> In any case, you must repeat the lesson and achieve an acceptable score on the lesson post-test before you will be allowed to take subsequent lessons.

How would you like to receive this feedback? The word *Failed* appears in a blood red color and jiggles on the screen, accompanied by a chorus of boos. Also notice the condescending tone.

Built using Adobe Dreamweaver. View example at horton.com/eld/.

Acknowledge partial success

Give learners credit for the questions they got right. Encourage learners to try again. Give them choices so they feel in control. Notice how this feedback acknowledges an almost-passing score and suggests alternatives for how the learner should proceed.

> Your score: 72
>
> Passing Score: 75
>
> Because your score was close to a passing score, we recommend you review the summary topic and then retake this test.
>
> Or, you could just retake this test. (You will see new questions.)
>
> If you feel you understand the subject well enough, you can proceed to the next lesson. Or, if you prefer a more in-depth review, you can restart this lesson.

Avoid wimpy feedback

Compared to the computer games that players love, much e-learning gives timid feedback. In a game, you always know exactly how well you are doing. If you fail to perform, the game mocks you or your character dies. I am not suggesting we abuse or decimate our learners; just consider a bit more direct approach. Avoid weak and vague feedback messages like these:

> Good try, but you could have done better.
> We're sorry, but that is not the best answer.
> Almost. Would you like to try another guess?
> Close, oh so very, very close.
> Oh, too bad.
> Bummer!

Simply say "Right" or "Wrong" and explain why the answer was right or wrong.

Give feedback at the right time

When will you tell learners how they scored on the test? Sooner is better, but sometimes delays are necessary even with automatic scoring. You can deliver feedback automatically after each question or after the whole test. Or, you can deliver feedback after evaluation by a human being. This section discusses the merits of each approach.

After each question

Scoring each question as the learner answers it provides immediate feedback but can interrupt the flow of the test. In general, I prefer this approach. It makes tests more fun and prevents misconceptions. It makes tests seem a bit more like games.

Immediate feedback corrects misconceptions before they take up residence in the learner's brain. If feedback comes only after answering a whole series of questions, learners will have transferred their answers to long-term memory before they realize which were wrong. Immediate feedback also keeps the learner from missing several related questions because of a single, simple misunderstanding.

Getting feedback piecemeal, however, can make the test take longer and prove frustrating to impatient learners, especially ones with a high level of knowledge who get few questions wrong. Immediate feedback can also make it harder for learners to answer a series of closely related questions. Interruptions for feedback break the continuity of the test. If you do choose to provide feedback after each answer:

▶ Make each question complete in itself. After reading the feedback, learners are unlikely to remember details of the preceding question.

▶ Let learners skip over lengthy feedback for correct answers. Make the feedback brief and let learners click a button to advance to the next question.

▶ Do not reveal too much. In the feedback to one question, do not give away the answer to another question.

▶ Do not require immediate remediation. Otherwise learners would bail out of the test after their first wrong answer. At the end of the test, provide a recap with links to let learners review material for questions they got wrong.

▶ If the test is timed, stop the timer while the learner is getting feedback and restart it only when the learner advances to the next question. Make sure learners understand that they can take all the time they want to read feedback.

After test is complete

Postponing evaluation until learners have answered all questions is more efficient and more economical, but less fun. By evaluating answers only at the end of the test, you reduce the number of screens the learner must view and the time required to take the test. Learners can quickly navigate back and forth among the questions, answering them at will.

Feedback at the end can comment on understanding of the whole subject of the test. By evaluating at the end, your feedback can be more targeted. If several questions test the same concept, learners see the feedback just once, not over and over again.

However, postponing evaluation can prove frustrating to some learners. Misunderstanding one question can cause them to miss other questions. Guess whom they blame!

If you do design tests with evaluation only at the end of the test, follow these common-sense guidelines:

▶ Make questions independent and self-contained. Misunderstanding one question should not lessen chances of getting other questions right.

▶ Keep tests short. Learners should be able to complete the whole test in 10 to 15 minutes.

▶ At the end, provide clear feedback on questions the learner got wrong with links to the original material or to new material on the subject.

After a delay for human evaluation

If a test question is complex and the teacher or fellow learners must carefully consider its answer, immediate feedback is not possible. For example, the answer must be transmitted to an evaluator who scores it and sends back a reply. Throw in time zones, weekends, holidays, and work priorities, and the delay can be several days.

For tests with delayed evaluation, use the strengths of human evaluation to offset the problems caused by the delay.

▶ Give priority to scoring tests. Guarantee 48-hour turnaround if you can do so without compromising the quality of evaluations. Find stand-ins if teachers are unavailable. Consider having learners perform non-critical evaluations. Base part of the final grade on the promptness and quality of such evaluations.

▶ Let learners proceed with the e-learning, even if a passing grade is normally required before beginning the next lesson.

▶ Schedule tests on days when the evaluator will be able to respond immediately. Some teachers like to schedule tests on Friday so that they can grade them during the quiet time over the weekend.

▶ Warn learners about potential delays. If learners decide when to take tests, publish a calendar indicating when the teacher will be available to grade tests. One course had this policy: "You will receive your grade within two business days at the office of the teacher."

ADVANCE YOUR TESTING

Combine advanced features of online-testing tools and sophisticated testing techniques to more accurately measure performance and to provide learners with better feedback.

Hint first

Instead of giving the correct answer as feedback to an incorrect guess, consider displaying a hint and challenging the learner to try again. Or include a **Hint** button to let learners request a little help answering the question.

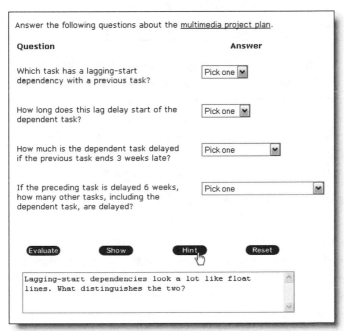

Notice how clicking on the **Hint** button reveals a fact that makes answering the question easier.

Built using Adobe Dreamweaver and custom JavaScript. View example at horton.com/eld/.

Use advanced testing capabilities

We can use computer capabilities to make testing fairer and more sophisticated. We can pick questions from a pool of available questions and can randomize the order of questions and choices within questions. These capabilities require a testing tool that provides these features or one that includes a scripting or programming language you can use to implement these features yourself.

Pool test questions

In *question-pooling*, test questions are pulled from a pool of available test questions. That is, the test designer creates more test questions than necessary for a single test. The test delivery system then selects questions from the pool at the time the test is delivered. For example, suppose we have created Questions A through H on a subject. Tests on this subject could pull questions from that pool as follows:

Test 1	Test 2	Test 3	Test 4
Question A	Question C	Question E	Question G
Question B	Question F	Question A	Question F
Question C	Question H	Question C	Question A
Question D	Question A	Question G	Question H

When should you use question-pooling? Question-pooling is great when tests are taken more than once. By drawing questions from a pool, we make sure that the learner does not see exactly the same questions time and time again. This is especially important when we are using pre- and post-learning tests to measure learning. If the post-test merely repeated the questions from the pre-test, we would not know whether results indicated learning or just familiarity with the test questions. Question-pooling is also useful when learners may need to retake a test, for instance, after failing a first attempt.

Another use for question-pooling is to make cheating harder. One student cannot tell another student what questions are on the test.

Question-pooling can pose some problems for test designers. It thwarts designers who want questions to appear in a specific order. Many designers want to start with simpler questions before more difficult questions or to put questions in a logical or chronological order. With question-pooling, one question cannot build on or refer to a previous question. If test scores are to be comparable between students and offerings of the test, all questions in the pool must be of the same difficulty. With question-pooling there is a statistical possibility that the questions on an individual test will not cover the subject evenly.

Don't forget that question-pooling requires test designers to create more questions. This requires more research, analysis, and testing. Budget and schedule accordingly.

A critical question to ask is how questions are selected from the pool. One way is randomly. Another way applies a scheme, such as picking questions from separate pools, ensuring that questions are not repeated on subsequent tests taken by the same learner, or picking from groups of related questions.

Just remember that question-pooling requires sophisticated technology and more work on your part.

Randomize questions

When you randomize questions, they appear in a different order each time a test is administered. For example, for a simple test:

Test 1	Test 2	Test 3	Test 4
Question A	Question C	Question D	Question B
Question B	Question B	Question A	Question A
Question C	Question D	Question C	Question D
Question D	Question A	Question B	Question C

Should you randomize the order of questions? Randomizing the order of questions can make the test seem fresh the second time taken, and it will make cheating harder. However, it does require you to design your questions independently. That means questions cannot refer to other questions. You cannot sequence questions in chronological or logical order. You cannot progress from simple to hard questions.

The randomizing feature is most often combined with the question-pooling feature so that questions are selected at random from a large pool of questions.

Shuffle answers

With randomized or shuffled answers, the choices for a pick-one or pick-multiple question appear in a different order each time the test is taken. For example, the answers to a pick-one question in chemistry might appear different on subsequent tests:

The element with atomic number 24 is:	The element with atomic number 24 is:	The element with atomic number 24 is:	The element with atomic number 24 is:
o Aluminum	o Dubnium	o Chromium	o Boron
o Boron	o Boron	o Boron	o Aluminum
o Chromium	o Aluminum	o Aluminum	o Dubnium
o Dubnium	o Chromium	o Dubnium	o Chromium

Should you shuffle the order of answers in your test questions? Shuffling the order of choices will make the test seem fresh the second time taken and will make cheating a little harder. However, it does require you to write questions so the order of choices does not matter. That means answers cannot refer to earlier answers (Be careful with pronouns like *it*, *these*, and *they* that refer to words in earlier answers.) It also means answers will not appear in alphabetical, numeric, chronological, or logical order. This can make scanning the choices harder, especially for test-stressed learners.

Automatically generate questions

Some advanced testing tools have the ability to automatically create fresh test questions from a formula or pattern. For example, with the learning management system called The Learning Manager (www.w-win.com), I can define a question in geometry with placeholders rather than fixed numbers.

> What is the area of a rectangle {number1} units high and {number2} units wide?

And I can then define a procedure to generate specific numbers to replace those placeholders in actual questions.

```
number1 = rndnum(1,10,1);
number2 = rndnum(1,10,1);
correct = number1 * number2;
format(number1, "%.0f");
format(number2, "%.0f");
format(correct, "%.0f");
```

The first line picks two whole numbers between 1 and 10 at random. The third line defines the correct answer is the product of these two numbers. The final three lines format the numbers as whole numbers.

The first time the question appears, a set of numbers is generated and a correct answer calculated.

> What is the area of a rectangle 6 units high and 2 units wide? 12

The next time the question appears, different numbers fill the placeholders and the correct answer is different.

> What is the area of a rectangle 7 units high and 5 units wide? 35|

Each time the question appears, different numbers fill the slots.

> What is the area of a rectangle 3 units high and 9 units wide? 27

Good uses for automatically generated questions include:

▶ Simple mathematics, such as arithmetic and unit conversions.
▶ Subjects requiring calculations, such as accounting and engineering.
▶ Drill and practice on estimating quantities.

Monitor results

One of the best ways to improve tests is to examine the log files after a reasonable number of learners have taken the tests. Look for the symptoms of easily corrected problems, such as these:

Symptom	Cause
Questions with lower than normal success rates.	These questions are too hard or are unclearly phrased.
Questions with higher than normal success rates.	These questions may be too easy or something is giving learners a clue to the correct answer.
Questions that many learners skip.	These questions may be hard to understand, take too long to read, or be too difficult to answer.
Large number of questions left unanswered on timed tests.	You may need to increase the time or decrease the number of questions.

Ask yourself this question: Do people who have the required skills and knowledge pass the test, while those without the skills and knowledge fail?

Make tests fair to all learners

Sometimes learners may feel tests are unfair. They believe that tests ask improper questions or do not give all learners an equal chance to answer questions correctly.

Test your tests

As a check on e-learning design, make each test question pass a test itself. This test has three questions:

▶ Which objective does this question test?

▶ Where was the learner taught this objective?

▶ Can someone with subject-matter knowledge but minimal reading skills answer the question?

Unless you can easily answer each item, rewrite your test question.

Solicit feedback from learners

Invite learners to comment on tests. However, request the feedback only after the test has been graded. This delay gives learners time to calm down so that their responses are more reasoned and less emotional. And learners can respond based on the actual grade rather than the anticipated one.

Let learners report questions they consider unfair. Require them to state why they feel the question was unfair. And ask them what change would make the question fair.

Prevent common complaints

Common complaints about unfair tests and test questions include:

▶ Questions outside the scope of stated objectives or unit of learning.

▶ Questions that depend on irrelevant skills or on knowledge not mentioned in prerequisites.

▶ Culturally biased questions that rely on knowledge that one culture might possess but another might not. Or complex, tricky language that is especially difficult for second-language readers.

▶ Unfamiliar terminology, such as unnecessary jargon, metaphors, and slang.

▶ Unreasonable time limits that unfairly penalize second-language learners and those with vision or reading problems.

Avoid trick questions

Trick questions are ones designed to trick learners into making an incorrect answer. Writers of such questions often claim that they are just trying to teach learners to pay close attention. Trick questions teach learners to fear tests and distrust the test-writer. Trick questions penalize even successful learners. Writing trick questions is unethical and probably immoral. If you do it, you should be sentenced to take an endless test made up entirely of trick questions where each incorrect answer triggers a sting by a big nasty wasp.

There is no limit to the number of tricks evil designers can play on learners. Here are a few of the most common abuses:

▶ **Red herrings** that embed cues to prompt incorrect responses. For example, asking, "Which consumes more oxygen, an 80 kg human jogging uphill or a 3 kg rabbit calmly browsing lettuce?"

▶ **Trivia questions** that ask for skills and knowledge that the learner will never need to apply. "What color eyes did Napoleon have?"

▶ **Late requirement,** which asks for something that was not taught in the course or in a required prerequisite.

▶ **Context-less queries,** which do not provide a specific enough context to enable an answer. For example, "How frequent are tornadoes?" Many such questions require a comparison but give no standard for the comparison.

▶ **Required confessions,** which require a response that admits to wrongdoing. For example, "How do you feel when you drive faster than the speed limit?"

▶ **Overlapping categories,** where the scope or range of choices overlap so that more than one pick-one answer could be correct. "What is the hardness of malachite on the Mohs hardness scale? (Pick one) (a) 1 to 2, (b) 2 to 3, (c) 3 to 4, (d) 4 to 5." The hardness of malachite can range from 3.5 to 4, so both the third and fourth answers could be correct.

▶ **Demoralization,** where the designer puts the hardest questions first to dishearten and fluster learners.

▶ **Duplicated distracters,** where the same wrong answer is restated in different words in subsequent choices. "Why was Brian fired? (a) He was rude. (b) He was discourteous. (c) He violated policy. (d) He was offensive. (e) He broke the law."

▶ **Linguistic lofting,** where the designer deliberately uses words that only some of the learners will recognize, even though understanding the terms is not a prerequisite or objective of the course.

▶ **Breakstep sequencing,** where numeric choices are not in numeric order. For example, "What is the altitude of the ozone layer? (a) 10 km (b) 20 km (c) 40 km (d) 80 km (e) 30 km."

▶ **Apples-and-oranges comparisons,** where completely different categories must be compared. For example, "Which is better, the climbing capacity of the V10 engine in the VW Touareg or the hill-descent electronics of the Land Rover Discovery?"

How do you know whether a question is unfair? Ask learners. Include only questions your learners will agree are appropriate.

Test early and often

As soon as you teach something, test on it. Help learners lock in learning and give them an opportunity to confirm their progress. Asking questions about knowledge learners have just acquired helps them consolidate and integrate the knowledge. Having learners perform procedures immediately after learning them makes performance fluid and sure.

Include more short tests, rather than just a few long ones. In a large course, include several tests evenly spaced throughout the course—not just one big exam at the end.

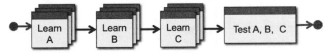

Many courses present a series of ideas and then test on them all. By the time learners reach the test, they have forgotten what they learned about the earlier concepts and are intimidated by the big test.

Instead of one big test at the end, sprinkle small tests throughout learning. Thus learners do not proceed without learning. Because these tests are small, they are less intimidating. After teaching and testing the final idea, present a brief review and a short test on all the ideas.

Design the smaller tests so that they accurately predict performance on the larger tests. Give learners lots of practice activities and just a few recorded tests. Tracking the learner's every attempt and recording every score discourages quick, spontaneous action. The rapid cycle of assessing a situation, forming a hypothesis, testing it, getting feedback, and revising the hypothesis is a valuable learning event in its own right. Give learners lots of opportunities to practice without the fear that their every mistake is being recorded in ink.

Set the right passing score

If your test is used to make decisions about learners—and not just to provide general feedback to them—you will need to set a passing score. This passing score (or cut score) is the number of points the learner must earn in order to adequately master the unit of learning covered by the test.

Before you set a passing score, consider exactly how you will use this score. Will you use it just as a goal for learners to shoot for? Will you require learners to repeat the module until they have achieved the passing score? Will the score be recorded as part of their job records? Will the score qualify the learner for a job-relevant certification? Obviously, the more effect the test score has on the learner's future, the more objective and systematic you must be in setting the test score—and in other aspects of testing.

One way to think of the passing score is as a target level of competence between minimal competence and complete mastery.

But what should that target threshold be? There are several ways to set the score. Here we list three in order of increasing rigor.

Professional judgment

If you are experienced teaching the subject of the test and know where and how learners will apply the knowledge or skills being taught, you can just use your professional judgment to set the passing score. You know the subject and how well learners must learn. Translate your professional judgment into a test score.

In setting a passing score, consider:

▶ How crucial is the skill or knowledge to future learning. A foundation skill must be mastered to a high level.

▶ What is the danger if the subject is not mastered? Will someone's life be put at risk? Will work quality suffer?

▶ How difficult is the subject to novices? Is a high score unrealistic?

Consensus of experts

Ask the help of subject-matter experts. Base the passing score on the judgment of a half-dozen experts in the subject of your test. An expert would be expected to score well above the passing score, a standard deviation or more.

One way to make more precise use of your experts is to have them examine each question and then specify the odds that a minimally proficient learner (someone who should just barely pass the test) would get this individual question correct. You can then add up the probabilities to get the number of questions necessary to pass.

For example, say a test has five questions and your experts estimate the probabilities of getting the questions right are 0.8, 0.7, 0.8, 0.4, and 0.6, respectively. Adding up these numbers tells us the number of correct answers needed for a passing score:

$0.8 + 0.7 + 0.8 + 0.4 + 0.6 = 3.3$ questions required to pass.

If questions have different point values, you would need to multiply each probability of passing by the number of points awarded for each question. Suppose the questions in the preceding example have point values of 10, 10, 20, 20, and 10, respectively. Now our required score becomes:

$0.8 \times 10 + 0.7 \times 10 + 0.8 \times 20 + 0.4 \times 20 + 0.6 \times 10.$

$8 + 7 + 16 + 8 + 6 = 35$ points required to pass

And while you are at it, have your experts take the test. Better still; have them take the test before making their estimates.

Contrasting groups

The contrasting-group method statistically compares the scores of experts and novices and sets the passing score between these two.

1. Recruit two groups of test-takers. The "expert" group consists of people who have mastered the subject of the test and should pass handily. The "novice" group consists of people who know little or nothing about the subject and who should fail the test. About two dozen test-takers should be sufficient.

2. Administer the test to the two groups under identical conditions. If possible, have them all take the test at the same time.

3. Compile test scores and identify the mean and standard deviation of the scores for each group.

4. Set the passing score between one standard deviation below the mean for the experts and one standard deviation above the mean for novices.

5. Nudge the passing score up or down within this range to make testing more or less stringent.

Define a scale of grades

Rather than a pass-fail threshold, give learners ranges of scores along with recommendations of how to proceed. For example:

90-100 points. Excellent! Please skip ahead to the <u>next lesson</u>. You may want to <u>attempt the test</u> for that lesson to see whether you can also skip that lesson.

80-89 points. Good. You understand the basics and can continue with the <u>next lesson</u>.

65-79 points. You should improve your score before beginning the next lesson. Please <u>review the summary</u> and attempt this test again.

0-64 points. You need to work on this subject before proceeding. You should *repeat the lesson* or explore <u>alternative learning resources</u> before re-attempting this test.

Pre-test to propel learners

A pre-test is a test taken before beginning a lesson or course. It covers the same ground as the associated unit of learning, just like the post-test or final exam that comes at the end of the unit. Pre-tests may test for prerequisites of the following unit, for the content of the unit itself, or for both.

Why pre-test?

Pre-testing offers several benefits to learners and to designers. Pre-tests:

▶ Motivate learners by challenging them to fill in the gaps revealed by the pre-test.

▶ Make clear what the unit of learning will cover.

▶ Ensure that learners take prerequisites before beginning the unit of learning.

▶ Streamline learning by letting learners skip material they already know.

▶ Help designers identify modules they can omit (because everybody passes the pre-test) or additional modules to develop (because everybody fails the pre-test.

Use pre-test results

Depending on your purposes for pre-testing and the sophistication of your learning management system, you can use the results of pre-testing to route learners to different locations within a course or lesson.

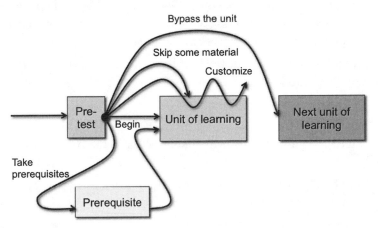

If learners ...	Route them to ...
Completely pass the pre-test.	The next unit in sequence.
Partially pass the pre-test.	A starting point within the current unit.
Show that they lack prerequisite knowledge.	A prerequisite course or lesson.
Pass the prerequisites portion of the pre-test.	The beginning of the current unit of learning.
Pass portions of the pre-test for the current unit.	A custom path through just the components the learner did not pass in the pre-test.

EXPLAIN THE TEST

One of the most common complaints about tests is that the rules are unclear or that the procedures are not explained fully. If learners do not understand the "rules" of a test, they may not score well and will blame the creator of the test. Take the time to tell learners how to take the test.

Prepare learners to take the test

Learners are curious beings, especially when it comes to tests. They want to know all the rules and regulations and restrictions—before they begin the test. But no one wants to read a bunch of boring rules. So keep the rules as simple as possible, express them concisely, and encourage learners to know the rules before they begin the test. Here is a comprehensive list of the kinds of questions learners ask.

▶ **Why am I being tested?** Learners who see the value of a test to them try harder and score higher. Tell learners that the test will give them confidence, help them quickly correct misunderstanding, and progress more quickly.

▶ **Is the test graded?** What effect will this test have on the overall grade? What is a passing grade? What grade should the learner achieve before going on to the next lesson?

▶ **What does the test cover?** Just the current lesson? All lessons up to this point?

▶ **Is the test timed?** How much time is available? What is the penalty for taking too much time?

▶ **When must the test be taken?** Before a deadline? During a specific period? At a certain hour and day? Before advancing to the next lesson?

▶ **How long is the test?** How many questions are on the test? (Especially important if the questions scroll off the bottom of the screen or are on subsequent pages).

▶ **How are answers scored?** How many points are awarded for each question? What are the penalties for incorrect answers, incomplete answers, and unanswered questions?

▶ **How accurate must my answers be?** Do spelling, capitalization, and grammar count? How precise must calculations be? Does the order of entries matter?

▶ **What form does the test take?** What kinds of questions are used: multiple-choice, true/false, fill-in-the-blanks, or others? Does everyone get the same questions or are questions picked at random?

▶ **Can I take the test later?** If so, how do I skip the test? How do I take the test later?

▶ **Should I guess?** Tell learners how unanswered questions are scored so they can decide whether to guess at answers. National testing services typically deduct one point for missing answers and three points for incorrect answers {Westgaard, 1999 #1951}.

▶ **Can I retake the test for a better grade later?** How many times? Which score is recorded: the first one, the last one, the best one, or an average of all attempts?

▶ **What resources may I use to take the test?** Specify what calculators, computer programs, books, Web sites, search engines, or other sources of information learners can use. Include links to these items so all learners have equal access.

▶ **Are questions weighted equally?** Do some questions score more points than others? If weightings vary, state the point value of each question as it appears.

▶ **How realistic are the questions?** Are drawings to scale? Are numbers realistic?

▶ **Must questions be answered in sequence?** Does advancing to the next question automatically trigger scoring the current question?

▶ **What if I experience a computer failure?** What if the computer, network, or the testing program crashes during the test? What effect will this have on my score? How do I restart or resume the test?

Keep learners in control

We want learners to feel in control as they take tests. That way they focus on the content of the test. The key to control is information and having appropriate choices.

▶ **Explain before starting the timer.** Give all the instructions learners will need for a test before starting the timer. After presenting the instructions, require learners to select a "**Start test**" button to actually begin a timed test.

▶ **Let learners skip optional tests.** If tests are optional, let learners skip them. Make this easy with explicit buttons.

▶ **Make status clear.** Let learners know how much they have done and how much they have left to do. Some systems display a console showing the time and number of questions:

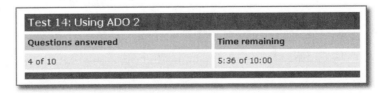

Test 14: Using ADO 2	
Questions answered	**Time remaining**
4 of 10	5:36 of 10:00

CONSIDER ALTERNATIVES TO FORMAL TESTS

Testing in e-learning obviously has limitations and is not always the best way to evaluate the progress of learners. Before you start designing tests, take a few minutes to consider alternatives to tests.

Use more than formal, graded tests

Not all assessments need to be formal, graded tests. Use a mixture of different forms of assessment:

▶ Formal graded tests.

▶ "Open-book" tests during which learners can consult reference materials.

▶ Performance tests requiring completion of actual work.

▶ Self-graded tests by which learners evaluate their own performance.

▶ Self-evaluations of practice activities or original work.

▶ Evaluations by boss, peers, subordinates, or customers.

▶ Learning games and puzzles that require learning to win or solve.

▶ Research projects that require gaining original knowledge.

▶ Tests taken by teams instead of individuals.

Help learners build portfolios

Instead of testing on knowledge, have learners create tangible evidence of their learning. Base grading on a work-ready portfolio the learner assembles during the course. The portfolio can consist of samples of a variety of work products or the completion of a single, complex plan or report.

For those already working in the field of the course, the portfolio can consist of materials immediately useful on the job. For those preparing for a new field, the portfolio can consist of samples that demonstrate competence to practice in the field.

Have learners collect tokens

Rather than requiring learners to pass a series of tests, challenge them to collect tokens that represent completion of activities. Each test or activity is worth a certain number of tokens in proportion to the scope and value of the knowledge it requires.

Adapt testing to social learning

Social learning will require a different style of testing than conventional e-learning. Here are a few suggestions:

Gauge performance in live online meetings. In online meetings, include activities that reveal the level of learning by students. Here are some activities you can use:

▶ **Polling**. Ask questions to see who "got it."

▶ **Application sharing**. Have learners demonstrate tasks with software.

▶ **Oral exams**. Ask specific learners.

▶ **Student teachers**. Have learners teach short segments.

▶ **Open-ended questions** that must be answered through chat.

Evaluate postings in discussion activities. For instance:

▶ **Take-home tests** that learners submit the next day.

▶ **Homework** that learners prepare and submit for grading.

▶ **Portfolios** of original work by learners.

Design group-tests. Create tests to be taken by groups. Allow time for the group to discuss the questions and come to a consensus.

Discuss the tests. Have learners take tests individually. After learners get their results, have them discuss the results within small groups. Allow groups to appeal questions they feel were unfair.

Have learners add test questions to a pool. Award extra points to the submitter if the question is relevant and appropriately challenging. Challenge can be measured by whether the desired percentage of learners answered correctly.

See Chapter 8 for more ideas on evaluating social learners.

Adapt testing to mobile learning

Make sure your test works on the mobile device learners will use to take the test (p. 519) and in the environment where they will take the test (p. 517).

Include performance questions done with real-world objects, devices, and environments. Have mobile learners enlist a human witness or proctor to verify their performance of assigned tasks. Or, have them record and submit video documenting their performance on a test.

See Chapter 9 for more on assessing performance of mobile learners.

IN CLOSING ...

Summary

▶ Develop and perfect tests by the same cyclical process used for other parts of e-learning.

▶ Use tests to let learners gauge their progress and administrators measure the effectiveness of your e-learning.

▶ Write test questions so they measure accomplishment of objectives, not the ability to decipher tricky phrases or to make lucky guesses.

▶ For simple questions, provide feedback immediately so that misconceptions are identified and corrected before they take root.

▶ Test early and often. Use unrecorded tests for frequent practice. Make tests more like challenging games and less like school examinations.

▶ Test your tests. At a minimum, make sure that experts pass the test and novices do not.

▶ As always, design first and then pick your tool. If you have already selected a tool to create and administer tests, do not moan, groan, or whine. Just do the best you can.

For more ...

For more sophisticated tests, consider using learning activities (Chapters 2, 3, and 4). Most activities will, however, require grading by the teacher.

Before buying a tool for authoring tests, try out the types of tests it provides and investigate how you can add tests of your own design. Consider these tools:

▶ Hot Potatoes (hotpot.uvic.ca/index.php).

▶ Perception Questionmark (www.questionmark.com).

▶ QuizPoint (www.learningware.com).

▶ Articulate Quizmaker (www.articulate.com).

▶ iSpring QuizMaker (www.ispringsolutions.com).

▶ Captivate (www.adobe.com).

▶ Flash (www.adobe.com).

If you have a learning-management or content-management system, be sure to investigate the types of test questions available and what additional features the system may provide. For instance, does the system allow for question-pooling, randomization of questions and answers, and the ability to design questions using a formula?

See Chapter 8 on social learning or Chapter 9 on mobile learning for more on how to evaluate learning and provide feedback for these types of e-learning.

Games and simulations (Chapter 7) integrate teaching and testing. Consider a learning game (p. 324) or whole simulation course (p. 396).

6 Topics

Accomplishing specific learning objectives

Topics accomplish individual learning objectives. They may consist of a single page or many. They may center on a single activity or may span multiple complex activities. They may mix text, graphics, voice, music, animation, and video. They may take minutes or hours to complete. But each topic accomplishes *one* learning objective and accomplishes it fully. That's what makes them topics. This chapter will show you how to design e-learning topics to accomplish your learning objectives.

WHAT ARE TOPICS?

A topic is the lowest-level learning object in a course or other knowledge product. It is the building block of instruction that accomplishes a single learning objective. Typically, a topic requires a combination of Absorb, Do, and Connect activities and includes a test to gauge accomplishment of the objective.

Topics are learning objects

We've said that topics are learning objects. But what exactly is a learning object? In e-learning, a learning object is a **chunk of electronic content that can be accessed individually and completely accomplishes a single learning objective** and can prove it. The most important part of this definition is "completely accomplishes a single learning objective." A learning object contains everything necessary to ensure that the learner meets the learning objective.

Not all learning objects, however, are topics. Some are whole courses or lessons. A course or lesson may have broad learning objectives that encompass lower-level, more-detailed learning objectives. A topic has only one main learning objective and no sub-objectives.

Another, perhaps more pragmatic definition is that a **topic is a micro-course designed to be combined with other micro-courses**. This definition emphasizes the idea that topics are self-contained enough that they can be reused in various versions of a course or in multiple courses.

Examples of topics

The term *topic* may still seem abstract and remote. Let's fix that by looking at some concrete examples of topics. One is very simple, another a bit more ambitious, and one complex indeed. As we look at each, we will point out its instructional design and its visible components.

A simple topic

Here is an example of a simple topic. (You might remember it from Chapter 1, where I used it to illustrate a low-level learning object, containing the three essential learning activities.) It consists of a single Web page and is about as simple as a topic can be.

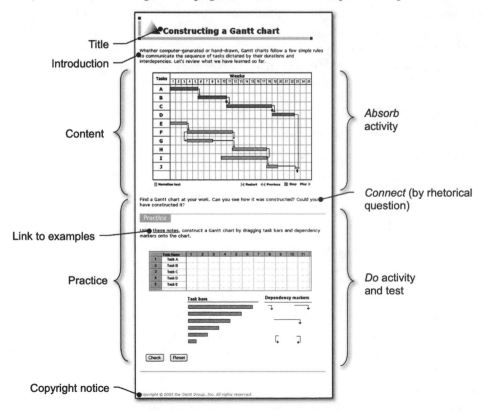

This simple topic accomplishes a simple objective, namely teaching how to interpret dependency markers in a Gantt chart. Though only a single page, this topic has the main components of a learning object.

It has a title that announces and labels the topic. A short paragraph introduces the topic and summarizes its content. Next follows a narrated animation that explains what dependency markers are and how to recognize them. After the animation is a short paragraph that emphasizes the key point and then links to another topic for more information on dependency markers. Next, the learner is invited to find another Gantt chart and interpret the meaning of dependency markers found there.

Although simple, this topic contains the necessary learning experiences. Learners absorb the concept by reading a definition and experiencing the animation. The practice provides both a Do activity and a test. Learners connect with future learning through the link to another topic.

A typical topic

Our next example is a bit more complex. It teaches the learner to make a difficult decision requiring research, analysis, and judgment.

This topic is from a prototype course for managers of wilderness areas. It is called a *micro-scenario* because it presents a situation based on real events that requires learners to make a decision just as they would in the real world.

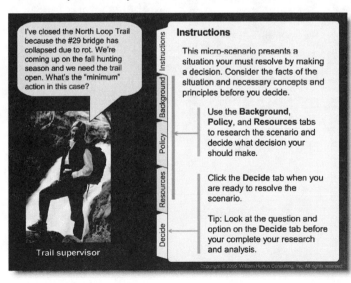

The **Instructions** tab welcomes learners to the main activity of the object and provides directions on how to complete the assignment.

Created in Microsoft PowerPoint and converted for Web delivery using Adobe Presenter. View example at horton.com/eld/.

The **Background** tab supplies details about the situation learners must investigate and find a solution for. Learners must absorb these details before searching for a solution.

The **Policy** tab reveals the most important constraints on a solution, namely regulations that govern the situation described in the Background. Learners must absorb this information before attempting to apply it.

The **Resources** tab presents a list of links to documents. Learners must research both the situation of the specific wilderness area as well as the generic information on regulations. This research connects learners to resources they will use in the future.

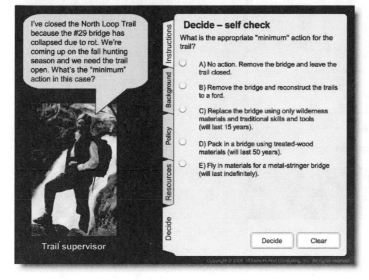

The final tab, **Decide**, lets learners choose a solution. These choices are all plausible, so learners must conduct research and carefully analyze the situation to pick the right answer. Learners' decisions provide an assessment on how well the objective was met. This is a Do activity.

Test was built using Adobe Presenter.

A complex topic

As an example of a complex topic, we look at the learning object that teaches how to set the material properties in a computer program called *GALENA*. The material properties are necessary for *GALENA* to analyze the safety of a dam or other slope. To enter material properties, the user of *GALENA* must make several separate entries on a dialog box in the program.

The topic has several tabs, each of which reveals a different part of the topic.

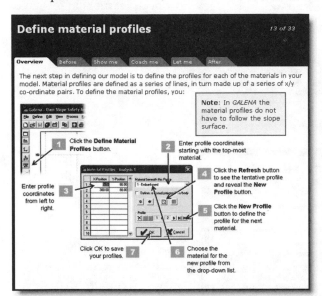

The **Overview** tab presents a concise preview of what learners will learn about how to define material properties. This overview serves as a summary as well.

Learners may absorb the instructions provided here. Or learners may print the page and use it as a job aid, which helps them connect to real work.

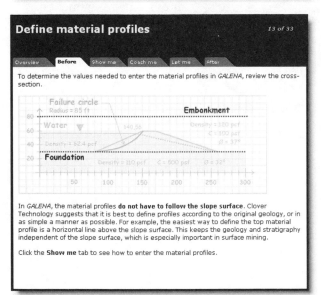

The **Before** tab supplies background information learners need before beginning the other activities. It explains the parts of the model that will be built in this topic.

Learners absorb this information.

Tabbed interface built using Adobe Dreamweaver and custom JavaScript. Screens captured with TechSmith SnagIt. Illustrations created in Microsoft PowerPoint.

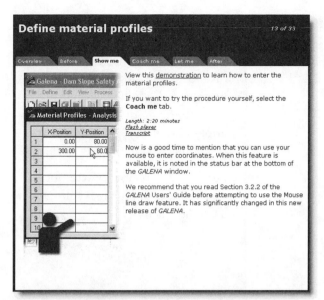

The **Show me** tab lets learners watch a demonstration of how to perform this step. This tab contains links to launch the demonstration and to display a transcript of its voice narration.

The demonstration appears in a separate window because the actual program requires a window larger than that of the course.

Experiencing this demonstration is an Absorb activity.

Demonstration built with Adobe Captivate.

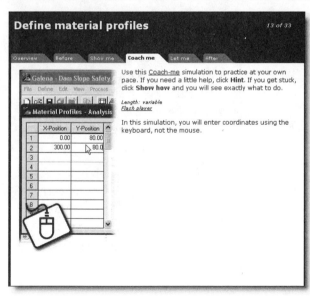

The **Coach me** tab lets learners practice performing the procedure. From this page, they launch a simulation in which they try to perform the procedure just demonstrated. Learners get feedback and can request hints or instructions.

Performing this simulation is a Do activity.

Simulation built with Adobe Captivate.

6

Topics

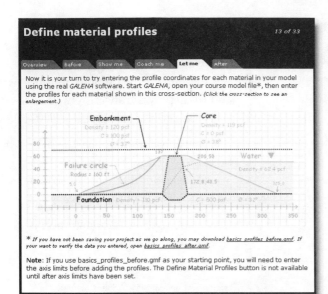

The **Let me** tab gives learners instructions for an activity to be performed with the real software. It provides a starting model and instructions of what learners are to do with the model. Learners must apply knowledge gained from the previous two tabs.

Performing an activity without assistance using the real software is a Connect activity.

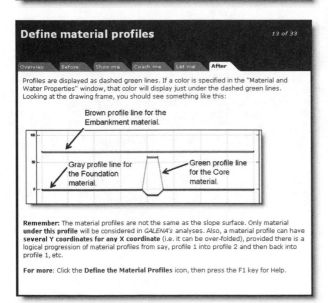

The **After** tab helps learners verify that the let-me activity was performed correctly. It also provides hints for how learners can verify their own success when using the software for their own models. And it suggests additional topics to pursue.

As a wrap-up, this tab helps learners connect to future learning.

Anatomy of a topic

Let's look at the components you might find in a simple, topic-level learning object. This list is comprehensive; so don't try to include all these items in every topic you create.

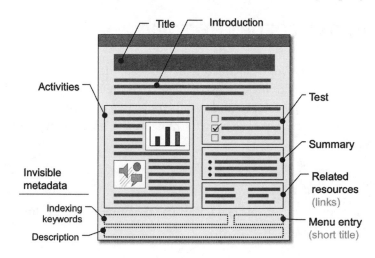

The first thing the learner might notice would be the title of the topic displayed as a banner or headline at the top of the page.

Following the title might be a brief introduction to help put the content in context or motivate the learner to consider it carefully. Further contextual information might be provided by some kind of you-are-here indicator.

The primary focus of the page will be the activities. This part of the topic may include text, graphics, and other media. These components will provoke the necessary learning experiences. A test will provide practice and feedback to let learners monitor how well they accomplished the objective of the topic. And a summary may be included to help learners retain key ideas from the topic and to make sure that those merely skimming are exposed to all critical ideas.

To be completely self-contained, the topic would need to include a lot of material of interest to only a few learners. As a compromise, the topic may link to related resources for those who want to follow up on personal interests or to dig deeper into the main subject.

In addition to these visible components, the topic may have invisible items, typically to make it easier for learners to find the topic. The topic may contain indexing keywords that can be compiled to present an alphabetical index or that may be searched for by search engines. The topic may also have a description that can, for example, be scooped up and displayed as an entry in a catalog of available topics. Invisible items like keywords and description are part of what are called metadata, that is, information about the topic.

Another part of the topic is the menu entry that the learner clicked to jump to this topic. Although the entry is displayed separately, it is properly thought of as part of a self-contained topic.

DESIGN THE COMPONENTS OF THE TOPIC

Although topics may differ widely, most contain some standard components, such as a title, introduction, learning activities, an assessment, and metadata. The objective gives rise to all the components of the topic, and it is the objective against which the results of these components are judged. Let's see how to translate the learning objective of a topic into these components.

Title the topic

A small but essential part of the topic is its title. The title announces the topic to the world and makes promises on its behalf.

Titles are crucial

Titles are crucial for success of the topic. The title is often the first part of the topic the learner sees, for instance, in a menu showing available topics or at the start of a lesson that lists the topics of the lesson. The title is displayed in search results. The title is almost universally cataloged by search engines and is the highest priority text for a search match.

The topic title is also important because it is a promise to the learner. The title strikes a bargain with the learner: Take this topic and you will gain what the title implies.

Base the title on the objective

Make the title appropriate for each type of objective.

Type objective	Format for title	Examples
Create an X that does Y.	Building a _____	Building trust among team members. Writing your first VB program.
Decide X.	Selecting _____ Choosing _____	Picking your prescription plan. Selecting your team members. Saying no to fraud.

Type objective	Format for title	Examples
Do procedure X to accomplish Y.	_____ ing _____	Interpreting dependency links. Replacing a trail bridge. Defining material profiles.
Know X about Y.	[Name of X] [Statement summarizing X]	Dependency links. VAT differs by province.
Believe X.	Why _____? [or just a statement of X]	Why slope stability matters. Leveraged investments are risky.
Feel X about Y.	[Statement that implies X about Y]	Everyone brings something to the team. Slope failures kill people.

Compose a meaningful title

The title is the first part of a topic that learners read. A good title efficiently tells the learner what question the topic answers. A good title is:

▶ **Distinct**. Easily distinguished from names of other topics, lessons, activities, and other components.

▶ **Context-free**. Do not depend on the context or other surrounding information to make sense of the name. For this reason, avoid pronouns in titles. "Why this is so" is meaningless out of context.

▶ **Understandable**. Use standard grammar and terms meaningful to the reader. Be careful about using official terminology that learners will understand only after completing the topic.

▶ **Scannable**. Make the meaning obvious in a glance without further reading. Put the most important words at the beginning of the title so they are noticed and not cut off if the list of titles is narrow. Change "How you can make friends" to "Making friends."

▶ **Thematic**. The learner can predict the contents of the topic from the title. See whether learners can match titles to the objectives of the topics.

▶ **Motivational**. The learner recognizes "what's in it for me." Compare "Filling in the 3407/J form" to "Reducing bank fraud."

Every topic should have a unique title that learners will understand, even when they see the title apart from the topic. Often learners must pick a topic from a list of topic titles. A knowledgeable learner should be able to guess the content of the topic from its title.

And a short title, too

When you title your object, take a few seconds to coin a shorter form of the title. This shorter form may better fit onto narrow menus. This may be more effective than having the display chop off all but the first few words of the title or else wrap the title to several lines.

Long title	Applying multiple analysis restraints
Long title chopped	Applying multiple an
Long title wrapped	Applying multiple an alysis restraints
Shorter form	Multiple restraints

To shorten a title, pick out the most important verbs and nouns from the long title. Abbreviate if necessary, but make sure learners will recognize the abbreviation. If possible, provide a tool tip or hover text that displays the full title when the learner moves the cursor over the short title.

Here are some examples of long and short titles:

Original title	Short form of the title
Interpreting dependency links	Dependency links
Replacing a trail bridge	Replace bridge
Defining material profiles	Profiles

Introduce the topic

Do you just dive into the heart of the topic, or do you provide an introduction to gently ease the learner into the subject? And how should you introduce the subject of a topic?

Do you need an introduction?

When learners may jump from topic to topic, introductions are especially important. How much of an introduction should you include? That depends on how the learner gets to the topic.

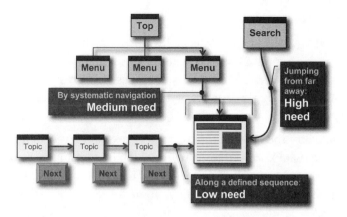

Learners may get to the topic along a trail of topics by repeatedly pressing the **Next** key. Because each topic introduces the next, very little introduction is needed. Sometimes the learner may get to the topic by systematically navigating a hierarchy of menus. Because the path is systematic, the need for an introduction is moderate. Other times the learner may jump to the topic from a distant topic or find the topic using a search process. In this case, the need for an introduction is high.

Examples of introductions

Here are some examples of introductions based on the objective of the topic and how the topic will be accessed.

Example: Interpreting dependency links

Objective	Teach how to recognize and correctly interpret dependency links to a mid-level manager or supervisor who can interpret task bars on a Gantt chart.
Introduction	Restatement of prerequisite knowledge to set the context: "Dependency links show the relationship between the start and finish of two tasks. For example, the requirement that Task A must be completed before Task B can start."

Example: Replacing a trail bridge

Objective	Teach how to decide the "minimum action" necessary to maintain a trail in a wilderness area to a wilderness manager who understands the principles of "minimum action" and has access to underlying regulations and Web-based resources.
Introduction	Immediate presentation of the scenario problem the learner is to solve. The problem is stated in a speech balloon over the image of a trail manager standing beside a stream.

Example: Defining material profiles

Objective	Teach how to use the Material Profile dialog box in *GALENA* to define the cross section for a layer of material in a slope-stability model to an engineer responsible for safety of slopes in open-pit mines who can use *GALENA* to create a model of a slope up to the point of defining cross sections.
Introduction	Context of the topic in the overall process and a restatement of prerequisite knowledge: "The next step in defining our model is to define the profiles for each of the materials in your model. Material profiles are defined as a series of lines, in turn made up of a series of x-y co-ordinate pairs."

Base the introduction on the type of objective

As with all other components of the topic, we look to the objective for guidance. Make the introduction appropriate for each type of objective.

Type objective	Type introduction
Create an X that does Y.	Why create X. Mention Y and its value to the learner.
Decide X.	Statement of the question or issue to be decided. When the decision is necessary. Statement that the decision is often made incorrectly.
Do procedure X to accomplish Y.	Why perform the procedure. What it accomplishes. When to perform the procedure. One-sentence overview of the procedure.
Know X about Y.	Context of Y into which X fits. Restatement of prerequisite knowledge. Question that X answers.
Believe X.	Current belief (that does not include X). Startling reason to believe X.
Feel X about Y.	Context of Y. What is Y? Statement of how the learner probably feels about Y now.

For more examples of introductions, see *Secrets of User-Seductive Documents* available at horton.com.

Design a good introduction

A good introduction welcomes and orients the learner. It helps the learner see how the topic relates to other topics and to the course as a whole. A good introduction should:

▶ **Confirm that learners are in the right location**. It lets learners verify that they jumped to the right topic. It provides enough information to let them decide whether to continue with the topic or resume searching elsewhere.

▶ **Orient learners** who jumped directly to this topic from far away. It provides enough of a preview that learners understand what the topic will do for them.

▶ **Set the context** for the rest of the content of the topic. Prepares learners to interpret what they read, see, and hear.

▶ **Motivate deeper study**. The introduction gives learners reasons to study hard.

For most topics, only a short introduction is necessary. A couple of sentences and a single graphic usually suffice.

Test learning in the topic

The topic should verify that it accomplished its objective. A simple test will do this. It will verify learning to reassure the learner and to assist the developer in improving the topic. Chapter 5 shows several types of formal tests you can build into your topics. In addition, many of the activities suggested in Chapters 2, 3, and 4 can help learners and designers gauge how much learning occurred.

Examples of tests based on objectives

The test used to measure success of the topic must verify that its objective was accomplished. Here are some examples:

Example: Interpreting dependency links

Objective	Teach how to recognize and correctly interpret dependency links to a mid-level manager or supervisor who can interpret task bars on a Gantt chart.
Test	Referring to a Gantt chart, answer five questions such as which task depends on a particular task or which tasks must be completed before another task can begin.

Example: Replacing a trail bridge

Objective	Teach how to decide the "minimum action" necessary to maintain a trail in a wilderness area to a wilderness manager who understands the principles of "minimum action" and has access to underlying regulations and Web-based resources.

Test   Require learners to decide among five courses of action. Selection will require judgment and compromise. Choices represent tradeoffs among invasiveness, economy, and longevity. For example, one choice is more disruptive of the environment but will not have to be repeated every few years.

Example: Defining material profiles

Objective   Teach how to use the **Material Profile** dialog box in *GALENA* to define the cross section for a layer of material in a slope-stability model to an engineer responsible for safety of slopes in open-pit mines who can use *GALENA* to create a model of a slope up to the point of defining cross sections.

Test   Assessment is provided in two ways:

The steps of the coach-me activity can be individually scored and an overall score reported (a la SCORM) to a LMS.

The final let-me activity tests learners' ability to perform the procedure unaided.

Pick test for type of objective

The type of test you use depends on the type of learning objective. Here are some suggestions to get you thinking along these lines:

Type objective	How assessed
Create an X that does Y.	Give the learner the assignment to create X and the resources necessary to do so. Observe whether the learner does so successfully.
Decide Y.	Give the learner situations that call for the decision and the necessary information and other resources and observe whether the learner makes the correct decision.
Do procedure X to accomplish Y.	Require the learner to recognize situations in which the procedure should be applied and to perform the procedure.
Know X about Y.	Test whether the learner can recall and interpret facts, principles, and concepts.
Believe X.	Verify that the learner's statements and actions are guided by the belief.
Feel X about Y.	Verify that the learner's statements and choices reveal the desired emotion.

Specify learning activities for the topic

Learning activities are the heart of the topic. They power the learning. Chapters 2, 3, and 4 can suggest specific activities for you to consider.

Examples of learning activities in topics

Once again, here are our titles and objectives. For each objective, there is a selection of Absorb, Do, and Connect activities listed.

Example: Interpreting dependency links

Objective   Teach how to recognize and correctly interpret dependency links to a mid-level manager or supervisor who can interpret task bars on a Gantt chart.

Activities   **Read** an introduction containing a definition of dependency links and a statement of why they are important.
View an animation that points out dependency markers and how they connect tasks.
Read a summary of what dependency markers are.
Think more about Gantt charts by finding them in your own work.

Example: Replacing a trail bridge

Objective   Teach how to decide the "minimum action" necessary to maintain a trail in a wilderness area to a wilderness manager who understands the principles of "minimum action" and has access to underlying regulations and Web-based resources.

Activities   **Read** a description of the situation and summary of the regulations. Situation is that a trail bridge has collapsed due to rot. Regulations permit actions to reopen the trail, provided they are the "minimum action" as defined in legislation.
Research the situation. Read about the wilderness area and the trail to learn how it is used. Examine maps to scout out alternative routes and to identify resources that could be used to rebuild the bridge.
Research regulations. Examine laws, regulations, articles, and case studies to identify issues that must be considered in making a decision.
Decide by choosing among five plausible alternative courses of action.

Example: Defining material profiles

Objective   Teach how to use the **Material Profile** dialog box in *GALENA* to define the cross section for a layer of material in a slope-stability model to an engineer responsible for safety of slopes in open-pit mines who can use *GALENA* to create a model of a slope up to the point of defining cross sections.

Activities	**Read** an overview of the steps of the procedure.
	Read about and view aspects of the ongoing example that will be filled in during this phase.
	Watch and listen to a demonstration of setting material profiles in *GALENA*.
	Perform a simulated procedure based on the procedure demonstrated. Receive feedback and hints as necessary.
	Perform the procedure for real. Learners define a specified material profile using *GALENA*. Learners then compare results to targeted results.

Pick activities for the type objective

Let's look at the kinds of learning experiences that you might need for each of the different types of learning objectives. This is only a starter set. Volumes have been written about how to pick activities to teach various objectives. Still, this should get you started.

Types of objectives	Learning activities to consider		
	Absorb	**Do**	**Connect**
Create an X that does Y.	Presentation of the requirements of Y. Demonstration of how to use tools.	Practice creating an X that does Y.	Create an X for the learner's Y.
Decide Y.	Read or watch presentations on: ▸ Rules for deciding. ▸ How to gather information. ▸ Reasons for each option.	Practice deciding using various assumptions.	See consequences of decisions. Decide for situations in the learner's life.
Do procedure X to accomplish Y.	Watch a demonstration of the steps. See examples of conditions that trigger the procedure.	Practice performing the steps.	Identify personal situations in which the procedure will apply. Identify how it must be modified to apply.

Types of objectives	Learning activities to consider		
	Absorb	**Do**	**Connect**
Know X about Y.	Read, listen, watch a presentation on X.	Practice identifying X in various situations.	Identify situations in which this knowledge applies. Apply knowledge to a personal situation.
Believe X.	Presentation or readings on: ▶ Reasons for X. ▶ Facts suggesting X.	Infer X from facts and reasons.	Acknowledge change of beliefs. Apply new beliefs to personal situation.
Feel X about Y.	Presentation and readings on reasons to feel X. Image associating X and Y.	Respond to situations in which Y triggers X.	State the personal effect of feeling X.

For more on choosing activities for specific learning objectives, go to page 55 in Chapter 1.

Summarize the topic

If a topic consists of more than a single scrolling zone of information, you may want to include a summary.

When to include a summary

The summary gives the learner another chance to learn. It also helps learners verify that they acquired the necessary knowledge. A good summary may be all that is needed by learners returning for a refresher or for learners who already know much about the subject and only need to extend their knowledge a little bit.

Include a real summary

Many topics have a page or section titled "Summary," but lack any true summary. A real summary states the key points the learner should know before ending the topic. Many so-called summaries merely restate the objectives. I think lazy designers are to blame.

Here is a comparison of two summaries. The first summary is just a restatement of the topic objectives. The second summary is a true summary that adds additional value for the learner.

☹ No	☺ Yes
This module taught how to: ▶ Set a starting time using the keyboard. ▶ Use buttons to adjust the time. ▶ Pick a person at zero time. ▶ Pick a team at zero time. ▶ Specify the people to pick from. ▶ Specify the teams to pick from.	To **set a starting time**, select the time and then type in minutes and seconds. To **adjust the time,** use the **up** and **down** buttons. To **specify what to pick**, select the **Team** or **Person** checkbox. To **specify people** to pick from, click the **Specify people** button. For teams, click the **Specify teams** button.

Combine overview and summary

One way to simplify your topic is to design the summary as an overview and put it early in the topic.

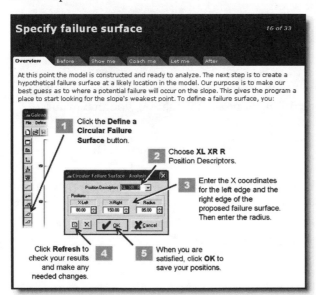

The *GALENA Slope Stability Analysis* course does just this. The topics for each procedure begin with an **Overview** tab that serves as both a preview of the steps to be learned and a summary of those steps.

Tabbed interface built using Adobe Dreamweaver and custom JavaScript. Screens captured with TechSmith SnagIt. Illustrations created in Microsoft PowerPoint.

Base the summary on the type of learning objective

The following job aid suggests how to base a topic's summary on the type of learning objective for the topic. For each of the six types, it suggests how to summarize the topic.

Suppose, for example, you are designing a topic to teach how to make a decision. You look in the Type column to find "Decide Y" and then move across to the right to find three suggested ways to summarize the topic.

Types of objectives	How to summarize
Create an X that does Y.	Generalized recap of the procedure or process for creating X. Format as a job aid.
Decide Y.	Brief recap of rules for deciding. If-Then table to guide decision. Mnemonic for the rule used to decide.
Do procedure X to accomplish Y.	Generalized recap of the procedure. Checklist, map, or flowchart of the procedure.
Know X about Y.	List of key facts to remember. Mnemonic to aid in remembering. Conceptual diagram.
Believe X.	Reminder of the evidence for believing X. Enumeration of what the learner should now believe.
Feel X about Y.	Congratulations from someone who feels the same way.

Link to related material

Real life is seldom simple. Problems defy simple solutions, and work demands a wide mix of skills and knowledge. Topics must provide a variety of learning experiences and reference materials.

Make it easy for learners to read related topics and materials. Put hyperlinks to other topics learners may need. In each topic, present just one main idea. Link to other topics, rather than include their information.

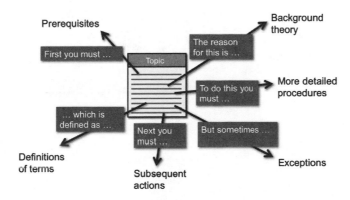

Link to reference materials or to other topics for background theory, more details for a procedure, exceptions to a rule, subsequent actions for a procedure, definitions of terms, and prerequisites or requirements before beginning an activity.

Connect related knowledge

Continually ask yourself, "What other information would help the learner?" Use hyperlinks to let learners quickly find all the different kinds of information they need to answer their questions. Consider linking these kinds of information (Notice some hyperlinks are two-way and others are just one-way):

Steps in a procedure	↔	Concept involved
A step in a procedure	↔	The next step in the procedure
One way of doing a task	↔	Another way
Overview	↔	Specific details
Term	→	Definition
Principle or concept	↔	Concrete examples that illustrate it
General rule	↔	Exceptions to the rule
Parent topic	↔	Child topic
Knowledge or skill	→	Prerequisite knowledge or skill

Let's look at how some topics and lessons expand the potential learning experiences by linking to related materials.

The *Designing Knowledge Products* course begins each lesson with references to prerequisites and related information. These links take the learner to topics in other lessons or to documents found elsewhere on the Web.

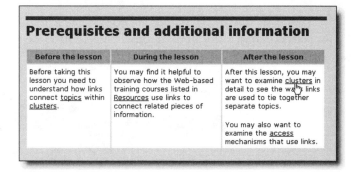

Prerequisites and additional information

Before the lesson	During the lesson	After the lesson
Before taking this lesson you need to understand how links connect topics within clusters.	You may find it helpful to observe how the Web-based training courses listed in Resources use links to connect related pieces of information.	After this lesson, you may want to examine clusters in detail to see the way links are used to tie together separate topics. You may also want to examine the access mechanisms that use links.

In the *GALENA Slope Stability Analysis* course, the topic on applying an analysis technique contains a link to a document explaining the method of calculation used in the technique.

Learners who were interested in learning more about the mathematics involved in the technique could download and read this document.

Limit free-form hyperlinks

Limit free-form hyperlinks. These are links that jump diagonally across the organizational hierarchy. Such links lead to the *tangled vine dilemma*. If you include a topic in your e-learning, you must include all the topics it links to. And all the topics they link to. And all they link to. And so on and on.

One mildly painful solution may be to enable free-form navigation only through the menu, the index, a search facility, or automatically generated next and previous links. The solution is painful because finding related topics now requires consciously searching for them. But the result is that the topics and lessons you create can be reused freely.

One technique to use is to suggest search terms to the learner who needs to find related topics, for example, "For more detailed instructions, search for *editing sentences and words*."

Write metadata

Metadata is just descriptive labeling. The term metadata means "information about information." It is just a fancy way to refer to the descriptive labeling that can be used by learners to find topics they want to take and by developers to find topics they want to include in their courses.

Industry standards define specific metadata items, and many authoring tools leave slots on their dialog boxes where you can enter metadata for your topics and other components.

Include keywords and a description

Two metadata items are especially important for designers of topics: the description and keywords. Although these items may not be visible to learners as they take the topic, they can help learners and developers find the topic when they need it.

The keywords may be used like index terms in a book. The learner may enter them in a search field to find a topic that matches these terms. The description may appear in a catalog of course topics. Here are some examples:

Example: Interpreting dependency links

Description Shows what dependency link markers look like and explains what they mean.

Keywords dependency links
dependency markers
links, dependency
markers, dependency

Example: Replacing a trail bridge

Description Teaches managers to conduct research necessary to decide the minimum action for maintaining a wilderness trail.

Keywords minimum action
trail bridge
ford
bridge outage
maintaining a trail
trail maintenance

Example: Defining material profiles

Description Teaches how to add a profile to indicate the cross section for a material in the slope.

Keywords material profile
profile, material
cross section

Assign indexing keywords

If your e-learning is large, you will need to include an index and possibly a keyword search facility. That means you must assign indexing terms to topics. The terms you assign depend on the content of the topic and on the objective it accomplishes.

Anticipate questions of learners

When do you use the index of a paper book? When do you do a Web search? When you are seeking the answer to a question—that's when. This suggests that we choose keywords to match questions learners may have and that our topics may answer.

1. Compile a list of questions that learners may have. Consider all the ways a learner might ask the question. Remember, the learner may not know the official terminology yet.

2. Identify which topics answer these questions.

3. Assign keywords to each topic by picking words prominent in the questions that the topic answers.

Add more terms

Consider additional terms. Here are some candidates:

▶ Unique nouns and verbs from the title, body text, and figure captions.

▶ Names of things. Include prominent proper nouns, official nomenclature, and parts lists.

▶ Objects and concepts shown in graphics, especially ones not explicitly named in the text.

Include more than standard words

Further enrich your keywords by including familiar:

▶ **Abbreviations**. How many people know what NASA or UNESCO stands for? How many would type out the full form of a more common abbreviation, like IBM or CIA?

▶ **Part numbers**. Many mechanics know the numbers of frequently replaced parts better than the names of these components.

▶ **Slang and jargon**. Learners may have a workplace vocabulary that does not square with the official terminology used in your topic.

Speak the learner's language

Remember, not everybody uses the same words or spells them the same way. Learners may not yet know the official names of things. So, in your keywords, include synonyms, that is, words with the same meaning. For example:

copy → duplicate, replicate, reproduce

build → create, make, generate

Vary the grammatical form of the words. Some search engines can do this automatically. If yours cannot, consider including multiple forms of each important word. For example:

> copy → copying, copies, copied
>
> build → building, built

Account for spelling variations. British and American spellings may differ. And some words may have competing spellings or different forms for the plural or collective. For example:

> color → colour
>
> appendixes → appendices

Do not over-index

These techniques are good for keyword searches, but can cause a problem in displayed indexes. If you plan to include an index, use a subset of your keyword list so that the displayed alphabetical index will not end up with too many nearly identical entries in a row.

Describe your topic

Another important piece of metadata is the description of your topic. This description may be displayed to the learner as a preview of the topic or an inducement to take it. There are no hard-and-fast rules for writing the description, but here are some commonsense suggestions:

- ▶ **Write the description for the potential learner**. It is easier for an instructional developer to understand a description written for learners than vice versa.

- ▶ **Tell learners what the topic offers them**. I do not recommend the usual boring recitation of the instructional objectives—in a bullet list, nonetheless—but a simple statement of what the learner will be able to do as a result of the topic.

- ▶ **Keep the description short**. A few sentences are usually enough. If learners are curious, they can examine the topic itself.

- ▶ **Choose terms that the learner will understand**. Do not use terms that the learner would understand only after completing the topic.

Design components logically and economically

In designing the parts of a topic, consider how components interact, what they do for learners, and how they fit together.

Design components in logical order

Design the components of the topic logically. That means designing components in order by logical dependencies.

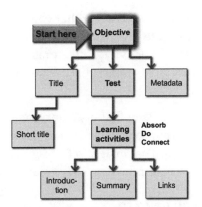

1. We start by defining the objective. The objective figures in every design decision, so this is where we start. We go nowhere till we nail down the learning objective.

2. Next, I like to pick the title and the short title. I do this because naming a topic requires me to focus tightly on the objective. By the time I have decided on a short title, I am familiar with the learning objective.

3. Now, I design the test. I use it to guide design of other content components.

4. Next come the learning activities. I design Absorb, Do, and Connect activities I need to accomplish the objective. I know I have the right activities when they enable the learner to pass the test.

5. Now, I zoom back and design the introduction to induct learners into the topic and the summary to send them on their way.

6. For special needs, I decide what links will be needed to provide access to related resources.

7. With all my content specified, I finish up by creating the metadata that describes the topic. I could do the metadata earlier, but I find it helps me to know the content of the topic before I craft a description or assign indexing keywords to the topic.

You may find a different order works for you. Just remember that the arrows show dependencies. You can start with the objective and work your way down any path you choose. Keep an open mind, and be ready to revisit any design decision.

Think verbs, not nouns

Here's an insight that will save you from painful experience: Think verbs, not nouns. What do I mean by that? To design the components of a topic, we must remember why topics contain content.

 No

☺ Yes

Components are **content** you must **create**.

Components are **tasks** you must **perform for the learner**.

For years I thought that components are content that you must create. Such an approach simplifies the design process to a rote procedure. Coin a title. Write an introduction. Create a presentation for the Absorb activity. Add a practice activity. Add a test. And so forth. Such a mechanical process yields topics that are minimally effective, but are seldom engaging, concise, or efficient.

My ah-ha moment came when I realized that my components are really tasks that I must perform for the learner. That is, components are a checklist of things that need to happen rather than a list of media to build. That insight sets designers free to creatively accomplish these tasks rather than to monotonously create content.

Don't create more than you need to

Here's a checklist to use when designing or analyzing topics. It also contains some good news that will simplify your task as a designer.

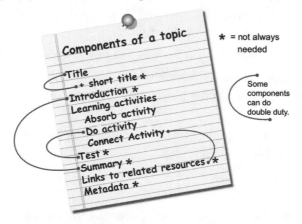

The standard components of a topic include a title, a short title, an introduction, learning activities (namely Absorb, Do, and Connect activities), a test, a summary, links to related resources, and metadata. Whew! That's a lot. The good news is that you seldom have to create every one of these items.

The asterisks in the checklist flag items that are not always needed. You can sometimes omit the short title, introduction, test, summary, links to related resources, or the metadata. Though generally useful, these items are not as critical as the others, namely the title and learning activities. Even if you do not omit these items, you can often keep them brief or incorporate them with other components.

And that leads to our second bit of good news. Some components can do double duty. In the checklist, lines connect components that can often be combined into a single component, which performs both functions. For example, if the title is concise, it can serve as the short title. Designers often put the summary first as an introduction to the topic. A well-designed Do activity can also serve as a test of accomplishment of the objective. And, linking to related resources can provide a Connect activity.

Next time you start to design a topic, use this checklist to plan what you must design and create.

DESIGN REUSABLE TOPICS

Just dumping content into templates does not make for effective learning. Just structuring topics as learning objects does not in itself make the content usable or reusable. To be useful and reusable, topics must be designed with reuse in mind. And reuse can only come if the topic is useful in the first place.

Craft recombinant building blocks

Reusable components are discrete chunks, not flowing passages. They are like building blocks that can be stacked to build a wall, a house, or a cathedral.

Design discrete chunks of reusable content

Effective topics are coherent, self-contained, complete, and consistent.

Reusable content is coherent. It aims to accomplish one purpose or answer one question. It confines itself to one subject and does not meander into non-essential material.

Reusable topics are self-contained. They may be consumed in any order. Sure, consuming topics in a specific order, such as the steps of a procedure, may make them more valuable and understandable, but no one should become hopelessly confused when encountering a topic out of sequence.

Reusable topics are complete. They contain everything necessary to accomplish their goal. They may contain the necessary presentations, practice activities, and other content directly. Or they may contain other more-specific topics.

Reusable topics are consistent. We can mix and match them with little concern that learners will become confused as they navigate the course.

Use recipe cards as a guiding metaphor

If you need a role model for reusable objects, think of recipe cards. Each recipe card is self-contained and complete. It contains all the knowledge necessary for a cook to prepare one dish. It is concise and focused. It does not mix too many different types of information or stray from the subject. Recipe cards follow a consistent format.

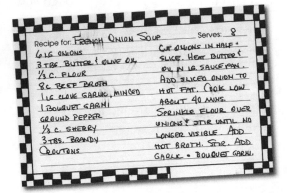

Imagine taking a stack of recipe cards and throwing them in the air. After they flutter to the floor, pick one at random. It still works. Sorting the cards out by type of dish or nutritional characteristics may add value, but a recipe card taken out of context will poison no one. That is a goal we should work for in designing reusable topics.

Design consistent topics

Prevent the whiplash experience that occurs when learners, moving through a sequence of topics, are buffeted by an unpredictable sequence of pedagogical designs, colors, navigation schemes, icons, writing styles, backgrounds, layouts, sound levels, media, and test questions. In developing your topics, standardize:

▶ Visual appearance.

▶ Navigation schemes.

▶ Instructional strategies.

▶ Testing approaches.

This advice goes double, if multiple departments create topics. And triple, if multiple companies are involved.

Avoid the "as-shown-above" syndrome

What happens if our topics are not self-contained? Imagine the introduction of a topic where you find the phrase "In a previous topic you learned how to …." But what if the learner chose to skip that topic? Or jumped directly to this topic from a search engine? The presumption that learners all follow a single path through the course indicates that the topics are not truly self-contained.

The *as-shown-above syndrome* is the tendency of a designer to assume that everybody takes the course in exactly the sequence the designer intended. You see it in phrases and assumptions like these:

▶ "As shown above" and "As shown below" (where the items mentioned are not on the current screen or even in the current topic).

▶ "Earlier you read that…."

▶ "By now you have learned how to…."

▶ "Repeat the preceding steps" (when the preceding steps are in another topic or have scrolled off the screen).

▶ "… will be explained later." (But will the learner be reading later?).

▶ Abbreviations spelled out only the first time they are used and terms defined only the first time they are used.

▶ Warnings, cautions, notes, and conventions in the beginning of the course.

▶ "The next step in the process is …." (when the learner arrived at this topic directly from a search).

▶ Links labeled <u>Return to X</u> (when we did not come from X).

The solution is to make no hard assumptions about which path learners will follow. If understanding one idea requires understanding another idea, state the other idea, or link to it, or at least signal the requirement. Make it easy for learners to find needed information out of sequence. Here's where an index pays for itself. As do a good menu and a search facility.

INTEGRATE FOREIGN MODULES

Sometimes the best way to build your e-learning is to include topics, activities, and lessons developed by others. Technically, you can do so just by linking to these "foreign" modules. However, content developed by someone else following different standards may look different, teach differently, and further different objectives than your topic or lesson. Such modules may prove confusing to learners accustomed to your e-learning's "native" topics and activities.

To ease this confusion, you should design a "docking module" to fit between the foreign content and your topic.

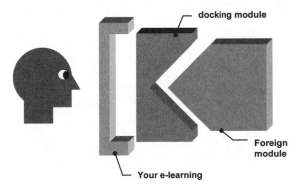

The docking module helps the foreign module fit into your course so that learners can make the transition from your course to the foreign module and back again.

Example of a docking module

Here is an example of a module designed for one course but appearing within another.

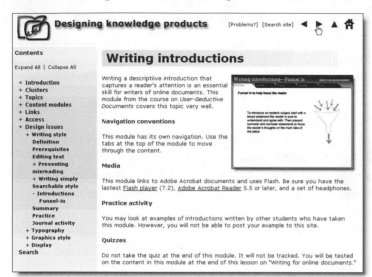

The brief introduction to the foreign module tells learners where the module comes from and guides them in navigating the module.

It also tells learners what file formats are used and what portions of the module should be ignored.

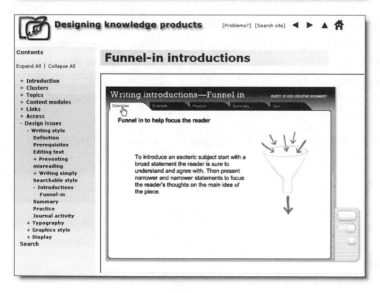

Here, the foreign module appears within the standard course structure.

Course created using Adobe Dreamweaver and Active Server Pages. Foreign module built in PowerPoint and converted for Web delivery with Adobe Presenter.

What to include in a docking module

A docking module consists of all the things you do to make the foreign module meet the needs of your learners. Some of the components of a docking module are:

A special display window. If the foreign module is of a different shape or size than your modules, you may need to craft a special frameset. You can also display it in a separate window alongside the window for the main part of your e-learning.

Introduction. You may need to create a preview, introduction, abstract, overview, or description of the module to tell learners what to make of the foreign module.

Cautions. Let learners know any limitations of the module that are different from those for native modules. What conventions does it follow? How accurate and relevant are its materials? Who owns it, and how is its use restricted?

Access aids. Give learners any help they may need in accessing the foreign module and displaying its content. Provide:

▶ Instructions on taking the module.

▶ A special menu and index linked to its content.

▶ Help obtaining any plug-ins or fonts it requires.

▶ Glossary to define different terminology used in the module.

Certification test. The foreign module may not provide a test, or its test may not measure what is important to you. Add your own test to measure what learners got from the module.

IN CLOSING ...

Summary

A topic is a unit of e-learning that accomplishes one learning objective. A topic that contains the activities and assessments necessary to accomplish the objective may be considered a learning object.

A topic consists of these components:

Objective A statement of what the topic will accomplish. This learning objective must be precise enough to guide design of all the other components.

Title The label of the topic. Must be clear enough to convey what the topic offers.

Introduction A transition into the content of the topic to welcome the learner and set the context for what follows.

Tests Activities to verify that the objective was accomplished. These can be formal tests or simple self-check activities.

Activities A combination of Absorb, Do, and Connect activities necessary to accomplish the learning objective.

Summary A recap of the main points taught by the topic. May appear as an overview or preview and be printed as a job aid.

Links Hyperlinks to related topics and other materials. Although such links can enrich the learning experience, they can make topics harder to reuse.

Metadata Descriptive labeling aimed at helping learners and instructional developers find this topic when necessary. Two main types of metadata are keywords and description. Keywords are like index terms for a paper book. The description is like a catalog entry for the topic.

To design effective topics, we must seek an effective compromise among competing goals:

▶ Make topics self-contained for greater reuse.

▶ Include links to related material at the risk of requiring the linked material in every course that includes the object.

▶ Balance the need for short-specific topics that precisely target objectives with the danger of having to create too many separate topics.

▶ Size topics to avoid sprawl and choppiness.

▶ Set and follow standards to ensure that topics appear consistent to learners.

TEMPLATES FOR TOPICS

The following are templates listing suggested content for topics to accomplish each of the six basic learning objectives.

Create an X that does Y

Title	Building a _____ Designing _____		
Introduction	Why create X. Mention Y and its value to the learner.		
Learning activities	**Absorb**	**Do**	**Connect**
	Presentation of the requirements of Y. Demo of how to use tools.	Practice creating an X that does Y.	Create an X for the learner's Y.
Test	Give the learner the assignment to create X and the resources necessary to do so. Observe whether the learner does so successfully.		
Summary	Generalized recap of the process for creating X. Format as a job aid.		

Decide X

Title	Selecting _____ Choosing _____		
Introduction	Statement of the question or issue to be decided. When the decision is necessary. Statement that the decision is often made incorrectly.		
Learning activities	**Absorb**	**Do**	**Connect**
	Read or watch presentations on: ▶ Rules for deciding. ▶ How to gather information. ▶ Reasons for each option.	Practice deciding for various assumptions.	See consequences of decisions. Decide for situations in the learner's life.
Test	Give the learner situations that call for the decision and the necessary information and other resources and observe whether the learner makes the correct decision.		
Summary	▶ Brief recap of rules for deciding. ▶ If-Then table to guide decision. ▶ Mnemonic for the rule used to decide.		

Do X to accomplish Y

Title	_____ ing _____		
Introduction	Why perform the procedure. What it accomplishes. When to perform the procedure. One-sentence overview of the procedure.		
Learning activities	**Absorb**	**Do**	**Connect**
	Watch a demo of steps. See examples of conditions that trigger the procedure.	Practice performing the steps.	Identify personal situations to apply the procedure. Identify how it must be modified to apply.
Test	Require learners to recognize where the procedure should be applied and to perform the procedure.		
Summary	Generalized recap of the procedure. Checklist, map, or flowchart of the procedure.		

Know X about Y

Title	[Name of X] [Statement summarizing X]		
Introduction	Context of Y into which X fits. Restatement of prerequisite knowledge. Question that X answers.		
Learning activities	**Absorb**	**Do**	**Connect**
	Read, listen, watch a presentation on X.	Practice identifying X in various situations.	Identify situations in which this knowledge applies. Apply knowledge in situations.
Test	Test whether the learner can recall and interpret facts, principles, and concepts.		
Summary	List of key facts to remember. Mnemonic. Conceptual diagram.		

Believe X

Title	Why _____? [or just a statement of X]		
Introduction	Current belief (that does not include X). Startling reason to believe X.		
Learning activities	**Absorb**	**Do**	**Connect**
	Presentation or readings on: ▶ Reasons for X. ▶ Facts suggesting X.	Infer X from facts and reasons.	Acknowledge change of beliefs. Apply new beliefs.
Test	Verify that the learner's statements and actions are guided by the belief.		
Summary	Reminder of the evidence for believing X. Enumeration of what the learner should now believe.		

Feel X about Y

Title	[Statement that asserts or implies X about Y]		
Introduction	Context of Y. What is Y? Statement of how the learner probably feels about Y now.		
Learning activities	**Absorb**	**Do**	**Connect**
	Presentation and readings on reasons to feel X. Image associating X and Y.	Respond to situations in which Y triggers X.	State the personal effect of feeling X.
Test	Verify that the learner's statements and choices reveal the desired emotion.		
Summary	Congratulations from someone who feels the same way.		

For more ...

To see some of the kinds of activities you may want to include, flip through Chapters 2, 3, and 4. To see the types of tests you can include, turn to Chapter 5. For help integrating topics into lessons, see online Chapter 12.

For more on creating topics as learning objects, search the Web for *learning object*.

7 Games and simulations

Learning by playing and pretending in virtual worlds

Games and simulations allow learners to practice tasks, apply knowledge, and infer principles—all while having fun. With learning games, people can learn from a personal tutor who demonstrates subjects, guides them through their initial efforts, monitors their growing skills, and certifies their mastery.

Games and simulations may provide a complete model of a real-world system or just a rapid-fire series of questions to answer. Games and simulations can be individual Do activities, tests, whole topics, sprawling lessons, and even entire courses.

GAMES AND SIMULATIONS FOR LEARNING

Games and simulations for learning can be fun, but they are always purposeful. They teach first and entertain second. Learning games can draw on the established conventions of quiz shows, board games, and video games to arouse curiosity and harness competitive urges. Simulations immerse learners in a work-related context and let them safely verify that they can perform a specific task or procedure.

How do you think most learners would respond if you asked them whether they would rather take a test or play a game?

Example of a learning game

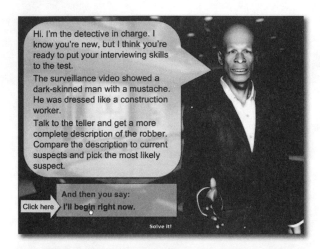

This game teaches interviewing skills in the context of a police investigation. Learners are assigned the task of interviewing a witness to a bank robbery to elicit clues to the identity of the robber.

The game provides the learner with choices that affect the course of the game.

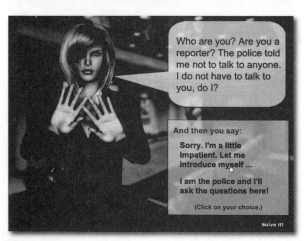

Most feedback is provided by events in the game. Events reveal whether the learner's previous action was appropriate.

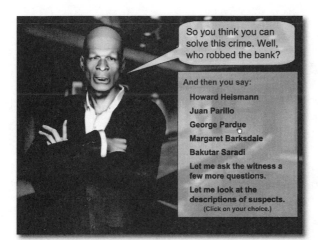

At any point, learners can try to solve the mystery.

Created in Microsoft PowerPoint and converted for Web delivery using Articulate Presenter. 3D characters created in SmithMicro Poser. View example at horton.com/eld/.

How are games, tests, and simulations related?

What exactly are learning games and simulations? How are they related to tests and demonstrations? The terms are used rather loosely, so we should define them before considering how to design them.

A game can be thought of as a simulation that involves a personally challenging task. A simulation can be used for several different purposes. Pairing it with the challenge to perform a task meaningful to the learner turns it into a game.

Another way to look at a game is as a test that provides immediate feedback but does not record a score. The test is any task the learner attempts. Immediate feedback guides the learner in performing the task. The absence of a recorded score encourages the learner to guess, take risks, and try alternative strategies—just to see what happens.

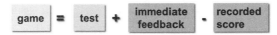

Do you call it a game or a simulation?

Experts and linguists will howl, but I believe the main difference between the terms *learning game* and *learning simulation* are just ones of positioning. True, simulations tend to look more realistic, while games tend to feature scorekeeping. However, pedantic reasons to distinguish the two are trumped by pragmatic concerns. Hence this recommendation:

If *game* sounds frivolous, call it a *simulation*.

If *simulation* sounds too stuffy or expensive, call it a *game*.

Just be sure to design it so it teaches. So, free to pick whichever term appeals to your learners and satisfies your chain of command.

Demos are not true simulations

Although the term simulation is used broadly to cover a range of activities, it is important to make a distinction between demonstrations and true simulations. The contrast is especially important in education and training. The key distinction is that, in true simulations, the learner controls the sequence of events.

Demonstration	True simulation
Learners watch passively.	Learners decide and act.
Learning results from clear explanation.	Learning results from practice and authentic feedback.
Useful for selling and informing customers.	Useful for educating and training workers.

In a demonstration, the learner watches passively as the task is performed. It is like looking over the teacher's shoulder. The learner may start and stop the demonstration, but does not actually perform the steps being shown. In a true simulation, the learner decides and acts. The simulation may animate the system's responses to the learner's actions, but it is up to the learner to decide what to do and how to carry out those actions.

In a demonstration, the learner learns from a clear explanation. A logical commentary or narration is essential in a demonstration. In a simulation, learning relies primarily on authentic feedback, like that provided by the actual system or by a coach who is experienced in using the system. Simulations let learners practice as much as they want to or need to.

Demonstrations are highly effective for selling products and for informing learners. They can make clear the great results possible with a product. And they can teach already experienced learners how to extend their existing skills. True simulations are ideal for serious training and education because retention is greater and understanding is deeper.

These distinctions between demonstrations and simulations are crucial for two reasons. First, you should never send a demonstration to do a simulation's work. Or vice versa. Each has its uses but they are not interchangeable. They are, however, complementary. A good demonstration prepares and motivates a learner to engage in a true simulation. Learners who have used simulations to learn basic operations can often pick up additional skills by watching well-designed demonstrations. (For an explanation of the role of demonstrations, see "Physical demonstrations" on page 72 and "Software demonstrations" on page 74.)

How do games and simulations work?

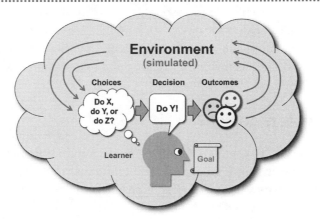

In a learning game, the most important factor is the learner. Perhaps this person is learning to use a piece of software or to interview job candidates. Or, learning how to apply calculus to solving problems in particle physics.

Note: In simulations, the learner is often referred to as the *user*—in games, as the *player*.

In the game or simulation, the learner has a goal. Usually this goal is presented to the learner by the computer. The goal is typically a task the learner is learning to perform. For software simulations, the goal typically requires the learner to perform a common task with a computer tool. For other tasks, the learner might have to interview a simulated job candidate or earn points by answering questions on the subject of study.

The learner operates inside an environment. That environment is simulated, of course. For a software simulation, the screen looks like the display the learner would see when operating the computer program. For the job interview, the screen might show the job candidate seated across a desk from the learner.

The environment presents the learner with choices. What do I do next? Which command do I use in this computer program? What question do I ask the job candidate? What approach will solve my problem? The learner must decide among choices and take action. The learner may indicate a choice by clicking a button, typing in text, or some other action.

The learner's actions have consequences or outcomes in the simulated environment. The learner may see the display change. Or the simulation may make a rude noise and an error message may appear. Such feedback is intrinsic to the game or simulation.

These outcomes may have additional effects in the environment, some of which may be invisible to the learner. These changes in the environment present the learner with new choices, and the cycle continues.

This cycle of making decisions and seeing results is the essence of the game or simulation. For software simulations, each cycle corresponds to one input from the learner. For the job-interview, each cycle consists of one question by the learner and an answer by the job candidate. In combat simulators used to train soldiers, an entire cycle may take only a second. In business simulations involving creating and marketing products, a cycle may represent months.

What do we mean design?

Games can be complex and expensive, requiring months and millions of dollars to develop. Or they can be as simple as a spreadsheet with instructions to adjust three values until a fourth value exceeds a limit. The goal of design is to find the simple solution that accomplishes your learning objective.

For games, as for other forms of e-learning, design and development are often separate activities. Design plans and specifies the game, and development builds it. Development may require hiring a software developer or just employing templates for common forms of games, such as puzzles and quizzes. In any case, though, the designer must thoroughly specify the game.

WHY GAMES?

Why and where are games effective ways to learn? Games and simulations enable types of learning not practical in classrooms or conventional e-learning.

What can games do for us?

Games provide specific educational advantages over all other forms of learning. For example, games:

▶ **Show consequences not normally visible**. With games, learners can experience the cumulative effect of widespread small changes. A course in ethics can, for instance, show the effects on an organization if everybody engages in a questionable practice that seems harmless if performed by only an individual. Use games to show consequences that are not normally visible because they occur too quickly, take too long, occur far away in physical space or in a distant part of the organization, are too small or too large, or are too abstract.

▶ **Let learners make mistakes without suffering permanent consequences**. Use games to let learners explore the consequences of risky behavior. Game players can learn from mistakes that, in the real world, result in death, injury, imprisonment, financial collapse, social rejection, or legal action. Such learning is especially important in work and social environments where failure is not tolerated.

▶ **Encourage learners to pause, reflect, and revise**. Often real-world experiences don't give the learner opportunities to rethink decisions and try alternative approaches, but games can.

▶ **Provide a laboratory** where learners can test different hypotheses, mental models, tactics, and strategies to see which work best and which are too risky to try in the real world.

▶ **Simplify complex situations** in ways that isolate the components and variables that learners should attend to and that make relationships explicit.

▶ **Give opportunities for abundant practice and feedback**. For tasks where "time on task" is critical to learning, games can provide 24x7 opportunities to practice and refine behavior. Games provide time and experience enough for learners to discover patterns, trends, and relationships for themselves.

▶ **Reawaken learning by play**. As children, we play with blocks to learn gravity and spatial relationships, we practice personal relationships with dolls and action figures, and use scale models to learn design and construction. Games extend the motivating effect of play to adults. Games can even seduce voluntary learners into taking tests.

As powerful as games are, they are no educational panacea. Even the best game cannot by itself teach large amounts of detailed information or replace books, classrooms, and other forms of learning.

When to use games

Developing effective games is difficult, time-consuming, and expensive—typically 100 times the cost of a simple multiple-choice text question. Getting games to work well over the Web is even harder. What can games do for the organization that must pay for their development? Consider games in these situations:

Costs of failure are high. Failures that endanger life, public safety, and financial success justify expensive remedies. Brain surgeons, nuclear power plant operators, and stock market investors must consistently perform at a high level of skill.

Learning with real systems is not practical. The real activity may take too long, for example, testing genetic modifications to plants. Training on real systems may be too expensive, for example, learning to fly the latest product from Boeing or Airbus. Failure may be too embarrassing, for example, triggering a false alarm in a security system that summons the police.

Learners need individual attention. Games can be self-customizing. Learners experience a unique series of events in response to their own knowledge, skills, and instincts.

Many people must be educated. Since the major costs for a game are in developing and perfecting it, additional learners add little to the total costs. Spreading the costs over a few hundred or a few thousand learners recovers those costs.

Tasks are complex and time is short. Games can telescope weeks of education into days. Games let learners skip rapidly through subjects they have already mastered and spend more time on just the areas in which they need improvement. Games are highly efficient coaches.

Skills to be taught are subtle and complex. Games work well for subjects when the greatest challenge is not acquiring factual knowledge but applying skills, knowledge, and attitudes in complex, unique situations.

You have time and budget to see the project through. Games may be effective, but they are seldom easy or inexpensive to develop. Sophisticated, realistic games can require 500 to 1,000 hours of development for each hour of learning. Even though simpler games require much less development time, they do require substantial time to design, plan, and specify.

TYPES OF LEARNING GAMES

The different types of learning games are limited only by the creativity of designers. Here are a few more examples to give you some ideas of the variety of learning games you can use in e-learning.

- ▶ Quiz-show games (p. 331).
- ▶ Word games (p. 332).
- ▶ Jigsaw puzzles (p. 333).
- ▶ Branching scenarios (p. 334).
- ▶ Task simulations (p. 335).
- ▶ Personal-response simulations (p. 337).
- ▶ Environmental simulations (p. 340).
- ▶ Immersive role-playing games (p. 341).

Quiz-show games

To make tests less intimidating and more engaging, restyle them as game shows, similar to ones common on TV.

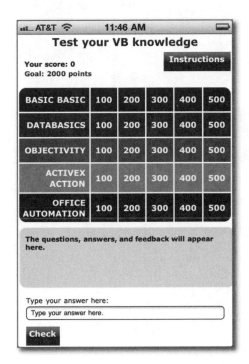

In this example, learners are challenged to score a number of points by correctly answering questions about Visual Basic. To reach their goals, learners can answer a lot of low-point questions or fewer high-point questions. They can answer questions from a few categories or across several different categories. Each correct answer adds to the total score, and each incorrect answer subtracts from the total score.

Built using Adobe Dreamweaver and custom JavaScript and jQuery. View example at horton.com/eld/.

Quiz-show games are good for testing factual knowledge, provided answers are clearly right or wrong. Such games can serve as tests. And they are efficient: In just a few minutes you can ask 25 fill-in-the-blank test questions. They provide incentive to study and learn. A quiz-show game might be a good sensitizing activity or pre-test at the beginning of a module. The desire to win the game provides incentive to learn the needed facts.

Answers in quiz-show games are not limited to verbal responses, as this next example shows.

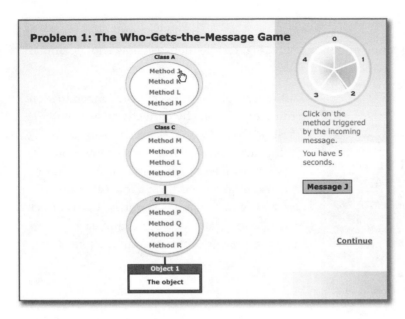

This game teaches principles by having learners click on a method in the correct class that can accept an incoming message. And, like many TV quiz shows, this one has a timer to require a prompt response.

Built using Microsoft PowerPoint and converted for the Web with iSpring Presenter. View example at horton.com/eld/.

Word games

Word games, such as crossword puzzles, make learning terminology fun. Most are just fill-in-the-blanks tests dressed up as a game.

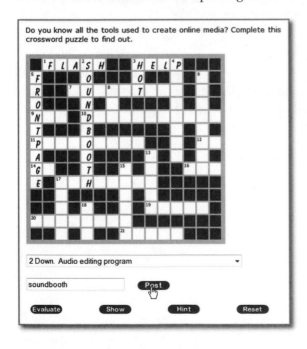

This crossword puzzle is from a course on technologies for creating online media. Here's how it works. You select a clue, in this case 2 Down. Then you type the answer into the answer field and click **Post**. The answer now appears in the puzzle.

Built using Adobe Dreamweaver and custom JavaScript. View example at horton.com/eld/.

Word games are good to test knowledge of terms. They are also good to motivate reading of text to identify names of people, products, concepts, animals, locations, and so forth. They combine well with scavenger-hunt activities where learners look up the answers to clues rather than merely recall answers (p. 198).

Jigsaw puzzles

Do you teach subjects that involve whole-to-parts relationships? Do you spend time telling learners how a product, business, or other subject is organized? If so, jigsaw puzzles and scrambled-tiles games offer a way to let learners discover such relationships and to test learners on such relationships.

A scrambled-tile puzzle can help learners recall images, visualize relationships, or notice discriminating details.

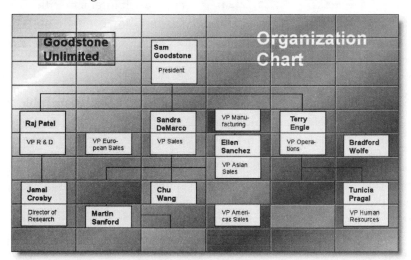

This activity on listening skills asks learners to assemble an organization chart based on an overheard conversation among company executives.

Built using Adobe Dreamweaver and custom JavaScript. View example at horton.com/eld/.

Learners click on the tile they want to move and then click where they want to move it. They continue the process until the picture has been assembled. The game directs learners' attention to specific reporting relationships.

This same kind of puzzle has been used to teach remodeling contractors how the components of a particular architectural style are combined in specific houses and to teach JavaScript programmers the Internet Explorer document object model.

Conceptual and abstract subjects require practice too, yet we often forget to provide realistic practice activities for such subjects. One way to do so is to create a concrete game for learning abstract concepts.

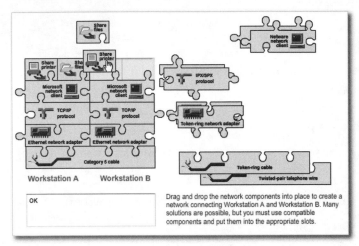

This jigsaw puzzle requires learners to drag and drop the puzzle pieces into place to configure a network. As they drop a component into place, they get feedback on how well the component works in the slot to which it is assigned and how it interacts with surrounding components.

Built using Adobe Flash. View example at horton.com/eld/.

The task is not as simple as it looks. There are more pieces than slots and only compatible components can be used together. There is no fixed solution: any combination of components that would work in the real world works here.

In this activity, learners explore the abstract world of multi-layered standards regarding data-communication protocols—but in a fun, tangible way. Games with such intricate rules are difficult to create but are very effective in teaching subjects that have more than one right answer.

Branching scenarios

Branching scenarios let learners proceed toward a goal by making decisions that help or hinder their progress. These games resemble the early computer adventure games in which the player sets out on a quest and must pick up objects and choose paths carefully. Such games are often called social-interaction simulators when they are used to simulate the interaction between people.

On page 390 we look more closely at designing a branching-scenario game.

This example lets learners practice their management skills by responding to an employee's request to take a sabbatical leave. Arriving at a correct response requires checking personnel files, reading company policy, and calling other managers.

Built using Microsoft PowerPoint and converted for the Web with iSpring Presenter. View example at horton.com/eld/.

Other examples of branching scenarios include *The Crimescene Game* (p. 324) and the interview game (p. 379).

Task simulations

Task simulations require learners to accomplish a realistic bit of work. There are two main types of task simulations: software simulations and device simulations. Though these two types may look different and require different tools to produce, their underlying instructional design, logic, and sequence of experiences are similar.

Software simulations are becoming a standard way to learn to operate computer software.

This simulator lets learners practice setting up connections between the operating system and various databases—without any risk of damaging data or the system. The simulator behaves like the real control panel—except the simulator restricts learners to the task being taught and provides instructions if needed.

In this step, the learner has selected the correct driver for the database and must now click **Finish** to continue.

Built with Adobe Captivate. View example at horton.com/eld/.

On page 386 we look more closely at designing a coached task simulation.

Device simulations teach how to operate a piece of equipment. In device simulations, learners simulate pressing buttons by clicking on images of the device. They may simulate turning a knob by dragging its edge left or right.

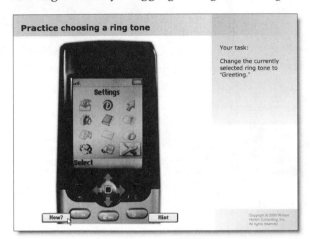

This example lets learners practice how to select a ring tone on a mobile phone.

Built using Adobe Captivate, PowerPoint, and Adobe Presenter. View example at horton.com/eld/.

And this one teaches how to operate an anesthesia delivery unit. Mistakes are a lot less costly in this simulation than in the real operating room. This is one case for which I would call this a *simulation*, not a *game*. If life is at stake, we do not play games.

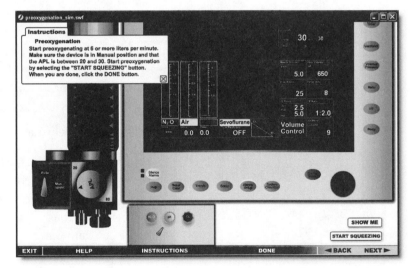

Designed by William Horton Consulting and built in Adobe Flash by Web Courseworks (webcourseworks.com).

Personal-response simulations

Personal-response simulations pose a series of complex decisions for learners to make. Decisions depend on many separate factors. Learners immediately see the results of the decision. Learners can then tweak and tune their answers to try to improve results.

In *The Diet Game*, learners practice ordering restaurant meals to meet complex dietary requirements. Meals consist of several different foods, each with different nutritional ingredients. After placing their order, learners see how well they did. They can then try other combinations of foods.

Built using Adobe Dreamweaver and Active Server Pages.

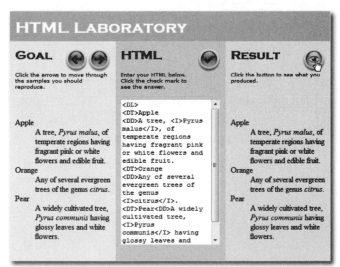

The *HTML Laboratory* is another example of a personal-response simulation. In the left column, learners are presented with formatted text and challenged to reproduce it by entering HTML code in the middle column. When they click the Result button, they see their results in the right column. Learners then refine their code until they match the goal.

Built using Adobe Dreamweaver and JavaScript. View example at horton.com/eld/.

Personal-response simulations are quite useful to help learners perform math in a fun, visual, intuitive fashion.

Would you rather learn to manage the finances of a corporate department by filling in numbers on a spreadsheet like this?

Selling e-learning

Product-revenue model

Decisions			
Enrollment fee		$100	USD
Relative quality		100%	% of competition
Service life of product		3	years
Consequences			
Enrollments		2250	
Development costs	$	300,000	
Financial results			
Revenue	$	225,000	per year
Amortized costs	$	100,000	per year
Profit	$	125,000	per year
ROI		125%	

Spreadsheet built using Microsoft Excel.

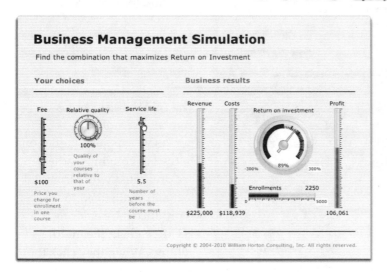

Or by dragging sliders in a game like this?

Built using SAP Crystal Dashboard Design and Microsoft Excel. View example at horton.com/eld/.

Another example lets learners develop better investment habits by repeatedly making risky investments until they discover the dangers of treating investing as gambling.

Learners decide what percentage of their net worth they want to invest and by how much they want to leverage it. Here a learner has decided to invest a quarter of his net worth and to leverage it by 5X, that is, to borrow $5 for every dollar of his own money invested.

The learner then clicks **Invest now**.

The game shows the fluctuations of the investment's value over time. At any point the learner can click the **Sell** button to sell the investment and reap the gain or loss. The game then reverts to the earlier screen where the learner's net worth is revised to show the gain or loss. The learner can then try again and again.

Built using Adobe Flash. View example at horton.com/eld/.

Possible subjects for such math-based simulations include finance, science, engineering, and medicine.

7

Games and simulations

Environmental simulations

Environmental simulations let learners experiment with a complexly interrelated system, such as a natural environment.

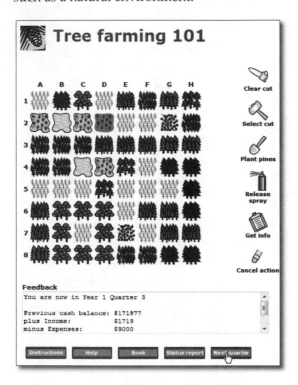

This game teaches private landowners in the southeastern United States to manage their forests more effectively, regardless of their particular goals. In it, learners manage a tree farm.

In the game, learners confront fluctuating prices, pine-beetle infestations, cash flow difficulties, and the fact that a tree takes 30 years to grow. This game lets learners discover both ecological and economic principles and learn to apply them in the simulated environment.

Built using Microsoft Notepad, Microsoft Paint, and a whole lot of custom HTML and JavaScript. View example at horton.com/eld/.

This simulation can replicate the changes that occur over hundreds of years if necessary. For each time period (one quarter of a year), the learner reviews the results from the last time period and decides what actions to take. Actions include things like selectively cutting an area, clear-cutting it, replanting it, or having the area appraised. Actions can be individually applied to each of the 64 plots on the map.

The results for a time period depend on actions taken by the learner, and also on variables such as rainfall, fluctuations in prices for saw timber and pulp wood, emergency needs for cash (daughter gets accepted at Harvard), forest fires, and disasters such as tornados and lightning.

Just as in the real situation, learners must look beyond the superficial appearances. To do so, they can call up a detailed status report.

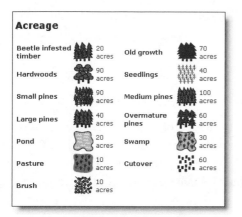

The status report shows the land use and condition of trees.

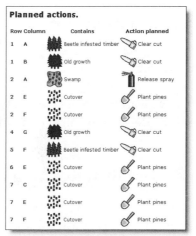

The status report also lists the actions ordered by the learner over the next time period. This list gives learners a chance to reconsider actions, just as in the real world.

This game is a bit unusual in that learners can set the goals. They can mix economic, aesthetic, and environmental concerns to most closely match their goals for their real-life timberland. By making the goals flexible, we encourage learners to try out various approaches.

Immersive role-playing games

Immersive role-playing games embed learners in a pretend world complete with complex goals, tools, allies and opponents, unpredictable events, and hidden motivations.

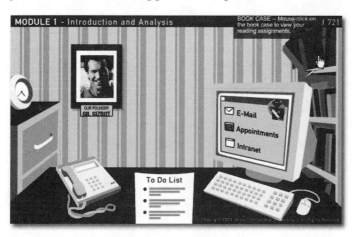

Here we see the opening screen for a game where the learner plays the role of a newly hired manager of a corporate department. The learner must pursue a strategic goal while dealing with occasional crises, winning management support, and interacting with peers in similar positions at other companies.

In this six-week simulation, the learner interacts with the teacher and fellow learners only in their roles in the game. For more on this game and its world, see page 351.

Such immersive role-playing games are good for teaching learners to prepare for complex work environments and evolving simulations.

DESIGN GAMES FOR LEARNING

Commercial computer and video games can cost millions of dollars and take years to develop. Few schools or training departments have budgets that large. On the other hand, I have seen effective learning games created by one person in a week. A good learning game requires good design more than it requires massive amounts of programming and intricate graphics.

Design to accomplish learning objectives

Designing effective games is as much art as science. A large part of that art comes in crafting experiences that both teach and test accomplishment of objectives.

From the beginning, make clear what the game must accomplish. List the goal and individual learning objectives the game must accomplish. This is the same step you perform for any form of learning. I mention it here because many game designers tend to forget about objectives and focus on just making the game fun. Be prepared to state how each element in the game supports the objectives, either directly or indirectly.

Here are a few examples of game activities to accomplish different types of learning objectives.

Types of objectives	Type game and how to use it in e-learning.
Create	**Jigsaw puzzle** – Require learners to assemble components into a non-obvious combination that solves a problem or meets requirements. **Environmental simulation** – Test whether learners respond flexibly to unexpected conditions and infer principles from experiences in the game. **Immersive role-playing game** – Challenge learners to achieve goals despite incomplete information, hidden rules, and distracting details.

Types of objectives	Type game and how to use it in e-learning.
Decide	**Branching scenario** – Let learners experience the consequences of strategies and principles used to guide decisions. **Task simulation** – Have learners practice making on-job decisions to carry out tasks. **Personal-response simulation** – Let learners experience consequences of decisions and revise their choices to incorporate discoveries. **Environmental simulation** – Encourage learners to discover principles and concepts that guide better decisions in the environment simulated.
Do	**Jigsaw puzzle** – Provide practice in an assembly procedure. **Task simulation** – Provide practice and feedback in a linear task.
Know	**Quiz-show game** – Exercise and test recall of information. **Word puzzles** – Exercise and test recall of names and terminology. **Jigsaw puzzle** – Test recall of spatial and logical relationships among components of a whole.
Believe	**Branching simulation** – Allow learners to experience the consequences of their beliefs within a realistic situation and to revise those beliefs by discoveries made in the simulation. **Personal-response simulation** – Provide immediate feedback on the correctness and consequences of beliefs. **Environmental simulation** – Let learners test their current beliefs about how an environment operates. **Immersive role-playing simulation** – Have learners exercise, test, and revise their beliefs by seeing the complex consequences of decisions within the simulation.
Feel	**Branching scenario** – Let learners experience the consequences of decisions influenced by their emotions. **Personal-response simulation** – Let learners see the effect of their emotions on decision-making and how they can improve results by consciousness of their emotions. **Environmental simulation** – Have learners experience widespread consequences of decisions affected by their feelings. **Immersive role-playing simulation** – Have learners make decisions and receive feedback in complex situations likely to trigger emotional experiences.

7

Games and simulations

Express the goal as a specific task

In the game, exactly what are learners to accomplish? Give learners a single, understandable goal against which their results can be measured.

☹ No	☺ Yes
Make money by investing in stocks, bonds, and real estate.	Re-balance a portfolio of stocks, bonds, and real estate to reduce federal taxes by 40%.
Order a balanced meal at the simulated restaurant.	Order a meal with less than 1,000 calories that has twice the daily-recommended amounts of iron and calcium.
Pick a diverse team.	Pick the smallest team with all the required skills for launching a new product simultaneously in Japan, China, and the United States.

Pick the right sized game

Some types of games are small and simple. Others are sprawling and complex. Some only work for narrow objectives while others are too expensive to use for only a small unit of learning. The following job aid recommends where to consider different types of games. Open circles indicate a good fit. Black dots represent a better fit.

Types of games	Use for ...				
	Do activity	Test	Whole topic	Whole lesson	Whole course
Quiz-show game	●	●			
Word puzzle	●	●			
Jigsaw puzzle	●	●			
Branching scenario	○	○	●	●	○
Task simulation	○	○	●	○	
Personal-response simulation		○	○	●	
Immersive role-play			○	○	●

Emphasize learning, not just doing

Make sure your games require applying what you are teaching. Make winning the game require creativity and careful decisions, not just fast reflexes.

Simulate the thought-processes, not just the physical actions. Avoid games that measure only how quickly and accurately the learner can move the mouse, unless that is the skill you are teaching.

Require the learner to make the same kinds of decisions as in the real activity. In most learning games, it is more important that the learner make authentic decisions than that the learner execute those decisions in a realistic way.

Avoid arbitrary limitations on how the learner accomplishes the goal. If there are three ways to do the task in the real world, allow three ways in the game.

Specify challenge and motivation

Early on, decide how the game will motivate learners to put forth the effort required and overcome the frustrations and difficulties posed by the game. Some common motivational techniques include:

▶ Competition with other players, other teams, or a player's "personal best."

▶ Supporting your allies, friends, team, company, department, or other organizational unit in the game.

▶ Solving a problem, such as a puzzle, mystery, or riddle.

▶ Meeting or beating a set standard.

▶ Success in the vicarious game world, such as advancing to the next level, winning a promotion, saving lives, or gaining possessions or territory.

Manage competitiveness

Excessive competitiveness can get in the way of effective learning. If learners are highly competitive anyway, the game may not produce the desired outcome. Sales representatives and trial attorneys may compete more aggressively than you anticipated. Other groups may feel uncomfortable competing directly against their friends or co-workers. Ask yourself whether it is more important for your learners to compete or to collaborate? Design the game accordingly.

Provide multiple ways to learn

Supplement the trial-and-error learning common in games with other methods. Learning by trial and error can be frustrating, and there is the danger that learners remember their first attempts, not the correct ones. To make learning more reliable, incorporate additional sources of learning into the world of the game, for example, business reports, memos and e-mail messages, technical manuals and industry standards, company policies and procedures, meeting minutes, and other sources.

Where possible, just link to real documents available on the network. Such exhibits provide a low-bandwidth alternative to video and sound. Or, for greater realism, make these exhibits available to learners only after they have taken actions that would make them available in the real world—such as asking for them or joining a professional association.

CREATE A MICRO-WORLD

Engage learners in an interesting, challenging, and fun alternative reality. Make this micro-world one that will capture the imagination of learners and let them pretend that the micro-world is real.

Specify the game's world

The game world can be simple or complex. It may resemble real life in every particular or may create an alternate reality with its own rules, values, and appearances. Specifying a complete world is a biblical effort. For your game, you will probably want to keep the world simple and small. At a minimum, you will need to specify:

▶ **Characters** or active agents in the game. The most important character is the learner. For some games that is the only character. Other games may have a cast like a Hollywood extravaganza.

▶ **Objects**, such as tools, equipment, furniture, and other things the learner and other characters interact with within the game.

▶ **Locations**, such as rooms, cities, environments, and other spaces through which game play can proceed. Locations may have their own objects and rules and may be used to subdivide game play or to represent progress toward a goal.

▶ **Relationships** among characters, objects, and locations determine how they may interact as the game proceeds.

▶ **Laws of math, physics, and nature** that determine physical interactions among objects, consequences of actions, and numerical results. The game world may selectively implement constraints of the real world, ignoring irrelevant limits in order to focus attention to the ones important to the learning at hand.

▶ **Other dynamics** that specify how things change and interact. For example, the tree farm game (p 340) specifies how the growth in one area depends on the current content of the area, on rainfall, on the content of surrounding areas, and on human interventions.

Specify characters and important objects

In games, people interact with characters and important objects. Ensuring that the interaction is truly educational requires careful attention to the design of those characters and objects. These items can include human, animal, and robot characters along with tools, tokens, and other objects that play roles in the outcome of the game.

Role in the game

Everything in the game should be there for a reason. The reason may be primary or secondary. It may be to further education or merely to support the flow of the game. Just make sure that you can say why a character or object appears in the game, that is, what is its role and how does it relate to other characters and objects in the story. Let this role guide design of the item.

Name

Give every significant character and object a memorable name. Even if the name is never used in game play, it may be valuable to the design and development team in referring to the item. The name should be easily remembered but not too odd. For names learners will encounter in the game, make the name easy to pronounce. Avoid names that imply more than you intend about the nationality or background of the character.

Observable characteristics

Carefully specify any observable characteristics that may be relevant to decisions made by the learner playing the game. Also specify any characteristics that you do not want to leave to someone else's imagination. Observable characteristics of characters include:

▶ **Gender**. Is a character male, female, or indeterminate? Remember that robots, some animals, and abstract characters need not display a gender if it is not necessary for the story.

▶ **Age**. Is the character an infant, child, youth, young adult, middle-aged, or older person? If age is an important part of the character's role, indicate it clearly; otherwise, disguise age or make it typical for the role the character is playing.

▶ **Race or skin color**. If you need to show a particular race, for example in teaching cross-cultural communication, specify the race exactly. For cartoon characters, you can subdue all indicators of race and use a skin color, such as green, not common on human beings.

▶ **Clothing**. The clothes worn by a character can reinforce the character's role and help learners keep characters separate. In general, keep clothing typical for the role: lab coat for a researcher or business suit for an executive.

▶ **Hair**. Head and facial hair is an easy way to visually distinguish otherwise similar characters.

► **Voice**. The way a character speaks can reinforce the role of the character and help express emotion. For each character, specify the tone and accent (everybody has an accent). Also specify any imperfections, such as a slight raspiness, that will give the character a more distinct persona. Make sure that the voice will match gender, age, and other characteristics.

► **Personality** and emotional makeup. Is the character calm or flighty, chatty or taciturn, outgoing or shy? Is the character rock steady or prone to emotional outbursts? Does the character have phobias or pet peeves?

► **Movement**. How does the character move? In moving from one part of the screen to the other, does the character skip, plod, limp, bounce, stagger, weave, glide, or shimmy? Does the character have a distinct pattern of movement, such as fiddling with a strand of hair falling across the face? When standing or sitting, does the character adopt a particular posture?

Design the character to epitomize the role. The character should look, sound, and act like what it represents. In general, this will require making each character a typical and familiar version of the item. Two exceptions apply: First, do not employ stereotypes that ridicule a group of people. Second, the hero (or the character who represents the learner) should be atypical in ways that increase the learner's willingness to identify with the hero.

In addition to the characteristics of people, you should specify characteristics for the environment, such as time period, architecture, décor, and simulation implements:

► **Time period** in which the simulation is set: past, present, or future. What characteristics of the simulation will set the stage in the learner's mind? If you are designing for the present, avoid depicting fads. Instead, keep environmental objects neutral to ensure that the simulation will not look dated a few years down the road.

► **Architecture**, such as building exteriors and street scenes that the learner will see. If learners interact with architectural features, how realistic do the features need to be? Are they representative of a real or imaginary place? Must the architecture convey a particular time period, culture, or social class? If architecture does not play a primary role in the simulation, then ensure that intended learners will not be distracted by the architecture to the detriment of learning.

► **Décor**, such as furniture, lamps, rugs, wall covering, pictures, and other accessories that learners will see and interact with. Should the décor evoke a particular style, culture, or social level? How detailed should the décor be? Will learners manipulate any of the items, such as file cabinets, desk drawer, or wall pictures?

► **Simulation implements**, such as file folders, writing implements, test tubes, dials and levers, or some other game piece. How realistic do they need to be? For instance, if part of a medical procedure involves manipulating the patient, is it necessary that learners actually experience the sensation of touch? Or will a simple animation suffice?

Design every aspect of your simulation to ensure that it plays its appropriate part and contributes to meeting the simulation's objectives.

Create a storyline

The "story" in a game is the sequence of experiences encountered by the learner. You must specify the starting and ending points in the game, the learner's role in the game, what occurs between start and end, and how to get the game started.

The **starting point** represents the condition of the learner as the game opens. For a quiz-show game, you might specify: "All questions are available on the game board and the learner has zero points."

The **ending point** of the game represents accomplishment of the goal of the game. For the quiz-show game, the ending point might be: "The game ends when the learner achieves a score that indicates expert-level knowledge of the subject or all questions on the game board have been attempted."

The **learner's role** determines how the learner interacts with the game world and how the actions of the learner can accomplish the goal of the game. For the quiz-show game, the learner's role might be defined as simply: "The learner is a contestant on the game show."

 The **path from start to end** represents the plot of the story. Unlike novels, games can have multiple paths through the story rather than a single plot line. And, in games, it is the learner who determines the path. As a designer, you must specify what kinds of things happen along the way. This step can require defining simple rules or drawing wall-sized flowcharts. In the quiz-show game, the plot is: "The learner repeatedly attempts questions. The learner picks a subject category (a row) and a point value (a column). The question at that intersection is displayed. The learner types in the short answer to the question and clicks a "Check" button. If the answer is correct, the learner's score is increased by the point value of that question; if incorrect, the score is decreased by the point value."

The final element of the storyline is some **incident to kick-start the action**. The learner may need prompting to take the first step. For the quiz-show game, the learner is given instructions for playing the game and asked what question to start with.

Create a back story

Some complex games may require a back story, which is a body of background information about what supposedly happened up to the point of the start of the game. The back-story may define hidden relationships, principles, and information that may come out in the course of play. It may provide motivation for characters in the game. It may be necessary to explain why things appear as they do in the game.

In *The Crimescene Game* (p 324) the back-story is the bank robbery that occurred before the start of the game.

Specify the game structure

Game structure determines how the events and possible pathways through the game are organized. Good structure keeps the game simple enough for learners to comprehend and concise enough for developers to complete on time and within budget.

Most games involve cycles of activity in which the learner makes a decision and experiences the immediate consequences. Beyond this atomic structure, games may be organized into linear pathways, a sequence of missions, or as limited or free-form branching. Multiple players may take turns acting or may proceed independently at the same time.

Assign the learner's role

Make clear the situation in which the learner must act. Set the stage. Base the game on a situation familiar to the learner from current work, home life, or popular media. Pose the learner a problem to solve in that situation.

Memo

From: Boss

To: You

Subject: Factor of safety for the MOHLUMA Embankment

Please take a look at this sketch of a cross-section of the MOHLUMA Embankment. Would you model this embankment in Galena and verify the factor of safety is 3.03?

The sketch is attached.

For example, a simulation on using software to assess the safety of mine slopes and road cuts begins with an assignment like that the learner might receive on the job.

The simulation further provides the learner with data in the form of a hand-drawn diagram of the sort common in this situation.

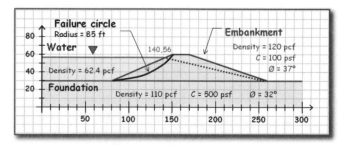

Make the game meaningfully realistic

Many novice designers equate realism with photo-realistically rendered 3D graphics or virtual-reality worlds. For learning purposes, though, realism has a somewhat different meaning. The game need not closely mimic the task for which it prepares the learner so long as it exercises the abilities and knowledge needed in the real task. A game is realistic (hence effective) if it:

▶ Implements the causal relationships and principles of the real-world system that learners must master.

▶ Contains details necessary for the learner to map components of the game to their real-world counterparts.

▶ Allows learners to control the aspects of the game they would control in the real world.

▶ Makes learners feel they directly control objects they manipulate within the game.

In other words, it is more important that the game work like the real-world system than that it look like the real-world system.

Specify rules of the game

Game rules determine what the player can do in the game and how the game responds. Specify clear rules for:

▶ What information is presented to the learner at each situation in the game.

▶ What actions the learner can take.

▶ What immediate feedback results from each action.

▶ What other, perhaps hidden, consequences occur for each action.

▶ How points are awarded.

Design a rich, realistic environment

Make the micro-world diverse and complex in a way that securely reminds learners of the real world for which the game prepares them.

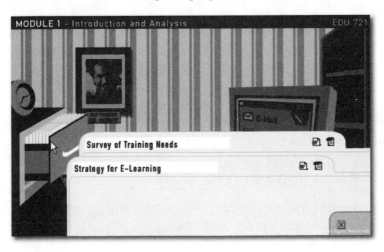

Here is an example of the opening screen from a six-week immersive simulation that taught departmental management skills.

The learner has just clicked the file cabinet to see its contents.

This micro-world was articulated through objects and components with which the learner interacted:

▶ A simulated social environment with a boss, a CEO, and fellow executives—one of who was trying to sabotage the player's career.

▶ Generic reference materials, such as research papers and a textbook.

▶ Scenario-specific reference materials including reports and proposals relevant to the learner's simulated job assignment.

▶ Company Web site containing a company history, policies, organization chart, code of conduct, and mission statement.

▶ Agenda expressed in terms of to-do lists.

▶ Managers at other companies (played by fellow learners).

Such in-depth materials make the simulated world seem true and real. The micro-world has the most important people and objects of the real world and they behave in fundamentally the same way they do in the real world.

Interaction in this game resembles interaction in a real company.

▶ Meetings are held online.

▶ The learner can interview fellow executives to try to gather information and win them over.

▶ E-mail messages from the boss make new assignments.

▶ Interruptions and crises occur just as in the real world.

Provide a deep, unifying challenge

Unify the game around a primary mission or goal. This assignment can keep learners focused on the overall goal of learning, target efforts, and integrate learning.

For a simple quiz-show game or puzzle, the goal is to win the game or solve the puzzle. A more complex game may require crating an explicit goal or assignment for learners. For example, in a business simulation, learners were assigned the task of crafting a business strategy. Learners were given the strategy document from an earlier, failed attempt and challenged to "do it right this time." The flawed example suggested the scope, structure, and format for the solution. It served as a model of what not to do and as a starting point for discussion and innovation. It also constrained the task so learners did not waste time on issues found acceptable in the prior attempt.

Define indicators of game state and feedback

Success of the game depends on the clarity of feedback given to the learner. Decide what kind of feedback you will give and where it will appear to the learner. If you can, respond directly in the game world through the words and emotional state of the characters. You can also respond through changing indicators on a console-display. Feedback can likewise come in indicators such as the current score, tokens won, levels achieved, time remaining, or attempts remaining.

SPECIFY THE DETAILS

The design process varies among the great variety of games possible, but some steps are common to most forms of games. None of these steps is especially difficult, but all require careful thought.

Sketch out the user interface

The user-interface is how learners see and control the game world. Usually it is a mixture of a direct view of the game world and a console. The direct view exposes learners to what they would see and hear if in the game world. The console view adds additional information not visible in the game world, such as the current score or the time remaining to play.

The user interface also determines how learners affect the game world, that is, through direct manipulation of game objects or by commands entered through the console. Direct manipulation may be more natural, but can require much more sophisticated programming.

Write the words

Though designers may not create all the media for the game, designers do typically write all the spoken and displayed words that occur in the game. These include:

▶ Labels and instructions displayed on the screen.
▶ Characters' speeches and thoughts.
▶ Questions and prompts put to the learner.
▶ Feedback to the learner.

If the game will incorporate spoken words, provide a pronunciation guide for the narrator. Include all technical and specialized terms.

Specify the graphical style

As a designer, you may not be the one to draw the graphics of the game, but you should specify the style they will take. Will the game look like a cartoon, illustration, photograph, abstract painting, mechanical device, control panel, game board, or some other type display?

What tone should the graphics suggest? Do you want the display light and airy with a white background and lots of pastel colors? Or should it look dark and serious with dark, rich colors with metallic surfaces? Do you want learners to describe the appearance of your game as cute, whimsical, businesslike, ominous, funky, or some other way?

If you can, sketch out the graphics. If not, use stick figures and clip art to help communicate to the artist what you need in the way of graphics.

Specify other media

Depending on the complexity of your game, you may need to specify other media to incorporate.

Medium	Use in games	Design issues
Sound effects	Add realism. Clarify visuals.	Volume level so they are heard but are not too distracting.
Music	Suggest emotions. Bridge scenes.	Where present and where not. Specify "Sounds like _____", but do not pirate other people's music.
Animation	To generalize or avoid distracting or easily dated particulars.	Make compatible with other graphics.
Video	Illustrate human interactions or things not easily animated.	Must script out video completely: characters, setting, movement (stage directions), dialog, sound, music, and transitions.

ENGAGE LEARNERS

To teach, a game must engage learners; that is, it must capture their interest, involve them in game play, and continually challenge them. Designers of educational and entertainment games have evolved tactics to quickly and effectively engage learners.

Hook the learner

Capture the learner's curiosity immediately. Forego a lengthy introduction and statement of objectives. Get the learner into the game as soon as possible and let the game introduce itself.

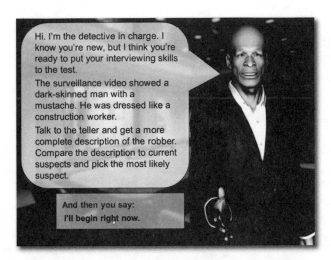

Notice how *The Crimescene game* draws learners in by immediately immersing them in the drama of investigating a bank robbery—no long-winded bullet list of objectives or boring recital of game rules.

Some common ways to hook the reluctant learner include these:

▶ Begin with an unresolved crisis.

▶ Briefly introduce the scenario and the learner's role in the scenario.

▶ Simplify the user interface so the learner does not have to search for the controls necessary to begin play.

Ask learners to suspend disbelief

No simulation is as rich an experience as real life. Learners must accept the limitations of the game or simulation. To get them to do so, we must ask them to pretend the game is real.

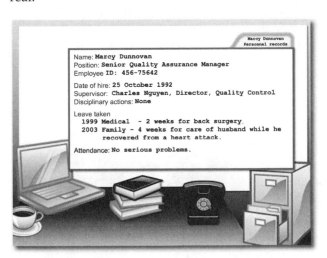

This branching scenario uses a cartoon style of graphics to suggest to learners that they will see simplified versions of real objects, devices, and documents.

To educe a willing suspension of disbelief:

▶ Give learners real, but highly simplified, details. Learners should recognize the details but know that they are simpler than in real situations.

▶ Use cartoon-style graphics rather than photorealistic images.

▶ Instruct learners to enter a fantasy world with phrases such as "Pretend that ..." or "Suppose that ...."

Set the context

Setting the context means making clear the situation in which the simulation occurs. For teaching use of a computer program, start with an overview of the workflow implemented by a program. By showing the overall workflow, the simulation prepares the learner to understand individual tasks in that workflow and which tasks are covered in the simulation.

For a simulation that covers a specific capability of a product, you might begin by stating the overall use of the product and showing how the individual capability contributes to that use.

For an individual command or other component in the user interface, you might start by showing where the component fits into the scheme of menus and toolbars.

Remember to answer the question, "Where am I?" If you are showing a part of a whole, identify the whole and show how the part relates to that whole.

Provide real-world prompting and support

Supply the same information learners will have in real situations. Do not, for example, ask a multiple-choice question about what button to click. Instead show a picture of the screen at the point where the learner would need to pick a button. Ask learners to indicate their choice by actually clicking the button.

☹ No   ☺ Yes

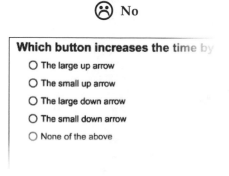

Provide access to reports, manuals, slide-presentations, and other materials available in the real situation. You may simplify these materials, but do provide access to the relevant information they contain.

Present solvable problems

Pose challenging, but solvable, problems to learners. Make these the types of problems learners might face in their work or daily lives. Problems may require multiple actions to solve. They should always require knowledge rather than guessing. To make difficult problems solvable by all, include links to resources where learners can find the parts of a solution.

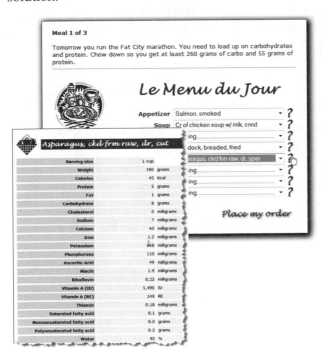

For example, in the *Diet Game*, learners can click a question mark beside a food choice to access the U.S. Department of Agriculture database for information about the nutritional ingredients of the food.

Adapt to the learner's needs

Where possible, adapt the game to the learner's needs rather than requiring the learner to conform to the rigid structure of a game.

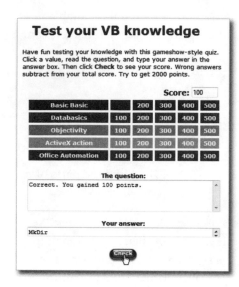

Notice how this quiz-show game provides challenge to a wide range of learners with different areas of specialization and different goals. The game provides flexibility in achieving the required score. Learners can achieve the target score by answering a few high-value difficult questions or by answering a larger number of low-value easy questions. Questions at different levels of difficulty provide challenge for both novice and expert. Different categories of questions let learners test their skills in the area they are most interested.

Other ways to adjust games to learners include:

▶ Offering a series of progressively more challenging goals as in the *HTML Lab* (p. 148). Learners can quit after reaching their desired level of skill.

▶ Letting learners set their own goals for playing the game. For example, *Tree farming 101* (p. 340) lets learners choose goals of environmental responsibility, short-term profit, long-term growth, bio-diversity, or many others.

▶ Permitting multiple solutions so learners can explore the ones of interest to them, as in the networking jigsaw puzzle (p. 334).

Challenge with time limits

Adding a timer to your game can add a sense of urgency to learning and require deeper learning of component skills.

If you do limit the time for certain responses, allow learners to make multiple attempts to accomplish a task. Also remember that timed tests may be illegal where they violate accessibility standards or discriminate against those with limited language skills.

Let learners try multiple strategies

Encourage learners to try different strategies and play multiple roles. Have them play once "by the book," again "on gut instinct," and finally "as bad as you can be." Games let learners experience the consequences of alternative behaviors. To teach the consequences of negative behavior, assign learners the persona of an evil or careless person, and let them experience life from that perspective. Instead of telling learners why they should follow rules, let learners break the rules and experience the consequences.

Program variety into the game

Design games so that the answer or response is different each time. That way, learners can repeatedly play the game. They cannot cheat by knowing the answers ahead of time. Either draw from a large pool of questions and situations, design the game to generate a new problem each time, or inject vagaries from the world being simulated: weather, equipment failures, outbreaks of the flu, or market fads.

Involve the learner

How do you keep learners engaged? Involve them in the events and outcome of the game. Experience and research with games suggests some simple tactics:

▶ Keep the outcome dependent on the learner's action until the end. Keep victory uncertain until the learner meets all of the learning objectives.

▶ Present a series of authentically difficult challenges rather than a progression of simple challenges.

▶ Make the learner a character in the game rather than just an observer.

▶ Provide dramatic, specific feedback rather than uniformly positive, supportive feedback only. If learners make a mistake, tell them so politely and clearly.

TEACH THROUGH FEEDBACK

In games, learning occurs because of feedback. Therefore, we must systematically design feedback that educates, informs, and motivates the learner.

Provide intrinsic feedback

The smooth flow of the game can be interrupted by delivery of feedback. Most good games deliver feedback naturally within the context of the game.

Within games, feedback takes two forms: intrinsic and extrinsic. *Intrinsic* feedback is feedback provided from people and things within the story of the game. *Extrinsic* feedback is provided from outside the game's story.

Intrinsic feedback	Extrinsic feedback
▶ Words, gestures, body language, facial expressions, and tone of voice of other characters in the game.	▶ Un-requested coaching feedback.
	▶ Gauges, dials, and other indicators not in the story.
▶ Responses by machines, computer programs, and other objects simulated.	▶ "Right" or "Wrong" after each step.
▶ Changes in the visual display of the game's simulated environment.	▶ Nagging by an irrelevant character within the game.

Where you can, use intrinsic feedback. It is more direct and does not interrupt the flow of the game or pull the learner out of the story at hand. With intrinsic feedback, correct actions continue the flow of the game in the direction the learner indicated. Indications of the correctness of the action may be subtle, such as body language or a facial expression of a character or the accomplishment of a minor goal.

The witness says:

"Who are you? Are you a reporter? The police told me not to talk to anyone. I do not have to talk to you, do I?"

She folds her arms in a defiant pose.

And you say:

■ Sorry. I'm a little impatient. Let me introduce myself ...

■ I am the police and I'll ask the questions here!

Here the witness's words and body language provide clear feedback that the previous question was too abrupt.

Likewise, negative feedback can be delivered in the context of the game: The intended action fails. A character responds through negative body language, gestures, or facial expressions. A door remains locked.

If you must inject explicit feedback, keep it short and clear. Just "Correct" or "Incorrect" is usually sufficient. Resist the temptation to explain why an action was wrong. Have the game play reveal the cause of the failure or record the reasons to a log that the learner can review after playing the game.

Inject educational feedback where needed

Another approach does interrupt play to provide explicit feedback aimed at delivering specific educational messages. For example:

> Correct. You can also use the keyboard shortcut **Ctrl-S** to save your file.
>
> No. **Save As**… would save your file under another name. You want the plain **Save** command.
>
> Incorrect. Let me show you what you should have done.

Such feedback may be justified to correct a misconception that could cause problems if not immediately corrected.

Provide continual feedback

Provide feedback frequently enough to prevent learners from believing they are succeeding when they are failing. Failing to flag incorrect actions can reinforce those actions and make them harder to unlearn.

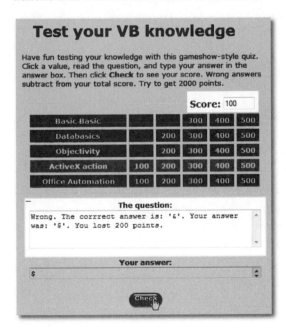

Notice how this quiz show game provides feedback after each question and posts a running score. (The score and feedback areas are highlighted.)

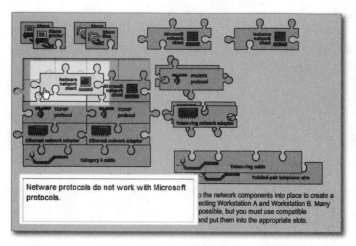

This jig saw puzzle game rejects attempts to insert pieces that do not fit with those already in place. And it briefly explains why the attempt does not work. (The incorrect puzzle piece and feedback are highlighted.)

Does this mean that you must provide feedback to every action by the learner? No, not at all. Here are some common-sense exceptions:

▶ If an action is merely irrelevant, you may want to let learners discover the mistake on their own.

▶ For tests, do not provide feedback that learners will not have in the real world.

▶ Omit feedback that learners consider distracting or annoying.

But give crucial feedback immediately

In games and simulations, immediately warn learners of the dangerous consequences of actions. By deferring feedback, learners may believe that their actions were harmless.

For example, in a simulation of operating-room procedures, any mistake that could harm the patient is immediately and forcefully brought to the learner's attention.

Make the feedback obvious, clear, and non-judgmental. Don't scold the learner, but point out the error and the correct action in the situation.

Confront bad behavior and choices

Allow learners to experience the consequences of negative behavior, dangerous actions, and bad choices. It is axiomatic that games cannot teach learners to avoid a choice if the learner is never allowed to make that choice.

In *The Crimescene Game*, the learner can make a clearly racist comment.

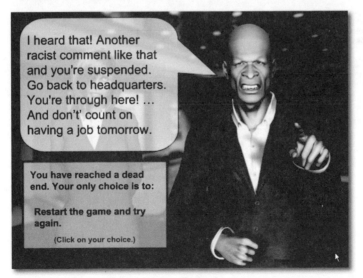

The feedback for choosing a racist comment ends the game with a stern warning to the learner's character in the game.

Give extreme feedback for extreme failures. If the learner does something severely wrong, correct the learner immediately lest the learner continue unaware of the severity of the failure.

Defer lengthy feedback

While we want to provide continual feedback to learners, we must be careful not to distract or overwhelm learners with the volume of our feedback. One solution is to provide minimal feedback within the play of the game and then provide more detailed feedback at the end of the game or at logical breaks in the action. This comprehensive feedback may take the form of an "after-action review" that comments on the learner's actions throughout the game.

The Crimescene Game

Ask the right questions and quickly solve the case

Situation	You chose ...	Feedback	Cost	Total
What happens: You sit down beside her. She seems a bit shaken but not hysterical.	Let me introduce myself, I'm ...	Good choice. You put the witness at ease.	0	35
The witness says: "Oh, I'm pleased to meet you Detective Parks. How can I help you." She smiles warmly.	I just need to ask you a few questions.	This was your only choice.	0	35
The witness waits while you decide which of the questions you want to ask.	What can you tell us about the robber's height and weight?	Good choice. This question may help the witness visualize the perpatrator and help her remember some distinguishing feature. However, estimating height and weight can be difficult and unreliable. Be prepared to ask a follow-up question.	0	35
The witness says: "He was about 5 feet 6 inches tall. And he weighed about 150	Tell me about your sister.	Bad choice. This question may tend to get the witness off the subject.	-5	30

In this alternative version of *The Crimescene Game,* the gameplay ends with just such an after-action review that recaps the learner's actions and provides detailed comments on them.

Built using Microsoft Notepad and custom JavaScript. View example at horton.com/eld/.

Anticipate feedback (feedforward?)

Prepare responses to expected actions by learners. Think about the mistakes learners will make and how they can best learn from these mistakes.

If the student does this:	It indicates:	Send the student feedback like this:
Suggests rewriting the entire plan or completely	They did not pay attention to executive's feedback on the	"The organization of the previous plan is just fine—it follows one of our corporate templates for proposals. It's what everyone at Gizbotics is used to. I would suggest that you stick with the
Refers to the old plan and discusses the opinions of the executives to that plan.	They did not understand that the plan is a business proposal— not a term paper.	"Your job is to create your own plan, not rebut the previous plan. Your plan needs to stand alone. I would not even mention the prior plan. The sooner executives forget about it, the better."
Requests interviews with executives before they are scheduled in the syllabus.	They are not sensitive to the time constraints on executives and are focusing on details too early.	"Don't worry. I'll arrange the interviews a bit later. I think it's a little too early to start talking to the executives. For now, concentrate on understanding their positions on e-learning and getting a feel for the politics, err I mean organizational dynamics, of Gizbotics."

Here is an example of feedback prepared for use by the facilitator who plays a role in a multi-player game.

Each item of feedback indicates exactly what action should trigger the feedback, what the action indicates about the learner's accomplishment of intended objectives, and the exact response to be given to guide the learner.

Enable learning through a variety of experiences

In games, players learn by experience: Their experiences in the game cause them to discover the concepts, principles, procedures, knowledge, and attitudes that lead to success. For experience to teach it must be meaningful and plentiful.

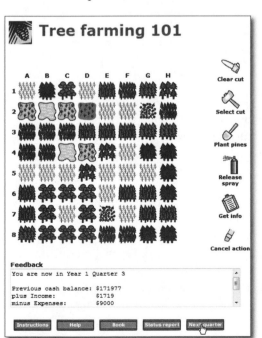

In this example the learner is the manager of a tree farm. To make the experience more meaningful, the learner can set the goals for the game: short-term profit, long-term estate growth, environmental protection, or some other goal. These flexible goals encourage learners to try different approaches, which provide a wide variety of experiences.

The experience is enriched by the problems that the learner must confront: fluctuating prices, droughts, pine beetles, and cash flow difficulties. Ample experience is ensured by the fact that the simulation can run for long periods of time as learners try different strategies and tactics. In an hour of game-play the learner can acquire the experiences of several centuries. Games like this are especially useful for teaching subjects for which a human lifespan is too short for learning by personal experience.

Provide complete, detailed feedback

Teaching complex, difficult objectives will require complete, detailed feedback.

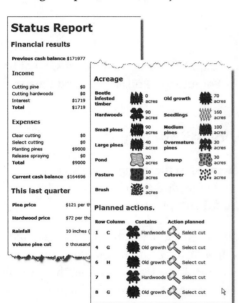

For instance, feedback for *Tree Farming 101* is multi-dimensional as shown in this status report.

Rich feedback, like this, encourages learners to confront the interconnectedness in systems and to adopt more sophisticated strategies to solving problems.

This example, from a game that challenges learners to order meals to meet specific nutritional goals, reviews the learner's choices.

Notice that it provides a complete explanation of the results for each choice. Specific differences between the goal and the results are noted. By clicking on an individual food choice, the learner can learn more about the nutritional contribution of that dish. The **Try again** button offers the opportunity for the learner to refine the results until the goal is met.

Help learners correct mistakes

Help learners understand and correct their mistakes, whether physical missteps or conceptual misunderstandings.

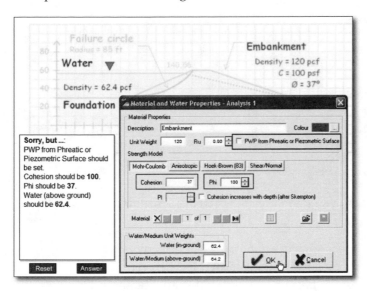

In this example, the learner made a mistake when filling in several different fields on the form.

Note that the error message points out exactly which field contains the error.

Specific error messages should identify the item or items in error. It should point out where to locate the error on the screen. It should spell out the type of error, for example that the value entered was too high or too low. An error message may also tell learners the correct response.

Keep in mind that the completeness of the error message should suit the learner's level of learning and your teaching strategy. You may want to withhold some information in order to challenge learners to diagnose and correct their own mistakes. You may even want to layer error messages. An initial message just points out that the learner made a mistake and suggests the general nature of the mistake. A second error message, when requested by the learner, spells out the details of the mistake and prescribes corrective action.

Offer abundant practice

Plentiful practice gives opportunities for discovery, helps learners refine their strategy and tactics, smooths and automates performance, and builds confidence. The key to offering abundant practice is to allow enough attempts for deep learning to occur.

Include a **Try again** or **Replay** button to let learners attempt the goal again, such as in this example.

Even successful learners may take you up on the offer, either to further hone their skills or to ensure that their success was not just luck.

You can offer two kinds of additional practice. One merely lets learners try again with the same conditions as before. This is especially valuable after learners have failed to accomplish a goal and do not want to give up until they succeed. The second kind of additional practice varies the conditions to present the learner with a fresh challenge to accomplish the same objective.

Acknowledge achievement

Videogames keep players motivated by recognizing improved performance; typically by letting them advance to a higher level in the game or by promoting them through a series of ranks. We can do the same.

Here we promote the learner to a higher rank to recognize that they have mastered some difficult material.

PROGRESSIVELY CHALLENGE LEARNERS

Design games to appropriately challenge learners both when they start the game and as they gain mastery.

Challenge learners

Design the game so it challenges learners at all levels of skill and phases of learning. You can design competition into the game so players compete against one another. Or challenge learners to top the best scores of others or their earlier best efforts. As learners gain more skill at the game, limit how long they can take for each turn. Another good technique for challenging all learners is called scaffolding and fading.

Scaffolding refers to the support we provide learners to ensure they succeed. As learners learn the task, we reduce scaffolding or support (*fading*) so they work more on their own.

These callouts illustrate three levels of scaffolding:

High scaffolding   **Medium scaffolding**   **Low scaffolding**

The low-scaffolding example provides a general prompt that requires learners to take several related steps at a time. Learners must decide what individual actions are required, locate the place to carry out each action, and perform them all. This is certainly more challenging and realistic than receiving detailed instructions for each action, as shown in the high-scaffolding example.

What do we let learners figure out on their own? In a computer simulation, we might start by requiring them to decide where to click. We let them find the needed button, icon, or other object on the screen. We might tell them to enter data, but let them decide in which field to enter it. We might also let learners decide how to format the data. We can also phrase our prompts so we tell learners what they must do, but not the order in which to perform actions.

It should come as no surprise that this advice requires sensitivity. You must balance the need to wean the learner from explicit prompts and instructions against the danger of leaving the learner clueless. Might we suggest a couple of rounds of testing?

Ratchet up the challenge

Make the game easy to start but hard to master. Learners, regardless of their skill levels, should find the game challenging throughout.

For example, this quiz-show game provides questions at various levels of difficulty. The low-value questions are easy enough for novices and the high-value ones challenging enough for experts.

BASIC BASIC	100	200	300	400	500
DATABASICS	100	200	300	400	500
OBJECTIVITY	100	200	300	400	500
ACTIVEX ACTION	100	200	300	400	500
OFFICE AUTOMATION	100	200	300	400	500

Progressive challenge can also come from a sequence of tasks, each more difficult than the previous.

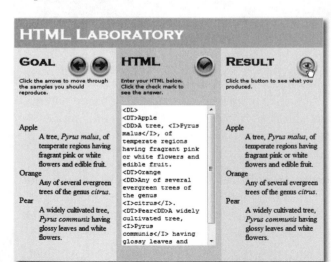

In the *HTML Laboratory*, learners are challenged to enter HTML code in the middle column to create progressively more complex displays, as shown in the Goal column. The buttons at the top of the Goal column let learners advance to more challenging goals or retreat to simpler ones.

Give closure between phases

Give closure between phases of a long learning sequence. Signal the end of phases in the overall sequence.

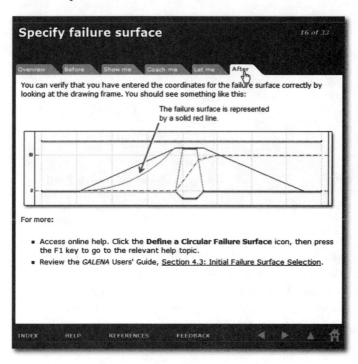

In this example from *GALENA Slope Stability Analysis,* the After tab announces the end of one phase of the activity before the learner begins the next phase.

To signal the end of a phase, we recommend you:

▶ State the results so far.

▶ Recap the steps of the phase just completed.

▶ Preview the next phase.

▶ Invite the learner to continue.

It is a good idea to have a closure point every 5 to 7 steps in a long task. However, the closure points should occur at logical breaks in the procedure, not after an arbitrary number of steps. Look for places where a piece of work has been completed and put the closure point there.

Control the rhythm of difficulty

A smooth learning curve is good, but a bumpy curve may be better. Learning improves if we alternate hard and easy activities.

Within each segment of learning, challenge increases. In the game, tension rises to a mini-crisis at the end of each episode or mission. This is followed by a relaxation. To implement this in a learning game, we simply follow difficult activities with simpler ones. The difficult activities drive learners to make breakthrough discoveries or accept difficult truths. The easier activities slow the pace to give learners time to reflect and to digest what they have learned.

Low-tension events can include:

▶ Congratulations to the learner for mastering difficult objectives.

▶ Review of what was learned.

▶ Pointing out how far the learner has come.

▶ Pleasant sights and sounds more like a vacation than combat.

Require consolidating small steps

Require learners to consolidate small bits of learning, such as the steps of a complex task. Once learners have learned the small steps, teach combinations of steps. Include activities that require learners to combine small actions to perform larger units of work. Merely teaching small, elemental actions may not be sufficient preparation for applying skills in the real world.

Early: Separate steps

> **Assignment**:
>
> (1) Set the time to **12** minutes.
> (2) Enter these teams: **Red Team, Blue Team, Green Team, Yellow Team.**
> (3) Set the **Pick team** checkbox.
> (4) Click **Start**.

Later: Whole procedure

> **Assignment**:
>
> Make the Timer-Picker count down for **12** minutes and then pick a team at random from these: **Red Team, Blue Team, Green Team, Yellow Team.**

Compared to the first example, the second example requires learners to fill in multiple fields in a dialog box—as one consolidated activity. It requires learners to map items of data to the appropriate fields and enter them there.

Such an approach helps you avoid needless repetition and keeps you from teaching microscopic details that learners already know or could figure out on their own. Remember: No amount of effort whatsoever will teach learners something they already know. Attempting will just bore them with needless repetition.

MANAGE GAME COMPLEXITY

Life is complex and the variety of potential experiences unbounded. Thus, the more realistic we make a game; the more complicated becomes its development. Clever design is necessary to keep the game easy to comprehend, navigate, and build. Clever design is especially important for branching games like task simulations and branching scenarios.

Beware combinatorial explosion

Games are subject to the mathematical phenomenon called *combinatorial explosion*. Imagine that we have a branching scenario where each scene presents the learner with a choice of four ways to proceed. From the starting scene, the learner can jump to one of the four resulting scenes. In each of these four scenes, the learner has four choices. So, two decisions with four choices would require 16 separate destinations. If each of these has four choices, 64 destinations are needed. Additional decisions require 256, 1024, and 4096 destinations scenes successively. A simple game that allows the learners only six decisions of four choices each would require creating over 4000 destination scenes!

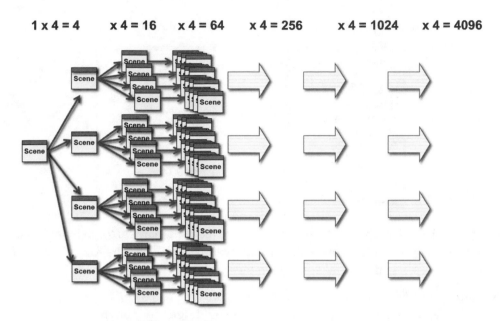

$1 \times 4 = 4$ $\times 4 = 16$ $\times 4 = 64$ $\times 4 = 256$ $\times 4 = 1024$ $\times 4 = 4096$

A simple outward-branching structure such as this is too complex to design, build, maintain, or navigate. This is where clever design comes to the rescue

Menu excursions

One alternative to prevent the combinatorial explosion is a menu-based excursion.

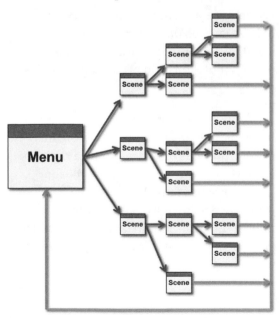

Here the learner chooses a path off the menu, makes a few steps, and then returns to the menu for another choice.

Each branch leading off the menu can accomplish a single objective.

In this map of the scenes of *The Crimescene Game*, you see arrows radiating from a central menu. After a few scenes, the arrows point to a circle with and A in the center. This represents the jump back to the central menu.

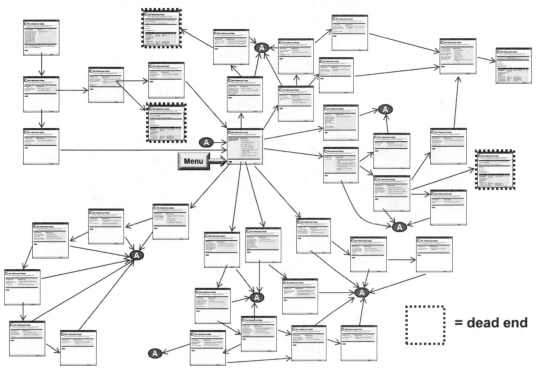

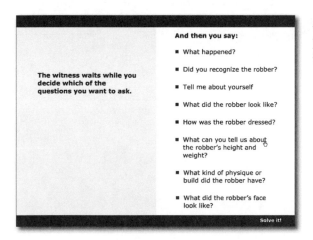

As you can see here, the menu offers plausible choices of questions to ask the witness.

Such a central menu is not ideal but is a pragmatic way to handle navigation. Most learners readily accept the fiction of the recurring menu—especially if we make the story engaging.

Mission-sequential structure

In the mission-sequential structure learners proceed through a series of missions. Each mission starts with a single scene from which learners branch out until they fail or succeed at accomplishing the objective of that mission. Their individual pathways then converge on a scene that recaps the just-completed mission and begins the next one.

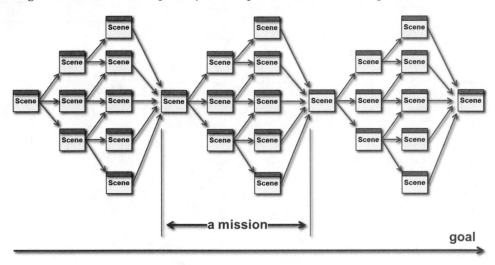

This structure works best for objectives that can be taught in sequence. Each mission can then accomplish one learning objective.

If learners must complete one objective (mission) before moving on to the next, you may require the learner to repeat the mission until successfully completing it. Before restarting the mission, learners may receive additional feedback or may just be admonished to think about what they learned in their unsuccessful attempt.

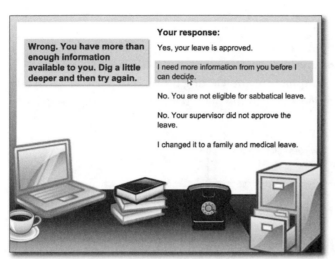

Here is an example of the end of an unsuccessful mission.

Short-leash strategy

In the short-leash strategy, learners are not allowed to stray far from the successful path.

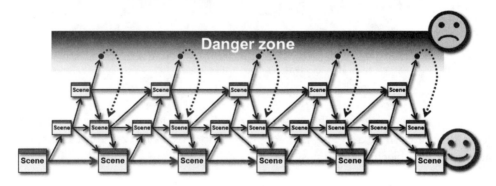

In this structure, the main path leads directly to successful completion of the goal. Learners, however, can stray from this main path. Getting more than a few steps of the path triggers corrective guidance that nudges them back toward the successful path.

This structure works well for teaching tasks where a series of missteps can lead to disaster. In the anesthesia-delivery simulation (p. 336), learners can make mistakes until they try an action that would endanger the patient. At that point, feedback steers them back on track (p. 362).

Safari structure

The safari structure gives the learner more leeway to err and to succeed than the short-leash strategy. In the safari structure learners can stray from the main path. The central path leads to an adequate but not triumphant result. Getting more than a few steps in one direction leads to disaster. Getting a few steps off the main path in another direction leads to immediate triumph.

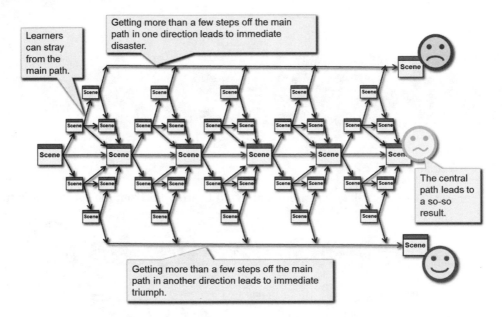

The safari structure limits complexity while providing plenty of room for learning the consequences of positive and negative actions. It also provides a way for learners who already meet the objectives to bypass game play that would teach them nothing.

Breakthrough structure

In the breakthrough structure, the internal state of the game triggers completion of the game. The trigger can be achievement of a target goal or the commission of too many mistakes.

Typically the game works like this. The story proceeds along a single path. Each decision along that path earns points for correct responses and costs points for incorrect responses. If the cumulative score exceeds a threshold, the game is completed and the learner receives congratulations. If the score falls below a lower threshold, the game is lost and the learner is given appropriate feedback.

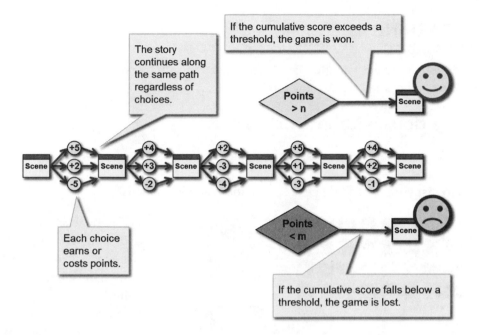

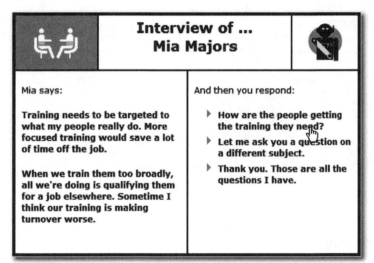

This interview game contains a hidden variable that represents the interviewee's level of anger. If that variable rises above a threshold, the interviewee abruptly terminates the interview.

The structure is simple to construct and simple to navigate. Learners need spend no more time on the game than necessary to achieve the goal or demonstrate that they need supplemental help.

SIMPLIFY LEARNING THE GAME

Make games easy to start and to play. Let learners concentrate on learning the subject you are teaching rather than on learning the game.

Guide actions with instructions

Give learners access to instructions for the game. Do not force instructions on learners, but let them request assistance when they need it. For example, *Tree Farming 101* has three buttons to dispense the full range of information learners may need.

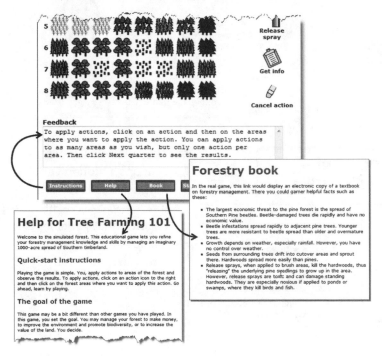

The **Instructions** button displays concise directions for interacting with the game. The **Help** button provides more extensive instructions. The **Book** button links to conceptual information needed to win the game.

Explain the game clearly

Provide instructions for your game. Explain the goal clearly. Make clear any limitations, such as the amount of time available. Learners may reject any game that imposes arbitrary or unfair rules. And it is learners who decide which rules are unfair. Cover these points:

▶ **What is the goal?** What is the learner to accomplish in the game? How is success defined? Can learners set goals for themselves?

▶ **What roles do learners play?** Are learners expected to play the role of a particular character? What are the motivations, values, and goals of that character?

▶ **How do learners get started?** Learners often hesitate to take the first step. To get the game under way, suggest a starting strategy like, "Why don't you begin with safe investments?" Or, provide a hint like, "Psssst! Look in your in-basket." Or require action within a short amount of time: "We need your decision in 2 minutes" or "An alarm just sounded on the master control panel. Better check it out." Smoothly and naturally propel learners into their role within the game.

▶ **What are the rules?** If the game mimics a situation, spell out the rules that people in that situation would know. If the game behaves in unrealistic ways, make these exceptions clear. You do not need to tell learners how to beat the game, just how to play it well enough so that they are learning the things they would learn in the real world.

▶ **How do they operate the game?** Tell learners how to operate the learner interface of the game. How do they translate real-world actions, such as making a phone call or selling a stock, into clicking, typing, dragging, and dropping? In some designs, this information is in a separate Help facility.

Start with training wheels

If game play is complex or the tasks simulated is difficult, take special care to get learners started successfully. One way is a training-wheels approach.

Tell learners new to the task exactly what to do. For learners who have never performed the procedure or any similar procedure, make sure you provide explicit directions.

What do you need to tell novices? Anything they do not already know or are not certain to figure out on their own.

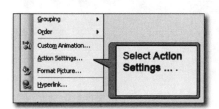

This example tells the learner exactly which menu item to pick. Notice that the menu is already exposed so the learner has a big hint as to where they will find the menu item.

For a computer task, these will include where to click, that is what button, menu, or icon to click.

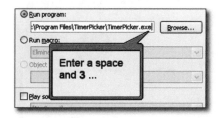

Tell novice learners exactly what to type and where to type it. For lists of options, tell learners which to select and which not to select.

If you want learners to notice something on the screen, tell learners where to look.

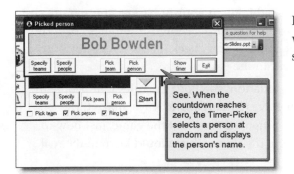

If several things occur at once, tell learners what they should notice and what they should attend to.

While we're being explicit, let's explicitly state that this advice can be overdone, especially if your learners are not novices or the skills you are teaching are advanced. Providing low-level instructions can distract learners from noticing patterns, trends, and principles. Just ask yourself two questions: What do I want learners to learn? And, what do they know already? Explicitly tell learners the things you want them to learn that they do not know already.

Assist when needed

Design the game so learners can begin with little preparation and continue learning about the game by playing it. Along the way learners may need assistance to understand the game display and how they are to interact with it.

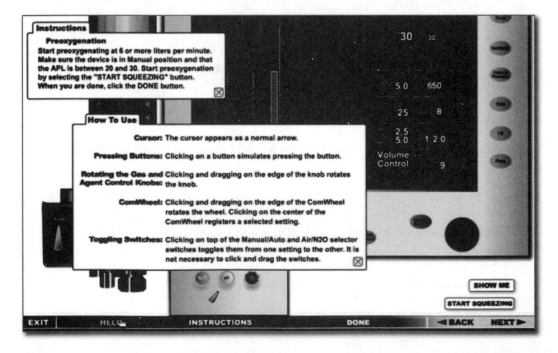

The previous example shows some of the common forms of assistance learners may need. At any point, they should be able to redisplay the goal they are to accomplish, especially if it is complex or contains precise specifications, as does this one.

You may also need to explain the symbology of the simulation, especially the controls that the learner can manipulate so that the learner can draw correspondences between the simulation and the real world. For novices, you may want to include a button to play a demonstration showing how they are to interact in the simulation. Typically this demonstration shows performance of an analogous task but not the exact one the learner is to perform.

Show solution after a few attempts

Require learners to attempt the task. Give learners one or two attempts before showing them the solution.

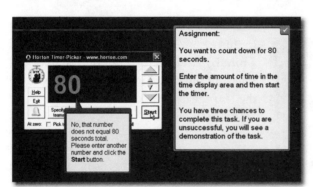

In this example, the learner has failed twice to carry out the instructions. After each attempt, the error was pointed out and the instructions redisplayed.

Here, the learner has failed the third attempt. Now the simulation demonstrates the correct procedure to attain the solution.

Do not let learners stall because they do not understand instructions or just cannot perform one step in a procedure. Correct the learner and move on after a reasonable number of steps. Or include a Show how button to demonstrate the correct response and a Next button to continue with the next step.

Let learners request assistance

Let learners get progressively more detailed instructions.

You might start the activity with general instructions that would be sufficient for an experienced learner to complete the task. If the learner requests a hint, you might tell them what to do to complete the next step. If the learner then requests more assistance, you could tell them exactly how to do it.

Three levels of assistance are usually sufficient. Making assistance available on demand lets learners perform as much of the task on their own as they can. It avoids delivering information that learners do not need.

Include pertinent hints

To encourage learning, you often need to guide and direct the learner's perception and thinking.

In this example, the learner has requested a hint by clicking the Hint button. Notice that hint implies, but does not tell, what the learner must do.

What are some other hints we can include? Comments about how the display is organized can help learners find individual items and make a sprawling display seem more logical and coherent.

Another hint is how to confirm success. Often, new learners will not know whether their last action was successful or not. We can include explicit congratulations at each step. Or, to make them more self-reliant learners, we can simply tell them how to monitor their own success by noticing changes in the user interface.

Simplify the display for quick response

Where learners must respond quickly, simplify the display to remove distractions and irrelevant click targets.

For example, during this financial simulation while the value of the learner's investment fluctuates, the user-interface contains only one button, **Sell**, because that is the only relevant action the learner can perform.

Simplify the display when quick response is required. Make clear how to respond and make that response a simple one.

Minimize distractions

Remove anything irrelevant to learning within the game.

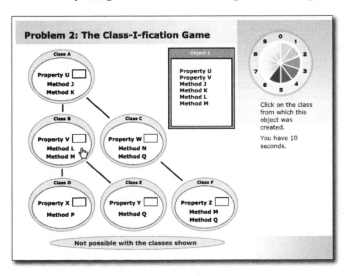

Notice the sparse display in this timed game that requires learners to select the correct bubble in the diagram.

Artwork is deliberately simple and drawn in soothing pastel and earth-tone colors.

Navigation buttons are hidden during game play and no background sounds or music interfere with the learner's concentration.

Accept all successful actions

Be aware of the alternative ways of performing actions. For example, make sure your computer simulations accept shortcut menus, right-click menus, control-clicks, and keyboard shortcuts.

In this example, the simulation accepts multiple ways of performing the required task. Once learners find one way to complete the task, the simulation challenges them to find an alternative way or two.

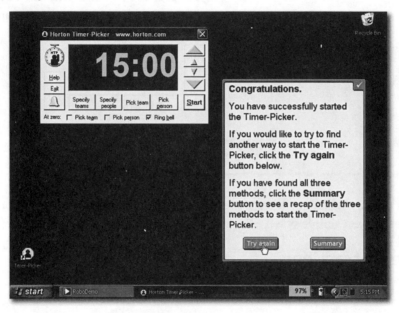

If accepting all successful actions would make the simulation too complex, omit alternatives but explain that they are not provided in the simulation though they would be present in the real system. In your instructions for the task to perform, you can mention restrictions, such as, "Use only the menus at the top of the screen."

DESIGN COACHED TASK SIMULATIONS

The coached task simulation (also known as a *coach-me* activity) guides the learner in performing the simulated task. It provides clear prompts for each step in the procedure and meaningful feedback on the success of each step taken by the learner.

Within the coach-me activity, you can provide varying levels of support or scaffolding. A coach-me activity for beginners might provide explicit instructions for each step ("Click here. Type '123' and press Enter"). Or it might provide only general instructions ("Enter the postal code."). The coach-me activity might withhold instructions until requested by the learner.

The key design principle of the coach-me activity is that the learner should never fail for lack of information or succeed without thinking.

Plan progressive interactivity

To lift learners from first acquaintance with the subject to advanced skills and knowledge, you must lead them through a series of progressively more difficult activities, each building on the last and providing appropriate challenge. Think of it as designing a ladder where you must decide the correct spacing of the rungs.

At the lowest rung, the learner performs the simulated procedure, but is given explicit prompts every step of the way. A more challenging coach-me activity offers prompts but requires the learner to specifically request them. Still more self-reliance results when learners follow open-ended prompts that suggest what to do but not exactly how to do it. Further up the ladder, coach-me activities provide no prompts, but allow learners to request hints when needed. At the upper limit of the coach-me activity, learners receive no assistance beyond hints that appear when they make mistakes.

Architecture of coach-me activities

Coach-me activities guide learners through performing a task by requiring them to do actions rather than just watch them being performed. For this reason, they require a different combination and sequence of experiences than do demonstrations.

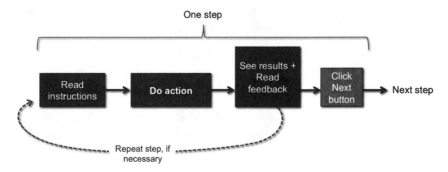

Most coach-me activities begin with instructions that the learner reads. Then the learner performs the necessary actions before seeing results and reading displayed feedback. The learner then clicks a Next or Continue button to move to the next step of the task.

Learners who perform the action incorrectly would read corrective feedback before attempting the action again.

One common variation is to omit the requirement to click a button to advance to the next step, especially for successful completion of the action where only minimal feedback is needed.

Another variation is to let learners request hints or instructions when needed. Let's look at the architecture for just such a coach-me activity.

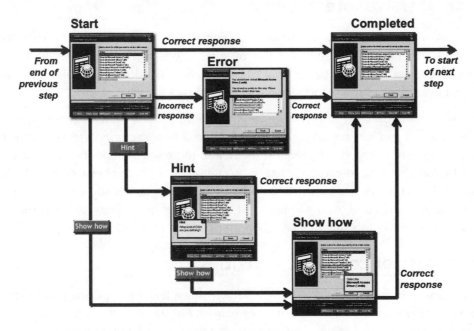

This diagram shows the common structure for each step in the simulated task. At the start of the step, the learner sees a simulated screen without any prompting. If the learner makes the correct response, the simulation shows the results and awaits the next step.

Learners, who need a little assistance, can click a **Hint** button to reveal a suggestion for what to do. The suggestion does not tell the learner exactly what to do, but does guide the learner to think of the solution. A correct response then puts the learner back on track.

If the hint is not sufficient, the learner can click the **Show how** button to receive precise instructions on where to click and what to type. Once the learner follows the directions, the simulation continues.

In this architecture, the learner does not have to request a hint before receiving explicit instructions. The learner can click the **Show how** button at any time.

The learner can also advance to the next step by pressing the **Next** button.

The diagram shown here is just one possible architecture for coach-me activities. You might choose to have three levels of assistance available—or only one. You might choose to display prompts or hints without requiring the learner to request them. Best practices do not ordain any particular architecture. Best practices suggest you select an architecture based on the difficulty of the task you are teaching and on learners' experience performing similar tasks. Learners should be challenged, but not frustrated.

Let the learner control coaching

In coach-me activities, provide buttons to enable predictable navigation. Do not use the linear playback control that is used for demonstrations.

The problem with the linear playback bar is that it advances through the simulation frame by frame. That means the control may step into the remedial (hint and directions) frames, even though the learner does not need them and has not requested them.

For a coach-me activity, we recommend a navigation control such as the one shown here. The exact mix of buttons may vary, but your navigation should provide these capabilities.

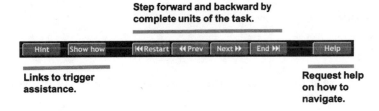

The navigation bar should include buttons to trigger assistance. This example provides a **Hint** button to display a suggestion and a **Show how** button to display explicit instructions.

The navigation bar should also include buttons to step forward and backward by complete units of the task. Usually these units are individual steps or actions. They seldom correspond to single frames of the underlying animation or simulation. This example includes buttons to restart the simulation from the beginning, to jump back to the previous step, to jump forward to the next step, and to jump to the end of the task.

You may also want to include a button to let learners get more help. This example includes a button to display a help screen that fully explains the buttons shown here.

Your choice of buttons depends on the design of your simulation. Factors that will affect your choice of navigation buttons include:

▶ Degree of control you want to give learners.
▶ Sophistication and experience of learners.
▶ Type activity: coached or test.
▶ Learners' eyesight.
▶ Special destinations: Hint, Show-how, and Help.
▶ Information learners need, for example, the page number.
▶ Space available for buttons.

DESIGN BRANCHING-SCENARIO GAMES

Branching scenarios let learners experience the results of their choices as they navigate a complex series of interactions. In branching-scenario games, learners experience a scene that calls for a choice. After making the choice, the scene changes in response to that choice and presents the learner with more choices. This cycle continues until the learner achieves the goal of the game.

Harvest storyline ideas

To create engaging and meaningful scenes and stories, gather ideas on which to base the story of the game. Talk to those privy to interesting incidents, such as supervisors, customer-support staff, classroom teachers. Ask "What was your _____est experience?"

▶ Happiest or saddest

▶ Funniest or scariest

▶ Most revealing

Search the Web for case studies, news stories, disasters, or triumphs from your field or an analogous one.

Pick a situation

Select a task for the learner within a simulated world. Here are some examples:

Learning objective	Situation
Teach interviewers to probe politely and persistently.	Police interview of a witness to a crime.
Teach mining engineers to calculate the factor of safety for mine slopes.	Assignment from pretend supervisor to calculate the factor of safety for a realistic mine slope with all relevant data.
Teach supervisors to decide whether to approve requests for time off the job.	Respond to phone requests for leave by accessing available information in files, within manuals, and from experts.
Teach managers of training departments to move to e-learning.	First 8-weeks on the job as chief learning officer for a company considering a move to e-learning. Replace failed CLO.

Map objectives to scenes

For each learning objective, specify a scene that teaches each objective. For an objective, the scene describes a situation calling for a decision by the learner. The choices available test accomplishment of the immediate learning objective. If learners make the right choice, it indicates they met the objective. A wrong choice indicates they have not met the objective. A correct choice triggers another scene that provides feedback that verifies accomplishment of the objective. An incorrect response whisks the learner to a scene whose feedback helps teach the objective.

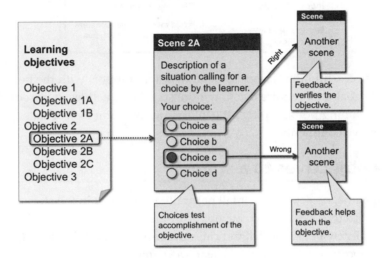

Derive specific objectives to teach

Before you begin creating scenes to teach objectives, you may have to refine your objectives so they are precise and expressed in terms that fit the chosen situation.

For example, to teach interviewing skills, we may start with high-level objectives based on what successful interviewers do. To accomplish these in a game, we may have to express more specific objectives that can be taught in a scene or two. We might ask, "How do successful interviewers do what is necessary for success?"

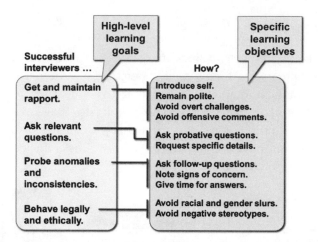

For example, successful interviewers get and maintain rapport with the person they interview. That goal may require meeting more specific objectives of introducing themselves, remaining polite through the interview, avoiding overt challenges, and avoiding offensive comments.

Translate objectives to a story

For a learning game, objectives must fall naturally into events in the story of the game. For each learning objective, we must create opportunities to show accomplishment of the objective, typically by behavior that indicates the correct ability, knowledge, belief, or feeling. Each opportunity becomes a scene in the game.

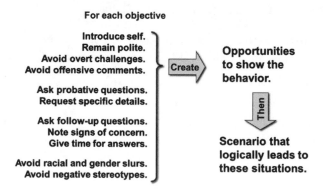

The next step is to organize these scenes into scenarios that logically lead to these situations. We organize the simulation by the scenario, not by the logic of the objectives. Our goal is to make the story seem plausible rather than to teach in the most logically efficient sequence.

Let's look at an example. We start by picking one of the learning objectives: "Avoid overt challenges." Next we think of a scene in the scenario of interviewing a bank teller who witnessed a robbery. This scene must test accomplishment of the objective. We do so by having the learner respond to the teller's claim that she did not recognize the bank robber.

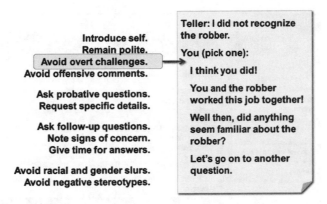

Choices range from directly confrontational and accusatory to completely accepting.

Next, we must craft scenes to provide feedback for each of these responses. To do so, we decide how the teller should react to each response. It is this response by the teller that provides the primary feedback to the learner.

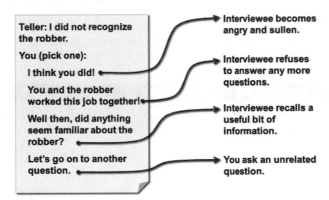

We would need to repeat this process for each objective and then weave the scenes and their responses into a branching network that provides a plausible story.

Specify each scene

As a designer, you must specify each scene in enough detail that the necessary media and linkages can be created. Here is a simple version of such a specification.

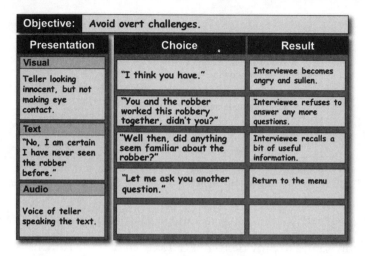

The Presentation column lists what the learner sees, reads, and hears in the scene. The Choice column lists the choices the learner can make, and the Result column sketches out the feedback the learner will receive in the following scene.

Before actually producing the media and linking the scenes, you may want to create a more complete specification, such as this one.

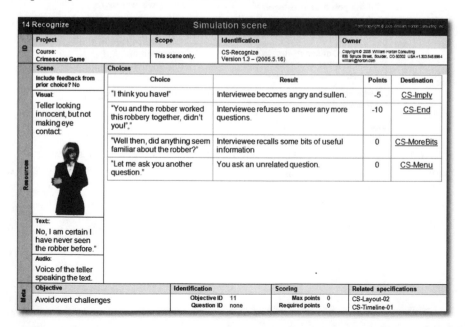

In addition to the information in the simple form, this one contains points awarded for choices and references to related specifications. Choices are hyperlinked to the specifications for the destination scenes so you can prototype the game using just these forms.

Thread together the scenes

Connecting the scenes in an entertaining and plausible way can require a lot of trial and error. One way to do this is to put each scene and its responses on index cards or *Post-it*™notes.

Then you can think about how to connect them, perhaps putting prerequisite objectives early in the sequence while maintaining the integrity of the story.

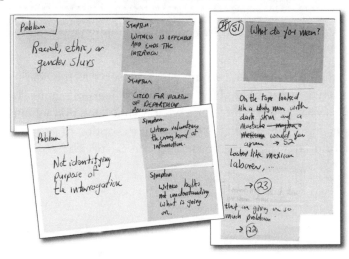

Add context-setting scenes

Such games typically need two types of scenes: scenes to test objectives and additional scenes to flesh out the story, called *context scenes*. Scenes to test objectives correspond directly with the learning objectives. The context-setting scenes help glue them together.

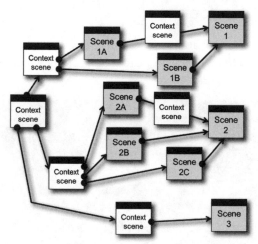

Once you have your basic structure set, consider adding context-setting scenes between the scenes where learners make choices. These context-setting scenes can set up the situation that calls for a choice so that it seems more natural and less rushed. Context-setting scenes can also provide more detailed feedback on the preceding choice. They also provide a bit of tension-relief between difficult choices.

USE GAMES AS E-LEARNING COURSES

Games can serve as the basis for an entire course—although many would call it a *learning environment* rather than a course.

Though seldom complete in itself, a learning game can serve as the heart of an entire e-learning effort. Here's how that might work: A typical learning game starts with a brief introduction that frames the game by telling what is simulated and what will be learned in the game. At this point, we might give the learner the option of learning by the game or by a conventional tutorial. Most would pick the game. Surprised?

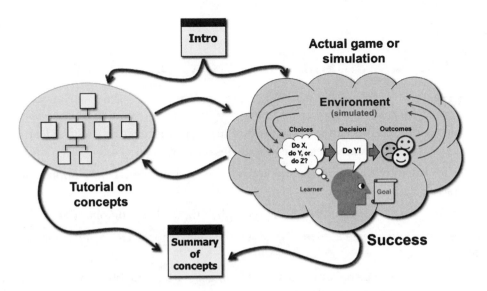

At some point, the learner realizes that to win the game it would help to know more about the subject of the game. Then the learner jumps to the conventional tutorial for a little study. After learning a bit more about the subject, the learner returns to the game. Learners may switch back and forth several times during the e-learning.

Once the learner achieves the goals in the game, there follows a quick review of the concepts. There is no test, because the game is the test. If learners can perform the task in the game, they can do it in the real world.

Of course, there are many variations possible in this flow. Some learners prefer to start with the tutorial and learn about the subject before trying their hand at the game. Others forgo the game altogether, and others never taste the tutorial.

IN CLOSING ...

Summary

- ▶ Games and simulations can provide practice, provoke discoveries, and test learning. They can serve as Do activities, tests, topics, lessons, and courses.

- ▶ Games for learning range from simple puzzles to environmental simulations and immersive role-playing games.

- ▶ Design the game so winning requires accomplishing the learning objective.

- ▶ For deep learning, create a micro-world with plausible goals, characters, objects, and rules.

- ▶ Design in progressive challenge so novices can get started reliably and even experts must struggle to master the game.

- ▶ Teach through feedback. Do not limit feedback to words. Use changes to objects in the display as well as body language and facial expressions of characters.

- ▶ Manage complexity to keep the game simple to learn and inexpensive to develop.

For more ...

For help designing questions and clues for quiz-show games and word puzzles, see Chapter 5 on tests.

For simple games, use available templates to reduce the amount of custom development required. Search for *e-learning game templates* or just *game templates*.

For more on designing games, search for *e-learning games design*.

8 Social learning

Learning as and from a group

Social media are changing the way we get news, entertain ourselves, and even find mates. Blogs have scooped national news networks and debunked their lead stories. Wikipedia challenges established commercial encyclopedias. Facebook and Twitter are necessities for many in today's society. No surprise, then, that social media and techniques are transforming learning and leading to another branch on the e-learning tree.

But social learning is not new and does not require social media. Social learning began in an ancient classroom when one child turned to another and asked, "What did the teacher just say?" That is, social learning is learning from other people—co-workers, fellow students, experts, consultants, customers, and consumers. It is also the process of learning in groups, both formal and informal. Technology just makes the learning more powerful, convenient, and fun.

WHAT IS SOCIAL LEARNING?

In the context of e-learning, the term *social learning* has several overlapping definitions. Sorry, the field is too new for precise categories.

A definition, sort of

Social learning involves learning by interacting with other people. Those people may be peers, such as classmates or others in the same profession; or they may be experts, such as a teacher or outside authority. An expert is anybody who can answer a difficult question or offer assistance. So, peers can be experts too.

Interaction is active. Politely listening to someone lecture is not social; engaging in a lively question-and-answer session is social.

The interaction can be through the direct exchange of messages, such as e-mail missives, discussion-forum postings, blog entries, or simple tweets. Interaction can occur through content created by others, such as student-produced slide shows or interviews.

Social learning is learner-driven. Virtual-classroom courses usually involve some social learning but are primarily expert-driven, the chief expert being the teacher.

Social learning advances the meaning of the word *learning*. Learning is not just putting information into the brain for later recall, but adding capabilities made possible through social interaction. The social learner's manifesto is: "I am what I can do alone—and what I can do with the help of others. You hire me; you get my social network for free."

So what?

The power of an individual lies in the ability to accomplish goals—either alone or with the help of others. The value of a workforce is its collective ability to accomplish the organization's mission. The strength of a population, society, or civilization is its collective ability to carry out the goals and ideals of the group. The effectiveness of a class is its ability to ensure that all members meet the organization's objectives and their own. Social learning leverages the energy and intellect of the group to accomplish those goals.

Consider the varieties of social learning

Social learning ranges from short, simple events to lifelong learning processes. Here are some forms and manifestations of social learning you may recognize:

- ▶ Feedback from other learners, especially if it takes the form of an open discussion.
- ▶ Dialog with an expert, coach, mentor or teacher.
- ▶ Consensus among group members on how to answer a question or proceed in a task.
- ▶ Collaboration on a single project, involving integrating the contributions of team members.
- ▶ Discussions embedded in other forms of e-learning.
- ▶ Group activities performed by a team or other group rather than as individuals.
- ▶ Performance support provided to individuals by an online community or professional network. The group answers questions and offers advice.
- ▶ Building a network of on-call advisors for help solving problems years into the future.
- ▶ Assistance in teaching by group members who critique work, enforce standards of behavior, and correct misconceptions.
- ▶ Individuals learning to function as members of a team by developing abilities to collaborate, share information, and motivate others.

▶ Team learning where a group learns to function as a unit, applying the full range of capabilities among members and developing abilities not possible by any individual.

The diversity in this list shows that social learning is not a specific technique or tool. It mixes well with other forms of learning; you have certainly encountered it in virtual-classroom courses and Webinars, for example. Functionally, the term *social learning* is more of an adverb than a noun because it concerns how learning activities occur but does not change which human experiences we wish to trigger.

What is not social learning?

It is easy to confuse social learning with some of its close relatives and ambitious imitators.

Not just using social media. Social is as social does. An electronic medium promotes social learning when a group uses it to communicate, collaborate, and coordinate. A spreadsheet can be social when used by a team who each contributes to its design and data. Twitter is not social if no one comments on the feed or retweets it.

Not just social networking. Social learning is not just using Twitter and Facebook in class. Social learning is not about making friends but building a community for learning and professional support.

Not just administrative uses of social media. Social media can be very helpful to make announcements, distribute course materials, submit homework, schedule office hours and appointments, and provide resources for reading and viewing. Though important, these uses are not in themselves social learning.

Not just for news. Using social media to communicate information is not enough to qualify as learning. Knowing that Version 3.2.1 of the software ships on Wednesday is useful information, but it is not true education.

What is the group?

Social learning takes place within a social group. That group might include just a mentor and protégé. Or it may include a work team, a class of students, an organizational department, a school or other organization, a nation, a profession, or even the entire population of this planet.

The social group where learning occurs may be called a team, network, or community. Several such groups are especially important when implementing ambitious social learning efforts:

▶ **Community of practice**. Like-minded practitioners engaged in the same endeavor or working in the same field. The focus is on performing work within the profession.

- ▶ **Learning community**. People working together to learn the same general subject. Sometimes called *learning cohorts* or a *learning team*. The focus is on learning the subject, rather than applying the subject. The community can include alumni and sometimes teachers.

- ▶ **Professional network**. One's personal contacts within a profession. These include people who can answer questions and offer advice.

- ▶ **Personal network**. One's friends and family. This group may use different tools and etiquette from the others. Its focus is on exchanging personal, rather than professional, information.

Each of these groups has its place in social learning. As designers we must involve the right group in each activity we prescribe.

HOW DO WE "DESIGN" SOCIAL LEARNING?

Social learning requires effective design. The electronic landscape is full of half-completed wikis, derelict Second Life meeting halls, and discussion groups either clogged with spam or gone silent. Good intentions and powerful technology fail without proper design.

What do we mean by design?

What is the role of design in the context of social learning? And what exactly is it that we design?

Designing social learning is a bit different from designing other forms of e-learning. Our goal is to engineer social processes rather than to configure tools or create content. Social processes include interactions such as asking and answering questions, posting and commenting on messages, and collaborating on projects. All social learning activities require at least two people, and most learning occurs as a result of feedback that occurs naturally as a part of their interaction.

Designing social learning is more like building the theater than acting in the play. The designer engineers circumstances that provoke the type of interaction necessary for learning. Most of the "content" of social learning is created by learners (and those they interact with) as they discuss, share, critique, and collaborate.

The role of the designer

Social learning is so new and broadly defined that writing a precise job description for a designer is not easy—but let's try. To the duties of the designer of conventional e-learning, we must add a mixture of new responsibilities. Some apply to any form of learning and others specifically to e-learning. As a designer of social learning, be prepared to:

► **Decide where and when to use social learning**. Social learning is seldom sufficient by itself for an ambitious goal or complex project. You, as a designer, must decide what objectives to accomplish by social learning and which objectives will require other solutions. (p. 404).

► **Define the target learners**. For social learning, the goal may be educating individuals or entire groups. As a designer you must precisely identify those you wish to educate and communicate that decision to others on the project. Keep in mind that the capability of a group of learners is not a mathematical sum of the capabilities of its members.

► **Clarify objectives**. What constitutes success? Is the goal to learn something specific or to learn how to learn independently? Is the goal to improve social skills, enhance team capabilities, or just to build up a professional network?

► **Decide where expertise will come from**. Cynics have defined social learning as the uninformed and confused teaching the ignorant and befuddled. To head off this real possibility, the designer must ensure that social interactions provide the needed expertise. This expertise can come from learners collectively, from outside experts, from an assigned coach or teacher, or from discovery activities. The designer must ensure that the expertise is available and gets to the targeted learners.

► **Decide and enforce prerequisite skills**. Social learning is not for everybody. It requires the ability to communicate clearly, work collaboratively, and learn independently. It also requires attitudes of openness and confidence. As a designer, you must set minimum requirements and establish mechanisms to ensure learners meet these prerequisites.

► **Decide what forms of social interaction best teach**. You must specify activities to accomplish specific learning objectives as well as activities to achieve general goals such as team formation. Start with the pattern of interaction you want to occur (p. 410).

► **Write the rules**. Heavy-handed procedures can doom social learning, but so too can a lack of structure. As a designer, you must set up policies, standards, procedures that guide social interaction. And you must encourage learners to set and enforce their own rules.

► **Set and clarify grading criteria**. How will learners be graded? What is the role of individual versus group performance in determining grades? How will you justify criteria to grade-conscious individuals? Grades must reflect the breadth and depth of learning and must appear fair to any objective observer.

► **Monitor and guide social learning**—without intruding. As a facilitator, you will need to model standards of behavior and coach social interaction.

▶ **Specify requirements for technology used**. Others may select and implement the technology, but you must ensure that the technology enables the types of social interaction required for learning.

▶ **Design templates and procedures for learners to create content**. For learners to create content they may need streamlined techniques to build slides, video clips, documents, spreadsheets, and many other types of learning materials.

▶ **Specify social-learning components in other forms of learning**, such as a physical classroom course, standalone e-learning, or mobile learning.

DECIDE WHERE AND WHEN TO USE SOCIAL LEARNING

Social learning works well in some circumstances and not in others. It can combine with other forms of learning to close gaps, solve unique problems, and make learning more reliable. As designers we must deploy social learning according to its strengths and weaknesses. Here are some goals for which social learning is appropriate.

Make learning more reliable

Social learning can make learning more reliable by clearing up misconceptions. It provides an instant source of feedback on ideas, and can thus filter out bad ideas and provide a second opinion. Social learning can refine ideas through discussion. And learners can continue discussion until the idea is completely clear. Social learning can mobilize thousands of minds to solve a difficult problem. As a bonus, it makes all activities Connect activities by linking learning to the larger world outside the individual.

Make learning more enjoyable

Social learning makes learning and work less lonely. It provides social interaction that extroverts crave and it provides emotional support to all learners. It lets learners work to standards set by peers they know and trust.

Keep in mind that social learning may seem alien to those from cultures with other learning traditions, especially ones based on the authority of the teacher and competition among learners.

And, social learning does not guarantee popularity among addicts of social networking. Merely using Twitter and Facebook in your courses will not make your programs more popular. Only well-designed programs will do that.

Teach difficult subjects

Social learning can teach high-level thinking and learning skills that are not easily reduced to simple rules and procedures. It can work well for enhancing creativity, innovation, problem solving, independent learning, judgment and decision-making. And, no surprise, it is ideal for teaching social skills, such as, conversation, interviewing, negotiation, and compromise.

Social learning lets e-learning tackle especially difficult topics or vast and ill-defined subjects. Social learning can prepare learners for:

▶ Decision-making in systems too complex to be fully understood.

▶ Constantly changing job duties and unique problems.

▶ Skills applied socially, that is, by a team rather than an individual.

▶ Assignments that require more talents than possessed by a single person.

Social learning cannot teach all subjects. It is not effective where learners must learn large amounts of information. Nor is it suited for getting started in a field where learners do not yet know the vocabulary and structure of the field necessary to productively interact with experts. Social learning is not effective where learners must be consistently educated to a specified standard, such as for certification or licensing. With social learning, it is hard to measure results and the causes for those results. So, depending on social learning alone is like playing the lottery as an investment strategy. Social learning may still have a part but not the lead role.

Implement learning quickly and inexpensively

Social learning can be created in less time and with less money than conventional e-learning. Social learning does not require first creating interactive content, and its coverage is not limited by the knowledge of a single teacher. The quickest and easiest way to teach some subjects is to have learners ask their professional and social networks.

Social learning can also lower teaching and administrative costs and time by delegating much of the management of learning to learners.

Because social learning can be implemented quickly and inexpensively, it works well to teach dynamic subjects, to respond to changing learning environments, and to incorporate current events and activities into learning.

With social learning, teachers and facilitators can manage larger classes, especially ones containing headstrong learners. The group or team counterbalances strong personalities and can deliver strong feedback and have it accepted. A learner can less easily shrug off the consensus of the group than the opinion of one individual. And many learners give more credibility to peers than to teachers.

Social learning is not a get-out-of-work free card. It seldom succeeds when the main purpose is to avoid the hard work of teaching by offloading work and responsibility onto learners and "the community."

Build a network to support the learning in the future

Perhaps the best use of social learning is for lifelong learning. Social learning helps learners build a network of professional contacts who can support them in the future. Social learning naturally sparks professional friendships with peers and experts. It establishes communities of learning and communities of practice that may endure long after the end of an individual course.

WHAT SOCIAL LEARNING REQUIRES

The advantages of social learning are not automatic or free. Effective social learning requires much of individuals and of the surrounding organization. Let's take a look at what personal characteristics and infrastructure are required for social learning.

What is required of learners

To engage in social learning, learners require certain abilities, attitudes, and technology.

Basic communications and thought skills

Social learning requires learners who can think logically and communicate clearly and efficiently with other individuals and with whole groups. The learner must be able to:

- ▶ **Read and write the language used in discussions, messages, and reference materials**. Learners must be able to use language to detect and express subtle meanings and nuances of emotion. In other words, they must read between the lines.

- ▶ **Speak and listen effectively**. Learners must make themselves understandable through audio and other media. And they must have the social sensitivity to go beyond the literal meaning of words and attend to tone of voice as well.

- ▶ **Ask and answer questions**. Discussion requires the ability to pose questions, listen to answers, and ask follow up questions. Likewise, it requires listening carefully to others' questions and crafting complete and concise answers.

- ▶ **Think deeply and efficiently**. Learners must assess the relevance of ideas, ignore irrelevant details, and draw logical conclusions. They must also recognize logical flaws in their own arguments and those of others.

Attitude of openness

Social learning requires being open to new and better ideas. Social learners must continually revise their opinions and refine their ideas. They must take criticism and face disagreement without becoming hostile or defensive. Above all, they must critique their own ideas and thought processes.

They must likewise share information and help others. Information hoarders make poor social learners.

A lack of openness can doom social learning efforts. Without openness, we tend to network with people like us—who don't challenge us and who know little more than we do. Because these people share the same biases and blind spots, interacting with them only reinforces groupthink.

Spirit of cooperation

Social learning is a joint venture that requires learners to put aside competitive instincts and to cooperate toward the goal of learning. As members of a team, learners must let go of the rank, status, or privilege they enjoy as individuals. They must align their actions to a common purpose, goal, or vision. And they must be willing to trust other team members in order to learn from them. Social learning often requires losing some control over results and grades. Unless learners have a spirit of cooperation, the time required to develop trust can be longer than the time allotted for learning.

Basic knowledge of the field of inquiry

To learn through discussions with others, learners must have the ability to ask questions and understand answers. That means they must have a grasp of the basic vocabulary, structure, and underlying principles of the field. Access to glossaries and primers can help, but a basic understanding is needed for fluent interaction, especially with experts who may have little patience with those who have not "done their homework."

Competence with social-media tools

Learners must be able to use common social-media tools and understand their terminology and conventions. Or they must have the ability to learn them quickly. Fortunately, the tools are simple and well documented.

Competence also includes following conventions of polite, professional online behavior or *netiquette*.

Work ethic

Social learning places most of the responsibility for learning on learners. This in turn requires active participation, not slacking off or "hitchhiking." It also requires the self-discipline to forego unproductive online social behaviors, such as flirting, bantering, provoking others, spreading rumors, or just wasting time (p. 457).

Social learning is not for dependent learners who will swap dependence on the teacher for dependence on other learners. This swap is not progress. At least the teacher was informed and motivated to help.

Something to contribute to the group

Each learner must offer something to the group. Some learners may possess in-depth knowledge within the field of inquiry. Others may have special social skills, such as the ability to resolve disputes among team members; or technical skills, such as the ability to teach others how to use advanced social media.

If learners cannot contribute to the group, they may feel isolated and insecure. They may withdraw or just fail to participate fully. To prevent this situation, first make sure everyone can contribute something. Have the facilitator work with team members to identify skills or knowledge they can offer the group.

What is required of the organization

Social learning does not work for all organizations. Both the organization that sponsors social learning and the environment in which learning takes place must meet some requirements for social learning to succeed.

Culture of sharing

To enable social learning, the organization must possess a culture of sharing information and helping others. A climate of secrecy and fierce competition hardens learners against the openness and collaboration required in social learning. People who are afraid to openly admit mistakes on the job or in the classroom are unlikely to overcome similar fears in social learning.

Organizational self-confidence

Social learning tinkers with the management structure, organizational culture, and established values of the organization. It provides lateral communication within an organization and abolishes rank and status as guarantees of respect or authority. The whole impetus in social learning is that the best idea wins ... until a better idea comes along. Authoritarian organizations with a rigid chain of command are not ideal for social learning.

Some executives object to the goofy names of social networking tools involved in social learning. Thus, they may feel that social learning trivializes education or is just fad-chasing. Or, that learners will just waste time socializing.

Legal security

Social learning can pose serious legal risks for an organization. It can expose the organization to legal liability if off-hand comments are used as evidence of fraud, harassment, or discrimination. Participation by learners in outside communities can raise issues regarding the ownership of intellectual property created in learning activities, the misrepresentation by learners of the organization's position on controversial issues, or the release of private or confidential information.

Information security

Social learning can pose problems of information security, privacy, and control—especially if performed using public tools and social networks. Organizations may fear learners will be exposed to spam or advertising. Or to inquiries by outsiders. Organizations may fear that private or proprietary information will be revealed. They may also have concerns that a social-networking site will cease operation, change its business model, or change privacy policy and procedures.

Availability of needed expertise

For social learning to succeed learners must have access to those with the needed expertise to guide them. This expertise can come from two sources:

▶ Learners collectively have the knowledge and just need to share it laterally.

▶ Experts are available and willing to share.

If the organization does not possess the needed expertise or cannot attract it, you may want to hold off on social learning.

Flexibility

None of these requirements are insurmountable provided the organization is willing to change. Implementing social learning may require compromise and adaptation. The organization can take small steps in opening up and encouraging sharing. It can communicate rules for social learning that protect the organization. It can give experts and learners incentives to participate.

Those implementing social learning can take steps to integrate social learning in a way that fits the organization's culture. They can also monitor early social-learning efforts to ensure that they produce effective learning while respecting the requirements of the organization.

PATTERNS OF INTERACTION

Within social learning, certain ways of interacting have proven especially productive. Other ways are also common because of their familiarity through traditional schooling and other human activities. This section catalogs some of the most common patterns of interaction. Use these as building blocks to create rich social-learning activities and lessons.

The elements of social learning

What are the patterns of interaction that recur throughout social learning? Here's a brief list of the main ones. Feel free to add to the list and experiment with hybrid types.

Tutoring interaction

 In the tutoring pattern of interaction, the expert and learner interact one-on-one. This pattern is common in coaching, counseling, mentoring, and apprenticeship.

Tutoring can occur in person, via e-mail or texting, as a phone call, or in a video-conference. The tutor can be a subject-matter expert, the teacher of a class, or an informed and caring classmate.

Though not an efficient way to teach, the tutoring pattern of interaction is good for delivering feedback privately, for getting answers to potentially embarrassing questions, and for issues of interest to only one person.

Presentation pattern

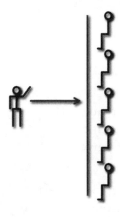 In the presentation pattern, one person directs information to others. The information may take the form of a course announcement, a live presentation, or a lecture. The presentation interaction is also used for speeches, lectures, and demonstrations. It is the mode used for presentation activities (p. 69).

By itself, a presentation is not social, but it may lead to other forms of interaction, such as question-and-answer, that are social. It may also be necessary in social learning to prepare learners to interact socially. It becomes social when learners, individually or as a group, take on the role of presenter.

Presentations can be presented in a physical meeting, by live or recorded video, or in an online meeting.

Use the presentation interaction to deliver information needed by all learners, especially where there is little need for interaction. Use it to set the stage for a productive discussion or other form of interaction.

Question-and-answer pattern

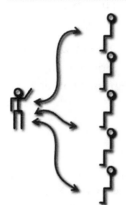

In the question-and-answer (Q&A) pattern learners ask questions of an expert. It can occur as an organized session at a specific time or as sporadically as needed. It is the core of questioning activities (p. 176).

Q&A can occur by any two-way media: e-mail, texting, chat, discussion forum, phone, audio- or video-conferencing, or micro-blogging. A Q&A session can be summarized as a frequently asked questions file.

Use Q&A to help learners answer questions that occurred while passively experiencing a lecture or other presentation.

Also use it to answer questions provoked by some other individual or social activity. Q&A can fill gaps caused by learners' different levels of background knowledge.

Post-and-comment pattern

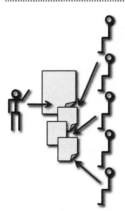

In the post-and-comment pattern, an expert, teacher, or discussion leader posts a message and learners comment on it. Everybody involved reads and analyzes all the postings. A learner can be the expert for an area just studied.

Post-and-comment interactions can also be implemented as a discussion thread or blog.

Post-and-comment interactions work to correct misconceptions and to refine ideas. A teacher can use the post-and-comment pattern to provoke discussion, to make assignments and collect results, and to direct attention to a specific aspect of the subject.

Learners can use this pattern to get feedback on a hypothesis, proposal, or interpretation; or to share private learning and insights with a group.

Collaborative-document pattern

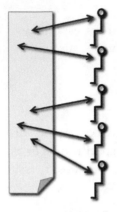

In the collaborative-document pattern, learners work together to create and refine a document or other piece of work. Such collaborative documents are often called *wikis*.

Collaborative documents can be implemented with software especially designed to enable multiple authors to create and edit an online document. Software for creating wikis fits the bill, as does Google Docs and equivalent collaborative authoring tools.

Collaborative documents let learners propose and refine ideas. They are especially useful in teaching subjects such as writing, visual design, and others that can be summarized in a diagram or other document.

Group-discussion pattern

In true group discussion, learners interact with one another. This pattern describes general discussions as well as specialized forms such as role-playing.

Group discussion can be implemented through chat, audio- or video-conferencing, or a discussion forum.

The group discussion is good to correct misconceptions, refine ideas, fill in gaps, and get feedback. It is also a place to practice social and interpersonal communications skills.

Small-group pattern

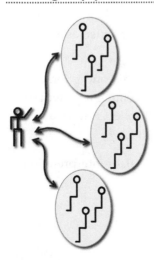

The small-group pattern is a legacy from classroom training. In it, the teacher assigns discussion topics or team tasks to groups of learners who work together and then report back to the class as a whole. The sub-groups are often called *breakout groups* and the virtual spaces in which they meet are called breakout rooms.

Breakout sessions are a feature in some online-meeting tools. They can also be implemented by using multiple chat rooms.

Small-group interactions are good for short-term teamwork assignments. They divide complex tasks into workable-sized units. They encourage teams to generate solutions independently and then to refine ideas by comparison. They provide a space where learners can practice social and interpersonal communication skills.

Panel-discussion pattern

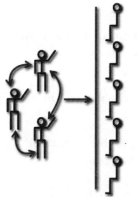

In the panel-discussion pattern, experts discuss a topic as learners watch and listen. This pattern is used for true panel discussions, debates, interviews, and role-playing.

Because the panel-discussion pattern does not require interacting directly with learners, it can be implemented with a live presentation or an audio-or video podcast.

Though not strictly social, the panel-discussion pattern is useful for modeling social behavior, illustrating social situations, exposing a range of opinions and viewpoints, and delving deeper into a subject.

Symposium pattern

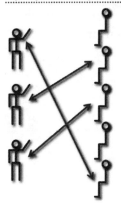

In the symposium pattern, a group of experts discuss a subject with learners. The symposium differs from the panel in that the experts interact with learners.

The symposium pattern can be implemented with audio- or video-conferencing, such as possible through an online meeting tool.

The symposium pattern is good for an extended question-and-answer session. It helps learners refine knowledge and meet individual learning needs.

Ask-expert-community pattern

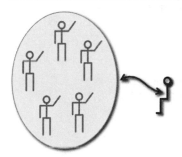

In the pattern of asking a community of experts, the learner consults a community of experts (of which the learner is not a member). The community might be a product user group or a discussion forum for a professional association.

Communication with the community is typically through its discussion forum.

Asking a community of experts is useful for answering advanced questions and getting professional advice. It is also helpful for suggesting alternative approaches to learners who feel stuck or out of their depth.

Ask-peers pattern

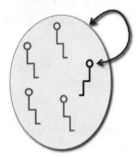

In the ask-peers pattern, a learner consults a group of which the learner is a member. The peers may be the learner's social network, professional network, or learning team.

This pattern is typically implemented with a discussion forum or social networking software.

This pattern of interaction is ideal for asking slightly advanced questions of interest to several members of the group.

With it, learners can get an explanation in understandable terms or receive needed encouragement and sympathy.

Combine patterns for complete activities

The power of these patterns of interaction emerges when patterns combine in a comprehensive learning activity.

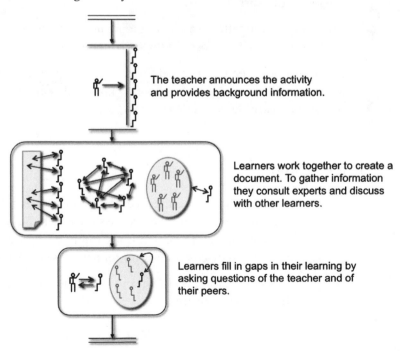

The teacher announces the activity and provides background information.

Learners work together to create a document. To gather information they consult experts and discuss with other learners.

Learners fill in gaps in their learning by asking questions of the teacher and of their peers.

This example shows the flow of interaction patterns in an extended activity. Teachers and learners work together to research and integrate information on a subject.

1. The activity starts with an announcement and mini-lecture by the teacher to clarify the assignment.

2. In the next phase, three types of interaction occur simultaneously.

   ▪ Learners work together to write and edit a document.

   ▪ To gain information and clarify issues, they ask questions of professionals in the field.

   ▪ To coordinate their research and writing, they discuss ideas and approaches.

3. In the third phase, learners round out learning. They meet privately with the teacher and ask questions of other learners to fill in any gaps left in their learning.

The interaction patterns are just building blocks and this was just one example. Imagine how you can combine these patterns to create effective social-learning activities.

SOCIAL CAPABILITIES OF SOFTWARE

Social media and tools provide channels for human interaction. In this section, we look at those capabilities. We do not consider individual tools, which are mixes of capabilities and which change rapidly. Instead, we look at the basic capabilities of communication and collaboration and the categories of tools that provide these capabilities. Along the way, we will offer advice on where and how to use each capability.

This section is rather long, so let's start with a preview.

Capability	Classes of tools	Page
Send targeted messages.	E-mail and texting.	416
Meet real-time.	Text-, audio-, and video-conferencing.	418
Discuss asynchronously.	Discussion forums.	425
Broadcast sporadic messages.	Micro-blogging and e-mail.	426
Post message sequences.	Blogs and podcasts.	428
Collaboratively create documents.	Collaborative authoring tools, wikis, whiteboards, and application sharing.	433
Share creations.	File- and media-sharing, social bookmarking, tagging or keywording items, and mashups.	440

Capability	Classes of tools	Page
Vote and rate.	Polls.	446
Filter messages.	Messaging tools with the ability to subscribe, block, and aggregate.	450
Establish a point of contact.	Social media tools with a profile or home page.	450
Administer a team or other group of learners.	Virtual classroom systems, online meeting tools, social media tools, and collaborative calendaring.	453

Use these capabilities to implement the patterns of interaction (p. 410), to adapt conventional activities (Chapters 2, 3, and 4) to social learning, and to add social components to virtual classroom courses (Chapter 10).

Send targeted messages

One of the basic actions in social learning is sending messages to specific individuals or to tightly defined groups. Typically e-mail or texting is used for such targeted messages. Though technically different, e-mail and texting serve the same social function. Voice messages, such as phone calls, can also target messages.

The ability to direct text messages to specific group members is part of many virtual-classroom, online-meeting, and social-networking tools. And e-mail and texting are standard features in most computers and mobile phones.

E-mail

E-mail is the most common method of collaboration in e-learning. E-mail includes private messages sent one-to-one, say from a learner to ask a question of the teacher. E-mail can also broadcast messages from the teacher to the class.

E-mail is simple, reliable, inexpensive, omnipresent, and familiar. Anyone who can use computer technology can use e-mail, and almost everybody has an e-mail address. Many mobile phones can get and send e-mail.

Originally, e-mail was limited to simple text messages, but today most e-mail readers can use HTML for formatting messages. That means e-mail messages can use the same rich mixture of media as Web pages. Most e-mail readers also allow senders to include other file formats in messages as attachments. E-mail is often overlooked as a collaboration mechanism in favor of flashier, more expensive, and less reliable mechanisms. Pity.

Texting

For purposes of social learning, think of texting as e-mail for mobile phones. It frees social learning from reliance on a desktop or laptop computer.

In a pure sense, texting involves sending short text messages to a mobile phone where it waits patiently for the recipient to read it. Like e-mail, texting has grown in scope and can include other media too.

Texting is especially useful for announcements to those not continuously connected to other social media.

Use targeted messages for immediacy, intimacy, and impact

Use one-to-one messages to ask and answer individual questions, but not for questions of general interest.

Do not use e-mail or texting for routine messages that do not require special attention from the recipient. If a response is optional and the subject is not critical, post the message to a discussion forum. If an immediate answer is crucial, use the telephone.

Use private messages for intimacy and discretion. Use private messages for responses that might embarrass the recipient if posted in a public discussion.

Use text messages effectively

Here are just a few points that become important when using texting and e-mail within e-learning:

▶ **Introduce yourself when sending unsolicited messages**. Begin by explaining who you are and your interest in the recipient. You do not want your message treated as junk mail. In e-mail, make sure the subject line makes clear why the recipient should read this message. A message headed "Welcome" is a lot more likely to be ignored than one that says, "Welcome to Geology Online."

▶ **Preview the message in the e-mail subject line**. That way, readers can recognize truly urgent messages, group similar messages, and begin thinking about the content of the message.

▶ **Require delivery receipts only in special cases**. Require delivery receipts for e-mail only where necessary. Some consider receipt requests a form of snooping. Do require delivery receipts if delivering a warning to a learner. You may need to document when the message was delivered.

▶ **Keep messages short and to the subject**. Enough said.

▶ **Make sure the recipient understands abbreviations**. Ensure that message senders take into account the profession, background, and culture of the recipient before shortening the message.

Meet real-time

Learners can meet and carry on conversations without being in the same location. The conversation may use text, audio, or video to convey messages. Unlike e-mail and text, which do not presuppose an immediate reply to messages, online meetings or conferences enable a real-time exchange among participants. And, unlike discussion forums, online meetings require all parties to the conversation to participate at the same time. That is, online conferences are synchronous events.

Text-conferencing: chat

Text-conferencing is commonly called *chat*. Every day millions of Internet users get together in chat rooms and instant-messaging sessions to whine, pontificate, flirt, and who knows what. Chat enables real-time conversations among a group of people over a low-speed Internet connection. Chat lets learners swap typed-in messages over a network. Chat sessions are like an instantaneous, real-time discussion forum. Note: Video-chat is a form of video-conferencing (p. 422).

In online learning, chat can provide a back channel for questions and feedback during a meeting (p. 469). Chat can also be a separate event, such as in a study-group meeting.

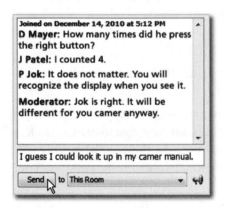

Here we see the discussion among learners watching a demonstration. Notice how they clarify what is going on?

This chat occurs within an Elluminate meeting.

Chat can be implemented via chat-room or instant-messaging tools, and is a common feature in many virtual-classroom, online-meeting, and social-networking tools. It can also be implemented in micro-blogging comments by appropriately tagging replies (p. 443).

Chat conversations are immediate and spontaneous. But they are limited to typed and pasted text. Nevertheless, many learners prefer chat to phone conversations because chat leaves a written record they can consult later.

The use of chat sessions in learning is different from their use for purely social purposes. Learners and instructional designers familiar with the social uses of chat may have to adjust their thinking to use chats effectively in learning.

In a typical chat session, everybody sees all the messages. However, some chat tools allow private messages—ones sent from one person in the chat session to another person in the session. Such messages are seen by the recipient but not by the others in the session. For example, the teacher can ask a learner to refrain from disruptive behavior or a learner can point out a typo on the teacher's slide—without alerting the whole class.

When to use chat in social learning

Use chat to let people at different locations on a network carry on a conversation. Use it when e-mail and discussion-forum exchanges are too slow. Here are some more *do*s and *don't*s for using chat in social learning.

Do use chat:

For simple conversations. Some common uses for chat include:

▶ Real-time question-and-answer sessions.

▶ Brainstorming, troubleshooting, and problem-solving sessions.

▶ "Oral" examinations.

▶ Interviews of experts by learners or researchers.

▶ "Study group meetings" among teams of learners.

To personalize learning. Use chat for other than whole-class meetings. Use it for study groups, team meetings, tutoring sessions, and private meetings with the teacher. Provide a procedure for reserving time slots on the class chat server or for setting up a private chat room. Encourage learners to use private chat to communicate to other learners, perhaps to suggest to teammates how the idea being discussed could be implemented in their class project. Keep the chat window available after the official end of the class meeting. And let learners schedule their own chat sessions.

For a small group. Chat can seem painfully slow if only two are chatting. If more than five or seven are chatting, however, it can be difficult to keep up, especially if you are a slow typist. That does not mean you cannot use chat as a back channel in a large meeting (p. 469), provided only a few people are using chat at once. I learned this lesson when I asked a complex question of 60 people in a meeting. For about a minute nothing happened. Then suddenly 5- and 6-line text messages poured into the chat window and the window began scrolling so fast that no one could read the messages before they disappeared off the top of the window.

For whispering to the teacher. Suggest that learners use private chat to ask a question or make a comment without interrupting the whole class or to remain anonymous from the rest of the class.

Don't use chat:

For lectures. Chat is for short, spontaneous thoughts. If the ideas are deeper than that, or if you require time to find just the right words, send the ideas as e-mail or discussion-forum messages. Nothing is worse than having to read a sporadically scrolling text narrative—awkwardly composed, inaccurately typed, and saying nothing a textbook does not say better. Using chat to narrate actions in an application sharing or whiteboard session can also be awkward. Having to stop using the visual application to go to the chat window and type a comment or instructions interrupts the flow of the task being demonstrated. Never use chat for lectures, OK?

With slow typists. All participants must be good typists. Otherwise the conversation is filled with awkward pauses. By the time a slow typist enters a reply, the conversation has moved on to a completely different subject. Do not rely on chat if all learners must type quickly and accurately or if responses must be complex.

Best practices for using chat effectively

Make sure that learners and teachers use chat in ways that advance learning. Even those who have used chat or instant messaging socially for years may not draw analogies to using it for learning. Here are some ways to use chat for learning:

▶ **Keep chat professional**. Chat for learning is not personal social chat. The light banter and heavy flirting that are common late at night on Twitter are hardly the kind of conversations you want to foster. Help learners to adopt professional behaviors that lead to learning.

▶ **Prepare "spontaneous" comments ahead of time**. If you know what questions you will ask or what answers you will give, prepare them in a separate text-editor window. At the appropriate moment, just cut and paste the comments into the chat window.

▶ **Monitor chat**. In most online meeting systems, the presenter or host sees all messages, even messages sent privately from one learner to another. You might want to warn learners about the teacher's ability to eavesdrop. Or, you might not.

▶ **Save a transcript**. Chat leaves a written transcript. You may want to save the transcript and post it to the class discussion forum so that learners can concentrate on the online meeting without having to make notes of what is said in chat. However, the transcript may seem crude when read later. Some participants may object to seeing their off-the-cuff remarks on display. Warn them ahead of time and ensure that providing transcripts does not inhibit discussion. Or, turn the transcript into a shared document and use collaborative authoring (p. 433) to edit it.

Audio-conferencing

Audio-conferencing lets participants talk with one another. Audio-conferencing can be conducted by a phone conference call or by using the Internet to communicate speech.

Audio conferences can be used for general and targeted discussions, for question-and-answer sessions, and for presentations—where words alone are sufficient. They can also be used to provide a parallel audio channel for online presentations (p. 69 and 545), whiteboard activities (p. 436), and application sharing (p. 438).

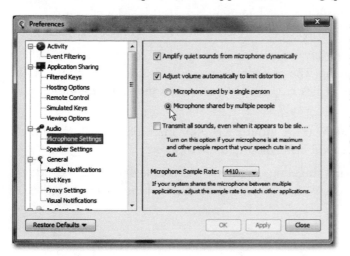

Audio-conferencing is typically provided by the online meeting tool used to provide other communication channels used in the meeting.

Here is the audio preferences dialog box in the meeting tool Elluminate.

When to use audio-conferencing in social learning

Use audio-conferencing when people need to hear and speak. The first question to answer is: When does someone need to hear someone else speak? Use audio-conferencing when:

▶ **Emotions are important.** A tone of voice can tell us whether the speaker is angry, excited, sad, or just joking. A text transcript cannot, for example: "Teacher: How's it going? Learner: Just great." Is the learner satisfied or just sarcastic?

▶ **Sounds are important.** You want to hear or demonstrate the sound that something makes—a computer disk drive or a healthy human heart, for instance.

▶ **Learners lack writing or typing skills** necessary to collaborate fluently by written media.

▶ **The discussion is complex.** A chat session would require too much typing and have too many delays that break the continuity of the conversation.

Best practices for audio-conferencing

Audio-conferencing puts strains on your listeners, your speakers, and your network. Plan how to use audio-conferencing within human and technological limitations. Here are some guidelines for presenters and other participants:

▶ **Reduce background noise.** Turn off the radio. Close the windows. Turn off unnecessary machinery. When not talking, mute the microphone.

▶ **Mute learners' microphones until they need to speak**. Entire classes have had to listen to intra-office gossip, parents disciplining children, and barking dogs because learners did not know how to mute their microphones.

▶ **Put emotion into your voice**. Poor audio connections make everybody sound bored and monotonous. Go a bit overboard. Exaggerate. Emote. Ham it up.

▶ **Speak slowly and distinctly.** Even the best telephone connection is low fidelity. E-nun-ci-ate! Repeat unfamiliar terms. Spell out words learners will not recognize.

▶ **Recruit a co-presenter**. Vocal variety can occur naturally when you have two presenters who alternate speaking. The presenters are less self-conscious and naturally speak with more emotion. Try to pick two people with voices that are different. Teaming a man and woman is one way.

▶ **Put the microphone below and near the mouth.** Keep the microphone just out of the breath stream. I recommend a good head-mounted microphone.

▶ **Wait before you respond.** Sound traveling over networks can be delayed a second or more. In audio-conferencing, silence does not always mean that the other person is waiting for you to talk.

Video-conferencing

In video-conferencing, distant participants can see and hear each other. Video-conferencing lets learners see at least a small video image of the presenter. Some systems allow larger images and two-way views.

This example of an online meeting shows video-conferencing used to demonstrate a physical procedure with a digital camera.

Learners can choose to view just the video or the entire meeting window showing the roster and chat area.

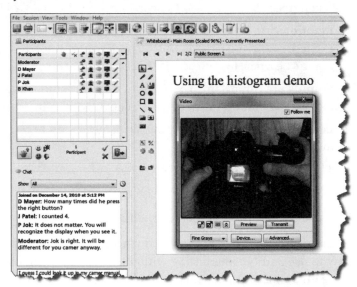

Meeting conducted in Elluminate.

Video-conferences are commonly used for demonstrations, role-playing activities, and for presenting feedback on physical actions.

The quality of the video images varies widely and depends on the speed and consistency of the network connection, the quality of the video camera, and the memory and processor speed of the computers involved.

Consider carefully whether you need video, whether it must be live rather than pre-recorded, and whether it must flow two ways.

When to use video-conferencing in social learning

What situations justify the use of video-conferencing? Use video-conferencing when people need to see someone talking or see objects moving. Use video-conferencing to:

▶ **Show moving objects**. Use video to explain how a piece of machinery works or to give instructions on repairing or manipulating a piece of equipment.

▶ **Make people seem real**. Use video-conferencing to introduce the teacher to remote learners and remote learners to the teacher.

▶ **Deliver powerful emotional messages**. Use video to motivate and counsel learners.

Do not use video-conferencing when a simpler, less expensive alternative works as well. Consider combining whiteboard (to show a series of still pictures) and audio-conferencing (to describe them). Or, display a still picture of yourself so people can view it as they listen to your voice by audio-conferencing.

Beware the talking head. Especially avoid long video segments that show nothing but the teacher talking, talking, and talking. In addition to the usual problems with video, the infamous talking-head shot makes the teacher seem egotistical. And there is no evidence learners watch the teacher for more than 20 or 30 seconds.

Best practices for video-conferencing

Video-conferencing requires careful presentation and even more meticulous preparation. Give learners and distant experts help to ensure they communicate effectively in video.

▶ **Prepare the "studio."** Plan how participants will record video. Even if they are broadcasting from a small cubicle, decide where the camera will go and how to light the scene.

- **Obtain a good camera**. A professional camera is better than a vacation camcorder, which is better than the average computer-store Web cam. Make sure your camera can connect to your computer.

- **Light the presenter evenly** from the front or slightly to the side. Either use diffused lighting or reflect light off an opposing wall.

- **Minimize background distractions.** Pose the presenter before a simple, static background. Place the background far behind the presenter so it falls out of focus. Or adjust the lights so that the background is dark. A noisy background or busy scene takes more work to transmit and display and can result in skips in the picture or stuttering in the sound. Avoid the common practice of showing the presenter in the middle of a room with people walking around in the background. Never pose the presenter outdoors or against an outside window with leaves fluttering in the breeze.

- **Frame the scene**. Position the camera so it will capture what is important. Consider the size video window learners will view. You may want to move the camera back to allow the presenter to move back and forth as in a classroom. Or you may want the camera closer to capture gestures or emotions. Make sure the video image shows a glint in the eye of the presenter.

- **Steady the camera**. Mount the camera firmly. Use a tripod to reduce shake. Point the camera precisely. If the camera must move to follow the presenter, make sure the tripod has a fluid head that glides smoothly and an operator with a good aim.

▶ **Prepare the presenter.** Help the presenter do the best job possible. Ensure that novice presenters avoid common mistakes.

- **Dress the presenter simply**. Avoid clothing with patterns. Use flat makeup and forego fancy jewelry that flickers and glints.

- **Rehearse the presentation**. Practice the presentation with cameras running. Then review the captured video and try again. Presenters may not realize how little is visible in a small video window or how annoying some of their gestures can be. Give them time to learn this new medium.

▶ **Prepare learners**. The effectiveness of a video-conference depends on the behavior and actions of learners—especially if they actively participate in the conference.

- **Explain video quality**. Explain to learners why the video quality may be lower than they are used to for broadcast television.

- **Tell learners to keep their video cameras off** until requested to turn them on. Too many video streams can clog the network and distract learners. There are few cases in which people need to watch more than two or three others.

- **Remind learners to keep their video images simple**. Warn against noisy or moving backgrounds.

▶ **Conduct the session smoothly**. During a video-conference presentation, the presenter and producer must use the medium efficiently and effectively. Here are a few suggestions:

- **Keep presentations simple**. Put details in separate Web pages that learners can read at leisure.

- **Keep props at hand.** Gather the objects you will show ahead of time. Put them out of camera view but within arm's reach. Practice grabbing and manipulating them.

- **Vary camera angle**. If one person must talk for more than a minute or so, periodically shift the camera angle. Have the person walk around. Cut away or pan to an object the person is describing. Insert a reaction shot showing the studio audience listening. Use close-ups to show details.

- **Move smoothly and predictably.** Move in fluid, steady, predictable motions. Start and finish movements slowly. Do not inexplicably shift the camera position. Make all movements seem natural and logical. Warn of shifts of locale. "We're now going to the workshop to show how to apply these ideas."

Discuss asynchronously

Discussion forums are another Internet collaboration mechanism that has found a role in social learning. Descendants of computer bulletin boards, e-mail list servers, and Internet newsgroups, today's threaded discussion forums support sophisticated collaboration. Their equivalent is an integral part of most virtual-classroom and blogging tools.

Online discussion starts when one person posts a question or an opinion. Others read it and attach replies. Then still others add comments to the replies. The sequence of commentary can go on indefinitely.

In this example, we see a learner's post indented beneath the Moderator's post.

Replying to the learner's post requires opening the post and clicking the Reply button.

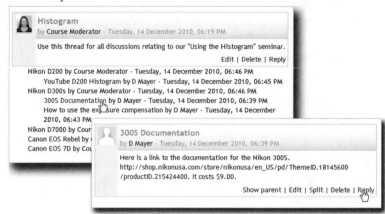

Discussion created in Moodle.

This pattern of indented messages is called a *thread*, and greatly simplifies following conversations. The idea of the threaded discussion forum is simple. A learner sees an indented list of messages. To reply to a message, the learner selects it, presses a reply button, and then composes the reply in a text window.

When to use discussion forums in social learning

If there is an unsung hero in e-learning, it is the humble discussion forum. Learners frequently cite discussion as the best part of the course, and it is not unusual for conversations to continue months after the formal end of a course. Discussion activities work well for subjects that involve collaboration, teamwork, and negotiation among multiple learners. Discussion forums:

▶ **Let learners interact with each other** even though they may be 12 time zones apart.

▶ **Allow discussions to continue as long as necessary**. Conversations do not have to stop at the classroom door. Discussion forums keep learners and the teacher talking between scheduled class events.

▶ **Give everyone a chance to join in**, even those who might not contribute in class: shy people too polite to interrupt others, those with limited language skills, those with a speech impediment or dyslexia, those sitting in the back row, those with soft voices, those put off by loud voices, and those whose schedules rule out class meetings.

▶ **Provide second-language learners a chance to practice language skills**. Such learners can take time to interpret messages, using a dictionary if necessary, and to compose and check replies.

▶ **Enable learners to discuss every topic of interest**. In a classroom, the class cannot waste time dealing with issues of interest to only a few. In a discussion forum, it takes only two learners interested in the subject to start a productive discussion.

▶ **Encourage full responses**. Threaded discussion forums allow time to compose responses, maintain separate threads for ongoing subjects, let everyone talk at once, and can manage discussions among hundreds of participants.

Best practices for discussion forums

Here are some best practices to help you get the most out of discussion forum activities:

▶ **Seed each thread** with a provocative statement or question to get a conversation started. For instance, start with open-ended questions that do not imply a simple answer.

▶ **Moderate but do not censor** messages. Guard against negative behaviors, but do not micromanage conversations. Charge the entire group with the responsibility for enforcing good netiquette.

▶ **Manage the conversation** as it develops. Probe, provoke, and prompt deep discussions. Continually ask, "Why do you say that?" and "What else?"

For more best practices, see the section on designing and moderating online discussion activities (p. 483).

Broadcast sporadic messages

Social learning includes making announcements to a large group or to the world in general. In the past, such announcements were handled with the equivalent of an e-mail blast, but now are more likely to occur using a micro-blogging capability (Think Twitter.) that keeps the announcements well organized and allows for replies from recipients.

Although this capability is used mostly for short, simple text messages, it may include links to longer messages and to other media, such as graphics and video.

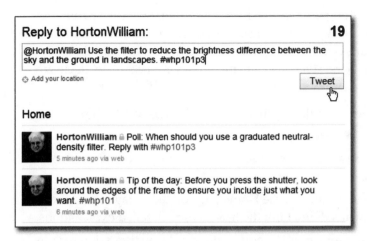

Here we see a micro-blogging service used for two kinds of sporadic messages: a tip of the day and a poll question.

Sporadic broadcast messages can be used for both deliberate and spontaneous communications, for example to:

▶ Make course announcements. Use broadcast messages for news and reminders of approaching tests, imminent deadlines, upcoming events, schedule changes, guest speakers, and other newsworthy items.

▶ Offer a daily tip, vocabulary word, fact, statistic, procedure, or principle.

▶ Share an inspirational story.

▶ Provide class-wide feedback.

▶ Poll the class on an issue.

▶ Correct a serious problem or widespread misconception.

Learners can use broadcast messages to:

▶ Publish real-time notes.

▶ Ask questions at any time.

▶ Initiate a discussion at any time.

▶ Share links and resources.

▶ Inform fellow team members of individual progress, questions, or concerns.

Use broadcasts for sharing *important* information

Broadcasting messages to entire groups can overflow message windows and overwhelm anxious learners. Use broadcast messages only for information important to the whole group receiving it.

Don't broadcast spam. Broadcasting unwelcome messages is what we call spamming. Teachers and facilitators should spell out when learners should broadcast messages to the whole class and when not. Learners wishing to communicate with all others should consider how the message will be received and whether another mechanism, such as a discussion forum or blog post, might work better.

Keep broadcast messages short. Keep them concise. Direct readers to a Web page or discussion forum for complete details.

Consider alternatives for course announcements. There are two other ways to make class announcements besides e-mail or micro-blog broadcasts:

▶ **Course home page**. If all learners stop at the Home page on their way into the course, put headlines of announcements there. Link the headlines to detailed explanations.

▶ **Announcement in discussion forum**. If learners regularly check discussion forums, you can set up a specific discussion forum for class announcements and post announcements there.

Keep messages organized. Establish rules for subject headings and hash tags to ensure that learners can filter and sort messages that may arrive from different sources.

Post message sequences

In social learning, participants may need to post a sequence of detailed messages available for others to read and comment on. This capability can be used to issue a sequence of messages that are kept available in chronological order. Message sequences composed of text and graphics are typically called *blogs*. Those including audio and video are called *podcasts*. These messages are kept available in chronological order.

Blogs and podcasts are conventionally used for presentations in Absorb activities as well as socially for learner-created content.

Blogs

A blog is an online journal containing periodic or sporadic entries on a specific subject. Messages are primarily text and graphics, but may include video clips. The term blog is a contraction of "web log."

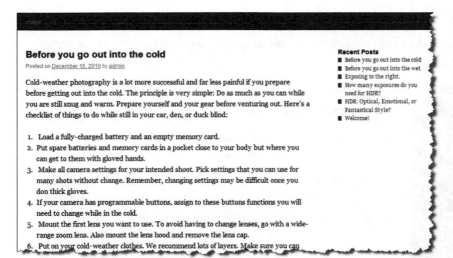

This blog on photography offers practical tips and techniques that learners can use to increase their skills as amateur or professional photographers.

Blog created in Tumblr.

8 Social learning

Technically, a blog is nothing more than a set of linked Web pages. Blogs are most often organized chronologically with more recent articles appearing more prominently, typically at the top of the home page for the blog.

Readers of blogs can "subscribe" to a blog. Doing so provides notifications of new articles. Notifications include links to display the articles. Learners can use a "blog reader" to access articles from all the blogs to which they have subscribed.

Tools to create and maintain blogs include WordPress and Blogger. A similar capability is included in some virtual-classroom tools.

In social learning, have **learners** use blogs to:

▶ Report progress on ongoing projects.

▶ Reflect on learning experiences by sharing discoveries, insights, and questions.

▶ Share work completed as part of a class project.

▶ Create mainstream course content for use by other learners.

Teachers can use blogs to:

▶ Pace the course by posting course announcements and assignments.

▶ Post resources needed for learning activities, such as presentations, readings, and job-aids.

▶ Keep learners on track by sharing insights, tips, solutions to common problems, needed bits of vocabulary, and points students seem to have missed.

▶ Post case studies or other thought provoking items for learners to discuss.

Audio podcasts

Audio podcasts are like radio programs for learning. Learners can listen to them and learners can produce them.

Here we see an audio podcast playing in iTunes. The visual is just the emblem for the podcast series.

Audio podcasts are used to distribute spoken-word messages of a few minutes up to over an hour.

The term podcast originally referred to programs intended for playing on Apple's iPod, though today such audio programs can play back on just about any computer or mobile device.

When to use audio podcasts in social learning

Audio podcasts work well when you can communicate your subject using just audio. They are especially useful for learners who must fit them into a busy life, say when riding on a train or on an airplane. I'm a little concerned about their use while driving an automobile, but they may be just the ticket for ignoring leering strangers at the gym.

Another argument for using a podcast may be economic. It may be easier and quicker to capture the expertise of authorities by having them talk rather than by requiring them to write it down. Some people are fluent speakers but hesitant writers. So let them talk. If you are worried they will ramble, record an interview where you ask specific questions to focus the responses.

Podcasts are a natural for subjects that involve sound, such as music or language. They may prove more difficult if the subject is highly visual.

Because audio podcasts require only simple audio-recording and -editing tools found on most current computers, they are ideal for learners to produce and share. Because some learners may find speaking easier than writing, audio podcasts may fill the same role as blogs.

Publically available audio podcasts can also provide independent sources of learning to those who need to obtain necessary prerequisite information, explore side streams of interest, or go deeper into the background or philosophy of a field.

Do not, however, use a podcast if your idea could be summarized to a page of text: use a blog instead. And stick to factual, procedural information. You are in the education business, not entertainment.

Forms of podcasts

Many podcasts take the form of lectures that explain a subject directly. But other forms are possible. Just listen to your radio. What do you hear?

- ▶ Interviews.
- ▶ Tips.
- ▶ Product reviews.
- ▶ Dramatizations of real or imagined events.
- ▶ Reading aloud like "books on tape."
- ▶ Live field activities.
- ▶ Trip reports.
- ▶ Summaries, overviews, and synopses of a field.
- ▶ News stories and research reports.

Best practices for audio podcasts

Here are some best practices for better educational podcasts:

- ▶ **Keep everything simple,** especially if learners may listen while driving their cars. No complex follow-along activities, please. Ten minutes per segment. Do not require writing anything down.

- ▶ **Make what you say memorable**. Repeat. Give mnemonics. Emphasize key points. Post URLs, names, and other details on a Web location that learners can find on their own.

- ▶ **Use only words that learners already know**. If you introduce a new term or concept, explain it.

- ▶ **Keep the introduction and close short**, especially if learners will listen to several episodes at once.

- ▶ **Do not just mimic radio**. Entertainment podcasts are radio. Informational podcasts must be more. Downplay the music, reverberating intro, and other radio effects. No advertisements, please.

- ▶ **Select music to please your audience not yourself**, especially if your audience spans several generations or cultures.

- ▶ **Make voices clear and pleasant**. Invest in a good microphone. Equalize and normalize voices. In a sound-editing program, adjust the frequencies of the voices and adjust volumes to a constant level. Speak in an upbeat, emotional voice. Speak to a simulated studio audience.

- ▶ **Smooth the flow**. Rehearse and rehearse again. Edit out mistakes and long pauses. Include short tips and other pieces to splice together for longer segments.

Video podcasts

Video podcasts are simply recorded TV programs (or films, if you prefer). They require recording and editing video. Simple video podcasts can be produced using a simple video camera and the video capture and editing tools built into most current computer operating systems. To see good and bad examples of video podcasts, visit iTunes, YouTube, or Vimeo.

This video podcast (displayed in iTunes) demonstrates a procedure with a digital printer.

When to use video podcasts for social learning

Video podcasts can be used to record and present information that requires motion. They can be used for any of the same purposes as blogs and audio podcasts. They can be viewed by learners to get information and created by learners to share information. Use them where the combination of audio and video is really needed, for example:

▶ Demonstrations of physical procedures.
▶ Role-playing where body language, posture, gestures, and facial expressions are crucial.
▶ Screencasts of software procedures.
▶ Emotional messages needed to motivate others.

Best practices for video podcasts

▶ **Build on audio podcasts**. Video podcasts add video to the capabilities of audio podcasts. The best practices for audio podcasts (p. 431) apply to video podcasts as well.
▶ **Have a reason for video.** Use it for subjects that must be seen moving. Video is seldom effective for talking-head reports that could work better as a blog or audio podcast.
▶ **Keep segments short.** If the procedure you are demonstrating is lengthy, consider breaking up the procedure into shorter video segments of just a few minutes.

▶ **Keep production simple**. Do not try for a Hollywood extravaganza. Use a simple set and limit camera movements and special effects.

Collaboratively create documents

One of the core activities in social learning is collaborating on a piece of work, such as a business document.

In many forms of teamwork, the purpose of collaboration is to create an artifact of value in itself. In social learning, we have additional goals of learning from the processes of researching, planning, drafting, editing, assembling, testing, critiquing, refining, and publishing the work.

Collaborating is easy when all participants are sitting around the same table. With distant learners, however, collaboration requires special mechanisms that enable widely distributed learners to collaboratively author documents, sketch diagrams and other graphics, share computer applications and data files, and schedule activities.

Collaborative authoring

Social learning often involves collaborative writing of documents, perhaps using Internet-hosted applications like Google Docs. The document can be the primary product of the activity or just a means of focusing and structuring learning activities.

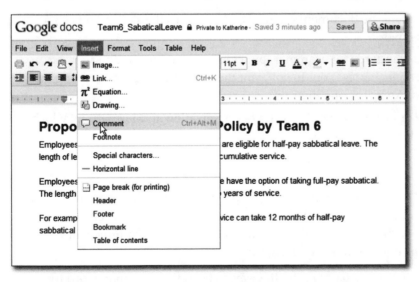

Here a team member adds a comment to a document the team is preparing for an ongoing business simulation.

Document hosted on Google Docs.

Collaborative authoring can be used to create a variety of documents, such as reports and white papers, proposals, specifications, spreadsheets, slide presentations, databases, project plans, blueprints, diagrams, audio and video podcasts, documentary films, job aids, and many more.

When to use collaborative authoring for social learning

Collaborative authoring activities are useful to teach:

▶ Basic teamwork skills, such as negotiation, compromise, and advocacy.

▶ Professional disciplines, such as engineering and management, which are applied as part of a team.

▶ Complex, multi-stage activities that involve integrating the work of separate individuals and teams.

▶ Communications skills such as technical and business writing, journalism, advertising.

▶ Use of a shared tool, like the one used to author the document.

Best practices for collaborative authoring

Keep in mind that collaborative authoring is different from solo authoring and that e-learning imposes its own requirements, too.

▶ If practical, author using tools that store the ongoing document in a shared, online workspace. That way the document is not locked up in one person's computer—which may be turned off or go offline.

▶ Establish and enforce a protocol for who can write and alter the document and when. Typically, this requires a checkout system whereby only one person can make changes at a time. For a long document or a large team, you may have to break the document into separately editable segments.

▶ Make sure that creating the document requires and exercises the skills you need to teach—not just busywork.

▶ Follow established standards for grammar, punctuation, spelling, and usage. Designate specific style guides. You do not want the team wasting time arguing the merits of British vs. American spellings.

▶ Supply a template or outline to handle issues of organization and formatting, which are not part of the learning objective.

Wikis

A wiki is a communally authored document, typically composed of separate entries, each tightly focused on an individual topic. With a wiki someone creates a new entry or modifies an existing one. Someone else then evaluates its accuracy and importance. Others may rewrite the entry to refine or extend it.

The epitome of a wiki is Wikipedia. *Wiki*, by the way, is from the Hawaiian word for "quick," as in quick information.

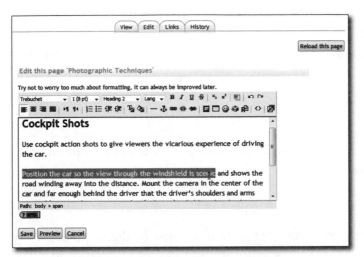

In this wiki on photographic techniques, a learner edits an entry created by another learner.

When to use wikis for social learning

Use wikis to teach teamwork, to share valuable knowledge, and to build a repository of verified information. Use wikis to:

▶ **Test and refine ideas** by commenting on them and rewriting them to improve accuracy and clarity.

▶ **Accumulate learning over time** by establishing a subject-based wiki that successive classes can refine and extend.

▶ **Consolidate separate learning results**, such as insights from individual team members or sub-teams.

▶ **Prepare materials for use later** in work or additional learning. For example, learners might establish, maintain, and extend a wiki to support work in a job category or profession.

▶ **Organize course materials**, including reference works and assignments.

▶ **Teach the need to cite sources**—and how to do it.

▶ **As a knowledge-management effort** when applied throughout the organization.

▶ **Make information more accessible** than it would be in a discussion forum or a library of separate documents.

Best practices for wikis

To create wiki entries that others will use:

▶ **Include a variety of entries**. Do not limit your wiki to encyclopedia articles. Consider including procedures, specifications, tips and shortcuts, overviews and summaries, research reports, essays, job aids, FAQs, insights, samples of effective work, exercises completed by previous classes, and clearly labeled editorials.

▶ **Make entries easy to retrieve**. Pick titles and headings with care. Add keywords that someone who needs the entry would use to search for it.

▶ **Make entries easy to understand**. Write entries so those outside the specialist field will understand. Avoid jargon and unfamiliar abbreviations.

Whiteboards

A whiteboard is a collaboration tool that simulates the process that occurs when the teacher draws on a wall-mounted whiteboard and then invites a learner to contribute to the drawing. All participants immediately see everything drawn on the whiteboard. In some online meeting tools, the whiteboard feature can be used as an overlay to annotate slides, Web tours, video clips, and even shared applications.

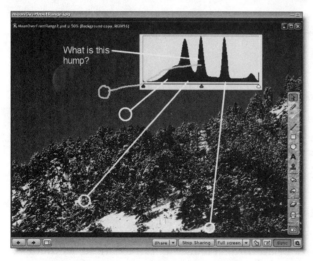

An Adobe Photoshop file is being displayed in Adobe Connect.

In this course on digital photography, the teacher poses a question to a learner and then passes control to the learner. The learner then answers by drawing on the whiteboard.

Use a whiteboard for visual learning

Whiteboards let learners and teachers sketch ideas they cannot express in words. Whiteboards are especially important for courses in science, engineering, mathematics, and other subjects that mix graphics and text. Whiteboards are also important for those with limited English language skills and those who express themselves well visually. Some common subjects include:

▶ **Visual appearance**. The color, layout, shape, or contents of any visual display.

▶ **Arrangement and organization of components** of a system. Participants can draw and edit a diagram.

▶ **Charts and graphs** showing numerical trends and patterns.

▶ **Visual symbols** that the learner must learn to recognize.

Use whiteboards communally

Whiteboards are not limited to one-way presentations to passive viewers. With whiteboards, learners and teachers can interact. Learners can complete a drawing started by the teacher. The teacher or learners can critique a graphic by annotating specific parts. Participants can mark up a slide, photograph, chart, or diagram to suggest improvements.

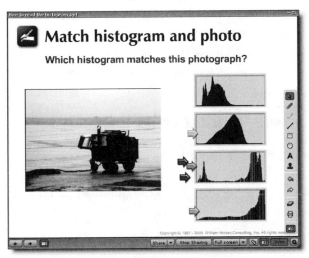

Some systems allow all meeting participants to draw at once. I use this for visual voting where learners can point to their choices. The flurry of arrows adds excitement as learners indicate and revise their choices.

Sounds chaotic, but it can be a productive way for immediate collaboration.

A Microsoft PowerPoint slide is being displayed in Adobe Connect.

Whiteboards make possible a variety of collaborative activities. Here's a list of whiteboard activities you can use to activate a class and get learners accustomed to using the whiteboard:

► Vote visually by letting learners indicate their choices on a graphic by pointing with an arrow, placing a checkmark, or highlighting their choices.

► Display a map and have students write their names and draw arrows to their locations.

► Present a grid with one square for each learner to write answers to a question.

► Ask questions visually. Have learners identify an item in a picture by pointing to it with an arrow. Have learners suggest where to navigate by pointing to a place on a map or a button on a Web page. Have learners identify errors in a display by highlighting areas for improvement.

► Create a collage by having learners contribute their own images to flesh out an idea or design.

► Let learners answer test questions. Have them rate items on a scale by pointing to the rating they would give. Or let learners match items in two lists by drawing arrows between them. Let learners select from multiple choices by pointing to the choice.

► Perform an "instant Delphi" survey by having learners vote on a whiteboard so they immediately see each other's votes. As the class discusses the issue, learners can change their vote as soon as they wish.

Best practices for using whiteboards

The secret to a successful whiteboard session is the same as that for any other live activity: careful preparation.

▶ **Prepare drawings and clip-art** in advance of the whiteboard session. Place them into a file or folder you can access during the session. Include: text for questions you know you will ask or comments you will make, objects you will discuss, symbols used in your profession, arrows, boxes, and other generic shapes.

▶ **Do not write by hand**. Avoid hand writing materials on the spot. Unless others unanimously agree that you can write very legibly very quickly, use the whiteboard's text tool. If you must write by hand, print in:

LARGE, THICK, SIMPLE, BLOCK LETTERS

▶ **Establish color codes** for drawings and text. Assign each learner a distinct color so that each contribution is recognized.

▶ **Keep graphics and backgrounds simple**. Textured backgrounds and intricate graphics take longer to comprehend than simple ones.

▶ **Define proper behavior.** Here are some rules to get learners started.

  ▪ **Ask learners to take turns.** Tell them to wait for others to finish before starting to draw.

  ▪ **Tell learners when they can all draw at once.** That way no one fears interrupting others.

  ▪ **Do not criticize someone else's drawing skill.** Re-draw the object for them if you can do better.

▶ **Summarize the session.** At the end, clean up the drawing to remove discarded ideas and arrange it to reflect the conclusion of the group. That way each participant receives a summary of the session.

Application sharing

Application sharing lets the presenter share programs, windows, or the entire screen with others in a meeting. The teacher can demonstrate a procedure or piece of software simply by running it on his or her computer. Learners see exactly what is displayed in the shared window. Learners, with permission of the moderator or teacher, can take control of the application and present to the rest of the group.

Here is an example of a shared application. It shows the view as the presenter modifies a photograph in Photoshop. The learner's computer does not require Photoshop to view this demonstration. Later the presenter may have a learner perform a similar procedure.

The meeting tool is Adobe Connect.

When to use application sharing

Use application sharing to demonstrate computer programs, computer data, pictures, and other material on a computer screen. Use application-sharing sessions to:

▶ Demonstrate computer programs and teach operations skills, especially for programs not released yet or not widely available.

▶ Let learners view data in applications that are not on learners' computers, such as a database not generally accessible.

▶ Let learners try out skills demonstrated by the teacher. Have learners talk aloud as they perform the activity. The teacher can take over if learners fail.

▶ Complete collaborative activities involving multiple learners. Periodically call on learners to conduct demonstrations. Have each learner in turn perform one step in a procedure. Share a game to make a multi-player game.

Application sharing is seldom fast enough to show any rapid animation or fluid motions. Use it for demonstrations that require only simple movements.

If your meeting system offers application sharing, you can use it in place of other capabilities that may be missing or inadequate in your tool.

If you lack:	Use application sharing to share:
Chat	A word processor or text editor.
Whiteboard	A slide or drawing program.
Slide show	PowerPoint or another slide program.
Web tour	Web browser.

Best practices for application sharing

Application sharing takes careful preparation and smooth execution. For best effect:

▶ **Rehearse the demonstration** until it flows smoothly. Learners do not enjoy watching the presenter's mistakes. An unrehearsed presentation communicates that the presenter is unprofessional and does not mind wasting learners' time.

▶ **Share just what you need to share**. Share an individual application or window rather than the whole desktop. Share only one program at a time. Do not let other windows cover the application you are sharing.

▶ **Quit unnecessary programs**. For better reliability and speed, exit other programs that require computer or network resources. Turn off video-conferencing.

▶ **Use audio to narrate**—if bandwidth permits. Continuously explain what you are doing. Let learners hear as well as see the demonstration. Speak slowly and clearly. Allow time for learners to listen and understand.

▶ **Keep security in mind**. If you grant control to others, they can open, modify, and delete files on your system. Do not hand over control and leave the room.

▶ **Move smoothly and pause frequently** so learners' displays have time to catch up with the presenter's display. Avoid dragging windows on the screen. If you must rearrange the screen, stop application sharing, move and resize windows, and then resume application sharing.

Share creations

Social learning invites learners to create and share learning materials, such as writings, photographs, and video clips. Learners can also share by providing others with links to online materials or by combining existing materials in original ways. Learners can also share by making materials and messages easier to find by assigning them tags or keywords that other learners can use to filter messages and other content.

File- and media-sharing

File-sharing and media-sharing capabilities let designers and facilitators set up online libraries of materials useful to learners. You may have used this capability when you shared your vacation photos on Flickr or just amused yourself by watching home movies on YouTube. File- and media-sharing can serve as a simplified wiki for less structured collections of materials.

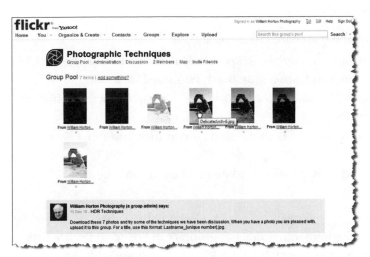

Here, in the photo-sharing site Flickr, the teacher shares nine photographs that will serve as the raw material for an exercise in digital photography.

Sharing can be done through public sites, such as YouTube and Flickr. Sharing can also be done using capabilities of a virtual-classroom system, a social-networking site, an online meeting tool, or a content management system. If the number of files is small, you can just put all the files in a shared online folder or post them to a discussion forum.

For social learning, the goal is to make it easy for members of a group to share documents and media. A secondary purpose may be to provide materials that learners can combine to create new learning materials, sometimes called *mashups*.

Share files and media to assist learning

In social learning, we need to share materials from the teacher as well as materials contributed by learners, such as:

▶ Presentations, lectures, speeches.

▶ Recorded discussions and debates.

▶ Documentary films.

▶ Stories.

▶ Homework posted for critique.

▶ Work samples.

▶ Screencasts of computer procedures.

▶ Videos modeling desirable behavior.

▶ Demonstrations of physical procedures.

▶ Templates for work products.

▶ Spreadsheets for complex calculations.

▶ Work from previous classes.

▶ Notes from class meetings.

▶ Archives of forum discussions.

▶ Clip-art and other raw materials for activities.

Best practices for sharing files and media

Make it easy for learners to find and use shared files and media:

▶ Make sure you have rights to share materials. Respect the intellectual property of others. Make clear how learners and teachers can used the shared materials.

▶ Simplify finding needed materials. Assign keywords and other metadata to enable learners to search for the files they need.

▶ Label files clearly. Make clear what the file contains, its file format, and what application can open it.

▶ Maintain the repository. Periodically remove outdated and duplicated items.

Social bookmarking

Social bookmarking is the process where individuals or groups can create and share lists of hyperlinks to useful online resources. Social bookmarking can be done with public tools such as Delicious or just by creating a Web page containing the links. Social bookmarking serves many of the same functions as file- and media-sharing, except that with social bookmarking only links to the files are shared, not actual files.

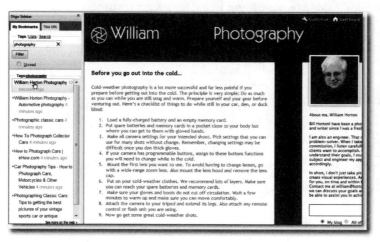

Here, the social bookmarking tool Diigo is used to publish links to advice on how to photograph classic automobiles.

When to use social bookmarking in social learning

Social bookmarking by itself teaches two valuable lessons: (1) much of the information and knowledge you need is readily accessible and (2) not everything online is equally useful.

In social learning, you can incorporate social bookmarking into a range of activities, such as these:

▶ Learners conduct online research and report best sources of information.

▶ Learners collect evidence for and against a claim, plan, or proposal.

▶ As a group, learners nominate, discuss, and vote to select the best links.

▶ Teachers and learners publish reading lists for topics of interest.

▶ Learners compare their lists of links to those prepared by the teacher or by experts.

▶ Learners scan links to brainstorm possible projects.

▶ Learners establish and maintain a link-library to support work in a profession or job category.

Best practices for social bookmarking

▶ **Discuss and publish criteria for which links to include**. Criteria may include accuracy, support by rigorous research, completeness, and political neutrality.

▶ **Suggest categories of knowledge to include**. While not restricting what learners can bookmark, give some suggestions of types of information that participants may find helpful, such as:

- Overviews, introductions, and summaries.
- Research reports and papers.
- Tutorials and training in the field.
- Standard reference works in the field.
- Classic books and papers.
- Contrasting opinions and dissenting views.
- Bibliographies and reading lists.

▶ **Monitor learners' work**. Make sure that learners have actually read and understood items they suggest including.

▶ **Publish lists of links**. These lists can be used by other classes, by the organization as a whole, or by the public.

Tagging or keywording items

One of the simplest, yet most effective, ways to collaborate in creating content is to label messages, documents, and media elements in a way that identifies the item's relevance to the learning effort. We do this by embedding tags into the message or assigning keywords to the file. Such labeling makes information easier to find and to combine. It can also suggest relationships among separate pieces of information.

In this Twitter exchange, the hash code #hcbus202B is used in a message and its reply. By filtering on the hash code, the learner is able to see all the messages that include that hash code. By including the code, the message's author ensures that the message is seen by other interested learners.

One of the simplest ways to label information is the hash-tag feature in Twitter. To flag a message, the author includes a label in the message itself. The label begins with the "#" character, which is called a hash character or pound sign. For example, to label something as relevant to the 2012 Olympics, you might tag it with "#2012Olympics" or the like. Others who want to see messages about the 2012 Olympics would opt to receive any messages that include that tag. They would receive your messages tagged with "2012Olympics" and messages of anybody else who used that tag. More and more social networking tools are adopting this hash-tag convention.

The older method of tagging information is by including keywords that describe the information. This information is usually entered in the metadata field for the document, file, or page. Learners can then search for items that include those keywords.

Mashups

Mashups combine and enhance already available materials and sources into a new derivative work.

For a simple example, consider Google Maps. Users can start with a basic map, add pins and other symbols to mark significant locations, provide commentary for these locations, and sprinkle on geotagged photographs of sites in the area of the map. The resulting enhanced map can be revealed to others on the Internet.

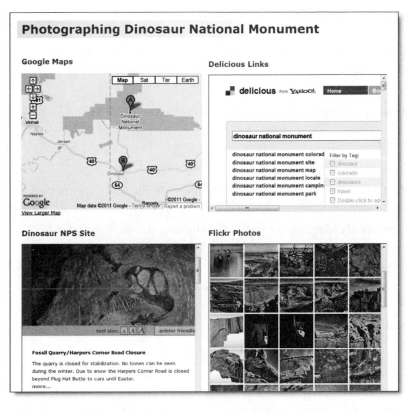

This mashup contains information collected from various locations to prepare photographers to visit Dinosaur National Monument on the Colorado-Utah border.

Simple to create, this mashup is a Web page that uses iFrame tags to pull in content from several Web sites.

Another example is business.gov, which provides a single Web site to access business-related materials on dozens of separate U.S. Government Web sites.

When materials of different types and from different sources are organized into a single display, the result is called a *dashboard* for its resemblance to the separate gauges and readouts in front of the driver of a car.

Any tool that can include network-hosted materials or just links to them can be used to create the kind of mashup useful in e-learning.

Creating mashups is inherently social. Individuals can construct documents and displays from materials created by other individuals. The process of identifying source materials, evaluating them, allocating space to them, and enhancing the result makes a superb team project.

When to use mashups for social learning

Use mashups in social learning to enhance and share available information, including information created in other social learning activities. Use mashups to:

▶ **Create a course dashboard** where learners can keep up to date on current assignments, schedules, and reading materials—and where they can submit completed assignments and receive feedback on them.

- **Reduce the time learners waste searching** for and navigating to individual sources of information.
- **Teach higher level skills** by having learners understand, evaluate, and combine information they find in online sources.
- **Create job aids** for use within a profession.
- **Compile survey reports** spanning a field of research, commerce, or art.

Best practices for mashups

Create and use mashups in ways that help meet learning objectives:

- **Carefully evaluate materials** included in mashups. Remember the GIGO principle? Well, here is an update: Garbage in, toxic sludge out.
- **Draw on materials previously identified** in your file-sharing, media-sharing, and social bookmarking efforts.
- **Respect others' intellectual property** by carefully screening copyright information. Do not use materials in ways that would violate copyright or reveal confidential information.
- **Identify the sources of information**, especially if they come from outside your organization.

Vote and rate

Learning activities often require learners to make a decision, express a judgment, or rank an idea. Polls provide a way that learners can rate and vote on items. Polls are on-screen displays that let learners select among alternatives. The choices are tallied and displayed in a composite view. Polls function like the keypads used by learners in some interactive video courses to indicate their answers to questions posed by the teacher. Online polls, however, require no special hardware.

Polling requires learners to make choices. Techniques such as *virtual voting booths*, *virtual response pads*, or *virtual show of hands*, let all learners see aggregate totals of how the group voted.

When to use polls for social learning

Polls are an effective way to encourage learners to research and think deeply about issues. They are also good to challenge learners to shape the opinions of others, thereby realizing the limitations of their own thinking. Polls can add a spark of interactivity by requiring the class to vote on the point under discussion.

Polling can be used to evaluate online learning materials such as Web pages and sites, blog postings, podcasts, profiles of individuals, and shared media. Such evaluations can provide feedback to the creator of the item. Polls can serve as informal tests. Polling can flag items worth learning and identify resources for future use. And, polling can assist in grading.

Use polls to force choices, administer surveys, and tally votes. Here are some uses for polls in e-learning:

▶ **Use spontaneous polls to survey learners instantly on an issue**. For example, let learners decide what the teacher should discuss or what the class should consider in greater detail.

▶ **Use polls for binary choices**. Have learners vote yes or no on items in a checklist. Conduct a mock trial and have learners vote on the guilt or innocence of the defendant. Hold a debate and let learners choose the winner.

▶ **Use polls to select among alternative paths** in a simulation or game.

▶ **Get instant feedback** on how well learners feel they understand a concept. Conduct before and after surveys to measure changes of opinion or knowledge.

▶ **Vote to narrow choices**. Then discuss the remaining choices and vote again to select the best choice.

▶ **Conduct emotional polls**. Ask learners how they feel about an issue. For example, use emoticons (smileys) to represent the ranges of emotion.

Types of polls

There are three forms of polls: spontaneous, synchronous, and asynchronous.

Spontaneous polls

Informal Yes/No polls in an online meeting ask participants to indicate their choices by clicking a **raise hand** button; or, a **Yes** button to indicate yes and a **No** button to indicate a no. Such spontaneous polls get immediate opinions from learners.

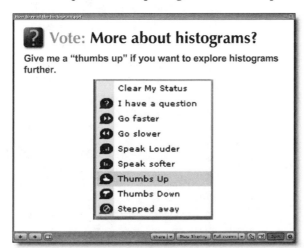

Here is an example of a spontaneous poll. The teacher displays a slide asking for learners to give a "thumbs up" if they want to delve deeper into the subject.

In addition to the poll question, the slide contains a graphic that briefly reminds learners how to indicate a "thumbs up."

The meeting tool is Adobe Connect.

Synchronous polls

Synchronous polls have learners pick from a list of alternatives and then see the results of the aggregate voting. Synchronous polls let members of the class answer informal test questions, make real-time choices, and vote on issues.

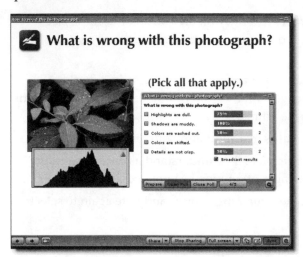

Here is an example of a synchronous poll. First, a slide appears to introduce the poll. Learners see the question and possible choices. Then, the voting area appears. Learners then vote and the results are displayed to the class.

Go to p. 437 to see how a whiteboard can be used for synchronous polling.

The meeting tool is Adobe Connect.

Asynchronous polls

Asynchronous polls are available for learners to vote over a period of time, say a week, before their votes are tallied. Asynchronous polls let learners research, discuss, and vote on their own schedule. Vote totals may be displayed after a voting period or continuously as they change.

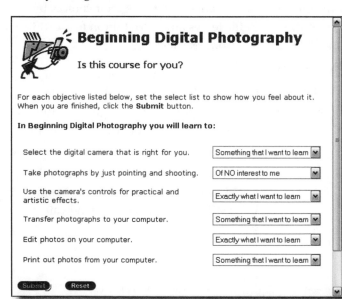

In this example of an asynchronous poll, we ask learners to state how much the objectives for a course overlap their objectives for study. It is asynchronous so learners can change their opinions as the course progresses.

Built using Adobe Dreamweaver.

Best practices for polls

Use polls in ways that let learners naturally express choices.

▶ **Collect opinions at the right time**. Record choices at the most revealing times: after an event, during an event, or both before and after an event. For example, let learners discuss a question before voting. And let them change their votes in response to comments in discussion.

▶ **Make sure learners know how to vote.** Include instructions, such as: "Select your choice and then click **Enter.**" Be sure to tell learners how to refresh their view to see the vote totals.

▶ **Phrase prompts and choices with extreme care**. Test to make sure learners understand the choices. Explain choices at the beginning of the activity. Test your questions on others to make sure they all interpret the question the way you intended. Refine questions until they are clear.

▶ **Display vote totals only**. Learners may hesitate to vote if they feel others can learn how they individually voted. However, the teacher may want to see how individuals voted. That way the teacher can call on a learner to speak for a particular position.

▶ **Track changes of opinion during an ongoing event**. Such logs can provide a valuable source for research.

▶ **Give learners time to make up their minds**. Do not force them to vote immediately upon receiving the question. Let them turn the question over in their minds, think of an answer, change their minds, figure out how to vote, and do so.

▶ **Require research and analysis for asynchronous polls**. Use them to provoke research and deeper learning.

▶ **Set up generic polls**. That way you will not have to create a large number of polls or re-create them each time you use a different meeting system. Put the actual questions on your slides. Then prepare polls with choices such as:
  - Yes and No.
  - A, B, and C (keyed to items on the slide).
  - A, B, C, and D.
  - A, B, C, D, and E.
  - More, The Same, and Less.

▶ **Ask open-ended questions**. Let learners give answers not included in the poll. I frequently include a poll choice of "Other (enter in chat)" to encourage learners to think beyond the list of choices I provide.

Filter messages

Social learning can fire-hose learners with a torrent of irrelevant messages and at the same time leave them anxious that they are missing part of a vital conversation going on somewhere online. To help learners organize and attend to important messages, ensure they are familiar with various ways of filtering messages.

Filtering lets learners decide which messages to see based on the sender, subject, or some other criteria. Different tools implement filters differently; however, certain filtering capabilities are common:

▶ **Subscribe or follow**. The learner may elect to receive sporadic work published by others. For blogs, the term is *subscribe*; in Twitter, it is *follow*; and in Facebook it is *fan*. The publisher does not have to approve the request.

▶ **Befriend**. One person can request to be considered a "friend" (in Facebook terminology). Once the request is approved, the two friends are mutually subscribed to each other's postings and announcements.

▶ **Block**. Learners may want to block messages they find offensive, distracting, or just uninteresting. Blocking is a standard part of e-mail and social-networking tools. It can pose a problem in social learning if learners filter out too many co-learners.

▶ **Aggregate**. Learners often need to consolidate streams of messages from separate sources. This is what an e-mail reader does. It organizes the messages into a single display, regardless of who sent them. Tools such as iTunes can aggregate podcasts you subscribe to into a single organized list. RSS readers can likewise list all new articles for all the blogs to which you subscribe. Some form of aggregator is crucial to consolidate all announcements and course materials into a single display—sometimes called a *console* or *dashboard*.

▶ **Tag**. Learners can filter messages to include only those labeled with specific keywords or hash-tags (p. 443).

Establish a point of contact

In a model popularized by MySpace, Facebook, and LinkedIn, people and groups publish a profile or home page describing them and serving as a point of contact. This profile serves as both a source and a destination for messages to and from the individual or group. This profile or home page creates an online identity.

Here is a home page for a course on digital photography.

In addition to the welcome message, there are links to important course documents, the teacher's profile, modules, and resources.

There is also a news feed and a link to the class roster.

Built using Moodle.

Uses for a profile or home page

In social learning, a profile or home page provides information and simplifies communication. A separate profile may be created for each learner, teacher, team, class, course, and school.

Profile for	Purposes	Include
Learner	Help other learners imagine this person. Help other learners assess this person's expertise and credibility.	Name. Professional and academic accomplishments. Areas of special skill and knowledge. Enough personal details to make the learner seem human. Photograph, especially if face-to-face meetings or video-conferences occur. Contact information.

Profile for	Purposes	Include
Teacher or facilitator	Establish authority for the teacher. Help learners decide what type assistance to seek from the teacher.	Name. Professional and academic credentials and accomplishments. Areas of special skill and knowledge. Photograph. Contact information.
Team or other group within a class	Help to form and administer the team. Coordinate activities of the team. Identify the team to those outside the team.	Name. Emblem or mascot (optional). Goal, mission, or unifying principle. Members. Contact information.
Class (group of people taking a course together)	Provide information to those in the class.	Designation or name. Syllabus. Course materials. Assignments.
Course (that may be taken by different classes).	Identify the course to those who might want to take it.	Name and number. Description. Objectives. Prerequisites. How to enroll.
School or training department	Provide information to learners taking courses from the school and those considering enrolling there.	Name. Mission. Course catalog. Policies and procedures. Rules and regulations. Contact information

Best practices for a profile or home page

Establishing helpful profile pages for e-learning requires focus on the goals of learning.

▶ **Give learners and teachers templates** with slots for recommended information to include. Let learners add to the template but encourage them to provide the suggested minimum information.

▶ **Discourage the use of pseudonyms** or "screen names" instead of real names. False names slow the development of trust and can create the suspicion that some learners are not who they pretend to be.

▶ **Keep profiles professional**. Some learners may just copy their Facebook profile. Besides providing way too much personal information, such profiles often hide the very talents, knowledge, and skills that will make the learner valuable as part of a team. And the photo of the learner hoisting a martini glass may suggest an unprofessional attitude.

Set up and administer a team or other group

Social learning takes place as a group. As such, it requires the ability to define a sub-group of individuals who can easily share information and exchange messages. Depending on your objectives, the group may consist of a class within a course, a learning team, a work team, a community of practice, or a professional association.

The capabilities used to manage groups vary among tools. Make sure the tools you use provide the capabilities you need. For social learning, group-administration tools should help:

▶ Form groups and update their membership quickly.

▶ Enable messages to be filtered by group membership.

▶ Enable a single address for messages sent to the whole group.

▶ Make member profiles or home pages available to all other group members.

▶ Let the group control access to materials it creates.

▶ Provide the group with a degree of privacy so it can limit what outsiders see of its proceedings.

▶ Form sub-groups within the main group, such as a task-team, committee, or breakout group.

▶ Let learners belong to multiple groups; that is, allow group memberships to overlap.

▶ Enable collaborative calendaring to schedule meetings, negotiate deadlines, reserve scarce resources, and accommodate interruptions.

FACILITATE RATHER THAN TEACH

In social learning, learners teach each other. In pure social learning there would be no need for a teacher. I say "would be" because pure social learning is an ideal, not likely to occur with us flawed human beings.

Here, now, in the messy ol' real world, social learning may need outside help. This help comes from a facilitator. The facilitator may have a title of instructor, teacher, or professor; but the actions of a facilitator differ from those of teaching. The facilitator's role is to help a group of learners learn socially—that is from each other.

Some groups, inexperienced in social learning, may require significant direct involvement of the facilitator. Others, comfortable and proficient with social learning, will require a lighter touch.

As designers, we must make sure that facilitators are available and that they know their responsibilities.

Define the duties of the facilitator

The facilitator's role is to do whatever is needed to ensure social learning occurs. Here are some likely tasks for the facilitator:

- ▶ **Set up groups**. Initially assign people to teams. Provide each team with its initial online identity.

- ▶ **Explain the goal and rules**. State the overall goal for the team. Spell out necessary rules, criteria, procedures, and protocols to get started. Point out that the group can make changes that do not violate laws, government regulations, or organizational policies.

- ▶ **Lead the group to become a team**. Reinforce responsibility for accomplishing the goal and for learning along the way. Suggest possible team roles, but let the team come up with its own roles and fill them. Encourage and guide the team in taking control of its operations.

- ▶ **Monitor for problems**. Review messages and comments. Watch for bad behavior by individuals and by the team as a whole.

- ▶ **Model and encourage desired behavior**. Listen patiently and deeply. Admit doubts and limits. Discuss rationally. Offer evidence for opinions.

- ▶ **Let the team learn from its members**. Never preach or lecture. Do nothing to embarrass team members. Do not debate or argue with learners. Don't eavesdrop more than necessary to monitor team health. Do not participate in student activities or solve participants' problems until they have exhausted their own resources.

▶ **Intervene where necessary to ensure effective learning**. Give the team time to discover, discuss, and resolve problems by themselves. Point out the problem politely and request the team to solve it. If the problem persists, act decisively to rescue learning.

The mantra for the facilitator should be "I am on tap, not on top. I am on call, not in control."

Establish a code of conduct

In social learning, a code of conduct sets expectations for behavior. It can prevent embarrassment or even disasters that can occur when learners are new to social learning.

Craft your own code of conduct to reflect the needs of your learners and the ideals of your organization. If possible, involve learners in drafting the code of conduct to ensure that they agree and commit to follow it.

Use the following as a starting point for your code of conduct. Note that it is addressed to learners, not to you the designer. I've written it this way to make it easier to adapt for your learners.

Be honest and open in all communications

Never pretend to be someone you are not. Make no inaccurate or deceptive statements. Disclose conflicts of interest. If you make a mistake, correct it immediately. Flag corrections in your posts so others know of the change.

Respect intellectual property

Working with the ideas of others raises ethical and logical issues. Disclose sources for opinions and information.

Do not violate the copyright of others or plagiarize their work. Take care to avoid self-plagiarism, which is republishing something you published elsewhere without identifying the source.

Do not reveal information inappropriately. Take special care when dealing with private, confidential, secret, or proprietary information.

Help others learn

Contribute to the learning of others. Do your share of the work. Conduct research, ask questions, perform experiments, and do other tasks so you have something to contribute to the group. Intervene when you can offer an insight, correct a misconception, or clarify an idea. Keep discussions on topic. Avoid spam or self-promotion.

Disagree professionally

Do not conceal disagreements, but always disagree respectfully and politely. Listen to what others have to say. Do not attack others or become emotional. Instead, just state factual and logical reasons for your disagreement. And, if you are wrong, admit it.

Use simple business-like language

Write and speak clearly and concisely. Limit your use of slang, jargon, and abbreviations to what all others will understand. Take care with grammar, spelling, and punctuation.

Use private messages appropriately

In general, make messages visible to everyone in your class or learning team. That way they can join the conversation and learn from it. However, use private messages for information only the recipient needs to know and to avoid embarrassing the recipient.

Require good behavior of yourself and others

You are responsible for your own learning and that of others. You are expected to behave professionally and to ensure that others do so as well. If you notice unproductive behavior in others, do not wait for the facilitator to intervene. Politely, but clearly, confront the behavior.

Intervene in cases of bad behavior

The facilitator is an on-call problem solver. One kind of problem is bad behavior by individual learners and by the team as a whole. Social learning poses as many possibilities for bad behavior as in any other social endeavor. Most are minor and are corrected by the group. Serious problems, however, require intervention by the facilitator.

Bad individual behavior

People are people. Sometimes they do stupid things. When they do stupid things in social learning, the facilitator should take note and prepare to intervene if the group does not solve the problem itself.

How to intervene

For bad behavior by individuals, intervene as stealthily and as light-handedly as possible. Always intervene privately and do nothing to embarrass the learner.

First, ask the learner what prompted the behavior. Start with the assumption that the behavior is rational and justified by circumstances you are not aware of. Point out the symptoms and see if the learner will identify their own behavior as the cause. If the reasons for the behavior are not justified, get the learner to take responsibility for the behavior and get a clear commitment to modify the behavior.

Analyze the learner's behavior. If it is a result of incentives, such as grading criteria, consider changing these incentives before more bad behavior results.

If multiple learners exhibit the bad behavior, ask the group to be on guard against the behavior and to act to correct it. When you point out the behavior, do not name names.

Correct specific types of bad behavior

Prepare the facilitator with guidance on how to respond to specific kinds of bad behavior by individual learners. Here is a list of observed bad behaviors and suggested ways to deal with them.

Behavior	Symptoms	Remedy or intervention
Off-topic comments	Learners are distracted and significant time is wasted by jokes, gossip, rumors, discussions about personal interests, and other irrelevant topics.	Monitor the number of off-topic comments. A few are OK. If such comments are hurting learning, request the learners to focus on their tasks. Counsel instigators and ask that they steer the conversation back on topic.
Pointless comments	A learner's comments contribute nothing to the conversation, for example: Gushing, vacuous praise. "Oh, that's the most brilliant idea ever. You are so smart!" The same comment is repeated again and again for other messages. Comments that just say "Me too" or "I agree." Comments that say "I disagree" or "I don't get it" but offer no reasons.	Remind the group to use messages and posts to contribute to the learning. Privately ask offenders to amend their posts to include reasons for the statements. Rework incentives to reward the value of posts rather than just the number.

Behavior	Symptoms	Remedy or intervention
Flirting	A learner makes suggestive or other inappropriate comments. At first this might seem innocent, but one person's flirting is another's sexual harassment—and it is how the message was perceived that makes the difference, not how the message was intended.	Intervene immediately. Remove the message. Require the poster to apologize. Explain the issue to the group. Point out that standards for social learning are stricter than for personal uses of social networking.
Hiding disagreement	A learner's actions contradict his or her comments in discussion. The learner agrees with (or fails to disagree with) both sides of an argument. Absurd ideas escape criticism.	First, make sure the learner is not being bullied or intimidated by other learners. Watch for signs of defensiveness on the part of other learners. Point out the behavior and encourage the learner to speak out. Demonstrate how to disagree.
Withdrawal	A learner works as an individual, not as part of the team. The learner hoards, rather than shares, information.	Find out why the learner has withdrawn. Does the learner perceive no value in social learning activities or feel intimidated by the subject matter or by other learners? Or, is the learner just introverted and shy? Does the learner feel the evaluation process is unfair? Once you know the reasons, the remedy will be clear.

Behavior	Symptoms	Remedy or intervention
Defensiveness	Instead of being open to ideas, the learner defends his or her current opinion. The learner's behavior includes: ▶ Emotional outbursts and rants. ▶ Not taking time for reflection. ▶ Not letting others finish a comment or question.	Slow down the conversation, for example, by moving from an audio-conference to a discussion forum. Redesign activities to require reflection. Point out the emotional nature of responses and request a rational argument.
Bullying	An individual learner dominates others in conversations and activities. The learner may use criticism, sarcasm, or just whining to get his or her way.	Ask the offender to "throttle back." Request a change of communication style: listening more, waiting longer for others to respond, and encouraging fuller responses from others.
Soapboxing	The learner repeatedly engages in self-promotion. Instances range from blatant spam to subtle resume-questions in which the learner prefaces comments with a statement of qualifications and credentials.	Point out the behavior and request the learner to change. Let learners rate the value of messages and of other learners—anonymously.
Social loafing (Also known as *social hitchhiking*)	The learner does the minimum necessary and leaves the hard work to others. The learner misses deadlines and fails to keep commitments to the team. The learner's work is sloppy, filled with factual errors, and implausible postings.	Make grades dependent on contributions to the team. Have learners rate contributions of other team members.

8

Social learning

Behavior	Symptoms	Remedy or intervention
Personal conflicts	Learner A constantly disagrees with learner B, rates B's contributions low, and complains about B.	Point out the pattern of behavior to the learner and ask for the reasons. Consider reconfiguring the team to remove the conflict.
Sabotage	The learner acts to disrupt learning. Common forms of sabotage include: ▶ Deliberately posting misinformation. ▶ Baiting the trolls, that is, making comments designed to provoke an emotional response from others. ▶ Misquoting others in replies.	Learn the reasons for the behavior. Is the learner perhaps frustrated with the slow pace of the course, resentful at having to take a required course, or unconvinced of the value of social learning? Or, perhaps the learner is mentally ill. Try changing the person's role within the team or let the learner try alternative ways of learning.

Bad team behavior

Teams, like individuals, can engage in unproductive behavior. Such behavior can be hard to notice as it requires time to manifest and requires careful attention to patterns of interaction.

In general, the solution is to point out the problem and ask the team to correct it. Some problems, however, may require changing policies or grading criteria. Here are some suggested solutions to specific problems:

Behavior	Symptoms	Remedy or intervention
No initiation of new members	New team members receive a brisk introduction and are left to catch up on their own. New team members are not given specific roles. They are not included in messages or their questions are ignored.	Intervene to integrate the new member into the team. Charge the team to create a process for inducting new members.

Behavior	Symptoms	Remedy or intervention
Loss of trust	Most of the team loses faith in a few of the team members. These members are shunned. Their ideas go ignored and their questions unanswered.	Privately, ask team members the cause of the problem. Reconfigure the team or request a change of roles. Once trust is lost, it is hard to regain. However, an apology for prior offenses can often help.
Fragmentation	The team divides into cliques, factions, sects, tribes, or clubs that communicate and act independently.	Reshuffle teams. Reassign team duties. Let each fragment be a breakout group. Require whole-team activities.
Debate rather than discussion	Communications resemble arguments more than conversations. Few learners change their initial opinions on any issue.	Point out the differences between debate and discussion. Show learners how to be open to new opinions. Reward discussions where learners can show they changed their minds or extended their initial ideas.
Log-jams	Learners make little progress on critical issues. Unresolved issues may trigger emotional outbursts.	Sidestep the disruptive issue by asking the team to brainstorm how to resolve difficult issues like this one.
Groupthink	Everybody sincerely agrees. Discussions are short. When prompted, learners can give only shallow reasons for their agreement.	Require more research to identify pro and con arguments. Have the team stage a debate. Increase perspectives among team members by having the group brainstorm with people from different cultures, life histories, or professional duties.

8

Social learning

Behavior	Symptoms	Remedy or intervention
False agreement (Also called the *Abilene paradox*)	The team decides in a way contrary to the unexpressed view of most team members.	Inject activities that require members to express their opinions before learning the opinions of others. Rephrase questions or restate issues in a way that provokes genuine discussion. Require learners to debate the issue.
Chit-chat	Tendency to discuss issues on which everyone agrees and everyone is knowledgeable rather than confront difficult critical issues.	Identify critical issues and inject activities that require discussing these issues. Also check for problems that would keep people from speaking out.
Talent gaps	The team makes obvious mistakes. Some activities succeed fully while others fail completely. Discussions show blind spots and obvious misinformation.	Add additional talent to the team. Or have the team conduct research to fill gaps.
Unclear mission	The team's activities and discussions bear little on the initial goal of the project. The scope of discussion ever widens. The team makes little progress toward the goal.	Have the team discuss and restate its mission. Ask the team to evaluate whether past work contributed to the restated goal.
No leadership	The team makes little progress, repeatedly misses deadlines, or lurches from logjam to logjam. Members exhibit poor time management.	Point out the problem. Remind the team that it is responsible for its own leadership. Have the team discuss the problem and then shuffle roles.

Behavior	Symptoms	Remedy or intervention
Lack of creativity	The team offers no original solutions, merely replicates earlier solutions. Discussions seldom encourage or even mention the need for innovation. Members show little pride in the work.	Slow down the pace of activities to allow time for reflection and inspiration. Add research activities to acquaint the team with a wider variety of ideas and solutions. Require and reward novelty, imagination, or just uniqueness.
No collective memory	The team makes the same mistakes over and over again. The team does not recognize patterns, generalize from one case to another, or state conclusions in abstract terms.	Add activities to require generalizing and abstracting results: Where else might this apply? What have we discovered earlier that might apply here? Slow down the pace and encourage learners to reflect on what they are learning. Require the team to produce a blog, recording what they have learned.

GRADE FAIRLY IN SOCIAL LEARNING

As designers of social learning, we must put in place processes to assess teams and other groups, assess individuals within the groups, and convince those individuals that the assessment process is fair.

To that end, our processes of evaluating learners and learning must account for the differences between social and solitary learning. For instance, social learning encourages learners to take risks, speak out, admit mistakes, and change positions. In conventional assessment regimens, these actions can lower learners' grades.

Learners may worry, correctly or incorrectly, that their grades will suffer in social learning. In some environments, such as traditional schooling and job applications, grades do matter. And even if grades do not matter to teachers, administrators, or employers, they may still matter a lot to learners.

Assess against objectives

Don't forget that social learning, like all other forms of learning, should evaluate against learning objectives. That is, did learners accomplish the designated objectives set at the beginning of the project?

Also remember that social learning projects may have two different types of objectives: to learn X or to learn how to learn X. For example, objectives may be based on acquiring a subject skill or acquiring a collaboration skill—or both. If the goal is to acquire collaboration skills, do not assess just subject skills and vice versa.

Use available evidence

Social learning leaves a track record of learners' actions and efforts, such as:

▶ Number and timing of posts and submissions.

▶ Text and other media of posts.

▶ Routing of all messages: Who communicated with whom?

▶ Contributions: original ideas, substantive comments, suggestions, or just trivia.

▶ Patterns of interaction: brainstorming, conversation, debate.

▶ Materials created and linked.

All the evidence necessary to form and justify a judgment is readily available.

Ways to assess learners

Social learning has evolved several ways to evaluate teams and individuals. Consider them carefully to see which work best for your social learning. Or use them as a starting point to brainstorm even more effective ways to gauge learning.

▶ **Group evaluation of individuals**. Each member of the group rates other members. The individual's grade is the sum or average of ratings by others. Group evaluations are simple to administer, but require some care. Many feel this technique evaluates popularity rather than learning and that it encourages trying to make friends rather than to help others learn. Cliques may form and agree to positively evaluate each other. To head off these problems, give specific criteria for evaluating others, require reasons and evidence to support ratings, and monitor the fairness of the process. You probably shouldn't use group evaluations as the only assessment for individuals.

▶ **Rating of posts and messages**. The group or a neutral outside expert ranks messages posted by learners. Rankings use criteria generated, discussed, and approved by the group. If the group does the evaluation, take care to avoid ratings that reward messages expressing agreement but not those pointing out gaps and mistakes.

▶ **Group test**. For skills applied as a team, the group takes a test as a group. They can discuss answers. The challenge is to answer questions as quickly as possible.

▶ **Group task**. The group is given a task that requires collaborative application of learning. They are evaluated on how successfully and quickly they perform the task. This assessment is valid only if the test accurately measures accomplishment of the objective.

▶ **Question pool**. Learners submit questions to a pool. The first person to answer the question correctly gets points. The questioner gets points if a specified range of learners get the answer right.

▶ **Evaluation to criteria**. With learners, establish objective rubrics to evaluate work in team activities. Criteria can include the nature, number, and timing of posts.

▶ **Applications of skills**. Conclude with a separate non-team activity that requires learners to apply what they should have learned. The activity can be a practical piece of work, a presentation, or a performance test. Learners might, for example, be tasked with creating and delivering a presentation summarizing the subject, showing a real-world application of it, or teaching it.

Set criteria for messages and posts

If messages and posts are to be used to assess learning, set objective criteria for evaluation. A facilitator may suggest criteria, and the team should then discuss, refine, and publish the criteria. Here are some criteria to start with:

Criterion	How to evaluate messages and posts
Substance	Is the message substantial or trivial? Does it add value to the conversation? Or does it just chime in, by saying something like "Me too!" or "I disagree"?
Timing	When did the post occur? Was it the first one to contribute an idea or surface a concern? Was a reply so quick that it was a reflex response rather than a reflective analysis? Was there a flurry of submissions immediately before a deadline?
Originality	Does the post offer a new idea to the conversation? Is it the first to contribute supporting evidence, an alternative interpretation, or an elegant restatement?
Tone	Is the post professional and helpful? If a disagreement, is the statement polite and direct? Or is the post filled with whining, sarcasm, and other emotional language?
Persuasiveness	Does the message offer evidence and logic to support a claim or opinion? Is the evidence from reliable sources?

Or, forego individual assessment

One approach may be to honestly admit the difficulty of assessing individuals engaged in complex social learning activities and just make the course pass-fail. If the team as a whole succeeds, all learners pass.

If individual assessment is required, mix individual and group activities. Assess based on individual and group activities, but include the scores of group activities only if they increase the individual's grade. Obviously this does not work when grading on a curve.

Remind learners that assessment occurs naturally as part of social processes. For feedback on their individual work, they can look to ratings and rankings by others, comments in discussion, success or failure in activities, and all the feedback they receive from other learners.

EXTEND CONVENTIONAL ACTIVITIES FOR SOCIAL LEARNING

Use the technologies and techniques of social learning to add depth and dynamics to conventional e-learning activities. Let learners perform activities as a team. Help individuals to create and share content with the group. Engage the group in vibrant decisions and engaging collaboration. Use social media to provide advice and feedback to learners.

Extend Absorb activities for social learning

To make conventional Absorb activities more social, encourage and enable learners to:

▶ **Experience presentations, stories, and readings through social media** that encourage comments, discussion, and feedback. Provide immediate feedback through a back channel.

▶ **Control a presentation or other absorbed experience as a group**. The group can pause for discussion and collaboratively decide where to go next in non-linear presentations and tours.

▶ **Provide content to absorb**. Learners can create content individually or as a team. Or they may work as a team to consolidate pieces created by individuals. Learners can capture absorbable content from others in their professional networks.

▶ **Comment on absorbed content**. Invite learners to restate, summarize, outline, rate, review generalize, or critique the content. Have learners publish notes they took, suggest applications, suggest better alternatives (safer, faster, more efficient, etc.), draw conclusions, and reveal what they learned.

▶ **Link content to related resources** that go deeper, offer contrary ideas, better express the same ideas, reveal the research or other basis for an idea, extend the content with visuals or other media, locate items on maps and satellite views, and supply external commentary (even if only Wikipedia).

▶ **Discuss what they absorb**. Let learners ask questions, assess validity and credibility, point out mistakes and ambiguities, offer corrections, debate conclusions, and brainstorm application.

▶ **Edit and annotate documents**. Let learners improve verbal expression, by altering grammar, spelling, punctuation, etc. Encourage them to embed comments, update factual content, highlight key points, link to supporting evidence and related resources, add new pathways, produce a summary or abstract, and translate to another language (or add subtitles).

Extend Do activities for social learning

To make conventional Do activities more social, encourage and enable learners to:

▶ **Get advice** on how to do the activity. Let them ask their team or extended social network. Have the group brainstorm, discuss, and vote on the correct approach to take.

▶ **Get feedback**. Have other learners rate and rank performance, demonstrate better techniques, and suggest alternative strategies.

▶ **Do activities as a team**. Subdivide work and combine results. Discuss and agree on actions or choices. Together plan risky or complex actions.

▶ **Engage in multi-person** activities.

▶ **Share what they learn**: insights, discoveries, difficulties, strategies, techniques, and applications.

▶ **Analyze results**. Have the group discuss results and draw conclusions. Encourage learners to compare experiences to notice differences and commonalities. Have the group generalize and abstract to derive underlying theories, principles, formulas, and rules.

▶ **Turn the activity into a game**. Let learners compete using criteria of time, speed, quantity, style, or score.

▶ **Create Do activities for others**. Have individuals and groups create games, puzzles, and other challenges for each other. Let teams or individuals contribute questions or challenges to a pool used in a quiz-show game. Involve the group in setting and reviewing criteria for success.

Extend Connect activities for social learning

To make conventional Connect activities more social, encourage and enable learners to:

▶ **Share results of Connect activities**, such as cited examples, stories, research findings, and original work.

- ▶ **Create content** used for Connect activities, for example job aids.

- ▶ **Perform the activity as a group**, for example, carrying out original work, applying a job aid, or asking questions.

- ▶ **Conduct group Connect activities** of brainstorming, role-playing, and comparison.

- ▶ **Use the group as support** or backup in Connect activities. If learners are stumped or frustrated, they can consult the group.

- ▶ **Discuss and review work** generated in Connect activities, such as original work, research, or stories.

USE PROVEN SOCIAL ACTIVITIES

Though online social learning is relatively new, certain types of social learning activities have proven effective and versatile. Some are simple and others are complex. Some are narrowly focused procedures and others are broad techniques.

Share what you learn

One of the simplest ways to introduce social learning is to have learners share what they have learned.

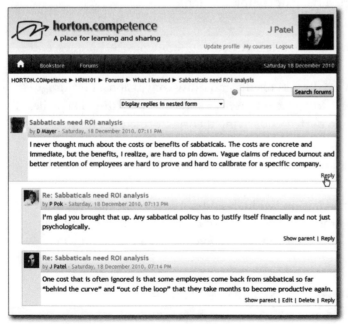

Here is an example of a simple "What I Learned" discussion thread where a learner reports an insight and others comment on it.

Forum created in Moodle.

Learners can share by making periodic posts to a blog, micro-blog, podcast, or discussion forum. The choice will depend on the nature of learning, the learner's technical abilities, and the amount of time available. A blog or discussion thread is a good choice because both are easy to set up and use. The critical feature needed is the capability for learners to comment on each other's postings.

Posts should report what the person has just learned. Posts can include insights, discoveries, summaries, restatements, hypotheses, informed opinions, ideas validated and invalidated, connections made and broken, reversals of opinion, refinements of prior ideas, applications of learning, and emotions experienced in learning. The only criterion is whether the post will help fellow learners.

Posts should answer questions fellow learners instinctively ask:

▶ What did you learn?
▶ Why is it valuable to you?
▶ How may it benefit others?
▶ How did you learn it?

For social learning, learners should read, digest, and comment on the posts of fellow learners. Comments should contribute to the learning of the group. As such, learners should forego the pointless "Me too!" and "Huh?" comments and instead contribute to the conversation with comments such as:

▶ How I would restate it.
▶ What it means for me.
▶ How I came to the same conclusion.
▶ How I came to a different conclusion.

Back channel for presentations

Social media can provide a back channel for live online or face-to-face presentations. A back channel can turn the presentation into a conversation. The audience can use the back channel to convey questions, comments, suggestions, and insights to the presenter.

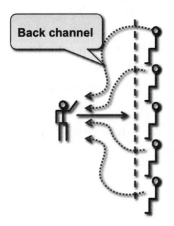

How does a back channel work? A back channel might let learners ask questions while someone is demonstrating an application or drawing on the whiteboard. The questions do not disrupt the person doing the demonstration and do not require a two-way audio channel. The person conducting the demonstration periodically checks for messages. Or an assistant does, so the presenter is not distracted.

Such back channels often occur spontaneously in the chat window of an online meeting tool. They can also be implemented easily by a separate chat tool or by hash-tagged messages within a micro-blogging tool such as Twitter.

Tools like PowerPoint Twitter Tools by SAP Web 2.0 and TodaysMeet can display back channel messages right on the PowerPoint slides used by the presenter.

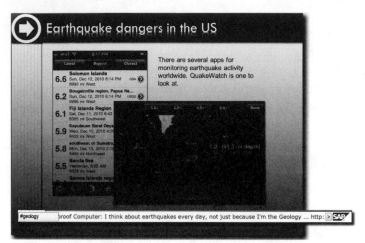

Here a presenter includes the back channel right at the bottom of the slides of a presentation.

Slide built in Microsoft PowerPoint. The Twitter ticker was created with PowerPoint Twitter Tools by SAP Web 2.0.

A back channel is more than a technical means to convey messages. For effective use, it must include a protocol followed by presenter and audience alike.

Have a good reason for the back channel

Use the back channel to make learning better, not just to show off technical fluency or to get by with an inferior presentation. Some valuable uses for the back channel are to:

▶ **Ask questions**. The back channel can be used to collect questions, which the presenter can answer at the next logical break or at the end of the presentation. Or, learners can jump in and answer the questions as they occur.

▶ **Correct or prevent misunderstandings**. An assistant can use the back channel to clarify the speech of an accented or inarticulate speaker.

▶ **Spell out details**. An assistant can define technical terms, spell out abbreviations, provide synonyms for unusual words, and provide URLs or search terms for references.

▶ **Communicate in a second language**. A back channel can be used for a translator to provide subtitles in a second language shared by a significant fraction of the audience.

▶ **Provide an ongoing summary**. Occasional summaries can help learners consolidate separate points made by the presenter.

A back channel can be distracting to the presenter and to many in the audience. Weigh carefully the potential benefits and drawbacks using a back channel.

Decide how to display the back channel

Think carefully about how you want to display the back channel. Here are some suggestions:

If ...	Then ...
Some audience-members have a history of making embarrassing or derogatory comments.	Display the back channel to an assistant who filters messages before passing them on to the presenter.
The presenter is easily distracted by incoming comments.	Display messages on a separate screen or hidden window that the presenter can consult periodically.
Members of the audience are easily distracted by comments and may engage in debates about them.	Display the back channel to the speaker only.
Messages are limited to just a few words, a la headlines on a news program. (And the presenter agrees.)	Display messages as a news-crawl along the bottom of the screen.
Messages are complete sentences. (And the presenter agrees.)	Display the messages in a scrolling window alongside the presentation—if space permits.

Do nothing to embarrass or hinder the presenter

The back channel can prove distracting and intimidating to some presenters.

▶ Always get the presenter's approval to use a back channel. Let the presenter know of your intentions well in advance.

▶ Schedule practice sessions to work out the best way to set up the back channel.

▶ Warn the presenter to avoid things likely to trigger distracting comments, such as unusual colors on slides, bad jokes, controversial comments, and confusing graphics.

▶ Take care of the technology for the presenter. Do not require presenters to install and configure special software or to modify their presentations.

▶ Offer assistance, for example, someone to monitor the back channel, to consolidate questions and comments, and to keep the technology working.

Spell out proper behavior for commenting

Announce and enforce a policy to ensure that comments contribute to better learning and improve the experience for learners and for the presenter. Here are some general guidelines.

▶ Make only helpful comments: Ask relevant questions, suggest examples, or cite sources. Use posts to help others learn.

▶ Post nothing to embarrass or distract the presenter: No whining or nitpicking.

▶ Make only one point per post. Keep the post short and to the point.

▶ Do not debate during the presentation. Defer discussion until after the presentation.

Hold learners accountable for their comments. Let them vote during replay: "Was this comment helpful?"

Take action quickly

Take action quickly if learners wander off topic in their comments or start to heckle the presenter. If possible, make the back channel feed private. Then, filter comments for the attention of the presenter. Track down the offending poster and counsel privately after the event. Insist that the poster apologize to all attendees for the poor behavior.

If you cannot make the back channel private, then turn off the back channel for the duration of the presentation. Periodically, ask learners if they have questions by "raising their hand" or through some other mechanism supported in the meeting tool. Open chat to allow learners to ask their questions. Filter the questions for immediate answer or for later consideration on a discussion forum thread.

Brainstorming activities

Brainstorming is a common part of most creative activities. Brainstorming is the process of generating lots of new ideas. In a brainstorming session, the leader poses a problem for which participants suggest solutions. The goal is to produce as many ideas as possible. In brainstorming, no ideas are rejected or criticized.

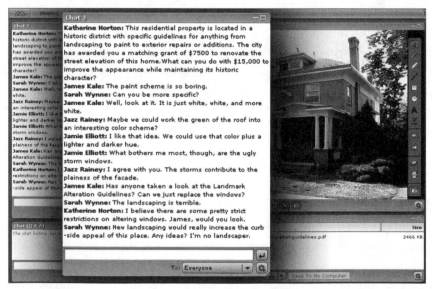

Meeting conducted with Adobe Connect.

This example of brainstorming is from a class for architects and building contractors on how to remodel homes. The purpose of the session is to show learners how creative thinking can help them work within a tight budget. The session starts as an online meeting using a whiteboard (p. 436) and a chat window (p. 418) where learners rapidly suggest ideas.

The brainstorming session shifts to a discussion forum (p. 425). Here we see the Brainstorming activity thread and the responses posted to it.

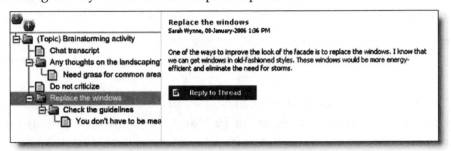

Discussion forum provided by The Learning Manager.

When to use brainstorming

Brainstorming can be taught as a valuable skill in its own right. It is an important aspect of teamwork, problem solving, and creative thinking. Brainstorming can also be useful anywhere learners need to solve problems in an original way.

How brainstorming works

Brainstorming sessions can take several forms. One common form involves both synchronous and asynchronous events. In an online meeting, the teacher presents the question to answer or problem to solve. Individual learners, using chat or audio-conferencing, contribute answers as fast as they can think of them until either the flow of ideas slows or the time allocated to the live phase of the activity expires.

The teacher then transfers the brainstorming from chat to a discussion forum in which learners continue adding ideas at their own pace. At the end of the allotted time, the teacher grades participants based on the quantity, not the quality, of the ideas they contributed.

Best practices for brainstorming

Brainstorming is a simple activity with great potential to motivate learners and develop creativity. To achieve this potential, consider some of these ideas:

Use more media. If you have the capability, use other media. Audio-conferencing (p. 420) speeds the process, as many people find typing slows their production of ideas. If you use audio, remember to record the session and post a typed transcript or summary to the discussion forum. A shared whiteboard (p. 437) lets learners contribute ideas by sketching or pasting in their drawings or clip art. For visual subjects, a whiteboard is especially valuable.

Skip the online meeting. If learners are familiar with brainstorming, you may want to conduct the whole brainstorming session in a discussion forum. This is a good alternative if it is difficult to get all learners together at the same time. Some brainstorming participants find it hard to be creative when it is four hours past their bedtime.

Set a context. You can give the brainstorming a more realistic flavor by situating it in a life-like scenario. Tell a story of a real problem. Ask learners to pretend they are characters in the story. Have them offer solutions from the perspective of their characters.

Enforce the prime rule of brainstorming. Make sure all participants understand the one and only rule of brainstorming: **There are no bad ideas**. Emphasize that participants cannot criticize ideas, but can add better ideas. Remind participants that they score points for the number (not quality!) of ideas.

Ask thought-provoking questions. Ask open-ended questions that can have many answers. For example: What if X? How do we make X better? Why should we do Y?

Keep ideas flowing. Prime the pump with a few ideas of your own. Periodically restate the question in a new way. Reverse the question. For example, after asking how to make something better, ask how to make it worse.

Team-task activities

Team-task activities are good to teach teamwork—or any skill that is practiced by a group rather than just an individual. Such teamwork activities require learners to work as a coordinated team to solve a single, complex problem. Team members communicate using online meetings and discussion forums in order to complete their assigned tasks.

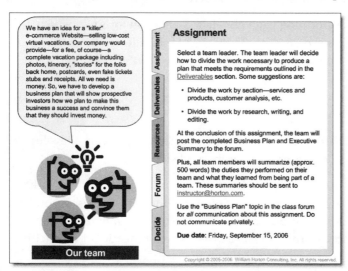

In this example, participants are given the task of preparing a business plan for a new venture.

Created in Microsoft PowerPoint and converted for Web delivery using Adobe Presenter. View example at horton.com/eld/.

In team-task activities, the teacher assigns a task and helps learners organize themselves into separate teams. Teams work independently, producing successively more refined versions of their work, which they submit to an integration team. The integration team merges the work of the other teams and submits the final project to the teacher for grading.

When to use team-task activities

Team-task activities are valuable to teach skills that learners apply as part of a team, rather than as individuals. Team-task activities are also valuable in teaching teamwork skills in their own right. As more and more work requires coordinating with distant colleagues, team-task activities will become a more common part of education.

Some common team-task projects require learners to create:

▶ A financial plan for a new type of business.

▶ A report on the feasibility of a new product.

▶ Recommendations on the use of a new medical procedure.

▶ Proposed laws to cover new technology.

Variations of team-task activities

Team-task activities are a broad category that you can adapt for classes of various sizes and for teaching various subjects. Here are a few suggestions:

Parallel teams. In a large class, have teams work in parallel. Divide the class into large teams and assign the same problem to each large team. Each large team must come up with its own solution and post it on the server for other teams to see. After seeing the solutions of other teams, a team may revise its own solution. At the end of the activity, each team must pick the best solution submitted by another team and justify its choice.

Mixed-language teams. For language learning, create teams of native and non-native speakers to solve a problem together. Teams must work in the language being learned.

Mosaic teams. Take a large book, Web site, or other complex work made up of somewhat independent pieces. Divide the class into teams. Assign each team a part of the whole to review. Each team can further subdivide the work by assigning parts to individuals, or all the members of the team can work on the team's assignment. Then:

▶ Each team prepares a summary of its part and a critical review of it.

▶ An über-team assembles the pieces and writes a review of the whole.

▶ Individual members comment on the consolidated review, and the über-team revises it.

Best practices for team-task activities

Make clear the grading criteria. Will grades be awarded to the class as a whole, to separate teams, or to individuals? Some learners may feel uncomfortable that largely unseen colleagues determine their grades.

Provide a suggested timeline for progress on the project. Lacking face-to-face contact, learners may not feel fully obligated to complete their share of work on time.

Challenge, but do not overwhelm. The goal of a teamwork activity must be appropriately challenging—not too difficult and not too easy. If learners have not worked in virtual teams before, they will require about twice as much time to complete an assignment as they would working together in a classroom.

For more advice on team learning, see "Promote team learning" on page 490.

Role-playing scenarios

Children learn much adult behavior by playing at being an adult. Likewise, adults can learn much by playing the role of someone else.

In a role-playing scenario, the teacher states a goal and assigns learners roles in achieving that goal. Learners research their roles. They then collaborate via online meetings and discussion forums to play out their roles to achieve the goal.

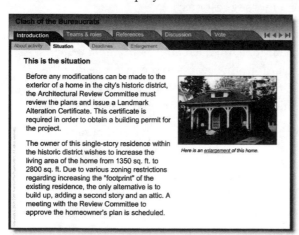

In this example, participants simulate the meeting of the town Architectural Review Committee to consider proposed renovations to a home in an historic district.

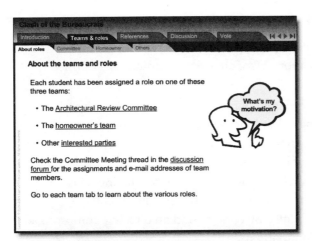

Each learner is assigned a specific role to play. Each role has specific duties and motivations.

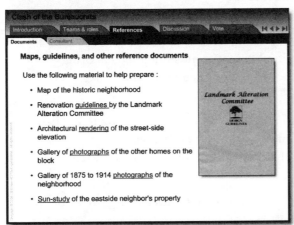

Learners have access to detailed reference materials, just as their real counterparts would.

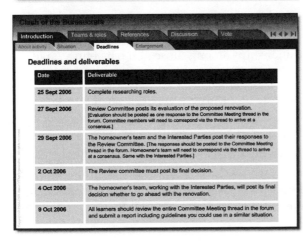

Learners must complete a series of activities in their roles and submit materials for others to examine.

Created in Microsoft PowerPoint and converted for Web delivery using Articulate Presenter. View example at horton.com/eld/.

When to use role-playing scenarios

Role-playing is a valuable way to teach subtle, interpersonal skills and to reveal the hidden complexity of many human endeavors. Here are some common uses of role-playing activities:

▶ Force someone to view events from a different perspective. Give an environmental activist the role of a real-estate developer. And vice versa.

▶ Allow someone to experience events online that they would not experience in real life. For example, let a man experience sexual harassment as a woman.

▶ Demonstrate the many perspectives necessary for a complex undertaking. Have a management team guide a project from initial idea to successful product.

▶ Teach interpersonal skills. Hold a committee meeting to find an effective compromise among competing ideas, groups, and individuals.

Variations of role-playing scenarios

Role-playing scenarios can be used to mimic all the different situations that bring individuals into contact and possibly conflict. Here are some forms that make good learning activities:

Behavior critique. Teach learners the correct behavior for a particular situation. Then model and critique bad behavior. Assign someone the role of demonstrating inappropriate behavior. Assign the rest of the class the role of reacting to the bad behavior.

Court trial. Put a concept, historical figure, or organization on trial. Assign roles of judge, accused, prosecutor, defense attorney, witnesses, and jury.

Board meeting. Simulate a meeting of the board of directors of a corporation, university, hospital, or other organization. Assign each participant specific goals, attitudes, and personality. Spell out known and secret relationships among those at the meeting. Give the meeting an agenda and a time limit.

Murder mystery. Teach investigative skills by having learners play roles in a murder investigation. Each member receives a role. For each role there are publicly known facts that everyone has access to and privately known facts that only the role-player knows. Role-players can be asked or tricked into revealing these hidden facts. Each role-player also has secret motivations. Role-players are either suspects or investigators. Investigators must solve the mystery by interviewing the suspects, examining artifacts, and exchanging notes. If a murder mystery does not fit your situation, substitute one of these investigations:

▶ Finding hidden treasure.

▶ Learning the cause of an airplane crash.

▶ Discovering the cure for a disease.

▶ Locating a missing person.

Who am I? Each learner picks and researches a different well-known person from the field of study. Each learner then writes a speech from this person's viewpoint and in this person's style. Learners post their speeches to a discussion forum. Learners comment on each other's speeches from the perspective of the person being impersonated. Learners defend the positions taken by their characters. At the end, each learner must guess the identity of the other impersonated characters.

Best practices for role-playing scenarios

Role-playing scenarios can be entertaining, energizing, and hugely educational—or, time-consuming and frustrating. The difference is careful design of the situation and assignment of the roles.

Introduce the scenario fully

Spell out the details of the scenario. What is the general situation and what problem does it pose for learners? What roles must learners play? For each role, what are the motivations and behaviors? How is success defined and how will the activity be scored?

Provide all the documents and other sources of information that would be available in the real situation. These can be abbreviated, but should contain enough detail to let learners carry out their roles.

Assign roles related to the subject

In team assignments, give learners roles that relate to the subject or metaphor of the assignment. Pick roles rich with interrelationships and opportunities for conflict and cooperation.

For example, the activity involving the Architectural Review Committee had the following roles:

Homeowners	Just want to build an addition to their home. Priority is getting more space for the least expense. Have a new baby on the way, so time is of the essence.
Architect	Wants to get the committee to approve plans already drawn. If plans are rejected, the architect will lose the commission. Really needs the job.
Building contractor	Wants to complete the job as quickly and inexpensively as possible. Does not worry much about architectural purity. Does worry about cash flow and completing the job before winter weather sets in.

City historian	Concerned with maintaining the architectural purity of the historic neighborhood. Classic bureaucrat with a fragile ego. Resents the power of the city attorney.
Head of committee	Also concerned with architectural purity. Has no formal architectural training. Just a busybody with lots of time on his hands.
City attorney	Insists that building codes be followed scrupulously and does not care that codes are somewhat vague and that they conflict with the guidelines of the Architectural Review Committee. Considers the city historian undisciplined and not too intelligent.
Neighbors	Concerned that the new addition will block their view of the mountains or shade their back yards. Generally get along with the homeowners but are jealous that the homeowners can expand and they cannot.

If you cannot use roles associated with the subject of the activity, you can always use generic roles that learners should find familiar (p. 495).

Match role to personality and skills

Assign roles carefully. Emphasize positive, creative roles rather than negative, critical roles. Be especially careful whom you assign to power positions, such as Manager, Judge, and Critic. Consider the personality of learners. Do they have the right mix of humility and assertiveness? Can they handle the power? Are their social skills adequate?

Also consider the basic skills of learners. If a role requires extensive writing, pick someone who can write clearly and quickly. If a role requires public speaking, pick someone with speaking experience and skills.

Have learners use their role names in messages

For class activities, have learners in e-mail, chat sessions, and discussion forums post their messages using the names of their roles (Teacher, Tech Support, or Juror 4), rather than their personal name.

Comparison activities

The comparison activity is a variant on the decision activity (p. 208). It lets learners compare their decisions to those of other learners or see how other learners did an analogous piece of work.

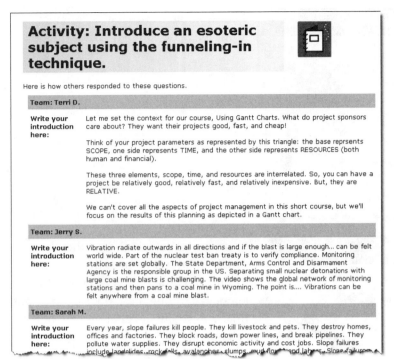

Activity: Introduce an esoteric subject using the funneling-in technique.

Here is how others responded to these questions.

Team: Terri D.

Write your introduction here:

Let me set the context for our course, Using Gantt Charts. What do project sponsors care about? They want their projects good, fast, and cheap!

Think of your project parameters as represented by this triangle: the base reprsents SCOPE, one side represents TIME, and the other side represents RESOURCES (both human and financial).

These three elements, scope, time, and resources are interrelated. So, you can have a project be relatively good, relatively fast, and relatively inexpensive. But, they are RELATIVE.

We can't cover all the aspects of project management in this short course, but we'll focus on the results of this planning as depicted in a Gantt chart.

Team: Jerry S.

Write your introduction here:

Vibration radiate outwards in all directions and if the blast is large enough... can be felt world wide. Part of the nuclear test ban treaty is to verify compliance. Monitoring stations are set globally. The State Department, Arms Control and Disarmament Agency is the responsible group in the US. Separating small nuclear detonations with large coal mine blasts is challenging. The video shows the global network of monitoring stations and then pans to a coal mine in Wyoming. The point is.... Vibrations can be felt anywhere from a coal mine blast.

Team: Sarah M.

Write your introduction here:

Every year, slope failures kill people. They kill livestock and pets. They destroy homes, offices and factories. They block roads, down power lines, and break pipelines. They pollute water supplies. They disrupt economic activity and cost jobs. Slope failures include landslides, rock falls, avalanches, slumps, mud flows, and lahars. Slope failures

Here is a comparison activity where the learner can see how other learners performed the same activity.

Built using Adobe Dreamweaver and Active Server Pages.

Often the comparison is a great source of inspiration. It lets learners reinterpret the activity in a more useful manner. It is also an important source of feedback in learner-led e-learning, where there is no teacher to critique the work, and in asynchronous e-learning where there are not enough learners at the same point in the course for a group critique.

Group-critique activities

The group-critique is the social form of the original-work activity (p. 207). Group critiques have learners help other learners to refine their work. Group-critique activities take advantage of discussion forums or other social media to help learners learn from other learners. In the simplest form of group critique, a learner prepares an individual answer to a question, posts it for others to critique, and then revises it before submitting the final version.

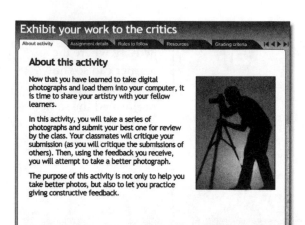

This example shows the assignment for a group-critique activity.

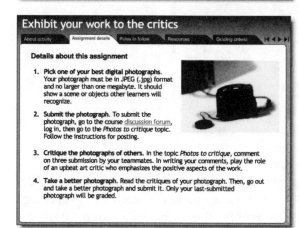

Learners are asked to select their best pictures, submit them to the discussion forum, view the photographs of other learners, critique these photographs, and finally to submit a better version of their original photographs.

Created in Microsoft PowerPoint and converted for Web delivery using Adobe Presenter. View example at horton.com/eld/.

A typical group-critique activity works like this: First, the teacher assigns an original-work activity for learners to perform. Individual learners then post their preliminary work to a discussion forum, where fellow learners can ask questions, critique, and suggest changes. Learners can then revise their work and resubmit it for another round of critique. In the end, the teacher evaluates learners based on the final quality of their work and on the helpfulness of their comments to others.

You can vary the basic group critique by changing how the critique is performed, what is critiqued, and what kinds of comments are solicited.

Group critiques teach learners to give and accept criticism. Use them to:

▶ Teach learners to refine their work by incorporating the ideas of others.
▶ Condition learners to accept and filter the criticism of their peers.
▶ Teach learners to offer helpful criticism.
▶ Offload from the teacher much of the work of evaluating and critiquing learners.

The value of group critiques depends on the quality of the comments offered by the group. For best results, guide participants in offering practical, encouraging comments. Monitor and moderate critiques. And be prepared to jump in if the comments degenerate into personal attacks. Remind reviewers that part of their grade depends on the helpfulness of their comments.

ENCOURAGE MEANINGFUL DISCUSSIONS

Online discussions are a staple of social learning, virtual classroom courses, and other forms of e-learning. Online discussions are one of the most evolved forms of social learning.

Discussion forums developed from the social and professional exchanges that took place in Internet list-servers and newsgroups. These intellectual watering holes attracted individuals with like interests but distant locations to a free exchange of ideas. And learning took place.

The use of discussion activities in e-learning builds on this informal exchange, but adds an efficient structure. Here's how an online discussion might be used in formal education:

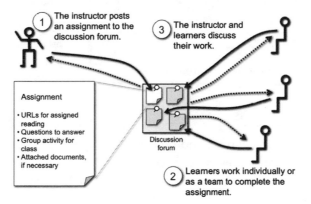

Learning starts as the teacher posts an assignment to the group. The assignment may include URLs or hyperlinks to assigned readings, questions to answer individually, and group activities. Assignments may also include attached reading and other necessary materials.

Learners read the assignment. They may work on it individually or in teams before posting their completed solutions back to the discussion forum where the teacher and other learners can see it, discuss it, and evaluate it. A typical course might consist of 6 to 12 such assignments.

Design discussion activities

Online discussions are an essential part of many different kinds of learning activities. The activity may take the form of a debate or brainstorming. It may involve few or many participants. It may cover factual or emotional subjects. The success of these activities depends on well-designed online discussions. But good discussions do not just happen. They are designed and crafted to provoke deep thought and continual improvement of ideas and opinions.

Start the discussion

Most important is the way the designer launches the conversation. Each discussion must start with a simple invitation to participate. The best invitation is a specific assignment. What makes a good assignment? Here are some techniques to use to create an assignment that entices learners to participate:

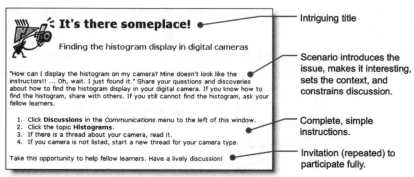

Prepare learners to discuss

Discussion activities can be complex and time-consuming for learners. To ensure you do not confuse learners or waste their time, provide complete instructions for each discussion activity. This example prepares learners to participate in a discussion in which they will critique the work of their classmates. Notice the different parts of this activity.

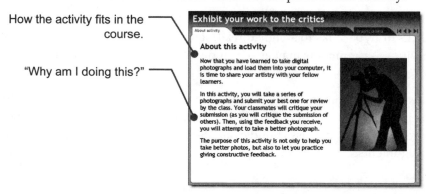

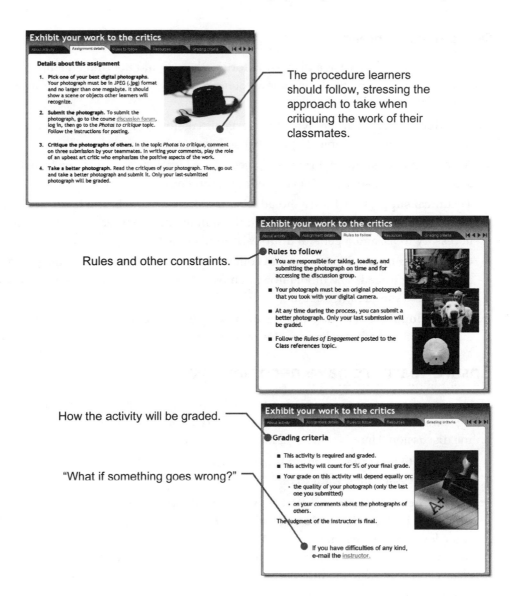

The procedure learners should follow, stressing the approach to take when critiquing the work of their classmates.

Rules and other constraints.

How the activity will be graded.

"What if something goes wrong?"

Allow enough time

Online discussions are not as fast as face-to-face conversations. As a general rule a 10-minute face-to-face conversation in the classroom would require:

▶ 20 minutes with audio-conferencing.

▶ 30 minutes with chat.

▶ One to two days in a discussion forum.

The same conversation in a one hour class meeting may require a week or ten days in a discussion forum.

Set up needed threads

When learners first arrive at a discussion forum, they should not find an empty warehouse. Put in some walls and a few rooms. Start a few conventional top-level threads, such as:

▶ **Introduction**. Tell learners what the whole discussion forum is about in more detail than on the welcome topic. Put any needed instructions here.

▶ **Administrative support**. Provide a place where learners can request help with any aspect of the course other than content or technology.

▶ **Technical support**. Include a thread for questions about tools and technologies used in the course. Start by posting the technical requirements, instructions for obtaining necessary tools, and a general troubleshooting guide.

▶ **General comments**. Plant a general comment thread to collect comments that do not fit any existing thread. The moderator can move these comments to the correct thread or use them to start a new thread.

▶ **Student lounge**. Set aside a discussion area where students can talk to one another on any subject—whether related to the course or not.

Ensure learners have necessary skills

Help learners new to your discussion forum learn to interact and to overcome their fear of doing something that makes them look stupid. Teach learners the essential skills for online discussion. Here is a survival kit of discussion skills:

▶ **Replying to messages**. Remind learners that they must click the **Reply** button for the specific message they want to reply to.

▶ **Posting new messages and starting new threads.** Learners must understand the difference between **New Message** and **Reply**. **New message** adds a message at the same level as the current message. **Reply** creates a new message beneath the current message. Not heeding this distinction results in tangled threads of messages with no clear context in which to interpret messages.

▶ **Writing a clear subject** for the message. For replies, the default is just to add "Re:" in front of the original subject line. Require learners to replace this with a meaningful subject. Otherwise you have messages that begin "Re: Re: Re: ...."

▶ **Editing posts**. Teach learners to correct small errors in their messages. They may not know they can click an **Edit** button to revise the message. Warn learners that it is not polite to make changes after a reply in a way that makes the reply look false or silly. The polite way is to add a message pointing out that the original submission has been revised and perhaps thanking those who suggested improvements.

Moderate discussion activities

In a *moderated* discussion forum the teacher—or someone else—watches over the exchange of messages. The primary duty of the moderator is to ensure that learners have productive discussions with other learners. Moderators perform two main tasks. First, they must set up the discussion forums and threads. Second, they must oversee the conversations that take place there.

Pick the right moderator

Normally, the teacher or facilitator for the course is also the moderator of the course's discussion forums. However, the requirements for a moderator are different from those for a teacher or facilitator. The teacher may be too busy to take on both jobs. And, in social learning, the group may be independent enough to elect their own discussion moderator.

A good moderator is knowledgeable, supportive, and articulate.

▶ **The moderator should be well-informed and on the ball**. The moderator must understand the subject matter, the computer system, and any software used by the discussion forum or other parts of the class. Or have ready access to those who do.

▶ **The moderator must have a caring nature**. The moderator must tactfully endure insults and rude behavior, patiently instruct fumble-fingered technophobes, continually inject enthusiasm into disheartened souls, and repeatedly calm abused and abusive respondents.

▶ **The moderator must be a superb communicator**. The moderator must be able to listen deeply and accurately gauge the knowledge and emotions of others. Not everyone can do this. The moderator must be someone whom others describe as tactful or diplomatic. And the moderator must be able to express complex ideas and subtle emotions in simple, unadorned prose.

So who are the job candidates?

Moderators can come from several different backgrounds. To pick a moderator, consider the following candidates:

▶ **Teacher**. About 90% of the time the teacher is the moderator. Make this your default choice.

▶ **Teaching assistant**. Often the teacher will delegate moderator duties to an assistant or teacher-in-training. Moderating a discussion forum is a great way for a junior staff member to learn about learners.

▶ **Recent graduate**. Learners who have completed the course may be good candidates, especially if they are continuing in the field of the course and want to stay in touch.

▶ **Outside expert**. A practitioner may not have time to teach a course, but may be willing to contribute by moderating a discussion forum.

▶ **Team member**. The learning team may take responsibility for its own discussion by nominating a member to oversee discussion activities.

If you cannot find an ideal candidate, perhaps you should split up the moderator duties. A technically adept assistant manages the technology, while the teacher spot-checks messages, and a learner helps out for extra credit.

Welcome learners

For each major area of the discussion forum, welcome learners to the discussion area and explain what and whom it is for. Make the welcome the first message in that area. Here is the opening message for a discussion topic on critiquing photographs:

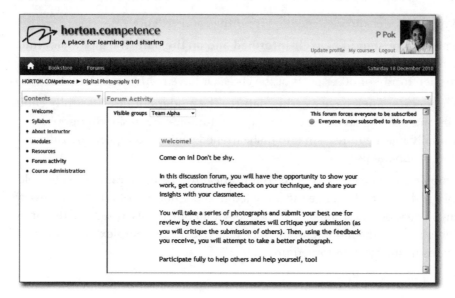

Make learners feel welcome. Invite them to participate. Help learners decide whether they are in the right discussion forum and the right thread, especially if a course has more than one forum or thread. Provide links to other discussion forums on the subject of the class.

Moderate actively but do not dominate

Actively moderate the discussion in order to activate learning. An active moderator should not lead to passive learners. The more actively the forum moderator critiques postings, adds comments, encourages participation, re-words messages, sparks creativity, resolves impasses, soothes tempers, challenges assumptions, and plays devil's advocate— the more active learners become.

Intervene when necessary, but only as much as necessary. Do not nit-pick. Let pass minor, first-time lapses. Many times social pressure will take care of the problem. If minor problems crop up repeatedly, post a gentle general reminder. And give it time to sink in. Deliver polite requests asking offenders to modify their behavior. Assume they are just careless or too busy to read the rules. Save high-power interventions for multiple-repeaters and for serious problems. Then pounce.

Keep the conversation lively

The role of the moderator may not be highly visible, but it is never passive. The moderator is like the mechanic for a complex piece of machinery, greasing a squeaky part here, clearing a jam there, flipping a blown circuit breaker when all motion stops. The moderator does whatever it takes to keep the discussion forum running at peak efficiency.

We have all known people who are always at the center of interesting conversations. Often they are not the ones who do the most talking, yet they do something to keep others talking effectively. The discussion-forum moderator can keep conversations lively by using a few proven techniques:

▶ Start new threads by posting interesting, deep questions.

▶ Recruit "guests" to add a fresh perspective or ask original questions.

▶ Respond to all inquiries that go unanswered for a few days.

▶ Correct all misconceptions before they propagate.

▶ Remind participants of the rules as necessary.

▶ Create new threads for interesting ideas that spring up deep within existing threads.

▶ Wrap up tired discussions by summarizing them (or assigning those duties to learners).

Challenge shallow thought

Do not accept mere opinions. Prompt learners to provide the evidence and logical thought behind their opinions. Challenge opinions by responding like this:

> I was intrigued by your answer [Quote it.] Can you explain why you feel so?
> Did particular experiences, research, or other evidence lead you to this opinion?

If everyone else agrees with an opinion, take the opposite opinion. Play devil's advocate. Learning teams often designate one of their members to fill this role. Here are some responses to stir up thought:

▶ OK, then answer me this …

▶ I claim the opposite. Can you prove me wrong?

▶ But what if …?

▶ Suppose just the opposite were true. What then?

Perform message maintenance

Messages dashed off in haste can sometimes go astray. A slight miswording can reverse the intended meaning. To maintain message quality, the moderator should:

▶ Reroute misdirected messages to the correct thread. And inform the poster of the change and the reason for it.

▶ Reword unclear or inaccurate subject headers.

▶ Fix (or have the sender fix) tragic typos or accidental misstatements.

Reject inappropriate postings

The moderator should reject postings that clearly violate course policies. Pacify or expel angry flamers. Remove messages that other learners complain about if you agree they are not appropriate. If you must reject a posting:

▶ Explain exactly why you rejected the posting. Remind the submitter of your standards for postings.

▶ Offer the submitter a chance to re-submit after specific changes are made.

▶ Require an apology if the posting unduly insulted or offended others.

▶ Point out any violations of a broader policy and the consequences of violating it.

If messages are posted immediately ...

In some discussion forums, messages are posted immediately without the moderator seeing them. In this case:

▶ Alert participants to this situation and warn them that some inappropriate messages may slip by.

▶ Read all new messages frequently, and immediately deal with inappropriate ones.

▶ If an offensive message slips by, remove it and post an apology to the group. Also require that the author of the message post an apology, too.

▶ Make learners responsible for policing discussion. Let them know that you will assist them, but remind them that it is they who decide what is and is not appropriate.

PROMOTE TEAM LEARNING

The team is a fundamental social unit in complex organizations. In many enterprises, the team is where most of the work gets done. No surprise, then, that team learning is a prominent part of social learning.

A team is a special kind of social group. It is not an arbitrary group of people saddled with a single work assignment. A team includes individuals working together to pursue a common goal or to realize a shared vision. A team is more tightly united than a school class or a business committee.

For social learning, two types of teams are important:

▶ Work teams whose primary purpose is to do work but who also have to learn in order to do that work.

▶ Learning teams whose primary goal is to learn but who do realistic work in order to learn.

Team learning is especially effective when learning occurs in the same team that will apply learning. The most valuable thing a team learns is how to allocate work and decision-making among team members. Team learning also works for teaching a skill that will be applied as a team, not individually.

Before going further, we should acknowledge that the term *team learning* is just a metaphor. Ultimately teams learn as individuals, and their collective behaviors become the behavior of the team. We must not forget our responsibility to educate each of these individuals.

Meet the requirements of a successful team

In learning teams, as in work teams, success depends on the membership and processes of the team. What, then, are the characteristics of a successful team?

▶ **Shared goal**. All members work together to accomplish a piece of work or to meet a learning objective. The goal can be large and complex, but must be shared by all members of the team.

▶ **Right size**. The team must have enough members to provide all the needed capabilities and to share the workload. It must be small enough to coordinate its own activities. For social learning, teams of 4 to 7 are practical. Larger teams are difficult for distant members.

▶ **Expertise or access to it**. Collectively the membership must have the needed skills and knowledge. Or it must have access to resources that fill any gaps.

▶ **Authority to question and innovate**. Within the team, learners must feel free to question, speculate, critique, admit mistakes or uncertainty, and speak their minds.

▶ **Time to form and operate**. Teams require significant time to form, mature, and operate. True teams are rare in short courses.

▶ **Ability to reach consensus**. Consensus is not resignation. It is not one opinion acquiesced to by all. It is not reduction to lowest common denominator. It is a leap to a new idea better than any initial ideas.

Form a team from individuals

Team formation is the linchpin of team learning. Before effective learning can take place, the group of selected individuals must transform themselves into a true team.

Difficulties in team formation

Team formation faces three main hurdles:

▶ **Time**. The transformation from group to team takes significant time. Time spent forming the team is time not spent learning.

▶ **Distance**. Lacking face-to-face contact, team members have limited ways to get to know each other.

▶ **Diversity**. To be effective, team members must possess a wide range of talents, knowledge, and perspectives. However, this same diversity can lead to conflict.

Required steps of team formation

To become a team, a group of people must:

▶ Get to know each other well enough to decide who should perform different work assignments and to develop trust in work done by teammates.

▶ Agree on a common goal, mission, or vision.

▶ Assign initial roles to team members.

▶ Devise and subscribe to standards of professional behavior and work results.

▶ Identify gaps of talent or knowledge and decide how to fill them, for example, by conducting research or by recruiting new members.

▶ Agree on initial team processes and procedures.

Align goals of team members

Team members must share a common goal. For a learning team, the goal is typically assigned by the facilitator. For a work team, the goal may be assigned by a higher level manager. In some cases, the team may be given a general or vague direction and asked to define its own goal.

In any case, team members must subscribe to that goal by aligning their individual goals to the goal of the team. They may also need to restate the goal in terms meaningful to the whole team.

In setting and aligning goals, a few team activities may help:

▶ **Consolidate interpretations**. Team members individually list what they want to accomplish as part of the team. Other members try to say how those items align with the assigned overall goal. The team comes to a consensus as to what the team's goal will be.

▶ **Refine the goal**. In a group discussion, have each team member state how his or her goal resembles the assigned goal and how it differs. Team members then refine the goal statement so that it can better apply to the group as a whole.

▶ **See the big picture**. In team learning, learners may focus on immediate needs or a looming deadline. To help them focus on the big picture, have learners submit examples of things that seemed important a few years ago but are not important now. These may include incidents or fads in popular culture, such as slang expressions, celebrities, or clothing. Then ask for similar items in the field of inquiry, such as theories, personalities, or tools. Ask the team to draw up guidelines to predict what will last and what will not.

Learn who can do what

To work as a team, learners must form accurate opinions of the talents, skills, knowledge, and character of fellow team members. This can be hard. Modest and shy individuals may downplay their capabilities. Others, fearing comparison, may exaggerate their capabilities. Many are unaware of their own strengths.

Forego traditional icebreaker activities

Avoid activities where team members learn irrelevant details about fellow learners, such as their favorite color, their middle name, or their favorite movie star.

Such activities don't reveal anything deep about the person. They waste time in team formation that could be spent learning about the expertise of team members. And, starting with an obviously trivial activity signals the unimportance of the activity and perhaps the work the team will do.

Explicitly reveal individual expertise

Provide ways learners can learn about each other. Have them post relevant information about themselves, for example:

▶ Credentials, such as degrees, licenses, and certifications.

▶ Work samples, including those from hobbies.

▶ Biography, résumé, or curriculum vitae.

▶ Questionnaire to elicit relevant information, such as: Prior jobs, side jobs, hobbies, volunteer work, artistic creations, interests, travel, awards, education, languages spoken, sports and physical activities, and organizational memberships.

▶ Self-classification activity. Using task-relevant criteria, such as expertise critical for a specific role on the team, have the members classify themselves along a scale or into defined subgroups.

▶ Self-assessment. For each critical area of expertise, ask each team member to identify the leading expert in the world and to say how he or she is like that person.

▶ Differences from the stereotype. Have members identify a way they have been stereotyped in the past and to list ways they differ from that stereotype. Remind participants that stereotypes apply to professions (engineer, accountant, and salesman) too.

▶ Favorites. Ask learners to identify items they admire. These should be in categories relevant to the subject of learning. For example, ask team members to identify their favorite non-fiction book, documentary film, businessperson, or scientist.

▶ Underutilized abilities. Have learners identify talents, skills, areas of knowledge that they possess but seldom get to apply.

But not too much information

Do not require learners to reveal information that could embarrass them, distract others, or lead to pointless conflict. If designing a course for people from cultures with which you are not familiar, do some research on conflicts within that culture. Take care before requiring learners to reveal their:

▶ Religion, denomination, or sect.

▶ Political affiliation or views.

▶ Membership in controversial organizations.

▶ Race, ethnic group, or tribal affiliation.

▶ Sexual preference.

As the team matures, learners will begin to trust each other and will naturally reveal more intimate details.

Have team members learn about each other

Once team members have revealed their expertise, consider assigning the team the task of assessing the expertise of fellow team members. Here are some activities to help them do that:

▶ **Matrix rating**. Have each team member rate his or her strengths and weaknesses in critical team skills. Then have team members rate each other. Consolidate and summarize ratings so each person sees how they rated themselves and how others rated them.

▶ **Make list of go-to people**. Have each person list the kinds of decisions the team will have to make and which team member's advice would help most in making that decision.

▶ **Compile an expertise catalog**. Agree on team members to serve as experts and checkers in each domain.

▶ **Match expertise and member**. Have members privately add their expertise to a list. Then let members ask questions of each other to try to match the expertise to the correct team member (or members).

▶ **Team-member bingo**. Have the team fill in a bingo card to identify one common item between each two members, such as a skill, interest, or background experience.

Adopt team roles

Let the team define and fill roles. A role on a team includes a cluster of duties. To keep the team small, each member may have to fill multiple roles.

Here are some customary team roles:

Role	Description
Coordinator	Identifies necessary tasks and dependencies among them. Schedules and tracks activities. Suggests assignments.
Compromise finder	Suggests ways to resolve conflicts. Can either suggest a new idea or a process of determining which of two competing ideas is better.
Devil's advocate	Guards against groupthink. Argues unpopular and unfounded positions. Challenges any hasty consensus. Identifies possible long-term or unintended consequences of any proposals.
Group-process monitor	Observes interpersonal communication, decision-making, conflict resolution, and other aspects of team operation. Points out where the team can operate better or where it is violating its own standards of conduct.
Morale booster	Monitors team morale and intervenes where low morale limits team performance. Works to reengage those who may have withdrawn or to counsel those who are too aggressive.
Discussion moderator	Monitors discussion activities. Takes steps when discussions stall, stray off topic, or become combative.
Journalist	Documents the team's operations. Writes a blog summarizing discoveries, obstacles, and routine operations of the team.
Summarizer	Crafts concise summaries, abstracts, outlines, and conclusions that condense extensive data and complex material.

Judge	Rules on the relevance and appropriateness of material. As a last resort, settles disputes for which no compromise or other resolution can be found.
Lawyer	Identifies and comments on legal issues raised by activities or proposals.
Liaison with outside experts	Coordinates discussions, interviews, symposia, and other communications with outside experts. Ensures that all contacts are professional and courteous.
Word-wrangler	Writes the text for formal reports. May also contribute text to presentations.
Picture-maker	Prepares photographs, drawings, diagrams, and charts needed for reports and presentations.
Presentation-maker	Creates and delivers formal presentations to outsiders. May include text, graphics, and other media from fellow team members.
Editor	Edits, enhances, and polishes the work of others. Does not criticize, but does offer better alternatives.
Quantitative analyst	Performs or verifies mathematical calculations. Computes statistics. Creates spreadsheets needed by the team.
Researcher	Tracks down sources of relevant information. Resolves factual disputes.
Technologist	Recommends, acquires, and configures computers, networks, mobile devices, and other tools needed by the team. Teaches team members to use these technologies.
Theory-former	Deduces principles, trends, concepts, and theories from concrete data. Generalizes ideas so they can apply more widely. Helps others see the big picture.
Theory-tester	Devises ways to logically and convincingly verify proposed theories and hypotheses.

Pick a leader, at least to start

A leaderless team is like a rudderless ship; it can only drift and spin. If a leader does not emerge through the process of team formation, a temporary leader must be chosen. The team may choose a team leader at random or may decide to rotate leadership through members. In any case, a temporary leader should be chosen to get the team moving.

Team processes

Once the team is formed and is ready to begin learning or real work, it will need processes to guide its operations. To reach its goal, the team must devise procedures, policies, and processes to:

▶ Recruit new members.

▶ Initiate them into the group, that is, to introduce them to each team member, to bring them up to date on the team's progress, and to assign them a meaningful role.

▶ Review and integrate work done by separate team members.

▶ Plan the next phase of work and allocate it among team members.

▶ Deal with unexpected events.

In addition, the team may need to revisit any of the decisions it made during team-formation.

Set norms of behavior

The team should set and enforce its own standards of conduct. One way is to chart a matrix of reactions. Have the team brainstorm to construct a list of common team behaviors—positive and negative. Then survey its members anonymously to see how each member feels about each behavior: Does the behavior help or hinder progress? How strongly do they feel, pro or con, about the behavior? Display results anonymously. Have learners discuss the implications and then derive specific norms of behavior.

Team warm-up activities

Warm-up activities are simple tasks that help team members get to know each other better, build trust among members, test team processes and norms of behavior, and develop leadership and communications processes.

Warm-up activities require learners to work together on meaningful tasks. Here are some typical warm-up projects:

▶ **Create a team symbol**. As a team, devise a symbol that represents subject-relevant expertise possessed by the team. The symbol can be an acronym, a portmanteau word, or a logo.

▶ **Plan a project**. Decide how to carry out a complex, but well-understood project in the field of inquiry, for example, to plan a half-hour TV documentary on some issue or aspect of the subject. Planning the project will require working together to identify the goal and starting point, defining necessary tasks, researching dependencies and other requirements, sequencing tasks, and revising the plan.

▶ **Survive after the fall**. Have the team imagine that a global catastrophe has left only the members of the team alive. What leadership scheme and roles would be needed? What laws?

▶ **Create a position application**. As a team come up with questions to qualify someone to join the team or to fill a role.

▶ **Play a game together**. Play a game or solve a puzzle as a team. For example, the team could conduct a simulation of a business process, assemble a jigsaw puzzle of a subject-relevant diagram, or complete a crossword puzzle involving vocabulary in the field. Members should discuss each move before making it. Any game will do so long as it requires thought or analysis.

▶ **Compose a poem**. As a team, write a poem that summarizes (or lampoons) an item of interest in your field of inquiry. The form can be a short poem, limerick (rhyme scheme: aabba), haiku (3 lines, 17 syllables), bumper sticker, or advertising jingle.

Fade out support

In unfamiliar situations, even the most independent learners desire structure and guidance. Provide leadership at the beginning, but fade out structure and transfer leadership to the group as soon as the group begins to function as a team.

Design activities for teams

A team activity is more than a multi-person activity or a single-person activity performed by a group. In designing team activities or adapting solo activities, ensure that learners accomplish the intended learning objectives.

▶ **Clarify the objectives** (yes, plural!). Team activities can be complex and time-consuming so use them to accomplish multiple related objectives. Objectives can include specific subject-related skills as well as general collaboration skills.

▶ **Supply written instructions for all activities**. Or record them so learners can play them back later. Provide enough information for learners to get started. Specify the results required. Clearly state time limits and other requirements.

▶ **Ensure that team members collectively have the expertise necessary to accomplish the objectives**. Or, provide access to the expertise.

▶ **Make the activities challenging and fun**. The best way is to make them resemble problems in the profession to which the learner aspires.

▶ **Allot enough time for team processes to work**. Typically team activities take three to ten times as long as an analogous solo activity.

- **Require collaboration to accomplish the goal.** Learners should spend the majority of time working together. Design the activity to provoke the kinds of mistakes from which the team can learn—ones that stymie individuals but which the team as a whole can overcome.

- **Require an observable result that can be objectively evaluated.** That way, learners know whether the team met the goal.

- **Make internal teamwork visible for analysis.** Archive discussions and chats. Record audio- and video-conferences.

- **Fairly evaluate individuals.** Decide how to determine whether the team accomplished its objective and how much each member contributed.

Engage in open inquiry

Team learning is potentially simple, flexible, and educationally effective. It is flexible enough to work for a variety of subjects.

In an advanced form of team learning, called **social inquiry**, learners probe more deeply into difficult subjects than anyone has before. As a team, learners go beyond existing guidelines and established knowledge. They advance into areas where there are no standards to tell them if they are on the right track. The goal is creating new knowledge, procedures, and processes.

This type of open-ended inquiry requires advanced teamwork skills where learners must readily let go of existing ideas in order to discover and prove better ideas. This does not require new procedures but advanced communications skills and emotional control. Team members must:

- **Listen objectively**, especially to critique of their ideas. They must not reflexively defend or advocate their own ideas.

- **Analyze the faults** of their own position. They must admit when they do not know.

- **Strive to synthesize** better ideas or at least more ideas.

- **Learn from failure** rather than blame others. The team as a whole must forget about blame and simply move forward to better ideas.

- **Raise valid concerns** about ideas of others and state clearly their reasons for concern. They must question others in a way that encourages them to analyze their opinions.

- **Admit to emotions** triggered by others' ideas and analyze the reason for the reaction.

Although these actions are helpful for any form of teamwork, they become necessary for inquiries where there are no teachers, experts, or best practices to guide them.

8

Social learning

IN CLOSING ...

Summary

▶ Social learning involves learning by interacting with fellow learners, the teacher, experts, and other professionals.

▶ Social learning occurs in a wide variety of forms, but some processes are common, namely, discussions, feedback, collaboration, and learner-created materials.

▶ Use social learning to teach collaboration and to tackle difficult subjects that lack established criteria.

▶ Engineer learning by sequencing patterns of interaction that create situations where learners learn from each other and from experts.

▶ Before picking software for social learning, list the social capabilities you need, such as targeting, filtering, and broadcasting messages, holding synchronous and asynchronous discussions, sharing created materials, voting, and managing collaborative teams.

▶ Facilitate social activities to encourage teams to take responsibility for their own learning. Monitor and intervene to correct bad behavior.

▶ Discussions are the lifeblood of social learning. Provide technology, procedures, and guidance to produce productive conversations.

For more ...

Virtual classroom learning is an application of social learning. See Chapter 10 for help designing this type of social learning.

For specific ideas on learning activities for social learning, see the "Design ... for social learning" sections in Chapters 2, 3, and 4

Mobile learning

E-learning for people on the go out in the world

Mobile learning frees people to learn at the place and time they choose and to learn from a world of teachers. This learning may be part of a non-mobile form of learning, such as a field trip during a classroom course. Or the course of learning may be entirely mobile.

WHAT IS MOBILE LEARNING?

Mobile learning has two main meanings: (1) participation in learning events while mobile and (2) learning from the world in which we move.

▶ **Participation in conventional learning by mobile individuals.** Mobile learning techniques and technologies allow mobile individuals to participate in established forms of learning including classroom learning, virtual-classroom learning, standalone e-learning, social learning, and performance support.

▶ **Real mobile learning**. In real mobile learning, we learn not from the mobile device but from the world around us. Real mobile learning requires learning from objects, environments, experts, and fellow learners that we encounter as we move about in the real world.

START WITH WORTHY GOALS

Creating mobile learning can be expensive, difficult, and risky. Before you dive into detailed design, ensure that the rewards justify likely costs—for you and your sponsor. What are potential rewards of mobile learning?

Learn from the whole world

Mobile learners have a world of teachers, coaches, and mentors—not just those embedded in a training course. In mobile learning, learning comes from interacting with:

▶ **Objects**. Buildings, machines, tools, automobiles, telescopes, cameras, instruments, and a whole lot more.

▶ **Locations**. Public and private spaces, museums, factories, stores.

▶ **Environments**. Natural and manmade.

▶ **Experts**. Professionals, practitioners, docents, executives, customers, consumers, and ordinary people.

▶ **Fellow learners**. In person and online, formal and informal. In the real world, everyone is a learner, and everyone is a teacher.

▶ **The Internet**. And all its connections.

Take advantage of teachable moments

Teachable moments occur when the learner is most open to learning and life is ready to teach the needed lesson. These moments happen when the learner wants to do something new or to do something better. They happen when something unexplainable occurs, especially when procedures that used to work now fail. Teachable moments occur any time curiosity is aroused—regardless of where the learner is located at that teachable moment.

Teach in the context of application

Mobile learning can teach subjects in the context and situation where learning will be applied. We can connect physical experiences with related recorded experiences to enhance subjects such as science, math, music, art, history, and architecture.

Teach "outdoor" subjects

Mobile learning is ideal to teach skills practiced outside the classroom or office, for example:

Agriculture	Cooking	Paleontology
Archaeology	Forestry	Photography
Architecture	Geology	Piloting
Art	History	Politics
Astronomy	Languages	Repair
Athletics	Manufacturing	Sales
Biology	Mapping	Surveying
Construction	Medicine	Tourism

Make learning healthier

By untethering sedentary learners, mobile learning improves the mental and physical health of learners.

▶ **Less physical strain**. Mobile learners vary their posture greatly throughout the day. Sitting still at a screen is just one of the thousands of postures in which people can learn.

▶ **Good exercise**. A mobile learner may walk to a site, move through it, take notes, physically manipulate tools and the environment, stretch to reach, scramble to climb, bend to examine, assemble, push, pull, lift, drop, drag, turn, open, close, and engage in a thousand other very active motions.

▶ **Improved blood flow to the brain**. Movement and exercise increase blood flow to the brain thus increasing alertness, attention, recall, and other mental processes crucial for learning.

▶ **Change of scene and environment**. Changes of location add mental stimulation. Even a subtle change of temperature, scenery, or background sound is enough to reinvigorate learners.

Don't go overboard in promising health benefits. Realize that mobile devices raise their own health concerns, such as repetitive-stress injury from thumb-typing, eyestrain caused by glare on the screen, and the uncertainty about the long-term effects of radio waves passing through our brains and bodies. Monitor the research and make an informed decision.

Learn more of the time

Mobile learning lets learners learn during more hours of the day and during those moments when learning is most effective.

▶ **While traveling**. When traveling and productive work is not possible, learning can still occur. Learners can consult mobile devices when riding in an airplane, carpooling to work or school, waiting in a station or terminal, riding on a train or bus, or waiting in a hotel.

▶ **When waiting for something**. Much of the annoying delays in life can be filled with engaging and effective learning activities. We can learn while waiting for a meal to arrive at a restaurant, while stuck in the lobby waiting for a delayed appointment, and while plopped down in a conference room waiting for meeting participants to arrive.

▶ **During found time**. Sometimes we expect to be busy but are not. Such moments can be put to advantage by learning. Found time includes cancelled meetings, arriving early for an appointment, or just occasional bouts of insomnia.

Enable virtual attendance

Mobile learners can participate in ongoing learning when they might not otherwise be able to do so because they are:

▶ **Performing competing duties**, such as completing mandatory work duties, keeping a doctor's appointment, or attending a child's softball game.

▶ **Out of the office** while on vacation, conducting field research, on a field trip for another course.

▶ **Coping with unforeseen circumstances**, such as bad weather, family emergency, recovering from illness.

Such virtual attendance may not be ideal for learning, but it keeps a dedicated learner from falling behind and dropping out.

Reduce infrastructure costs

Mobile learning can reduce the costs of real estate, electronics, and other physical infrastructure needed for learning. Mobile learning reduces the need for:

▶ Physical campus.

▶ Classrooms.

▶ Faculty offices.

▶ Desktop computers.

▶ Wired networks.

▶ Physical laboratories.

▶ Libraries of physical books.

Mobile learning also reduces the difficulty of engaging qualified teachers. Mobility allows more people to serve as teachers, experts, mentors, advisors, and critics. Mobile individuals do not need to alter their travel plans and can more easily fit teaching in among their other professional and family duties.

Prepare for an increasingly mobile world

Mobile learning prepares learners for the way they will live the rest of their lives. In this future anyone, anywhere, at any time can:

▶ Communicate directly with anyone else via voice, text, or video.

▶ Capture and edit text, voice, sound, music, and video.

▶ Post and receive messages from anyone.

▶ Look up any information needed.

▶ Determine his or her exact location and learn how to navigate to any other location.

More importantly, mobile learning prepares learners to take responsibility for their own learning and work schedule.

ADAPT EXISTING LEARNING FOR MOBILE LEARNERS

Proven effective learning efforts can, with some changes, accommodate mobile learners. Here, organized by goal, is a checklist of changes to ensure effective participation by mobile learners.

Enable participation in classroom learning

To enable remote participation in classroom learning:

▶ **Use an online meeting tool** to broadcast and to record class meetings. Let remote learners participate that way. Note: This approach does not require a full virtual-classroom system, just a simple online-meeting tool. At a minimum set up a phone conference so remote learners can listen in.

▶ **Publish materials and summaries of meetings**. Include separate audio and video recordings of lectures and discussions. Also make available slides with notes of what was said with each slide. If this seems like too much work, let in-class learners take on the task—in exchange for extra credit, of course.

▶ **Format materials for easy reading on mobile devices**. One way this can be accomplished is through separate style sheets for the mobile versions of pages.

▶ **Provide ways for mobile learners to ask questions**, for example, by e-mail, through social networking tools like Twitter and Facebook, or via text messages. For class meetings, define and publish procedures for mobile learners to request attention and communicate their questions.

▶ **Set up homework-submission procedures** for mobile-learners to hand in homework, such as attachments to an e-mail sent to a drop-box address.

▶ **Assign an in-class "study-buddy"** for each mobile learner. The study-buddy ensures that the mobile learner's concerns are addressed in a timely manner. Give extra credit for study-buddies.

▶ **Design activities so mobile learners can participate**. For example, don't require extensive writing or access to local resources, such as books on the reserve shelf of the library. Allow audio submissions.

▶ **Post assignments well in advance** of their due dates so mobile learners can fit them into busy schedules.

▶ **Make tests "open-book"** so there is no suspicion that mobile learners are cheating.

▶ **Convert the entire course to a virtual-classroom format** (Chapter 10) if a significant number of learners are mobile.

Accommodate mobile learners in the virtual classroom

To make virtual-classroom learning work for mobile learners, follow the same steps as for classroom learning. In addition:

▶ Make sure that a client for the online meeting tool or virtual-classroom system works on the mobile devices of your learners.

▶ Do not require attendance in online meetings. Make recordings of meetings available for mobile learners who could not attend.

▶ Conduct discussions over days, not minutes. Use discussion forums rather than chat.

Let mobile learners take standalone e-learning

To make standalone e-learning courses available to learners, make sure that the e-learning plays on the mobile devices learners carry.

▶ Simplify pages for easy reading on mobile devices in the actual environment where learning will occur (p. 520).

▶ Minimize typing and simplify entering text (p. 526). Let learners interact by pointing to items on the screen.

▶ Make selection targets ("tap areas") large enough and far enough apart.

▶ Allow learners to download entire lessons and courses and take them while not connected to a network (p. 525).

▶ Design the course so it works for learners with intermittent and slow network connections (p. 525). Provide text transcripts and other alternatives for high-bandwidth media (p. 524).

Make social learning mobile

Mobile learning and social learning are a natural combination, especially among young learners who have grown up with mobile phones and social media. To make social learning mobile:

▶ Make clients for social-media tools available for mobile devices or at least a browser-based interface to the social-media tool.

▶ Rotate the meeting time so no group of learners always has to get up in the middle of the night.

▶ Require detailed profiles with photos for all participants. Also include a voice greeting if practical. Help learners get to know one another.

▶ Limit long real-time meetings. Replace meetings with ongoing forum discussions.

See Chapter 8 for more on designing social learning.

Performance support

Mobile workers need performance support at the place where they do work. Mobile devices are well suited to deliver that support. To ensure that mobile workers get the support they need:

▶ **Provide access to information needed** to perform meaningful work. Make it easy to find job aids, instructions, procedures, checklists, and standards.

▶ **Publish documents targeted at critical tasks** and frequently performed tasks. These can include concise recipes, troubleshooting guides, summaries, and FAQ lists.

▶ **Provide access to background information** needed for fluent and efficient work. For example provide links to glossaries, pronunciation guides for technical terms, names of people the worker may need to meet, and biographies of critical people.

▶ **Enable workers to download information** for use while off the network (p 525).

▶ **Format information for use**, not just reading. Do not require scrolling to see all of a step. Never require horizontal scrolling. Place warnings before the step to which they apply. Consider audio instructions for steps that must be performed while looking away from the device.

▶ **Ensure that search-engines work from the mobile device** either by supplying a client for the mobile device or a Web interface to the search engine.

▶ **Convert content to job aids** to both reduce theory and shorten long readings. Provide clear criteria and procedures for making decisions. Include links to details, reasons, and alternatives.

USE THE CAPABILITIES OF THE DEVICE

Mobile devices offer a wide palette of capabilities that we can use to engage and educate learners. The capabilities vary among devices, but even moderate-cost mobile phones can accommodate mobile learning.

Use the following table to compile a list of capabilities you will need for your mobile learning. Then make sure that learners' devices have these capabilities.

Capability	Description (what the user can do)	Uses in mobile learning
Screen display	Display text, graphics, and video.	To display readings, presentations, assignments, graphics, tests, Web pages, job aids, any other visual content.

Capability	Description (what the user can do)	Uses in mobile learning
Audio playback	Play voice, music, and sounds.	Let learners listen to lectures, instructions and assignments, feedback, critiques, coaching, advice, overviews and previews, class and team meetings.
Video playback	Play video segments.	View lectures, presentations, demonstrations, documentary films, assignments, and critiques.
Clock	Display time, measure time, and schedule events.	Display reminders of scheduled events, study times, and time limits.
Calendar	Schedule activities and display reminders.	Track class meetings, due-dates for assignments, and project milestones.
Contacts list	Catalog the name, address, e-mail, phone number, and other contact information for participants.	Easily communicate with teachers, experts, advisors, mentors, fellow learners, and others important to the learner.
GPS	Detect latitude and longitude coordinates. Note: It can take 10 minutes to acquire an accurate GPS signal.	▶ Suggest an item of interest near the learner. ▶ Provide information and activities related to an object approached or an area entered (geofencing). ▶ Guide learners to a location or object. ▶ Track learners for safety. ▶ Record location where data is recorded. ▶ Teach navigation skills and Cartesian coordinates. ▶ Verify attendance or accomplishment of location-finding objective.

Capability	Description (what the user can do)	Uses in mobile learning
Map display	Show streets, roads, buildings, and terrain. Can pinpoint the learner's location with GPS capability.	▶ Help learners find locations for learning to occur. ▶ Keep learners oriented and confident while moving through and unfamiliar environment. ▶ Locate classmates for physical meetings.
Navigation	Get instructions on how to get from one place to another.	▶ Direct learners to a site where learning can occur. ▶ Ensure learners are on time for physical meetings.
Bluetooth	Connect to another Bluetooth-enabled device.	Supplement a device by adding capabilities not built in. Bluetooth enables use of accessories such as data probes, separate mobile phones, and ultra-accurate GPS units.
E-mail	Send and receive e-mail messages and attachments.	▶ Ask questions of teachers, experts or fellow learners. ▶ Receive assignments and submit work. ▶ Give and receive feedback.
Web browser	Access Web servers and all that they provide.	▶ Access Web-based lessons, documents, job-aids, and other learning content. ▶ Communicate with server-based tools such as online-meeting tools, virtual-classroom systems, and learning management systems. ▶ Communicate via Web-based social-networking tools.

Capability	Description (what the user can do)	Uses in mobile learning
Radio-frequency identification (RFID) reader	Read a short message encoded in a RFID tag. Tags are tiny (4 cu. mm.) devices that transmit an identifying message triggered when a RFID reader comes within a few centimeters.	RFIDs can be used for object- and location-based activities. The mobile device can use the identifying message to retrieve: ▶ A lesson on the object or location. ▶ Background information. ▶ Instructions for an activity involving the object. ▶ Instructions to find next object. ▶ A job-aid for performing a task. ▶ A you-are-here map to help navigation. ▶ Scavenger hunt with verification and extra information.
Bar-code reader	Read a short message encoded in the bar code. The mobile device's camera reads the bar code and interprets its short message, typically a URL or other identifier to guide retrieval of information. (Common bar-code types include: Linear, QR code, Data Matrix code, and Ezcode.)	Bar codes can be used for object- and location-based activities. The mobile device can use the bar code to retrieve: ▶ A lesson on the object or location. ▶ Background information. ▶ Instructions for an activity involving the object. ▶ Instructions to find next object. ▶ A job-aid for performing a task. ▶ A you-are-here map to help navigation. ▶ Scavenger hunt with verification and extra information.

Capability	Description (what the user can do)	Uses in mobile learning
Text messaging	Send short text messages to another mobile device.	▶ Ask questions of teachers, experts, and fellow learners. ▶ Vote or take a poll. ▶ Send and receive reminders. ▶ Conduct a single-question short-answer test.
Audio recorder	Record voice, music, and other sounds using the built-in microphone or an external microphone.	▶ Record learners' work, including poetry, music, reports, and speeches. ▶ Record notes and reminders. ▶ Record podcasts.
Still camera	Take photographs.	Photographs can prove accomplishment of an objective by showing: ▶ Learner at an assigned location, such as in front of house with specific style of architecture. ▶ Something created. ▶ Sequence of work activities completed. ▶ Items in a scavenger hunt. ▶ Photographs can also capture data and take notes.
Video camera	Record motion and audio.	▶ Produce documentary films. ▶ Create video podcasts. ▶ Tell stories. ▶ Record demonstrations and presentations. ▶ Record data from lab experiments. ▶ Provide instructions for others. ▶ Create reports or proof of completion of assigned activities.

Capability	Description (what the user can do)	Uses in mobile learning
Edit and format text	Enter, organize, and format text.	Create reports, stories, poems, scripts, essays, and other textual works.
Edit photographs	Adjust photographs: crop, straighten, change brightness and contrast, alter color, and apply special effects.	▶ Learn photography. ▶ Improve images for inclusion in reports, presentations, and blogs.
Edit audio	Shorten, combine, and adjust volume and tone of audio recordings.	▶ Learn audio production. ▶ Improve audio for inclusion in reports, presentations, and podcasts.
Edit video	Cut, sequence, overlay, and adjust video clips.	▶ Learn video production. ▶ Improve video for inclusion in reports, presentations, and video podcasts.
Keyboard (screen)	Enter small amounts of text.	▶ Fill in forms. ▶ Enter user ID and password. ▶ Write short messages, such as, brief e-mails, status updates, tweets, and the like. ▶ Respond to short-answer test questions.
Keyboard (external)	Enter large amounts of text.	Write reports, stories, essays, blog entries, and other substantial works.
Battery charger	Charge the device's battery.	Use the mobile device over periods longer than its battery life. Mobile learning tends to use battery-draining capabilities.

Capability	Description (what the user can do)	Uses in mobile learning
Extra batteries	Replace a depleted battery.	Enables usage over periods longer than battery life—when not able to recharge, such as when in the wilderness or moving too rapidly or sporadically to pause to recharge the single, built-in battery.
Phone call	Talk to other people.	▶ Ask questions of teachers, experts, and fellow learners. ▶ Participate in conference calls and online meetings.
Social networking	Connect to social-networking sites and tools, such as, Twitter and Facebook.	▶ Participate in social learning activities that require these social networking tools. ▶ Communicate with teachers, experts, and fellow learners.
Wireless networking	Connect to the Internet and local-area networks via Wi-Fi, EDGE, 3G or other wireless protocols.	▶ Connect to networks while traveling. ▶ Download materials and assignments. ▶ Upload completed work.
Calculator	Perform common calculations.	Perform mathematical calculations required in subjects such as science, engineering, architecture, statistics, finance, and construction.
Spreadsheet with charting	Perform math with rows and columns of numbers and display charts of results.	▶ Perform complex calculations required in subjects such as science, engineering, architecture, statistics, finance, and construction. ▶ Analyze data for trends. ▶ Prepare charts for reports.

Capability	Description (what the user can do)	Uses in mobile learning
Voice control	Activate and direct functions of the mobile device with voice commands.	▶ Record notes and other data while hands are occupied. ▶ Operate when touch is not possible, such as when wearing mittens to fend off extreme cold.
Text-to-voice synthesis	Have the device speak aloud words stored as text.	▶ Supply instructions when the learner cannot look at the screen. ▶ Relieve eyestrain when reading from the screen is difficult. ▶ Assist learners with poor vision.
Voice-to-text	Convert spoken words to text.	▶ Enter text quicker and more conveniently than by keyboard. ▶ Enter text when hands are needed for other tasks. ▶ Enter text when typing is not practical, for example, when wearing gloves for cold.
External microphone	Record sound through the microphone jack on the device.	▶ Record voice in a noisy environment. ▶ Isolate one specific sound out of many. ▶ Capture environmental sounds.
Augmented reality	View relevant data superimposed on the image recorded by the video camera.	▶ Supply information about buildings, monuments, and objects in the learner's vicinity. ▶ Reveal pattern among objects in view, for instance, the lines connecting stars of a constellation. ▶ Provide instructions on how to interact with objects near the learner.

Capability	Description (what the user can do)	Uses in mobile learning
Interface for TV	Play audio and video on a television.	▶ Relieve eyestrain and muscle cramps caused by hunching over a tiny screen. ▶ Share mobile-learning with a group.
Interface for projector	Play audio and video on a screen projector.	▶ Share e-learning content with a group. ▶ In social learning, perform activities as a group.
Data probes	Measure physical data such as: temperature, air pressure, pH, salinity, O_2, CO_2, acceleration, force, light, color, and sound level.	▶ Collect data for use in an analysis, discovery, or research activity. ▶ Enable classical laboratory activities.

DESIGN FOR THE LEARNER, ENVIRONMENT, AND DEVICE

Mobile learners have the same retina, eardrums, and brain chemistry as sedentary learners. And mobile learners learn by the same kinds of experiences. They do differ in their situation, environment, and choice of communication device. As designers, we must account for those differences as we strive to provide learning experiences. This section provides guidelines. There are a lot of possible issues, but fortunately, only a few will apply in any given situation.

Design for the mobile learner

The learner's situation and work activities may require special design efforts.

Characteristic	Issues	Guidelines
Busy, engaged in activities they consider more important than learning.	Learning must fit between "higher priority" activities.	▶ Design short, self-contained sequences. ▶ Let learners quit at any time and resume where they left off.
Traveling	The learner may be out of contact for hours or days.	▶ Enable learners to download entire lessons and courses and play them offline (p 525). ▶ Announce deadlines well in advance. ▶ Include FAQ and Help so learners can solve their own problems.
	Learners may suffer fatigue and jet lag.	▶ Set generous deadlines for activities. ▶ Do not base grades on participation in real-time meetings.
Distracted	Other tasks limit attention available for mobile learning. Eyesight and hearing may likewise be occupied.	▶ Make content available as text and as audio. ▶ Let learners decide when to advance. ▶ Make the "replay" function clear.
In remote locations, possibly off the grid.	Slow speed connection.	▶ Provide alternatives to high-bandwidth media (p 524). ▶ Publish a low-bandwidth version of each lesson or page.
	Intermittent connection. Or none.	▶ Enable learners to download entire lessons and courses and play them offline (p 525). ▶ Do not enforce prerequisites.
	Battery life is limited.	▶ Provide a solar charger and extra batteries. ▶ Allow learners to work from paper for simple reading activities (p 526).

Characteristic	Issues	Guidelines
In a different time zone.	Out of sync with class meetings.	▶ Minimize required meetings. ▶ Meet in the middle of the day or at a time that accommodates most remote learners. ▶ Acknowledge that remote learners may be half asleep. Publish notes. ▶ Do not base grades on participation in real-time meetings.
Using a personal, rather than a corporate, device.	The learner determines the device and how it is configured.	Design for the mobile devices learners already have (p 522).

Design for the environment where learning occurs

Environmental conditions will affect how well mobile learners will learn. Here are some conditions learners may face, the issues the conditions may pose, and design strategies to deal with them:

Condition	Issue	Design solution.
Noise	Hard to hear voice and other sounds.	▶ Have learners use earphones with ear buds or enclosing earmuffs. ▶ Provide a text transcript for all voice segments.
	Hard to record sound.	Provide a noise-cancelling microphone or directional microphone.
Vibration	Difficult to read small text.	Simplify the display and design for easy reading (p 520).
	Difficult to point precisely or use a small keyboard.	▶ Use larger selection targets for clicks or taps. ▶ Require less typing.
	Small details are obscured.	Require devices with a high-legibility display.

Condition	Issue	Design solution.
Bright light	Extreme brightness and screen glare make reading hard and obscures details.	Require a high-contrast display and an anti-reflection coating.
Darkness	The screen may be hard to read and physical buttons must be located by touch.	Require a backlit display and provide extra batteries.
Dust	Can obscure small details and scratch the screen.	▶ Provide a protective coating. ▶ Limit drag-type interactions.
	Can clog ports and crevices.	▶ Provide a protective case and screen coating. ▶ Use only the on-screen keyboard.
Moisture and humidity	Can short-circuit the device.	▶ Provide a waterproof container for the device. ▶ Use only an on-screen keyboard.
Heat	Device can overheat. Perspiration can cause a moisture problem.	▶ Suggest that learners defer learning till a cooler time of day. ▶ Limit the time spans that the device must be turned on.
Cold	Learner wears gloves.	▶ Enlarge targets for clicks and taps. ▶ Provide a stylus.
	Extreme cold can cause the device to fail and batteries to run low.	▶ Provide a heated case for the device. ▶ Supply extra batteries.
Wind	Dust, vibration, and noise.	(See the entries for dust, vibration, and noise.)
Electromagnetic fields	Interference	▶ Provide shielding for the device. ▶ Ensure your e-learning works with intermittent or slow connections (p 525).

Design for the mobile device

As a designer, it galls me to compromise the design of learning to fit limitations of technology. However, the benefits of mobile learning are so compelling that compromise is justified. Limited learning beats no learning any day.

Limitation	Description	Guideline
Screen size	The display screen will be small for a smart phone and moderate for a tablet.	▶ Design for easy reading (p 520) and fit content to the small display (p 523). ▶ Minimize navigation controls, logos, and emblems. ▶ Put unessential navigation controls and content at the bottom of scrolling content. ▶ Minimize use of wide photographs, diagrams, and tables.
Battery life	Learning and other uses may exhaust the battery before it can be recharged.	▶ Publish battery-conservation instructions. ▶ Provide a solar charger, car charger, or extra batteries. ▶ Minimize battery-draining activities, such as video, audio, GPS, or wireless access. ▶ Instruct learners to turn on battery-draining features only when needed.
Intermittent connection or none	Learners may not have continuous network connection. Connection may be unreliable. Some LMSs require continuous contact.	▶ Let learners download lessons and courses to take while they are off the network (p 525). ▶ Design short, self-contained learning objects. ▶ Publish procedures for uploading work when back in contact.

Limitation	Description	Guideline
Slow connection	Wireless connections especially at remote locations may be slower than wired connections at home.	Provide alternatives for high-bandwidth media.
Pointing device	A fingertip cannot point precisely.	▶ Enlarge selection targets and leave space between them. ▶ Consider providing a stylus.
Storage limitations	Limited on-device storage.	Provide alternatives to high-bandwidth media (p 524).
File formats supported	Not all devices support Flash, PDF, Java, or highly-formatted Microsoft Office documents.	Stick to widely supported industry-standard formats, such as HTML, CSS, JavaScript, and JPEG.
Browser support of standards	Not all devices have browsers that support industry-standards.	Don't depend on precise layout and format.

DESIGN GUIDELINES FOR OVERCOMING LIMITATIONS

This section offers suggestions to make mobile learning more engaging and effective and to overcome the limitations of learners' situations, mobile devices, and environments where learning occurs.

Design for easy reading

Reading from a small, glare-stricken screen can be error-prone and downright painful. Do not require lengthy reading by mobile learners. Use other ways to present verbal information.

▶ **Reduce the amount learners must read**. Provide overviews and summaries.

▶ **Format for scanning**. Let learners quickly find the small piece of text they really need. Use lots of headings. Convert paragraphs to easily skimmed tables and lists.

▶ **Present words as audio**. Record text and distribute audio files. If this is not practical, look into text-to-speech synthesis.

▶ **Use a more legible medium or device**. Consider upgrading learners from a small-screened smart phone to the more spacious display of a tablet or laptop. Or just enable learners to print out content they must read carefully.

▶ **Establish and follow standards of legibility**. For more on designing the visual display, take a look at online Chapter 14.

▶ **Let learners adjust the display**. Provide instructions on how to customize the display. Prefer authoring tools that embed controls to let learners adjust the display.

▶ **Use simple high-contrast backgrounds**. Avoid graphics behind text. Remember black and white provides the highest contrast.

Maintain contact with learners

Mobile learners can feel isolated and lonely. They cannot swing by for a soothing cup of herb tea during office hours. They cannot ask the person sitting next to them. They may be out of contact for days at a time. They may be ten time zones away and jet lagged. Provide ways that remote learners can get assistance and support when needed.

Some suggestions:

▶ **Arrange 24-hour technical support** for the mobile device and any software the learner may use with the device, including the learning management system, online meeting tool, and social-media sites and clients.

▶ **Redefine "office hours" to allow electronic participation** via text messaging, chat, voice conferencing, or just a phone call.

▶ **Respond promptly to messages** from mobile learners. Promise a response within a certain amount of time—and keep this promise. Set realistic expectations: teachers need sleep too.

▶ **Enlist all learners in supporting mobile learners**. Make all learners, mobile and non-mobile, responsible to help their fellow learners. If necessary, give extra credit to the most helpful learners.

▶ **Let mobile learners communicate on their own terms**. Set up multiple channels for learners to ask questions, request help, or just vent their frustrations. Let learners communicate via voice mail, text messaging, e-mail, chat, Twitter, Facebook, and any other means they may be able to use. Imagine your learner perched at the top of a jungle peak frantically trying to acquire mobile-phone signal as their battery-level display drops to its last chiclet.

Design for the devices learners already have

Mobile devices are personal devices. Learners will prefer the device they already know, love, and carry everywhere, not the one you prescribe—even if you give them the new device free, gratis, and at no charge.

▶ Learn what devices learners already have. Designing e-learning for an Android device can be a disaster if 90% of your learners have iPhones.

▶ Design Web content to display in a variety of mobile and desktop versions of browsers, such as Firefox, Safari, or Internet Explorer.

▶ Forego use of features not widely available among learners' devices. Provide alternatives for those who lack specific capabilities.

▶ Test learning on the full range of devices learners will use. At a minimum test on the least capable device.

Use learners' time efficiently

Mobile learners are busy and often distracted. They may have little patience for activities with no obvious benefit. A learner who asks, "Why am I doing this?" is lost to you.

☹ No	☺ Yes
Waste learners' time moving from location to location.	Maximize learning at a location and while on route to a new location.
Much time spent just collecting data.	Increase time spent analyzing data and drawing conclusions.
Require extensive text entry.	Let learners pick from a list.
Require precise text entry.	Accept typos and abbreviations.
Require complex formatting of text, formulas, tables.	Accept plain text.
Require complex media editing.	Accept raw clips.
Assign repetitive activity without learning benefit.	Supply a starting point or sample data that eliminates the need for repetitive activity.
Assign any activity whose benefit is not obvious.	Tell learners why they need to do the activity.

Fit text and graphics to the display

Screen-size can become a critical issue in mobile learning, especially when presenting complex information on a mobile phone held so the screen is taller than wide.

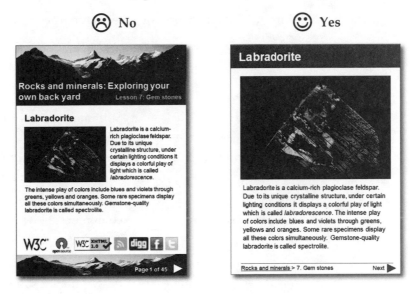

- **Present only core material**. Cut out anything not required to accomplish your learning objective. To compensate for possible gaps, make it easy for learners to ask questions.

- **Use space for meaningful content only.** Eliminate unnecessary banners, IDs, buttons, legal warnings, copyright notices, and logos. This may require confronting the legal department and visual-identity committee. Include a **More ...** button to reveal removed items.

- **Put secondary content at the bottom of the page**. This way it does not distract learners or waste space in the first scrolling zone. The bottom is a good place for optional navigation controls, emblems, badges, copyright notices, and other legal notices.

- **Reduce content to display**. Crop and simplify graphics. Edit text. Replace a large graphic with an overview and series of close-ups. Summarize.

- **Present a brief version linked to a complete version.** For example, link thumbnail graphics to an enlargement. Or link an overview to a complete article.

- **Test pages at small sizes**. Make sure pages display well on the smallest and narrowest screens likely.

- **Design a flexible layout.** Ensure that the display adjusts well to different screen sizes. This *may* require a separate version for mobile devices, but can often be accomplished by a separate style sheet for mobile devices.

- **Design a single-column flow.** Avoid sidebar articles or tables of contents that display in a separate column to the left or right of the main content.

Provide low-bandwidth alternatives

Media designed for an always-on, high-bandwidth connection can prove useless for many mobile learners, who may have a slow connection.

Make available lower-bandwidth versions and alternative media for crucial content.

High-bandwidth medium	Lower-bandwidth version	Alternative media
Video	▸ Shorten clips. ▸ Reduce width and height. ▸ Compress more highly.	▸ Stills and audio. ▸ Still photographs and a transcript. ▸ Just a transcript if the visual component is not essential.
Video chat or conferencing	▸ Smaller window. ▸ Only the current speaker visible.	▸ Audio chat or phone conference. ▸ Text chat.
Audio	▸ Shorten segments. ▸ Convert stereo to mono. ▸ Compress more highly. ▸ Choose a file format like .mp3 that is designed for small size.	▸ Text transcript or description of sounds. ▸ Text summary of a discussion.
Photographs	▸ Crop the image to just the essential part. ▸ Reduce the width and height. ▸ Compress the graphic more highly.	Include a thumbnail image linked to the full-sized graphic.
Slide presentation as video.	Slides at smaller size and audio more compressed.	Still pictures and transcript.

The key here is thinking about these issues and alternatives before you create high-bandwidth media. For example, it is easier to initially record two versions of video rather than to have to restage and reshoot a low-bandwidth version later.

Design for imperfect network connections

Learners moving about in the world may skirt areas of connectivity or move from hotspot to hotspot. They may stray off the grid or into areas of overloaded urban networks. As a result, they may have only sporadic, occasional, and unreliable network connections. Learners may connect for only short periods. They may experience dropouts and network failures.

These are technical problems and usually require technical solutions. The following suggestions will require efforts by your technical support staff.

- ▶ **Allow multiple types of network connection**. Pick mobile devices that let learners use both telephone and computer network protocols such as Wi-Fi, EDGE, 4G, and 3G. Keep in mind that the network protocols and frequencies common in one part of the world may be absent in other parts.

- ▶ **Break content into many small files** rather than one big file. Enable a single action to trigger download of the entire package. Clearly label which files are required for which activities.

- ▶ Enable learners to resume a download operation that was interrupted.

- ▶ **Provide for on-device storage of learning content**. This is not a simple matter on some mobile-device operating systems.

- ▶ **Do not enforce time limits for tests**. Let learners resume an interrupted test.

Try this: Set alarms on your mobile device to go off every few minutes. Start taking your e-learning. Every time an alarm goes off, turn off the network connection. Wait a few minutes, and then turn the network connection back on. How was your e-learning experience?

Enable "download and go"

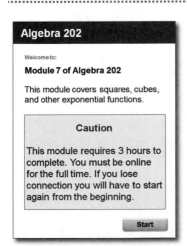

Long periods of continuous network connection are not possible for many mobile learners. Requiring them to learn only while continuously connected to the network is not practical. So, we must enable learners to download units of learning content to their device and interact with them while not connected to the network. The common name for this feature is "download and go."

Make sure that your learning management system and authoring tools support this feature. Some SCORM-conformant systems require a network connection in order for completions of each unit or results of each test question to be recorded.

Simplify entering text

Smart phones and tablet devices lack a full-size keyboard. Some devices have no physical keyboard and instead rely on a keyboard displayed on the screen. Typing is typically hunt-and-peck or limited to thumbs. OK, some learners can type quickly and accurately with just opposable digits, but many cannot. Problems arise when mobile learners must type quickly, enter large amounts of text, or type accurately.

▶ **Relax the rules of writing**. Allow abbreviations and minor typos. Tolerate incomplete sentences and elliptical expressions. Just insist on clarity.

▶ **Minimize required text entry**. Replace essay questions with short-answer and multiple-choice questions.

▶ **Give learners enough time**. Eliminate time limits on test. Set generous deadlines for activities that require extensive typing.

▶ **Allow voice submissions**. Let learners record and upload their responses. At least let learners record answers to an answering machine.

▶ **Use voice-to-text technology** to let learners create text by speaking into the mobile device. Such voice-transcription tools are not perfect but they do provide another way to generate text on a mobile device.

Follow established user-interface guidelines

Users of mobile devices expect learning content to look and behave like other content on their device. They resent having to learn new rules and conventions. Where possible, follow the user-interface guidelines for the device.

Conformance to the user-interface standards of the device is largely an issue for your authoring tools: Can they conveniently produce content that complies with the standards?

To see what standards apply to a device, search for "iPhone user interface guidelines" or the equivalent for your device.

Remember, paper is a mobile device

Paper is not the enemy of mobile learning. Paper has a highly legible display. It tolerates heat, cold, dust, and electrical interference. Its battery life is near infinite. And it is biodegradable and recyclable. Get over your paper guilt and just print it out—if that's the best way to effect learning.

Here's an example of a paper-based mobile learning activity.

Systematic shelving		
Batavia Books		New-employee training
Our stores are divided into areas by the type of book shelved there. Walk around the store and record what is shelved in each area indicated on this map:	Area	What is shelved there?
	A	
	B	
	C	
	D	
	E	
	F	
	G	

Paper is good for mobile learning when:

▶ Learners lack mobile devices.

▶ Learning must take place in environments where mobile devices are not allowed, do not work, or might be damaged.

▶ Learning will take longer than the battery life of the device.

Reuse existing content

Mobile phones and tablets are consumer devices. Their immense popularity has spurred the development of vast amounts of content that plays on these devices. Much of this content is free or inexpensive. Some of it is potentially educational. To see examples, peruse the iTunes store, especially the App and iTunesU sections. Or search *public domain learning content*.

Before you develop content, consider whether available content can be adapted to your purposes. So, what kinds of content are available for mobile devices?

▶ **Academic content**. Many universities and colleges now make available substantial works by their faculty and students. These include dissertations, theses, papers, and slides.

▶ **Publicly published materials**. The Internet has enabled a world of publishers of personal and corporate content. Such publications provide presentations and case studies. Just remember to respect the copyright of the publishers of such materials. These include blogs, podcasts, lectures, speeches, product demonstrations, product tutorials, interviews, panel discussions, reports, white papers, and executive briefings.

▶ **Entertainment media**. Media produced for entertainment may have secondary uses for education. Good candidates include world music, movies, TV shows, eBooks, and audio books. Just remember to review copyright restrictions.

▶ **Reference works**. Consulting a reference need not occasion a trip to the library. Many kinds of reference works are available online for use in education and as performance support. These include dictionaries, reference books, textbooks, job aids, reports, Web sites, stock-market reports, historic photos, speeches, flash cards, periodic table, anatomy diagrams, classical music, newspapers, and news feeds.

▶ **Applications**, or *apps* for short, are programs that add capabilities to the mobile device. Some are especially useful for mobile learning, for instance, spreadsheets, presentation slide players, measurement tools, maps, calculators, audio-book players, eBook readers, games, word processors, and bar-code readers.

REAL MOBILE LEARNING

In real mobile learning, we learn from the world rather than from mobile devices. Real mobile learning occurs when people engage objects, locations, and other people outside the classroom or office. The mobile device can provoke and assist such learning activities, but it is not the focus or locus of the activity. Real mobile learning activities are as varied as the things people do out in the real world. Here we consider just a few examples of mobile learning that goes beyond access to conventional learning.

Mobile discovery learning

Discovery learning activities lead learners to discover and develop principles and concepts through observation and experience.

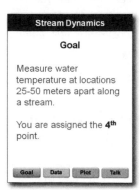

In this example, learners discover principles by interacting with real-world objects, namely temperature probes and a stream.

Five learners (or teams) are assigned the task of analyzing temperature variations along a stream course. They are provisioned with mobile devices equipped with temperature probes. Each learner is assigned to sample a point along the stream.

At the sample point, each learner inserts the probe into the water and taps the **Record** button, which captures the temperature at that point along with its latitude and longitude.

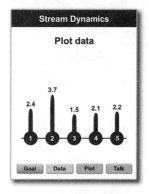

Once the five sample points are captured, each device displays all the data gathered.

Learners then discuss the gathered data, notice trends and anomalies, and hypothesize on the underlying causes.

This hypothesis leads to another round of observation and analysis.

The flow of actions here is much the same as for the virtual-laboratory activity (p 147) as both are based on the classic scientific method.

The mobile discovery activity begins with the concrete assignment to gather data. The device then graphs the data in a way that provokes comparison and analysis.

Discussion leads to a hypothesis or two to explain observed results. Naturally there follows the proposal for more observations to test the hypothesis.

This proposal becomes the assignment for another round of testing.

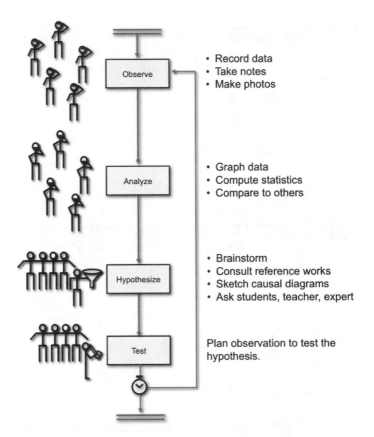

Distance apprenticeship program

For 50,000 years or so, human beings have learned a trade, an art, or a survival skill through apprenticeship, in which an expert or master oversees the work of less-skilled apprentices as they perform successively more difficult pieces of work.

Though widely acknowledged as an effective and enjoyable way to learn, apprenticeship fell out of favor because it was considered too expensive for widespread use. Mobile devices have revived this ancient form of learning. With mobile devices, a single expert can guide the work and learning of many, widely distributed apprentices. Let's see an example of how.

Learning can be initiated by a question from the learner.

The answer may include text, voice, graphics, statistics, or video.

A complete discussion can occur without either expert or apprentice leaving their current location and without a painful interruption of other activities of either expert or learner.

The teacher can enrich learning by asking questions of the apprentice or by assigning the apprentice a specific piece of work.

The apprentice completes the real-world assignment and submits a photo, video, or other evidence of the work.

The expert can provoke and assess learning by asking application-related questions that require thought by the learner.

The expert can offer more than instructions and knowledge. The expert can send encouragement and sympathy as well.

The basic template for distance apprenticeship activities is quite simple, as this diagram shows:

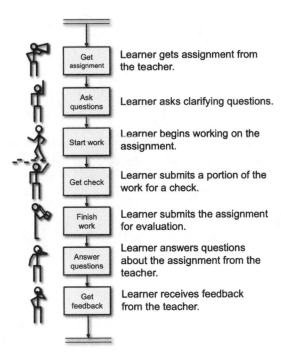

Architecture tour

In this self-guided architectural tour, the learner is guided to discover examples of common styles of domestic 19th Century architecture.

The lesson begins with a simple introduction to the objective.

The learner is told where to go to begin the tour. Both street and GPS coordinates are given.

The lesson reminds the learner to use capabilities of the mobile device.

The learner uses onboard maps and GPS navigation to find the starting point.

The lesson directs the learner to a specific location on the tour.

The learner is required to analyze the construction details of a house and decide its predominant architectural style.

The learner receives feedback. Feedback for the incorrect response would direct attention to architectural features that define the house's style.

The learner receives instructions to a new location. The learner can use the device's maps, GPS, and compass to find the location.

The learner is instructed to verify that the correct house has been found by taking a photo of it—including the learner in the picture.

The learner takes the requested photo, and then uses the built-in e-mail feature of the device's camera to submit the picture.

Inject mobile activities into other forms of learning

Mobile activities can occur within conventional classroom and e-learning lessons. The following diagram shows how the excursion out into the world is sandwiched between activities that prepare the learner for the mobile activity and ones that reconnect the learner with the flow of conventional learning.

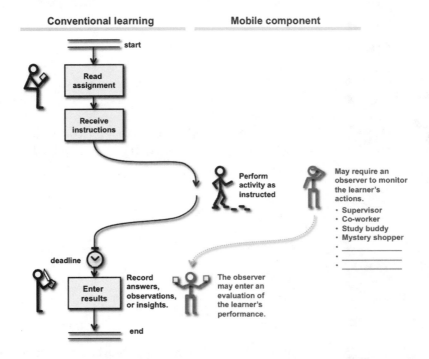

EXTEND CONVENTIONAL ACTIVITIES FOR MOBILE LEARNING

Use the capabilities of mobile learning to enrich and expand conventional e-learning activities. Allow learners to perform activities in any location. Involve real-world objects, people, locales, and events in learning activities. Use the media of mobile devices to capture and share real-world experiences.

Extend Absorb activities for mobile learning

For mobile learning, have learners absorb transmitted information while mobile, capture real-world content for others to absorb, and absorb from real-world experiences.

▶ Make sure that all recorded and live presentations, demonstrations, readings, and stories can be experienced through the mobile device that learners possess. Let learners absorb content where they will apply it.

▶ Have learners in remote locations originate and record content for Absorb activities. Have them, where permitted, use mobile devices to capture speeches, stories, lectures, presentations, demonstrations, workflow procedures, debates, and walkthroughs of public spaces.

▶ Direct learners to locations and events where they can absorb useful content. Have them attend educational events, such as lectures, presentations, demonstrations, plays, and discussions among experts. Direct them on tours of museums, battlefields, libraries, factories, rock quarries, archaeological digs, historic neighborhoods, and other educational spaces.

For more specific ideas for Absorb activities in mobile learning, see sections titled "Design … for mobile learning" throughout Chapter 2.

Extend Do activities for mobile learning

In mobile learning, Do activities can be performed with real-world objects, people, and situations.

▶ Use the mobile device to prove remote performance to an evaluator. Submit a photograph, video clip, or audio recording of physical performance for evaluation. Offer feedback and encouragement to mobile learners by voice, text, or other media.

▶ Provide instructions, job-aids, advice, and background information for real-world mobile activities.

▶ Encourage learners to apply skills in real-world situations, for example, to speak a foreign language on vacation.

▶ Help learners fill in knowledge gaps that prevent fluent performance. For example, provide access to a foreign-language dictionary, a list of keyboard shortcuts, or blueprints for a construction project.

For more specific ideas for Do activities in mobile learning, see sections titled "Design … for mobile learning" throughout Chapter 3.

Extend Connect activities for mobile learning

Use mobile-learning techniques to connect learners with real-world people, situations, problems, objects, and opportunities to apply learning. Here are a few examples to get you started:

▶ Direct learners to environments and places where they can meditate peacefully, contemplate applications of what they are learning, find relevant examples, and evaluate the quality and creativity of work. Use GPS and other location-based technologies to trigger display of related information.

- ▶ Use the calendar function to trigger Connect activities. Periodically have the calendar present a rhetorical question, amazing fact, question to answer by research, or riddle to answer.

- ▶ Enable learners to ask questions, access job aids, and conduct research from the location where they attempt to apply learning.

- ▶ Ensure that all Connect activities can be performed at any time, regardless of the time zone of the learner.

For more specific ideas for Connect activities in mobile learning, see sections titled "Design … for mobile learning" throughout Chapter 4.

IN CLOSING …

Summary

Mobile learning has two meanings: (1) letting mobile learners participate in conventional classroom and e-learning courses and (2) having people learn from objects, places, and people they encounter out in the world.

Mobile learning has compelling advantages: People learn from the whole world, they learn when teachable moments occur, they learn where they will apply learning, they benefit from exercise and variety, and they have many more opportunities to learn.

Before beginning a mobile learning endeavor, consider whether the potential rewards justify the likely costs involved.

In your designs, take into account the situations faced by mobile learners, the environments where learning will occur, and the limitations of learners' devices. Design for learners in noisy, distracting environments with slow, intermittent network connections, using devices with small screens and smaller keyboards.

For more …

Social learning and mobile learning are a natural combination. See Chapter 8 for some ideas on making mobile learning activities more social.

For specific ideas on learning activities for mobile learners, see the "Design … for mobile learning" sections throughout Chapters 2, 3, and 4.

For more on designing mobile learning, search for: *mobile learning design* and *instructional design of mobile learning* or similar phrases. For information on a particular mobile device, search either *features* or *capabilities* and the name of the device

10 Design for the virtual classroom

Designing and delivering instructor-led webinars and courses

Virtual classrooms bring the medieval classroom into the 21st Century. Virtual classrooms use collaboration tools to re-create the structure and learning experiences of a physical classroom. When well designed, they preserve the orderly structure and rich interaction of the classroom while removing the requirement for everyone to be in the same location.

Virtual-classroom programs can be as simple as one-shot, ad hoc Webinars or as complex as formal, semester-long academic courses. In either case, a teacher leads a class of learners through an explicit syllabus of material on a predetermined schedule. While these programs may include many of the activities in Chapters 2, 3, and 4, virtual classrooms also provide new possibilities and require additional design and management.

Virtual classrooms are a special application of social learning. If you have not done so already, scan Chapter 8 before diving into this chapter. You will need to refer to that chapter for some aspects of social learning that are not unique to the virtual classroom, especially discussion-forum activities. This chapter does repeat and restate some of the information from that chapter so you don't have to continually flip back and forth.

CREATE A VIRTUAL CLASSROOM

Why should you use a virtual classroom in your e-learning plans? And how do online presentations and meetings play into the virtual classroom course? Let's see.

Why create a virtual classroom?

Why design e-learning as a virtual classroom? Virtual-classroom programs (events, activities, and entire courses) require a teacher who can lead learners through the subject and learners who can attend online meetings. If you can meet this requirement, virtual-classroom programs offer several strong benefits over standalone e-learning or learner-led social learning.

The teacher can adapt learning to learners. The teacher can directly monitor everything going on in the classroom. The teacher can answer questions and address concerns immediately. The teacher can adjust content and presentation immediately in response to subtle feedback from learners.

The virtual classroom provides the community and discipline some learners need. Being part of a visible group embarked on a common endeavor appeals to a sense of community and tribalism. The requirement to show up at a specific location on a definite schedule enforces a discipline on learners. Direct contact with the teacher along with peer pressure help keep learners on schedule.

Classroom learning is familiar and proven. Learners are familiar with the procedures, rhythms, and presentation methods used in the classroom. Classroom courses have been the standard in education for 500 years or more.

Learning is flexible and active. The class can combine lecture, question and answer, individual and team activities, reading, and testing. Learners can work directly with fellow learners and gain from meaningful conversations with them.

What are Webinars and virtual-classroom courses?

Virtual-classroom programs come in two main types: Webinars and courses.

Webinars are individual online meetings. They typically center on a presentation and include opportunities for learners to ask questions. They may also involve individual and group activities during the meeting. Webinars tend to be informal in tone and lightly structured. Participants are seldom graded rigorously. Think of them as "virtual conference room" meetings.

Virtual-classroom courses are complete programs of learning. They consist of sequences of synchronous and asynchronous events. Among the synchronous events are online meetings, which may include online presentations, Q&A sessions, and both individual and group activities. The asynchronous events may include discussions and individual or group activities between meetings. Virtual-classroom courses typically have the formal structure and rigorous grading of their physical counterparts.

Of course, these two definitions are really ends of a spectrum ranging from a hastily called online meeting intended to deal with a momentary crisis to a detailed and lengthy program of study to cover a large subject.

Let's recap the differences between the two main forms of virtual-classroom programs:

Characteristic	Webinars	Courses
Meetings	One.	Several (or none).
Objectives	One or just a few.	Complete hierarchy of related objectives.
Meeting contains	Presentation and Q&A. May include individual and group activities by learners.	Presentation, Q&A, and individual and group activities by learners.
Outside-the-meeting activities	None.	Individual, group, and discussion activities.
Tone	Informal.	Formal.
Assessment of learners	None.	Rigorous, based on work done.
Time span.	30 to 90 minutes.	6 to 18 weeks.

Think of virtual-classroom courses as a series of Webinars, each with "homework" consisting of a mixture of discussions and individual and group activities.

Decide whether you need a live meeting

You need a good reason to require people to work together. You need an even better reason to require them all to log in at the same time. Should you conduct an online meeting?

No	Yes
Teaching explicit knowledge.	Teaching unstructured, implicit knowledge.
Content requires detailed study.	Learners have many questions.
Learners lack language skills.	Isolated learners prefer learning with others.
Learners have unpredictable schedules.	No time to develop standalone materials.

Laziness on the part of the designer is not a good reason for a meeting. Sad to say, many online meetings occur because the teacher lacked the skills or self-discipline necessary to create materials for learners to consume on their own. If information is simple, post it in a well-designed Web page. If your material needs a little interactivity, the computer can provide that interactivity. Require a good reason for an online meeting.

SELECT AND USE COLLABORATION TOOLS

Computer and network technologies provide a wide range of collaboration tools for person-to-person interaction. These range from simple e-mail to complete online-meeting environments.

Select your collaboration tools

Collaboration tools make it possible for distant learners to communicate freely and to work together on tasks common in the virtual classroom. You will need to consider the various tools and how to use them productively. First, you must decide what kind of person-to-person interaction best furthers the objectives of your project. Then, you must implement this interaction in the form and technology appropriate for your situation.

Consider a variety of tools

By incorporating rich communication and collaboration into our e-learning, we can ensure that learners never lack for that human touch, which is often cited as the reason why face-to-face classrooms are necessary for teaching advanced skills.

Collaboration tools can link a teacher and an individual learner, as well as linking groups of learners.

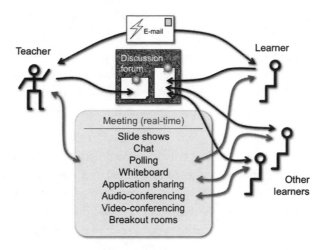

The simplest mechanism is e-mail between the teacher and learner. Often e-mail messages are broadcast, typically from the teacher to announce a change or an event to all learners in a class. Learners can also post messages on a class discussion forum, as can the teacher. Other learners can then read and reply to these messages.

Meeting mechanisms provide real-time exchanges among teachers and learners. Teachers can present slides, much like they would in a physical classroom. Participants can use chat (text-conferencing) to exchange text messages—something like instant e-mail. They can use polls to vote on issues and make choices. Through whiteboard or application-sharing tools, learners can discuss and work together on visual subjects. Learners can use audio-conferencing much as they would a telephone conference call. Those with fast networks can use video-conferencing to swap video images of one another. And, where the group is large, smaller groups of learners can meet in virtual breakout rooms to discuss an issue or work on an activity before rejoining the main meeting.

Pick tools to suit learners

Collaboration tools are technology, but human beings operate them. The most important factors in your choice of collaboration tools are human factors. Let me list a few.

Language fluency. Some collaboration requires greater language skills than others. Unless learners are all fluent in a language, real-time collaboration mechanisms like chat, audio-conferencing, and video-conferencing may frustrate those who would prefer e-mail or discussion forums, which allow more time to comprehend a message and then compose a response.

Accents. Internet audio quality can exacerbate difficulties in understanding speakers with a distinct accent. I took part in one international audio-conference conducted in English in which the Swedes could not understand the Pakistanis, who could not understand the Texan, who could understand everybody except the British, who thought all the Americans sounded like "bad Hollywood movie characters." If accents are a concern, post presentation, transcripts, and Q&A sessions to a discussion forum.

Typing skill. Chat is a spontaneous medium—for fast typists. Unfortunately, many learners are not proficient typists. Some can be embarrassed by their lack of typing skill or left behind by faster typists. If spontaneity is not an objective, move comments and discussion to e-mail or a discussion forum. Or consider using audio-conferencing for fast-moving discussions.

Technical expertise. Some learners have been chatting, texting, and social networking for years. Others are still trying to master the double-click. You need to consider how comfortable learners are with computer and network technologies. How much must learners extend themselves to master collaboration tools? If learners already know how to use a whiteboard, then application sharing is not much of a stretch. If they have just learned to use e-mail, expecting them to master chat, whiteboard, and video-conferencing is probably too much.

Also consider what technical support you can offer. If learners must master collaboration tools on their own, they may become discouraged. If you (or the tool's vendor) provide tutorials and phone support, the task is less daunting.

Enable interpersonal communication

Consider the nature of the interpersonal communication needed. Different degrees of communication require different media. Consider what you need to communicate your message.

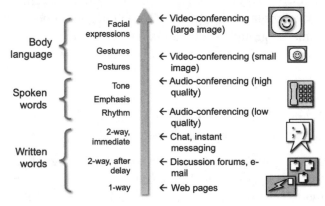

If an exchange of written words is sufficient, you can get by with chat, discussion forum, or just e-mail. On the other hand, if your message involves subtle emotional cues such as gestures, facial expressions, and tone of voice, you may require video-conferencing.

Slide shows

Chat, polling, whiteboard activities, application sharing, audio-conferencing, and video-conferencing are covered in Chapter 8 on social learning. Slide shows and breakout rooms are covered in this chapter because they are most often used as parts of online meetings.

Online slide shows present slides to a distant audience. Instead of watching the slide on a screen at the front of the room, learners watch it on their computer or mobile device.

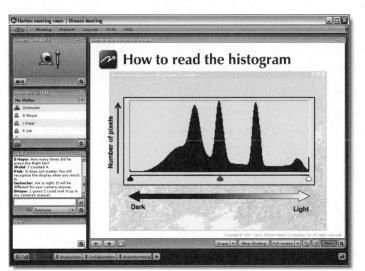

Here we see a slide being given by a presenter. Learners see the slide and hear the presenter speaking about the slide.

The PowerPoint slide is displayed in Adobe Connect.

The slide show feature is among the simplest collaboration mechanisms to use. The presenter creates slides, typically in Microsoft PowerPoint. The presenter may add graphics and animations.

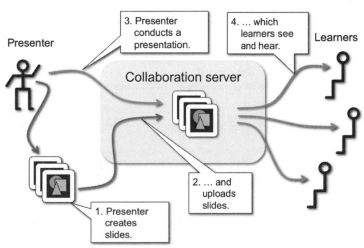

The presenter then uploads the slides to the online-meeting tool. Once the slides are uploaded, the presenter conducts a presentation, that learners see and hear as if in the same room as the presenter.

The presenter can be the teacher, an expert, a guest speaker, or a learner.

When to use slide shows

Use online slide shows for:

▶ Content that is changing right up to the last minute. The teacher can customize the presentation based on learners' responses to previous activities.

▶ Efficiently presenting information on spatial, logical, and mathematical subjects.

▶ Showing visual examples, such as photographs, sketches, or diagrams.

▶ Proven presentations with capable presenters to give them.

▶ Overviews of a subject area or previews of a collaborative activity.

▶ Briefing learners who have not yet learned to use other collaboration tools or are not ready to collaborate.

Unless you have good reasons to use a live presentation, record the presentation and let learners take it at their convenience.

Best practices for using slide shows

If using slide shows as part of your online meetings:

▶ **Keep slides simple and visual**. If possible, include meaningful animation. Do not just fill slides with text and bullet lists.

▶ **Keep text legible**. Make sure a learner with less than perfect vision can read all text even when leaning back with feet propped up on the desk.

▶ **Include some interactivity**, such as a poll or whiteboard activity, every 3 to 5 slides.

▶ **Use the whiteboard feature** to write and draw on slides. Fill in blanks. Check off answers. Complete drawings.

▶ **Make some change to a slide every 20 seconds or sooner**. Trigger an animation. Add a new element to a drawing.

▶ **Test your slides beforehand**. Your slides may look or behave differently depending on the tool you are using.

▶ **Record the presentation** either in the online meeting tool or another tool. Make the recording available to those who cannot attend the live presentation or who want to see the presentation but not attend the course.

Special tip: If you repeatedly give the same presentation, wait and record the third presentation before making it available to learners. Why the third one? It should be smooth by then, but still fresh.

Breakout rooms

Breakout rooms let small groups of learners conduct their own meetings within the main meeting. They are a feature of some online meeting tools. Breakout rooms may be instigated by the teacher or by learners.

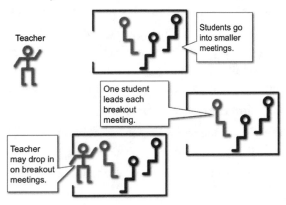

One student leads each meeting. The teacher may drop in on the individual meetings. After a while, the teacher ends the smaller meetings and resumes the original meeting.

When to use breakout rooms

Use breakout rooms for small-group work. Breakout rooms are especially good when the size of the overall meeting is inhibiting some learners and when activities benefit from a more intimate scale. They are also good for compound activities when part of the activity is done in a large group and part in a small group.

Use breakout rooms for:

- ▶ Teamwork and small-group projects.
- ▶ Competitive problem solving. Each group tries to solve a problem quicker or better than other groups.
- ▶ Small-group brainstorming.
- ▶ Team design of components of a system.
- ▶ Analyzing situations from different perspectives.
- ▶ Preparation for debates between pro and con groups.
- ▶ Alternative scenario resolutions where the teacher presents a general scenario calling for a decision. Each breakout room is free to come up with a different solution.

Do not use breakout rooms in one-time meetings or short courses. Use them throughout a longer course when learners have time to master the operation and conventions of breakout rooms.

Best practices for breakout rooms

Breakout rooms are relatively new in online meetings. If you use them, make sure the experience is a positive one for learners.

- ▶ Specify the goal and time available for the breakout activity. Give learners a clear assignment. Not "Discuss the issues," but "Suggest 3 improvements."

- ▶ Plan what learners will do before, during, and after the breakout activity. For example, start by introducing a problem to the class as a whole and dividing it into sub-problems. Then, in breakout rooms have each team find a solution to one of the sub-problems. Finally, require the whole class to consolidate individual group work.

- ▶ Assign three to seven learners to a breakout room.

- ▶ Appoint a room leader. Train the room leader beforehand. Teach the leader how to summon help.

- ▶ Ensure that the teacher visits breakout rooms often, especially during the first few breakout sessions.

- ▶ Streamline the process of moving into and out of the room. Warn learners before moving them into or out of the breakout room.

CONDUCT ONLINE MEETINGS

Online meetings are live, real-time sessions that use some combination of chat, virtual polls, whiteboards, application sharing, and audio- and video-conferencing. Online meetings are complex endeavors that require painstaking preparation, management, and follow-up.

Plan the meeting

Whether part of an ongoing virtual-classroom course or a one-time Webinar, online meetings require careful planning.

Decide roles

Before any online meeting, spell out the roles of the teacher, learners, guests, and others. For each phase of the activity, decide who will lead, who will speak, and who will listen. Also decide who will summarize and evaluate the event.

Phase	Person			
	Instructor	**Learner**	**Guest**	**Other**
Introduction (5 min) The instructor introduces the guest speaker.	Presents	Listens		
Presentation (25 min) The guest speaker presents original material.		Listens	Presents	**Producer:** Controls the cameras, monitors the schedule, and cues the instructor and the presenter.
Question & answer (20 min) The instructor moderates as learners ask and the guest speaker answers questions.	Moderates	Asks	Answers	
Summary (5 min) The guest speaker recaps the presentation and answers to questions.			Summarizes	
Evaluation (5 min) The instructor reviews the event, notes successes, and suggests improvements.	Evaluates			

Here is a simple plan for a one-hour guest lecture. Though simple, this plan spells out the main responsibilities and roles of participants during each phase of the event. It forms the basis for more detailed plans.

If the event is complex or involves tight interaction, you may want to prepare and distribute an agenda or script detailing the exact sequence of events.

Schedule the meeting

The ideal online meeting would be a 60- to 90-minute meeting held sometime between 9 AM and 1 PM on Tuesday. I've never been able to schedule a meeting that was ideal for everyone involved. So, read on.

Pick the best day of the week

Most experienced participants of online meetings feel Tuesday is the best day to schedule an online event. Everybody is still fresh. Monday has been used to take care of start-of-week emergencies. Avoid weekends and Friday afternoon—potential attendees are disengaged from work-related activities. (Note: If the workweek for your learners is not Monday through Friday, adjusts these recommendations, for example substituting the first workday of the week where I wrote Monday.)

Pick the best time of day

Start the meeting at 9:00 AM or later. People are at work, have checked phone messages and e-mails, and consumed the requisite number of caffeinated beverages.

Try to end the meeting before 1:00 PM so that everybody still has time to get lunch. After lunch, learners may be too drowsy to participate fully.

By all means avoid normal sleep time (9 PM to 8 AM) if at all possible.

Set the meeting length

The shortest time for an online meeting is usually 60 minutes. Anything shorter and little of value gets accomplished. Remember that introductions and set-up take time out of that hour.

Try to conclude the meeting within 90 minutes. Longer than that, people fidget and lose concentration. Longer meetings are hard for busy people to fit into their schedules. If you must make the meeting longer, try to keep it to no more than 2 hours and allow a couple of 5- to 10-minute breaks.

Adjust for time-zone compression

Consider where your learners are. It is seldom a problem if learners are spread over a few time zones; say across Europe, within Australia, or within the contiguous United States. Within the contiguous United States, for example, learners may span four time zones. That means you would need to hold your meeting from noon to 1:30 PM Eastern Time, which would be 9:00 to 10:30 Pacific Time.

Whatever you do, try to hold the meeting while everyone is normally awake. And consider whether learners in more distant time zones can log in from home.

Prepare learners for the meeting

Help learners get ready for the meeting—before the meeting. Do not waste meeting time on things that could be done before the meeting.

Inform learners of the meeting

Provide learners the information they need to participate in the meeting. This gives them fair warning and ensures they have time to prepare for the meeting. What should you do before the meeting?

- ▶ Advise learners of the goals and objectives of the meeting.
- ▶ Conduct an audience survey to identify who will attend and what they need.
- ▶ Publish the biography of the teacher and guest speakers.
- ▶ Tell learners how to set up their computers.
- ▶ Publish standards of behavior.

Make pre-meeting assignments

One way to make meetings more productive is to give learners an assignment to complete before the live session. Begin the live event with a discussion of the assignment. Reward learners who complete the assignment and are well prepared for the opening discussion.

Send related information ahead

If learners must refer to information during an online meeting, send that information ahead of time so that they can review the material and think of questions to ask the presenter. What kinds of materials should you send?

▶ Handouts so learners have a place to take notes.

▶ Reports, white papers, position statements, and other reference documents.

▶ Detailed examples and case studies.

▶ Biographies of the speakers.

At a minimum, provide learners with a copy of the slides in a format that lets them comfortably follow along with the presenter. This way the presenter's slides can use smaller text and more detailed graphics.

Introduce participants

Do not waste time introducing everyone during an online meeting. Have participants send or post biographies before joining the meeting. Include a biography of any guest speaker along with the announcement of the live event. That way the teacher's introduction of the guest speaker can be brief.

Plan follow-up activities

Do not waste valuable meeting time performing closing activities that could be done after the meeting. End the meeting with a strong, memorable activity. Afterwards, perform the routine follow-up work, such as:

▶ Gather learners' feedback with an asynchronous poll.

▶ Post reference materials to a discussion forum along with a transcript or recording of the meeting.

▶ Publish revised handouts.

Make contingency plans

The best way to prevent problems is to anticipate them. Brainstorm to list things that could go wrong. Plan what you will do if any of these events occur. Here are some not-too-remote possibilities:

▶ The speaker has laryngitis. Have a backup speaker ready to take over.

▶ The speaker's computer crashes. Switch to a backup computer. While correcting the problem conduct an impromptu Q&A session. Switch to a second copy of the presentation on the moderator's computer.

▶ Hecklers or nitpickers disrupt the meeting. The moderator can cut-off an individual learner's access to specific meeting tools or expel a disruptive learner from the meeting.

▶ Phone-conferencing or Internet audio fails. Switch to a backup audio channel. Send attendees on a break. Provide instructions on how to re-join the audio portion of the meeting.

Pack a conversational first-aid kit

Sometimes the best spontaneous comments are the ones you prepare ahead of time. Prepare comments or questions that will start useful conversations or revive flagging ones. Have them ready in case the conversation stalls. Here are some conversation resuscitators:

▶ Why do you say so?

▶ Where else might that idea apply?

▶ Do you have any doubts?

▶ What if X were different?

▶ Does the idea have any side effects?

▶ What else?

▶ How much would that cost?

▶ What are the practical applications of this idea?

Prepare for the meeting

Planning the online meeting is not enough. You must still prepare to conduct the meeting. Good planning and preparation almost guarantee a successful live meeting. It certainly lowers the anxiety and blood pressure of the presenter. Expect to spend 5 to 10 hours preparing for each hour of the event.

Rehearse completely

About three days before the meeting, rehearse the whole presentation and all collaborative activities with a remote assistant who plays the role of a learner. Hold the practice session at the same time of day as the real meeting. Test for speed and reliability of the network as well as the ability of the remote assistant to participate fully. Make sure the tools work reliably and that the presenter is confident using them. Be sure to:

▶ **Upload materials for the presentation**. At the end of the rehearsal, do not delete these materials. More than once, I have been unable to load materials on the day of the actual presentation. The rehearsal materials saved me.

▶ **Practice showing all media**. That means go through all slides, polls, Web sites, and applications. Practice interacting with your assistant.

▶ **Make a list of things that could go wrong**. Write them down on index cards and shuffle the deck. Every five minutes during the rehearsal, draw a card and pretend that the problem on the card just occurred. Practice your response.

▶ **Time the rehearsal**. The actual class will take 20 to 40% longer than the rehearsal. Learners interrupt to ask questions. Minor technical glitches occur and have to be dealt with on the spot.

▶ **If you discover problems, fix them and repeat the rehearsal again**. I like to schedule my first rehearsal three days before the actual event. That way I have time to fix problems and conduct another rehearsal or two.

Enlist help

It is difficult for a lone teacher to carry out all the duties of conducting a vibrant online meeting. Get help.

▶ **Hire a producer**. Have an off-screen producer guide all on-screen activities. The producer can time and pace the event. Using hand signals or earphones, the producer can cue and coach the teacher. If a guest speaker conducts the session, the teacher can serve as the producer.

▶ **Hire a sidekick**. Have a second on-air person to interact with the teacher, ask the teacher questions, and take over if the primary teacher runs into a problem. While one person is presenting, another can be answering questions in chat or loading material to address an issue raised earlier by learners.

Set up the workstation

Arrange the presenter's workstation to encourage a lively, professional performance. Here is the setup we use:

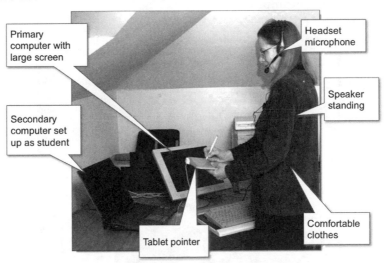

Dozens and dozens of online presentations have taught us some valuable lessons:

▶ **Present standing up**. You can rock and sway. Your chest gets a full dose of air. Your voice sounds more resonant. You can gesture fully.

▶ **Wear a headset microphone**. That keeps the microphone at a constant position relative to your mouth, minimizing the annoying variations in audio level that keep learners adjusting the volume on their computers.

▶ **Run your presentation on a powerful computer** with lots of memory and a large screen. You do not want to risk overloading your computer, which is a real risk if you use application sharing and Internet audio.

▶ **Monitor your presentation from a secondary computer** set up to mimic the computer and connection experienced by learners. Time actions and tailor comments to the way the presentation appears on this secondary computer.

▶ **Wear comfortable clothes**. For me, comfortable clothes are baggy shorts and a Hawaiian shirt. My partner is most comfortable when dressed to the nines. Whatever makes the presenter comfortable makes the presentation better.

▶ **Use a tablet pointer** if drawing or writing in whiteboard activities. The difference in legibility and writing speed justifies the expense.

▶ **Keep emergency supplies near at hand**. These include tissues, a glass of water, and a phone set to silent mode with the meeting tool's tech support number on speed dial.

About half an hour before the meeting, I shut down and restart all the computers and network equipment I will be using. Perhaps I am just superstitious.

Arrange your screen

About 15 minutes before you begin the meeting, arrange your screen to get everything where you can find it. For example:

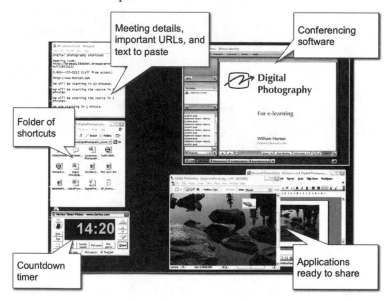

What do you need to have ready at hand?

▶ **Meeting software**. Start the meeting software early. Get logged in and set up. Then shrink the window of the conferencing software until you get ready to start.

- **Folder of shortcuts**. Create shortcuts to documents you will share, to slides you will show, and to anything else you might need to refer to during the meeting. No one wants to see the teacher rooting through folders looking for a file to show. Be sure to include a shortcut to the text file containing all the text you might need to paste.

- **Countdown timer**. I use an on-screen timer to count down the time remaining until the meeting starts. Then I reset the timer to the time remaining in the meeting.

- **Applications to share**. Start up all the applications and open all the documents you will share. If your computer does not have enough memory to run that many applications at the same time, consider not using application sharing. At least have shortcuts to the items you will share.

- **Text to paste**. Put all the text you might need to enter into a plain text document. For most of us without perfect typing skills, it is easier to copy and paste text. Include the URL of the meeting, account and meeting IDs, passwords, and announcements you will need to make in chat. I also include the phone numbers to join the phone conference and to report technical problems.

Set up the meeting room

Open the virtual meeting room early, especially if people need to download materials, obtain players, or phone in separately. Half an hour is not too much. Ten minutes is not nearly enough.

If possible, set up a private meeting for the presenter and producer before the main meeting begins. That way they can talk and rehearse without the rest of the participants noticing.

Specify how to pass control

For chat, audio-conferencing, video-conferencing, whiteboard, application sharing, and other multi-participant activities, make sure all participants know who has control and how control is passed. Otherwise, frustration dances with chaos to a tune played by confusion.

It may help to define modes of control, each with clear expectations and protocols for passing control. Here are some common modes:

- **Lecture mode**. The teacher alone can present. Everyone else watches and listens. No one can interrupt the teacher. Questions can be typed into chat, but the teacher is not expected to stop and answer them until a Q&A session.

- **Q&A mode**. Learners ask questions that a presenter answers. Learners may type their questions into chat or raise their hands to request the microphone.

10

Design for the virtual classroom

▶ **Moderated mode**. The moderator leads a discussion. Although all learners have a chance to speak, they can do so only after being recognized by the moderator. Learners can make statements, respond to earlier statements, ask questions, or answer questions.

Announce the meeting

Announce the live event in plenty of time for learners to prepare for it and to fit it into their busy schedules. Provide all the information learners will need.

▶ **Purpose**. What exactly will learners get out of attending the event?

▶ **Time**. When does the event begin and how long does it last? Remember to specify a time zone or use UTC or GMT times. How early should learners log in? Ten or 15 minutes should get everybody ready to go.

▶ **Procedure**. How do learners join the meeting? What is the address of the event and how do participants enter the event? (Include a hyperlink in the announcement.) Are specific user IDs and passwords necessary? If the meeting uses a separate phone connection, what is the phone number? Make sure you provide a number that works internationally.

▶ **Required**? Is attendance mandatory or optional? How much does the event count toward a final grade?

▶ **Learning preparation**. What must learners do before the event? What must they read? Are there course topics or pre-tests they should complete?

▶ **Computer setup**. How should learners configure their hardware and software for best results? Must learners download and install any special software? Are there sample files they need to acquire?

▶ **Tools to be used**. Will the event use chat, audio, video, application sharing, whiteboard, polling, or other technologies? Learners should learn to use these technologies before the event, not during it.

▶ **Alternative**. What should learners do if technical difficulties prevent them from entering the meeting or force last-minute cancellation? What should they do if they are not available at the specified time?

▶ **Contact**. Whom should learners contact for more information?

Manage the live online meeting

It's show time! You have prepared. You have rehearsed. You are ready to go.

Rely on your producer. Have someone other than the teacher, or main presenter, manage the live event. A producer can mind the agenda, call time on long-winded speakers, and handle minor emergencies. An active producer allows the presenter and teacher to concentrate on the needs of learners.

Keep learners active. Make presentations dynamic. Use visuals and other media to focus attention on key concepts. Never become a talking head. Or worse, an automatic typewriter. Explain any pauses over five seconds.

Interact frequently. Never present for more than five minutes without some form of interaction with learners. Spend 40 to 60% of the time interacting with learners. Answer questions every 15 or 20 minutes. Or state that you will do so at the end.

Call on learners by name. In a physical classroom, the teacher can call on people by just pointing to them or just looking their way. In the online event, the teacher must call on people by name. That means the teacher must have a list of the names of all participants, not just the screen names or e-mail addresses displayed by the meeting tool.

Ask more questions than you answer. If you answer a question for a learner, immediately ask the learner a question to test whether he or she understood. Clear up any misunderstandings and point learners to resources they can use to answer their own questions.

Be spontaneous. Script out every session, but leave 30 to 40% of the time free to answer unanticipated questions, go into more detail about issues that deeply interest learners, and interject insights that occur to you at the moment.

Keep a back channel open. In face-to-face meetings, we scan the eye gazes, nodding heads, and smiles of meeting participants. And we listen for vocal utterances like "uh-huh" and "OK." In online meetings, teachers must find substitutes to test whether their message is getting through. Keep open an interactive communications channel such as chat so that learners can interrupt if they do not understand something. Consider pausing after each stage of a presentation to get feedback. (See "Back channel for presentations" in Chapter 8 for more on designing a back channel.)

Turn off unused media. Turn off media you are not using at the moment. If you are just talking, turn off the video and leave the audio on.

Maintain control and focus. During online meetings, learners must all be "on the same page." If questions or discussion drift too far, re-establish the subject under discussion. Terminate activities that continually drift off subject; but, give learners a chance to explore the limits and fringes of ideas before jerking them back on course.

Attend to all learners. Give attention to all learners, not just those who stand out. Greet participants as they enter the session. Learners who have their microphones turned up will sound louder than others. Those who sit close to their video cameras will seem larger. Learn to ignore these false cues and give equal attention to all learners. Respond to a raised hand in 30 to 60 seconds.

Stay organized. Pause before speaking. Clear raised hands before proceeding. Remember to save polls, markups, and chat. Use available time, such as while learners are filling in a poll or thinking of answers to a question, to relax and gather your thoughts. Run through a mental checklist of what you may want to do next.

Activate meetings

Most online meetings are as dull as the worst classroom meetings. Do not accept that as the norm. Activate your e-learning meetings.

Avoid one-way lectures

Do not conduct one-way lectures—or if you do, prerecord them and let learners play them at their own convenience. We have all heard of learners sending their camcorders to class. Learners record the lectures so they can view the presentation at their convenience and fast-forward through the useless parts. There is no reason to require learners to adhere to a schedule merely to receive information.

Move lectures and slow activities outside the meeting. Let learners listen to recordings of earlier recorded meetings. For presentations, record the presentation. Rather than perform lengthy activities during the meeting, have learners perform the activity before class and use class time to discuss the results.

Turn lectures into workshops

Convert passive presentations to active learning. The only real requirement is creativity. Here are just a few ways to transform boring lectures into engaging workshops:

- ▶ Pick learners randomly to answer questions.
- ▶ Periodically call on learners to recap or summarize the meeting so far.
- ▶ Perform audience-completion activities by chat. Have learners fill in the blanks on slides, for example.
- ▶ Require communal responses. Let the class vote on the outcome of a scenario, what to talk about, how to solve a problem, the next step to take in a simulation. Let the class rate solutions to problems. Treat bullet items as true/false questions. Have learners raise hands to signify true.
- ▶ Have a learner highlight your slides as you talk.
- ▶ Require a response: "Raise your hand if you do **not** have a question."
- ▶ Have learners make short presentations. Give learners a template to guide the content and format.
- ▶ Let learners suggest alternatives to scenarios and examples. For instance, let learners suggest different figures in a calculation, different assumptions and theories to explain

an event, different wording of text in an advertisement or contract, and different ways to solve a problem.

▶ Use debates to promote deeper learning. Before the meeting, have learners prepare both pro and con positions. Pick speakers randomly for each position. Or choose learners at random to play the devil's advocate by arguing assigned positions.

▶ Play the Who-Wants-to-Be-a-Learner game. Pick one learner to be the contestant. Ask the learner questions. The learner can use a lifeline to ask another learner or can poll the audience.

▶ Make learners spot truth. The teacher makes plausible sounding statements that learners must label as true or false.

Make participants visible

Participants in an online meeting need a way to know who's there. Since classmates are not physically present, learners may not be sure who is listening and watching. They may feel alone or may hesitate for fear of offending unseen watchers. To enhance awareness:

▶ Publish a roster.
▶ Periodically require everyone to say something, even just "I'm still here."
▶ Reveal the screen names of participants.

Equally, respect people's privacy. Do not require them to reveal their identity if they do not want to. Let them pick their own screen names by which they are known in the meeting.

Use icebreaker games to get learners started

Getting started in an online meeting can be difficult if learners are strangers or are anxious about the technology. Consider some quick, simple activities to engage learners, relieve anxiety, and introduce fellow learners.

▶ Put a world map in a whiteboard and have learners point to where they live now, where else they have lived, and where they have visited recently.

▶ In chat, have learners enter their job titles and the organizations they work for.

▶ In whiteboard have learners create a communal painting or graffiti. Consider using an image related to the subject of the meeting.

▶ Have participants pronounce their names in audio or video.

▶ Invite learners to upload pictures of something they have created.

Avoid trivial activities that communicate nothing substantial about learners. Remember, the purpose of such activities is to give learners a non-threatening way to use the collaboration tools while sharing information about themselves.

Include follow-up activities

After the meeting, direct learners to perform follow-up activities:

Assign make-up work

Assign make-up work for learners who could not attend the meeting. As a minimum, have truant learners play a recording of the live meeting so they can read, hear, and see what they missed. You might also require that they write a summary of the meeting and post it to the class discussion forum.

Continue the discussion after class

To encourage learners to continue conversations started during a meeting, start a chat session immediately after the class. This gives learners a chance to ask the teacher questions they were too shy to ask in class (or just thought of) and enables learners to discuss points that especially interested them during the meeting. During the meeting, invite participants to contribute to a discussion thread on the subject. Start the thread with transcripts of the meeting and its follow-up chat session.

Evaluate the event

To improve live events, conduct a formal evaluation, something like this:

- ▶ The teacher critiques the meeting, noting what worked well and what could be done better next time.
- ▶ Learners suggest how they could have done better.
- ▶ The teacher privately comments on participants' behavior, especially if not appropriate. Common problems might include verbally abusing others, dominating the scarce time, and asking questions outside the subject of the meeting.

Thank outside helpers

The teacher (or learners) should write thank-you notes to all those besides staff members who helped them in the meeting. A token gift is appropriate for experts who made presentations or consented to interviews.

DESIGN WEBINARS

The term *Webinar* is a contraction of "Web seminar." A Webinar is usually a single online meeting devoted to accomplishing a specific goal. (Multiple related Webinars are called a Webinar series.) Webinars are not restricted to learning. They are common in sales and marketing too. In this chapter, we will restrict ourselves to Webinars whose purpose is to educate participants rather than to sell them something.

When to use Webinars

Webinars are good for quickly and inexpensively accomplishing simple goals, where anything more extensive would be overkill. Consider a Webinar when these conditions occur.

▸ **To accomplish a single learning objective** with only a few sub-objectives. If you identify more than a handful of objectives, consider some other form. Use a Webinar to teach a single procedure, task, product feature, policy, principle, process, or regulation.

▸ **For a one-time need**. If you only need to accomplish the learning objective this one time, a Webinar may be the most economical and effective way. Consider events that occur just once but do require learning. For example, you might hold a Webinar to prepare workers to upgrade from Version 1.1.1 to 1.1.2 of an accounting program.

▸ **For a limited audience**. If you have to teach only a couple dozen learners, a Webinar should be your first choice. For any number up to a hundred, a Webinar should still be considered.

▸ **To teach *how* to learn a subject**. If your goal is not to teach learners all of a subject but to teach them how to learn that subject on their own, a Webinar may be the right balance of instruction and answering questions. Such Webinars typically define the subject, introduce the terminology and structure of the field, and tell learners where and how to search for learning materials.

▸ **To convey incremental information**. For accomplishing a Know objective for learners already familiar with the basics of a field, the Webinar may be ideal. Use a Webinar to report a new discovery, point out new resources, refine interpretations of a policy, update a procedure, or announce a new rule. Learners must be knowledgeable enough to apply the new information.

Webinars are short and simple. They work best for accomplishing a specific objective for a small group of people over a brief period of time.

Pick activities to teach

Webinars typically consist of a presentation followed by a Q&A session and possibly some other activity by learners. Each of these activities serves to accomplish the learning objective of the Webinar.

Presentation

The core of most Webinars is a presentation, such as a slide show or demonstration. In the presentation part of the Webinar, the presenter leads the Webinar while learners watch and listen. The two important elements for successful Webinar presentations are the presenter and the content of the presentation.

Pick the best presenter

Pick the best possible presenter for your Webinar. Ask, "Who can best convey the required information and best inspire learners to apply it?" Consider these candidates:

- ▶ **Teacher, instructor, or trainer**. Pick someone proficient in leading online meetings, in presenting information visually and verbally, and in encouraging learners. Allow enough time for the presenter to perfect the presentation.

- ▶ **Subject-matter expert**. Someone who knows the subject can often be ready to present on short notice. The subject-matter expert may, however, have trouble simplifying the subject to fit the level of learners. Subject-matter experts can include specialists from other departments in your organization or outside consultants.

- ▶ **Business leader**. For business subjects, a presentation by an executive or senior manager may add credibility and excitement. The presence of a high-ranking leader says that the event is important and that participants are lucky to participate.

- ▶ **Inspirational speaker**. If learners are discouraged or skeptical—or if you are trying to accomplish a Believe or Feel objective, consider a presenter who can convince and motivate learners.

- ▶ **Interviewer**. The presentation may consist of an expert answering the questions of an interviewer. Bring in an interviewer when the expert is shy, disorganized, or not accustomed to presenting.

- ▶ **Panel of experts**. Rather than one presenter, use multiple. Let them present by discussing the subject among themselves or by answering questions posed by the teacher. A panel works well for complex subjects that require multiple perspectives.

- ▶ **Learner**. In social learning, learners take on the role of teachers. Consider having a learner prepare a presentation and give it as part of a Webinar.

In picking a presenter consider the candidate's knowledge of the subject and ability to convey that knowledge in a convincing and engaging way.

Pick the right kind of presentation

Select the type presentation to match the objective of the Webinar. Consider live versions of the kinds of presentations suggested in Chapter 2. These include slide shows, physical demonstrations, software demonstrations, interviews, panel discussions, speeches, and stories. If there is not time to develop a presentation from scratch, see if you can modify an existing presentation.

Question-and-answer (Q&A) session

The second essential component of the Webinar is an opportunity for learners to ask questions. (See page 176 for how to design questioning activities.) Typically, questioning occurs immediately after the presentation during a designated question-and-answer session. If the subject is complex, the speaker may pause at logical breaks in the presentation to take questions from learners. A third possibility is to set up a back channel (p. 469) so learners can pose questions as the presentation is going on.

A special form of questioning and discussion occurs in the symposium pattern of interaction (p. 413) where the audience asks questions and discusses issues with a panel of experts. This form of questioning can be extended to encourage learners to answer questions posed by other learners.

In-meeting activities

Webinars can also have learners engage in both group and individual learning activities to practice what they are learning. Learners might be given a small piece of work to do and asked to rejoin the meeting in 10 minutes to show their results. Or small groups of learners might move into breakout rooms (p. 547) where they meet privately to perform an assigned group activity before rejoining the main meeting and reporting on their results.

In-meeting activities are more common in virtual classroom courses than in Webinars. This is not surprising. Webinars are typically short, usually an hour in length. After the presentation and question-and-answer activities, there may be little time left for other activities. The lack of time is compounded by the fact that in a one-shot Webinar, learners may be strangers to one another and may be unfamiliar with how to operate the online meeting tools. In Webinars, consider shortening the presentation and using time to have learners practice what they are learning.

DESIGN VIRTUAL-CLASSROOM COURSES

Successful virtual-classroom courses depend more on human interaction than on technological infrastructure. The secret of success seems to be a carefully orchestrated set of learning experiences and a responsive teacher who attends to the learning needs of all members of the class.

We have already reviewed techniques for two important parts of a virtual course, namely meetings (p. 548) and discussions (Chapter 8). Now we will look at best practices for the course as a whole.

Select a qualified teacher

The quality of instruction in the virtual classroom depends on the preparation and talent of the teacher. No amount of instructional design can compensate for an unprepared or incompetent teacher. The skills required in the virtual classroom are similar to those used in the physical classroom—but with some crucial differences.

These differences include:

▶ **Learners are not physically present**. The teacher must "read" them not through posture and facial expressions but through tone of voice or even their hastily typewritten words.

▶ **The teacher must communicate through the media available**: displayed words, spoken words, slides, sketches, demonstrations, and video. The teacher must be technically proficient in producing these media and the tools that transmit them. A commanding stage presence may be less effective than a well-modulated voice, swift typing skills, and coordinated operation of multiple computer programs.

▶ **Learners rely less on the teacher**. Lacking direct face-to-face contact with the teacher, learners will communicate among themselves. The teacher must encourage such "talking in class" and make it productive—even if this makes learners less dependent on and attentive to the teacher. The teacher must be willing to move from classroom commander to virtual valet.

What attitudes do teachers need?

Success as an online teacher is as much a matter of attitude as knowledge and skills. What are some necessary attitudes for online teachers?

> **Egolessness**: "I want to help people, not just be a sage on a stage."

> **Validity**: "E-learning is a valuable form of instruction."

> **Confidence**: "I can do this!"

Egotistical teachers are more of a problem than a solution. Be on guard against signs of too much ego, such as statements like these:

▶ "Just point the camera at me."

▶ "I don't need to rehearse. I've taught this 20 times in the classroom."

▶ "Students want to see and hear me, not some stupid animation."

What skills are required?

The skills of an online teacher are not the same as those of a classroom teacher. Here is a comparison of the main skills of each:

In a physical classroom

▶ Subject-matter knowledge.
▶ Authoritative tone of voice.
▶ Gestures and body language.
▶ Legible handwriting.
▶ Basic PowerPoint skills.

In a virtual classroom

▶ Subject-matter knowledge.
▶ Well-modulated tone of voice.
▶ Writing and typing.
▶ Ability to operate collaboration tools fluently.
▶ Advanced PowerPoint skills, such as animation.

Require experience first

Teaching in the virtual classroom is a challenge for even experienced teachers. Before letting teachers teach solo, require potential online teachers to:

▶ Experience a dozen online meetings.

▶ Rehearse three times with an experienced online teacher.

▶ Assist in three online meetings conducted by a proven online teacher.

▶ Teach once with a backup teacher available.

▶ Review their online performance with a proven online teacher.

It can take months before teachers become as capable, fluent, and confident online as in the physical classroom. Start developing your online teachers now. And do not quit. Technologies will continue to develop as fast as teachers can incorporate them into their classes.

Teach the class, don't just let it happen

The teacher must actively lead the class by setting the pace, making sure that learners are participating, and overcoming problems.

Contact learners individually. Call or e-mail learners individually to let them know you view them as individuals and to listen to any concerns they may have. If possible, meet them in person. For one online class, I discovered that half my learners would be at a professional conference I was attending. We spent a few productive hours together.

Help classmates get to know one another. Have learners post their biographies. Then have learners examine the biographies of their classmates to find one common interest or other significant similarity.

Stay on the published schedule. If you publish a schedule, stick to the schedule. Remote learners and those with busy schedules depend on the course schedule to arrange their work and personal calendars to fit the course.

Keep office hours. Make yourself available certain times during the week. Learners may feel reluctant to call you unless you sanction the activity. Unless you set specific hours, calls may come while you are dining or sleeping.

Pace learners. Space out assignments and deadlines. Ensure that the amount of work required of learners is consistent from week to week. Remember that earlier activities may seem more daunting than later ones after learners have become familiar with the course and its technologies. Enforce deadlines so the whole class is working on the same material and can help one another.

Let learners work ahead. Publish the entire syllabus at the beginning of the class. Assign class-long requirements, such as large projects and general readings, at the beginning of the class so that those who want to can start early. Those who have to miss a week can do work ahead of time so it is easier for them to catch up.

Do not spend too much time teaching the course software. Learners become frustrated when too much course time is spent learning how to operate the course software. Refer learners to other sources or teach such skills outside required events.

Plan predictable learning cycles

A course is not a one-shot event. Nor should it be an aimless ramble through the subject. The best structure for an online course may be a predictable learning cycle, synchronized with class meetings. For example, here is the cycle of events for each week of a course:

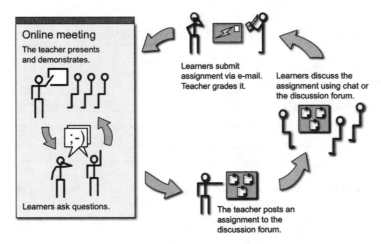

Such a cycle of repeated events makes the learning more predictable and lets learners concentrate on their studies rather than continually mastering new types of learning experiences or responding to surprising new requests. Variety comes in the actual assignments.

In designing your e-learning, you must specify the learning experiences that will teach— and you must decide what materials—online and otherwise—will be necessary to effect those learning experiences.

Here you see a synopsis of such a plan for a 6-week digital photography course. Each item shown here required more detailed specification before it could be created for use in the course.

	1 The new world	2 Shoot to edit	3 Edit to show	4 Fixing problems	5 Histograms	6 Artistic effects
Class meeting						
Presentation	How digital is different	Capturing the most editable image. Demo of difference in Photoshop.	Demo: Editing your image.	Demo: Correcting exposure, contrast, perspective, blur, noise, color, and cropping.	How histograms help prevent and correct problems. Demo in camera and in editing program.	Demo filters in Photoshop. Plea for voluntary restraint.
Activities	Identify assumptions carried over from film photography.	Identify camera settings that produce an editable image.	Identify edits needed in a series of photographs.	Identify problems and suggest ways to fix them.	Match histogram and photos. Suggest ways to edit the histogram.	Match effect and filter. Suggest effects to use.
Assignments						
Hands-on (individual)	Submit your best and worst digital photo.	Submit images shot to edit and shot to show.	Edit the photograph shot to edit.	Fix three of your worst photographs.	Use the histogram to improve a shot and to edit it.	Apply effects to three photos.
Discussion (group)	List and prioritize differences between digital and film photography.	Create a checklist for shooting with editing in mind.	Advice on using Photoshop or other tool to edit photographs.	Post a bad photo, suggest edits for others' photos, and post a fixed version.	Catalog the locations of histograms in cameras and editing tools.	Ethical rules for modifying photos. Best practices for artistic effects.
Scavenger hunt	How digital photography is different.	Characteristics of an editable image.	Instructions on editing digital photographs.	Books, tutorials, and demos on fixing photos.	Find histograms in your camera and editing tool.	Good examples of artistic effects in photos.
Resources						
Web sites and searches	Web sites for Nikon, Canon, and Olympus. Search: **digital film photography.**	Sites for editing programs, such as Photoshop. Search: **edit digital photograph.**	Sites supporting editing tools, e.g., photoshopuser.com. Search: name of the editing tool.	Sites with tutorials on fixing problems, e.g., photoshopuser.com.	Sites for camera makers and editing software. Search: **histogram digital photograph.**	Sites where professional photographers give advice on using artistic effects.
Other	Articles on the digital workflow from Adobe and Apple.				"Your friend the histogram"	Tutorials and demos on using specific Photoshop filters.

Respond to learners

For learners, the most important element in the virtual classroom is the teacher. Make sure that learners can ask questions and get help when needed.

▶ **Set reasonable expectations**. Tell learners what the turn-around time will be for responding to e-mail, say 24 to 48 hours. Some learners think their teachers live online, just waiting for a message from a student. Once you set expectations, meet them.

▶ **Respond promptly**. If you cannot respond quickly, send a short message acknowledging the question and promising a full reply later. Be sure to say when. If you will be out of your office for several days, use the auto-reply function of your e-mail system to notify senders when you will respond.

Provide complete instructions

For some learners, opening an e-mail message is a struggle. Others daily text-message co-workers from their mobile phones or instant message their friends from their computers, listen to podcasts while updating their blogs, attach video clips to their e-mail, and use their Webcams to show off their latest digital cameras. Both groups need clear instructions on how to use collaboration tools for learning. Those inexperienced with collaboration tools need simple, explicit instructions and encouragement on getting started. Those fluent in these media need direction on using these tools for learning purposes rather than social exchanges.

Virtual classrooms typically require three main documents to guide learning: Student's guide, Teacher's Guide, and Class Syllabus.

Student's guide

The student's guide provides instructions for learners and team leaders. It consolidates instructions that might otherwise be scattered among FAQs, e-mails, policies, discussion posts, and replies to questions in meetings or forums.

When do you need a student's guide?

A student's guide is especially important when:

▶ Learners are new to the media and collaboration tools of your course.

▶ Learners do not know the conventions and netiquette of e-learning.

▶ Bad student behavior could expose your organization to legal liability, for example, charges of bias or harassment.

▶ You lack support staff to coach each learner in the routine tasks of e-learning.

Explain essential actions

Ensure learners can perform all required actions. Make sure learners know how to prepare and send the kinds of messages necessary in the class. Provide step-by-step instructions for each of these actions:

▶ Send a message to an individual or to a whole group.

▶ Reply to messages.

▶ Format the message.

▶ Quote from an original message.

▶ Embed links in messages.

▶ Attach files to messages.

▶ Post a message on a specific thread of a discussion forum.

Provide a complete online manual for the discussion, e-mail, chat, and online-meeting tools used in the course. Unless you have created your own custom system, you can probably link to the online manuals and tutorials provided by the vendors of your tools. I say "probably" because not all vendors have good instructions written for first-time learners.

Make it easy for learners to print out these instructions. Either combine all topics into one file or assemble them into a special printable file. Better still; consolidate all the manuals for all the systems used in the course into one file with a comprehensive table of contents.

Supply computer setup instructions

Live events can tax the capabilities of even powerful computers and networks. Teachers and learners need to tune their computers for collaboration. The following example, from an announcement of an upcoming online session, alerts learners to the event and tells them what they need to do (technically) to get ready for it:

Special tools?	We will be using Elluminate for our online meeting. To participate, you will need a headset microphone (for voice-conferencing) and a 100 kbps connection or faster.
Computer set-up?	Test your setup by going to: http://www.elluminate.com/Support/?id=62. If you need an updated version of Java, you will be prompted to install it. On the day of the meeting, turn off any scheduled maintenance tasks and screen savers. The fewer programs running while you are in the meeting, the quicker will be the response time.

Explain how to e-learn

E-learning may be new to some learners, who may not realize the high degree of self-motivation and time-management skills it requires. Point out the specific learning behaviors and attitudes needed and suggest ways to develop them. Tell learners how to:

- ▶ Verify that their goals can be met in the course.
- ▶ Set their own objectives and timetables and milestones for achieving them.
- ▶ Constructively interact with fellow learners.
- ▶ Actively seek new knowledge and skills rather than waiting to be taught.
- ▶ Master new technologies like a child. Explore, experiment, and look things up in Help.

Guide message writers

Not all learners know how to craft effective messages and how to manage their message-sending activities. You may want to monitor how well learners send messages. If problems arise, recommend specific training. Or provide instructions yourself.

Include specific instructions on appropriate ways to exchange messages—or refer to a separate, more general guide, such as *Guide to Messaging*. Go to horton.com/eld/ to see an example.

Spell out collaboration policies

If students must work together as teams or comment on each other's work, provide guidance on recommended ways of working together and required behaviors. You may include this material in the student guide or publish a separate guide. Go to horton.com/eld/ to see an example.

Teacher's guide

The teacher's guide provides instructions for the teacher, discussion moderator, meeting producer, and guest speaker.

The teacher's guide tells instructors and facilitators how to set up the course, conduct online meetings, moderate discussions, and perform other activities. It should also cover the duties of others involved in administering and delivering the course, such as the producer of online meetings, guest speakers, and teaching assistants.

When do you need a teacher's guide?

Create a teacher's guide when those conducting the class are new to some aspect of the class. Create a guide when:

- ▶ Teachers or experts must teach a course they did not design and develop.
- ▶ Teachers are new to online teaching, to the subject matter, or to the specific course.
- ▶ Teachers might otherwise try to "wing it."
- ▶ Learning occurs mainly in feedback from the teacher.

Explain how to set up the course

The teacher's guide should provide directions for setting up a new offering of the course. Tell teachers how to:

▶ Register learners and other participants. This will include setting up roles and assigning security privileges.

▶ Announce the course to learners and to other participants.

▶ Upload course resources.

▶ Post biographies for the teacher and others responsible for the course.

▶ Welcome learners by e-mail or phone.

▶ Publish a student's guide, messaging policy, and collaboration guide.

When practical include models, examples, and templates that the teacher can use as a starting point in creating required materials.

Explain how to conduct the course

Conducting a course is more than teaching. It requires many activities. Some are mundane and others complex. Tell teachers how to:

▶ Monitor learners' performance, behavior, and attitudes.

▶ Moderate discussion forums.

▶ Intervene with unmotivated learners and those behaving badly.

▶ Grade learners. This may require detailed rubrics for scoring complex activities.

▶ Give feedback. Some feedback can be anticipated, and some can follow guidelines and policies.

Explain how to set up meetings

Each meeting requires careful preparation. Make sure teachers can:

▶ Adjust the syllabus and remind learners of meetings.

▶ Update materials. Revise assignments. Prepare or revise slides. Define new polls.

▶ Upload materials.

▶ Publish a detailed meeting agenda. Send a general schedule to learners and a more detailed one to producers, guest speakers, and so forth.

Explain how to conduct meetings

The teacher must conduct meetings smoothly and efficiently for learners accustomed to the flawless production of network talk shows.

The teacher must know how to perform all the basic functions of all the necessary collaboration mechanisms, such as audio-conferencing, slide shows, application sharing, chat, polls, and whiteboards. The teacher must know how to use these tools in a way that involves learners and provokes thought.

The teacher's guide cannot replace the presenter's guide published by the vendor of the meeting tool, but it can summarize the most important operations.

Explain how to moderate discussions

If discussion plays an important role in the course, the teacher must establish discussion threads, kick off the discussion, and keep it going. Make sure teachers know how to:

- ▶ Establish standard threads such as Introduction, Administrative Support, Technical Support, General Comments, and Student Lounge.
- ▶ Establish threads to support individual meetings and learning activities.
- ▶ Answer questions from learners.
- ▶ Post resources, such as reference materials and templates, needed for learners to complete activities.

Syllabus

For virtual classroom courses, the syllabus is the skeleton that articulates the course. It is the most important page in an online course. It serves as both menu and home page. It lays out the schedule, requirements, and activities of the whole course. It is the one place where learners can find all the requirements of the course. The syllabus may be long, but it should be clearly organized and attractively formatted.

When do you need a syllabus?

Having taught dozens of online classes, I cannot imagine a situation in which a syllabus is not the most valuable document in a course. It gives students a safe home base from which to start. They know that the syllabus will direct them to everything necessary to pass the course. The syllabus can also provide an overview of the course and set the context for activities. It shows how the course is organized and how each component fits into that whole. It answers the question, "Where am I?" The syllabus serves as a well-organized course menu. Hyperlinks connect learners directly to all parts of the course.

What the syllabus should contain

Here is a sample that contains most of the elements needed for an effective syllabus. The notes to the right label the content and suggest alternatives.

Syllabus
Beginning Digital Photography

Instructor: <u>William Horton</u>

Contents

<u>Objectives</u>
<u>About the course</u>
<u>Modules</u>:

1. <u>The new world</u>
2. <u>Shoot to edit</u>
3. <u>Edit to show</u>
4. <u>Fixing problems</u>
5. <u>Histograms</u>
6. <u>Artistic effects</u>

<u>Weekly events</u>
<u>Resources</u>
<u>Notes</u>

Objectives

In this course will learn basic and advanced techniques to help you take better digital photographs. You will learn to:

- Select the digital camera that is right for you.
- Take photographs by just pointing and shooting.
- Use the camera's controls for practical and artistic effects.
- Transfer photographs to your computer.
- Edit photos on your computer.
- Print out photos from your computer.

About the course

Make sure you understand the policies and procedures governing this course and that you meet the requirements—before the first class. Also take a few minutes to get to know your instructor and and fellow students.

<u>Policies</u>
<u>Technical requirements</u>
<u>Grading criteria</u>

Week 1: The new world

Events	Readings	Activities
<u>Presentation</u> "How digital is different" ✱ ☑ Be prepared to identify assumptions carried over from film photography. ✱	☺ Explore Web sites for <u>Nikon</u>, <u>Canon</u>, and <u>Olympus</u>. ☺ Search: *digital film photography* ▣ Read articles on the digital workflow from Adobe and Apple.	☑ <u>Submit your best and worst digital photo.</u> ✱ Due: Wednesday ▤ <u>List and prioritize differences between digital and film photography.</u> Due: Anytime ☑ <u>How digital photography is different.</u> ✱ Due: Friday

Title and identifying information

10

Design for the virtual classroom

Links to each week's events and to other materials

Because the syllabus may be quite long, include a local table of contents with entries linked to sections of the page.

Objectives

Remind learners what the course is all about.

About the course

Link to materials about the course that the learner may need to refer to before or while taking the course.

Week identifier

Events, readings, and activities

Events are real-time meetings. They can include video-conferences, chat sessions, and other live events.

Week 2: Shoot to edit

Events	Readings	Activities
📺 Presentation "Capturing the most editable image" * 📺 Presentation "Capturing the most editable image" * ☑ Be prepared to identify camera settings that produce an editable image. *	◉ Explore Web sites for graphics editing programs, such as Photoshop. ◉ Search: *edit digital photograph*	☑ Submit images shot to edit and shot to show. * Due: Wednesday 📋 Create a checklist for shooting with editing in mind. Due: Anytime ☑ Find the characteristics of an editable image. * Due: Friday

[Weeks 3 and 4 are similar]

Week 6: Artistic effects

Events	Readings	Activities
📺 Presentation "Demo filters in Photoshop " * 📺 Presentation "Plea for voluntary restraint" * ☑ Be prepared to match effects with the appropriate filter. * ☑ Suggest effects filters you would use. *	◉ Explore sites where professional photographers give advice on using artistic effects. 📖 Read tutorials and demos on using specific Photoshop filters.	☑ Apply effects to three photos. * Due: Wednesday 📋 Ethical rules for modiiifying photos. Due: Friday 📋 Post best practices for artistic effects. Due: Friday ☑ Find good examples of artistic effects in photos. * Due: Friday

Weekly events

These events and activities occur every week, but may not be listed in the week's detailed description:

Lecture: Monday at 20:00 GMT. Required *
Post-lecture chat: Immediately after the lecture
Open forum: Monday at 20:00 GMT
Discussion group: Open all hours

Resources

As you take the class, you may find these general resources useful:

About the instructor	Course discussion group
Roster	Technical support
Biographies of students	Administrative support

Notes

Assignments are due at midnight (00:00 hours UTC) on the day stated. For example, if we say an activity is due on April 15, then that would make it due by 7:00 PM (19:00 hours) New York time on April 14th (the evening before), or by 1:00 AM (01:00 hours) Berlin time on April 15th.

Lectures are required. We do not take attendance, but we do present information not available through readings or other resources.

Readings are materials learners must read or view. They may include local or Internet materials. Some may be simple Web pages, while others are elaborate multimedia productions.

Activities are things people do. Activities may have deadlines, but learners can generally complete activities on their own schedule. Activities include tests.

In Events or Activities, include milestones or intermediate products for a multi-week project.

Recurring events

List events and activities that occur each week, such as class meetings, lectures, chats and other scheduled meetings, and lab sessions.

Resources

List resources learners may find useful while taking the course.

Notes

Include any notes, cautions, warnings, or other material that you need to bring to the attention of learners.

Best practices for a syllabus

I have seen courses saved by a revision of the syllabus—it is that important. Give the humble syllabus the attention it deserves.

Make the syllabus comprehensive. List all activities, resources, support contacts, and administrative requirements. Link to mentioned documents and forum threads. Include phone numbers and e-mail addresses of faculty and support staff. And remember to test all links, e-mail addresses, and phone numbers.

Organize the course into bite-sized chunks. If learners are given the complete set of course materials from the start, the very mass of the materials may discourage or overwhelm them. Use the syllabus to divide the mass of course materials into understandable pieces, sort the pieces into logical categories, arrange the pieces into meaningful learning sequences, and set an appropriate schedule for mastering them.

Even if you do not include a formal syllabus, at least suggest a sequence and schedule for consuming the materials—and clearly distinguish high-priority "required" materials from optional ones.

Specify exact dates. When does the week end and begin? Be careful about international differences and time-zone shifts.

> Weeks begin just past midnight Monday morning—GMT!

If practical, fill in actual dates rather than just saying Week 1, Week 2, etc.

Link to everything. Do not require learners to go searching for materials mentioned in the syllabus. Link to the materials so that learners can jump to them. For lectures and conferences, link to the meeting site. For activities, link to the form learners must fill in and submit to complete the activity.

Flag required items. Use a distinctive icon for required items. Flag any mandatory or date-specific activities in the syllabus and course announcements. Make crystal clear which items affect the final grade and which do not. If an item is optional, but learners who perform the activity can win extra points, is the activity really optional?

Simplify tasks for learners

Learning is hard under the best circumstances. Make learning as easy as possible. Keep your course simple so learning is productive and efficient.

Keep the class small

Most teachers recommend keeping virtual classes small, say 7 to 10 students. However, small class sizes can thwart economic goals that may best be served by larger classes. You must weigh the immediate revenue of a large class versus the reputation engendered by the quality of learning experiences possible in intimate groupings.

If you cannot afford a small class, take steps to ensure that learners are still treated as individuals. Include lots of small-group activity so the scope of the class does not intimidate learners.

Offer a textbook (or equivalent)

One of the most valuable components of an online course can be an old fashioned textbook.

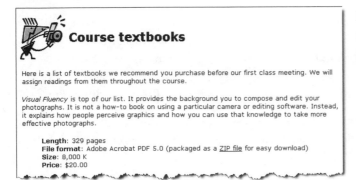

In this example, learners are referred to textbooks to be read for specific assignments.

A textbook is familiar to learners. An electronically accessible textbook helps with accessibility requirements. Screen readers for the blind can speak the text aloud. Hearing-disabled can read the textbook to learn what they could not get from voice in the meetings. And, yes, some learners would rather read a well-organized book than struggle with technology.

Respond promptly and reliably

Make and keep promises to punctually respond to learners' e-mail messages, discussion forum postings, tests, and exercises. Here is such a promise:

> I will check my e-mail in the morning (Taipei time) and evening on weekdays only. I will scan forum postings on Mondays and Thursdays. All exercises and tests that are not automatically scored will be returned to you within three business days.

If you need help on anything, just contact your instructor. Your instructor will try to respond within 24 hours. If you have not heard back in 48 hours, contact the support desk.

This example lets learners know how soon to expect a response to their e-mail messages.

Set realistic expectations for replies from the teacher. After all, some teachers may want to take the weekend off. Some may be nine time zones away in a country with different political, business, and religious holidays.

Teachers who will be unavailable for a longer period should arrange for someone else to handle messages while they are away. Or they should set up their e-mail programs to automatically respond to incoming messages with a reply like this:

> I will be out of the office until 27 January. I will answer your message then. If you need an immediate response, contact <u>administrative support</u>.

Tell learners where you will post critical announcements and how often they are responsible for checking them. Be reasonable. Giving less than 48 hours' notice is seldom sufficient.

Deal with problem learners

Most learners diligently pursue their education. Some, however, exhibit disruptive behavior, just as in classroom courses. The opportunities for bad behavior are magnified by the power of technology. Take steps to ensure that a few angry or confused learners do not ruin the experience for others.

Give fair warning

Make clear to learners what behavior is acceptable and what behavior is not acceptable.

Behavior

RACISM Make people of all backgrounds, ages, races, religions, national origins, genders, sexual orientations, and beliefs feel welcome. Refrain from statements of hatred, bigotry, and racism--even in jest. Make no defamatory statements or any that infringe the rights of others.

DISRUPTING LEARNERS AND LEARNING Avoid any behavior that makes learning harder for others: Sending provoking, distracting, misleading messages is forbidden. Messages designed to provoke angry or irrelevant responses are not allowed.

Send only messages that help others, further a conversation, or resolve an issue. Avoid messages that are:

- Irrelevant to the topic under discussion
- Are unclear or misleading
- Just repeat an earlier posting
- Vulgar or suggestive
- Rants, diatribes, and temper tantrums

Though not forbidden, such messages may be removed by the moderator.

SPOOFING AND FORGERY Never pretend to be someone else in your interactions with other learners. (Role-playing activities are an exception.) Never alter documents of others. Never post documents under someone else's name.

PROFANITY Behave the way you would in a classroom or boardroom. Avoid obscene and profane language.

PORNOGRAPHY Send no pornographic materials.

This portion of a collaboration policy attempts to head off bad behavior by laying down clear rules for what kind of behavior is expected. Although such rules do not prevent bad behavior, they do ensure that there is no question about whether such behavior is acceptable.

Deal with bad behavior

Bad behavior is as rare in online courses as in the classroom—but potentially more disruptive. Here are some proven techniques for dealing with misbehaving learners.

▶ **Plan responses for common bad behavior**s. Anticipate problems and have a consistent, thought-out response ready.

▶ **Publish a standard for behavior**. Many learners may not know the conventions and expectations for online learning. Enforce policies consistently.

▶ **Cool off first**. Never respond in anger. Do not assume a learner's behavior is baseless. Ask why. Perhaps the learner was ignorant of the rules or just unable to use the technology as expected. Perhaps the learner is just trying to get your attention.

▶ **Progressively respond to bad behavior**. Politely remind first-time violators. Privately counsel serious or repeat offenders. If these learners' bad behavior continues, do not recognize them. Block their chat. Finally, expel incorrigibles.

▶ **Distinguish intellectual disagreement from abusive behavior**. Teach learners to disagree professionally and politely. And teach them to respond to legitimate criticism.

Handle common problems

Here are some common problems encountered in collaborative activities and some suggestions on how to handle them. For more suggestions for handling problems in social learning, read "Intervene in cases of bad behavior" in Chapter 8.

Problem	Description	Solution
Latecomers	Some learners join meetings and discussions late and insist that the entire process start all over again.	Start meetings on time. Do not re-start for latecomers. Point out that their tardiness is disruptive. Be prepared for some interesting excuses.
Dominating	Some learners may try to dominate the conversation by intimidating others or by trying to answer every question.	In private e-mail ask the sender to post questions for others to answer. At the same time, encourage others to join in.

Problem	Description	Solution
Spamming	Sending self-serving messages, such as advertisements and sales pitches, to the whole group.	Yank the message and remind the sender that it violates course policies. Make sure your policy is specific. Is it OK for one student to send a resume to another who is a potential employer? Can students recruit other students for permanent or part-time work?
E-mail bomb	Posting messages designed to disrupt a group by provoking angry responses. Comments on abortion, gun control, political correctness, sexual preferences, or nationalities are all guaranteed to wreck a discussion forum for a week.	Remove the message and warn the submitter. Require an apology. Remind other learners how much time they wasted commenting on such messages.
Nitpicking	Participants find fault with the work of others but never offer solutions. They may continually point out typos and small grammatical errors. Such nitpicking distracts everyone from the subject of the e-learning.	Remind nitpickers to focus on higher-level issues. Discover why they nitpick. If they lack knowledge to critique at a higher level, recommend prerequisite courses.
Sloppiness	Learners are lazy and inconsiderate of others. They forget to mute their phones or give meaningful subjects to their messages. They fail to read instructions and write incomprehensible stream-of-consciousness entries. They reply without reading previous posts.	Point out that learners have a responsibility to fellow learners. Show how sloppy learners are wasting the time of others. Institute a neatness-counts policy in grading activities.

Problem	Description	Solution
Plagiarism	Learners submit the work of others as their own. Typically learners will just copy material from the Web for an activity that should require original work.	Use a Web-based service, such as Turnitin (turnitin.com), to spot plagiarism—and let learners know that you do. For the first offense, explain the policy. Better still: rework the activity so it cannot be answered by simply copying information.
Copyright violations	Learners submit material owned by others. Similar to plagiarism except that learners are violating laws, not just ethics.	Warn learners and require replacing the material and redoing the activity. Also follow the steps for plagiarism.
Flaming	Making abusive and emotional attacks on someone else.	If the attack is mild, let the group deal with it first. Step in as necessary. Require an apology and warn the sender.

Follow up after the course

The microphones are all turned off and the screen-savers are playing, but learning can continue. Learning should not stop at the end of the course—just when learners are beginning to apply what they have learned. Use collaboration tools to let teachers and learners stay in touch and to monitor how successfully knowledge gained in the course is applied on the job and in subsequent courses.

Maintain communication with learners after the class ends. Encourage alumni to share success stories, ask for help, and offer help to others. Make it easy and inexpensive for learners to stay in touch.

▶ Keep discussion forums open or set up alumni-only forums.

▶ Maintain a roster of alumni who are willing to share their contact information. Make it available only to other alumni.

▶ Conduct alumni-only meetings to discuss how they are applying ideas from the course.

▶ Let alumni sit in on future offerings of the course.

▶ Invite alumni to serve as special tutors, mentors, or teaching assistants.

IN CLOSING ...

Webinars and virtual classroom courses use computer and network technologies to implement the structure and activity of conventional classroom courses.

Summary

▶ Use a Webinar to accomplish one simple learning objective, to meet a one-time need, or to teach a single group of learners.

▶ Use a virtual classroom course when a teacher is necessary to motivate learners, monitor their progress, and answer their questions immediately. Or when the discipline provided by a familiar structure and peer pressure is necessary to motivate learners.

▶ Publish a comprehensive syllabus listing all the events, activities, and readings of the course. Link to Web pages, forms, and other required resources. Likewise, include links to the roster, policies, requirements, grading criteria, discussion forum, and other resources of the course.

▶ Actively conduct the class. The teacher should contact participants directly, keep them on schedule and focused on the course, and manage collaborative activities.

▶ Plan live events carefully. Ahead of time, assign roles, allocate time, spell out a protocol for passing control, rehearse the event, and send materials needed during the event.

▶ Keep live events lively. Vary the presentation. Require learners to participate.

▶ Follow these Top 10 best practices for virtual teachers:
1. Prepare well: Do not try to wing it.
2. Rehearse, rehearse, rehearse … and then relax.
3. Less presentation, more activation.
4. Check your ego at the door.
5. Motivate, motivate, motivate.
6. Quickly deal with bullies, bigots, and buttheads.
7. Insist on professional, adult learning behaviors.
8. Encourage students to learn from each other.
9. Schedule for the convenience of your learners.
10. Monitor learners. Or have someone else do so.

For more ...

For more ideas on how to teach actively in the virtual classroom, consider using some of the activities explained in Chapters 2, 3, and 4. Even the asynchronous ones can be adapted for use by a teacher.

To find more on designing and delivering virtual-classroom courses, search the Web for combinations of these terms: *virtual classroom, online meeting*, and *synchronous e-learning*. Also search under the names of individual collaboration tools, such *as application sharing, whiteboard, video-conferencing*. Be sure to try alternative spellings, especially for compound terms.

For online meetings, you will need an online meeting tool. There are many to choose from. Here are a few popular ones to get you started.

- ▶ Adobe Connect (www.adobe.com).
- ▶ Elluminate (www.elluminate.com).
- ▶ GoToWebinar (www.gotomeeting.com).
- ▶ Live Meeting (office.microsoft.com).
- ▶ WebEx (www.WebEx.com).

Virtual school tools provide an entire package for meetings, discussion, and other collaborative activities, all structured as a familiar school or campus.

- ▶ Moodle (www.moodle.org).
- ▶ .LRN (www.dotlrn.org).
- ▶ Blackboard (www.blackboard.com).
- ▶ Desire2Learn (www.desire2learn.com).
- ▶ eCollege (www.ecollege.com).

Conclusion

The future of e-learning

E-learning is not just a change of technology. It is part of a redefinition of how we as a species transmit knowledge, skills, and values to younger generations of workers and students. I will end this book by daring to make a few predictions of how e-learning and the functions it serves will continue to develop.

HOW WE WILL LEARN

Where we are headed

The new models lead us to some interesting new visions of how education will be acquired in the future. One scenario goes like this:

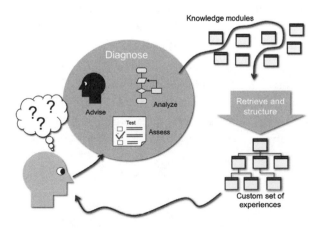

Learners will have access to millions or billions of knowledge modules. Some will be Web pages with simple text and graphics. Others may include multimedia simulations. Some may consist of coupons for a video-conference with a human expert.

When learners have a need for knowledge, they will engage in a diagnostic procedure. This diagnosis may be performed in a few nanoseconds by an algorithm in their computers. Or this diagnosis may involve taking an exam or filling out a questionnaire to assess their current knowledge level relative to their needed level. It may involve working with a counselor or advisor over a period of days.

The result of this diagnosis will be a request to a database containing millions or billions of knowledge modules. The needed modules will be rounded up and herded into a structure comprising a lesson or document custom-tailored to the needs of the individual who requested it.

This cycle of requesting and receiving knowledge may take place dozens of times a day. The custom set of experiences may take minutes or months to consume. The result, though, will be a shift from mass-manufactured to handcrafted education.

How we will get there

As interesting as where we are going is the journey we will take to get there. Here are some predictions of social and technological changes we can expect:

▶ E-learning will fade away. E-learning has entered the mainstream. In many fields, e-learning has become the default way to conduct training or to provide education. Few areas are unaware of its benefits. The question of whether to use e-learning will be replaced by a decision of what types of learning experiences best accomplish goals. The emphasis will drift back to learning. And e-learning will be all the stronger.

▶ Advances will come more and more from grassroots designers, developers, and learners. The success of projects like Wikipedia shows the possibility for consumers of information to create their own documents. Many small organizations have found success in customizing open-source tools to meet their own needs. Communities of designers share techniques, tips, and inspiration.

▶ E-learning will grow by incorporating technical and social progress. New products, trends, and innovations from fields like entertainment and mass communication will continue to be adapted for use in education. Just as audio CDs led to CD-ROMS and the Internet to Web-based training; today mobile phones, videogames, and social networking are contributing new possibilities to e-learning. So too will the technological advances and social fads of the future.

WHAT HAS TO HAPPEN

For e-learning to continue to advance, and not stagnate, practitioners must continue to innovate and institutions must embrace the benefits that e-learning offers.

▶ Digital natives or the digitally fluent must achieve positions of power in all institutions from shipping clerk to chairman of the board, from local school-board member to university chancellor, and from city council to … (I almost wrote "White House," but then I remembered the incident where President-elect Obama's insistence on continuing to use his Blackberry caused a panic among the Secret Service and White House technical staff.)

▶ Designers must insist on fundamental instructional design and not just cram content into authoring tools. At every stage, we must ask, "Why am I doing this? How does it help my learners to learn?"

▶ Designers must accept social learning, mobile learning, and learning games as valid forms of e-learning, deploy them where they work best, and strive to design them well. And designers must be open to new ideas while avoiding chasing fads for popularity's sake.

▶ We must redefine learning as adding to people's capabilities rather than cramming information into their long-term memory. The focus must shift from what people know to what they can do—all the things they can accomplish alone and all the things they can accomplish with everything they can access electronically, including reference materials and social networks.

SECRETS OF E-LEARNING DESIGN

I've tucked four secrets here. You found them because you have persisted through a very long book or else were smart enough to flip to the last page. These secrets are special insights, not commonly known or widely practiced. They provide leverage points where a little effort has far-reaching results. They can form the basis for a successful career in e-learning design. They represent areas where your creativity and persistence are rewarded and where you can make significant progress.

The first secret is to teach what learners need to learn in the way they most naturally learn. To do so, we can test real learners in real situations. A technique for doing this is explained in the Appendix, right after this chapter.

The second secret is to define clear learning objectives. Here the term secret is a bit ironic as all instructional design methodologies preach this but few projects practice it. The key is not just to define objectives as a check-off item in a list of tasks, but also to put the objectives to work to guide and inform every decision on the project. Clear objectives are like GPS navigation for your project.

The third secret builds on the first two. It is to focus on the right objectives. Too many projects merely teach people to recite facts and figures or to follow rote procedures. Today, people can look up information and simple procedures. Today we need to teach people to create things and to make difficult decisions. And to do so, we often have to attend to what people believe and feel, not just what they know.

The final secret is in the power of testing. Only a small percentage of e-learning today incorporates valid testing. A mere recital of facts is seldom valid testing. Valid testing requires performance of the actual learning objective (remember secrets 2 and 3!). Valid testing measures learning. It can more precisely target learning activities. It provides learners with vital feedback and designers with an assessment of the effectiveness of their e-learning. The power of testing is amplified when we develop tests before content. That way tests make objectives more concrete and specific so they can better guide the development of learning activities and media.

JUST THE BEGINNING

We are just at the beginning of e-learning. We are using Version 1,364,287.4.6 of classroom learning. It is highly refined and efficient. We are only on Version 2.0 of e-learning. It is crude, buggy, and full of limitations. But every day it gets better. Creative designers are just now warming up.

I can't wait to see what you do.

Appendix

Essentialism

Teach just what people need to learn

Essentialism calls on us to teach the essence of any subject rather than unimportant, distracting, and peripheral details. By teaching essentials, we enable learners to master the subject quickly and surely.

ESSENTIAL ESSENTIALISM

At all stages of design, you must ask yourself, "What do learners need to learn?" Analyzing learners' needs—as well as their potential and limitations—requires careful study. The most efficient and reliable method of identifying just what you need to teach is to test potential learners in the environment in which they must apply learning.

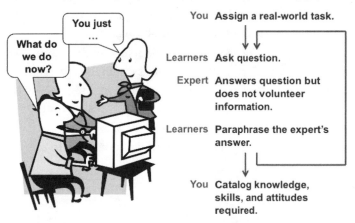

Over the years, I have refined this process to a simple, quick, and inexpensive procedure. You gather a pair of test subjects to simulate those who need the skills, knowledge, and attitudes you are charged with conveying. You put them in the environment in which they must perform tasks that require those same skills, knowledge, and attitudes. You give the test subjects no training or other resources they would not have in the real environment. However, you do bring in a subject-matter expert who can answer any questions the test subjects may have.

You begin the test by assigning the pair a realistic task. The test subjects proceed until they feel the need for help. At that point, they may ask a question. The expert answers the question but does not volunteer information. The test subjects then paraphrase the expert's answer to make sure they understood. The subjects proceed until they need help again. Throughout the test, you catalog the help required by the test subjects.

Understanding how learners think about things and how they refer to them (as shown by the test subjects) will prove useful in developing knowledge products for them.

It really is that simple.

SET UP THE TEST

To perform an essentialist analysis, you will need five main ingredients:

▶ **Test subjects** who represent your learners. These test subjects should have the same abilities and motivations as your intended learners.

▶ **Tasks** that require what you are charged with teaching. These tasks should require accomplishing the top learning objective of your project.

▶ **Environment** that simulates where learners will apply learning. Setting up the environment may require the physical space, furniture, and tools available in the real situation. The environment may also include other people to play roles in performing the task, especially tasks performed in a social setting.

▶ **Sources of information** that are accessible in the real situation. In the test, test subjects may need access to all the resources they could use in the real world to answer questions and overcome obstacles. These sources may include product documentation, a simulated help line, phone access to friends and co-workers, and access to a social network of potential advisors.

▶ **Expert** who can answer questions. The expert must know how to perform the task and answer questions about the task.

SUPERVISE THE TEST

Directing the test requires a light hand and a watchful eye. Test subjects must feel in control so they act naturally. Here are the steps to follow in conducting the test:

1. **Prepare the test subjects**. Make the test subjects comfortable and confident. Introduce yourself and the expert. Have subjects introduce themselves. Give test subjects a little time to get to know each other. Familiarize them with the physical environment of the

test and the resources they can call on during the test. Remember to get written permission to record the test.

2. **Explain the rules**. The rules of essentialist testing are simple and few:

    a. **Test subjects** can do whatever they feel necessary to accomplish the goal.

    b. **Experts** can answer questions but must not volunteer information.

    c. **The test conductor** should not intrude, except when necessary to keep the test on track.

3. **Assign the task**. Explain the goal of the task clearly to the test subjects. Answer any questions they have about the goal but do not give any hints they would not receive in the real task. Remind them of any restrictions, such as a time limit. Wish them luck and begin the test.

4. **Monitor the test**. Observe as the test subjects proceed toward the goal. When they encounter a problem, they will try to find a solution. Let them. If they ask a question of the expert, make sure the expert answers fully, but does not volunteer information not asked for.

5. **Conclude the test**. When the test subjects reach the goal—and recognize that they have met the goal—call a halt to the test, stop recording, and thank everybody involved.

The roles of the test subjects, expert, and test conductor are further explained in the following sections.

The role of test subjects

The following is the briefing given to test subjects before a test.

Test subjects

Your role in this test is to be yourself. By doing so you will help us design the most effective learning possible. Keep these points in mind:

▶ **You are in charge**. In the test, nothing *you* do is wrong. There is no way *you* can fail.

▶ **Accomplish the goal** by whatever path you and your partner see fit. If there are any restrictions, such as what tool to use or how long you have to complete the task, these will be spelled out to you before the test begins. Other than these specific limits, you are free to accomplish the task by whatever method you prefer.

▶ **Get help when you need it.** Feel free to seek information by whatever means seem most natural to you. You can discuss the issue with your partner. You can just guess or can apply a trial-and-error strategy. You can look up information in documents present in the test environment or search online. You can use the provided phone to call friends, family, or co-workers. You can access any social network or professional network to which you belong. You can also ask the expert. There is no

recommended
method of getting help. Just do what works for you.

▶ **Ask the expert only if you want to**. The expert is willing to answer any question you pose—or to wait patiently in the background.

▶ **Talk through the expert's answer.** If you ask a question of the expert, please discuss the answer with your partner to make sure you both understand the answer to mean the same thing.

The role of the expert

The following is the briefing given to experts before a test.

Subject-matter expert

Thank you for agreeing to participate in this test. Your role, as a subject-matter expert, is to respond to requests for help from the test subjects. As you participate, please keep these "rules" in mind:

▶ **Do not interrupt the test subjects.** Even if you feel the test subjects are doing something wrong, do not give assistance until they explicitly ask for help. The only exception is if they seem about to injure themselves or damage expensive equipment.

▶ **Do not volunteer information.** Answer questions fully, but never go beyond the scope of the question. If in doubt, cut your answer short and wait to see if the test subjects ask another question.

▶ **Listen for implied questions.** Do not require the test subjects to phrase queries as grammatically correct questions. A question is any overt sign that the test subjects are asking for specific help. It can be an incomplete sentence, for example, "And then we …." It can be a simple request for confirmation, for example, "Then we press the Eject button, right?"

▶ **Count to three before answering any question**. Often, in that short delay, the subjects will discover the answer for themselves. The delay reveals what they *almost* know.

▶ **Answer in the most natural way possible.** The best answer may be a simple nod or gesture. The answer does not have to be in words; you can draw a picture or demonstrate a procedure.

Role of the test conductor

The following is the briefing given to the test conductor before a test:

Test conductor

Thank you for agreeing to participate in this test. Your role, as a test conductor, is to engineer a successful test. As you direct the test, keep the following suggestions in mind:

▶ **Make test subjects comfortable**. Introduce yourself to the test subjects and then introduce them to each other and to the expert. Familiarize them with the test environment. Explain the purpose of the test and emphasize that the test subjects are not being evaluated or graded. Give the test subjects time to relax and feel at home.

▶ **Explain the task fully**. State the goal and let the test subjects ask questions. Answer fully about the goal, but do not give any hints about how to achieve it.

▶ **Monitor the test once it begins**. Observe the problem-solving strategies of the test subjects. Keep in mind that they may be nervous at first. Results will be valid once the test subjects relax their posture and start speaking in incomplete sentences.

▶ **Interrupt only where necessary**, for instance:
  - Test subjects are about to do something dangerous.
  - The expert volunteers information not requested by the test subjects.
  - The expert fails to respond to a, perhaps subtle, request for help.
  - The expert cannot answer a question but you can.

ANALYZE TEST RESULTS

For each test you perform, carefully review the results and draw conclusions. Analysis usually requires three steps: 1. Record what the test subjects needed to learn. 2. Identify how they preferred to learn. 3. Infer principles to guide your design.

Record needed learning

The first step of analyzing results is to record needed learning. That is, what abilities, knowledge, beliefs, and feelings were necessary for success? And, what were not necessary?

Start by listing three things:

▶ What test subjects **needed to know** as shown by the questions they asked of the expert.

▶ What test subjects **figured out on their own**, for example, by trial and error, by discussion, or by online searches.

▶ What the test subjects **did not need to know**—even though experts and designers predicted they would.

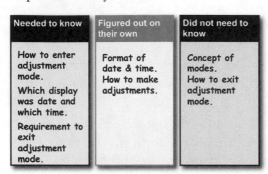

Here are the results of a single test where test subjects were challenged to set the date and time on a multi-function digital watch.

First, what did the test subjects actually need to know, as demonstrated by their questions? They needed to know how to enter the adjustment mode. They were confused about which display was date and which was time. They were unaware of the requirement to exit the adjustment mode after making a change. That's it.

What did they figure out on their own? They puzzled out the format of date and time without too much effort. And, once they got into adjustment mode, they figured out how to make adjustments on their own.

We also want to note the things they did not need to know—even though we expert instructional designers thought they would. One issue that never arose was the concept of modes. It just never was an issue. Perhaps other devices had taught the concept fully. The second surprise was that the test subjects did not need to know how to exit adjustment mode, just that it was required for them to do so. This is a subtle distinction, but one that can spell success for failure for the unwary designer.

OK, what do we do with this analysis? As a broad strategy, we should teach the things that the test subjects really needed to know. For the things they figured out on their own, we can provide online documents in case some learners are not as perceptive or persistent. The things that they did not need to know can be omitted.

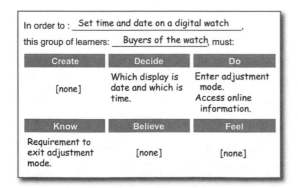

As a refinement of our observations, we can restate learning needs in terms of types of learning objectives.

Subsequent tests would, of course, add additional objectives.

Identify the learning approach

The next level of analysis looks at the learning approach taken by the test subjects and what it implies for how we teach similar learners.

What did test subjects need?	☐ ☐ ☒ ☐ Concepts Procedures Facts Attitudes _____
In what order did they do tasks?	Set time and then went on to set date, though not requested to.
When did they ask questions?	☐ Before trying a step ☒ When stumped ☒ After failing at a step ☐ _____
How did they prefer to learn?	Asking questions ◀ Pick along scale ▲ ▶ Trial & error
How did they learn as they went along?	Successfully applied time-setting procedure to set the date.
How did test subjects interact?	☐ One dominated ☒ Shared ideas ☒ Alternated ☐ _____

First, we ask what kind of help did the test subjects need? Did they need concepts, complete procedures, individual facts, attitudes, or something else? In this case, you might say they needed procedures, but a careful review of the video showed that they never asked for whole step-by-step procedure, only specific facts or individual steps.

The next question is in what order did test subjects do tasks? In this case they set the time first and then went on to set the date, though not requested to perform operations in this order. This is significant since the maker of the watch assumed users would set the date before setting the time.

When did test subjects ask questions? Was it before trying a step, when stumped, after failing at a step, or at some other event or situation? In this case they asked questions only when stumped or after failing at a question. This shows they wanted to learn by trying it out on their own.

How did the test subjects prefer to learn? Where does their behavior fall along a scale from asking questions to trial and error? In this case, test subjects leaned toward the trial-and-error approach.

Another important question is how did test subjects learn as they went along? Did they ignore what they learned earlier or did they apply it fully to subsequent challenges? In this case, they successfully applied the time-setting procedure to set the date. They were learning as they went along.

Finally, how did the test subjects interact? Did one person dominate? Did they share ideas? Or did they alternate leadership of the procedure? In this case they shared ideas. They also alternated control, handing the watch back and forth.

Answers to these questions can go a long way toward picking an instructional strategy that is most effective for learners like these.

Infer design principles

To put our testing and analysis to work, we need to infer design principles to guide design of our learning. The first step is to compile a list of essential learning objectives. What exactly must we teach? In this case, three main objectives emerge from our analysis: We need to teach learners how to get started. We do not need to teach much, just the first few steps. After that learners can figure out subsequent steps on their own. The next learning objective ensures learners can correctly interpret the overall format of the display. A final objective is that learners be able to verify successful completion of steps so they have confidence in their efforts and so they do not repeat steps unnecessarily. These objectives are fewer and more focused than the ones suggested by experts and designers before the test.

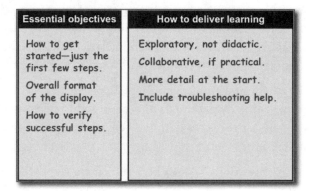

Essential objectives	How to deliver learning
How to get started—just the first few steps.	Exploratory, not didactic.
Overall format of the display.	Collaborative, if practical.
How to verify successful steps.	More detail at the start.
	Include troubleshooting help.

Next, we can use our test results to guide us in how we deliver learning. Results suggest that our learning program should be exploratory and not didactic—more like a video game than a college lecture. Activities might benefit by being collaborative, if practical. Our test subjects worked the assigned task as a team, not as individuals. Chances are they would prefer to learn that way too. We should provide more detail at the start of tasks and procedures and less once learners are underway. This may mean violating the unwritten rule that requires the same amount of "training" for each and every step in a procedure. Finally, we should provide lots of troubleshooting help. Learners are likely to seek help only after they have made a mess of things. We should provide tools to get them unstuck and back on track.

Of course, your test results may be different, and so too will be your analysis and the principles you infer from that analysis. The important thing is to base your educational strategy on the experience of real learners in real situations.

MAKE TESTING BETTER

Though testing for essentialism is simple, it is subject to the usual constraints of schedule and budget. It is also subject to human failings and misinterpretations. Not to worry. In this section, I'll guide you through the difficulties so you can conduct effective tests on a tight schedule with a limited budget and an undeveloped subject.

Overcome the Hawthorne effect

So, what could go wrong? One problem with usability testing was observed before usability testing was even a term. This problem goes by the name of the *Hawthorne effect* after a series of experiments that were conducted from 1927 to 1932 by Harvard Business School Professor Elton Mayo at the Western Electric Hawthorne factory in Chicago. The experiments measured changes in the rate of production of telephone relay switches by a team of workers as a result of changes in the work method or environment.

Workers were shifted to piecework, … and production rose. Workers were given more rest breaks, … and production rose. The rest breaks were lengthened, … and production rose. A hot meal was supplied, … and production rose. The workday was shortened, … and production rose. Then all the changes were reversed to return to the original conditions, … and production rose. Huh?

What Dr. Mayo discovered had little to do with worker fatigue and nutrition but had a whole lot to do with worker psychology. Observing human behavior tends to modify that behavior. It is a psychological analog to the Heisenberg Uncertainty principle of particle physics, which states that you cannot measure the position and momentum of a subatomic particle because observing one modifies the other.

Leave the lab-coat behind

Another experiment, this time conducted by Yale University, also undercuts the basic premise of testing. In this test subjects were tested in pairs. One subject was strapped into a chair with electrodes attached to his body. The other test subject was located in front of a control panel with a dial indicating electrical voltage and a button to deliver a shock to the first test subject each time he missed the answer to a test question posed by the test-conductor wearing a stereotypical white lab coat. After each mistake, the second test subject, the one administering the shocks, was instructed by the test-conductor to increase the voltage.

The real purpose of the test, unknown to the shock-delivering test subject, was to see how far people would go in causing pain. Sounds cruel, but the first test subject was just an actor and was not receiving shocks.

The frightening result was that many of the test subjects kept raising the voltage and delivering shocks as instructed by the test-conductor—even after the first test subject was screaming in pain or even appeared to be unconscious.

What this experiment showed is that in laboratory tests, the person conducting the test has enormous authority over the test subject. It further shows that test subjects will do things in the laboratory that they would never do in ordinary life.

As testers, we whisk test subjects up the elevator to an interior room with no outside windows but with a mirror along one entire wall. We point four video cameras at the test subjects and tell them to "act normal." Yeah, right.

In such tests, subjects do not act normally. They follow only approved procedures and follow instructions literally. They hide their doubts, fearing they may appear ignorant or look foolish. They work mightily to please the tester.

Test a twosome

One of the simplest and most effective ways to overcome the difficulties posed by the Hawthorne and Lab-Coat effects is to test with pairs of test subjects.

Having a buddy along side greatly reduces self-consciousness. Within a few seconds the pair have forgotten about the video camera and one-way mirror and are engrossed in the task. When they are puzzled, they do not grow silent. They ask questions of one another. They offer hypotheses. They suggest solutions to problems. They talk, talk, and talk. And from that talk, you can form a clearer understanding of what they know and what they need to know.

Provide all real resources

Provide test subjects with all the resources available in the real world, for example: books and manuals, both on paper and online; intranet and Internet, including social networking sites; and common job aids. Likewise, make sure the test environment includes realistic work materials. If employees receive assignments by e-mail, then provide such an e-mail as part of the test. If phone support is a possible source of information, simulate a customer-support phone line. Also simulate access to knowledgeable co-workers, either through a simulated friend in the room or through a phone line to a waiting colleague.

Reassure test subjects

For the most accurate results, test subjects must behave normally. They will not do that if they feel they are under the microscope. Reassure your test subjects. Remind them that they are not being judged.

Do not say, "We're not testing you." They may not have thought that they were being tested or they may not believe you. Instead, say something like, "Help us find ways to improve our educational program." Explain that what you are doing is research, not testing performance.

Do not say, "Don't worry. Your boss won't see the results." This just introduces a new worry. A better approach is to say, "We really want our program to work for people like you." Most people like having things centered on them.

Watch the video fully

If practical, record the test on video. Try to capture the test subjects' facial expressions, body language, and gestures. These are even more important than recording their interactions with equipment or computer programs.

To get the most from your testing, watch the video fully. Watch it several times and in different ways. Watch it once casually just to see what is there. Then watch it critically to observe small incidents. Once you think you have observed all there is to observe, watch the video with the sound off to notice motions, such as gestures and facial expressions. Watch again with the visuals off to notice the tone of voice of test subjects. Play the video in fast forward to notice patterns of motion, gestures, and shifts in body language. Play it in slow motion to notice the precise sequence of events and the delays between related events.

Look for signs of anxiety, enthusiasm, uncertainty, discovery, anger, relief, and embarrassment. Then track down the sources of these emotional reactions.

Conduct enough tests

Obviously you would not base an entire educational program on one test, but if subsequent tests replicate initial results, you would have a demonstrable rationale for the learning objectives you need to accomplish and the ones you can forego.

How many tests must you perform? That depends greatly on the vastness of your subject matter and the diversity of your learners. There are some break points in the numbers of tests.

One test is a lot better than no test. One test can raise potential problems and ward off a disaster.

Six tests can be practically, though not statistically, significant. A half-dozen tests can invalidate bad theories before you implement them and can flag critical issues that require special handling or more research.

With a couple of dozen tests, you can verify trends and gather firm evidence to support your approach. Two-dozen tests can be statistically significant.

Pick valid test subjects

Your results depend completely on your choice of test subjects. Pick test subjects who resemble your eventual target audience. Here are some tips for picking test subjects:

▶ Pick test subjects with comparable background knowledge and experience. If you were developing a new computer programming language, you would not use test subjects who had never used a computer. If you were developing a product for use by newly graduated nurses, you would not test it with senior surgeons.

▶ Vary factors like the age, gender, and language skills of the test subjects. Also keep in mind that cultural differences may affect how a class of people learns most effectively.

▶ Pair up similar people for a test. Then pair up very different people for the next test. Does the pairing make a difference?

▶ Do not use professional test subjects. Once people have participated in a few tests, they are no longer representative of your potential learners.

Here's a tip for those of you developing training and documentation for a product sold to your existing customer base. Walk over to your training center and invite customers to participate in tests. If you are working on GrottoGlop 2.0, who better than a user of GrottoGlop 1.0 to serve as your test subject.

RECAP: MASTER THE ESSENTIALS OF ESSENTIALISM

Let's recap. What are the essentials of essentialism?

▶ Do not try to teach everything everybody might possibly someday need to know.

▶ Teach what people do not know and cannot figure out on their own.

▶ Figure out what to teach by testing with potential learners.

▶ For testing pick, a task that requires what you need to teach.

▶ Test with a twosome.

Keep these five points in mind and you are well on your way to delivering essential learning.

Index

A

Q

R

T